Rethinking the Enlightenment

Joseph T. Stuart

Rethinking the Enlightenment

Faith in the Age of Reason

SOPHIA INSTITUTE PRESS

Manchester, New Hampshire

Sophia Institute Press
Box 5284, Manchester, NH 03108
1-800-888-9344

www.SophiaInstitute.com

Sophia Institute Press® is a registered trademark of Sophia Institute.

Paperback ISBN 978-1-622828-227
eBook ISBN 978-1-622828-234
Library of Congress Control Number: 2020941910

First printing

For my wife, Barbara Stuart

Contents

Acknowledgments

Mike Aquilina inaugurated this book by recommending my name to the publisher. His example and friendship have shown me the importance and the possibility of writing history for a general audience. If religious people do not tell stories that help them to know who they are, they will find themselves "out-narrated" by the secular culture — as Bishop Robert Barron wrote in his introduction to *Evangelization & Culture* (Spring 2020). Thank you, Mike Aquilina, for your incredible work and your wise counsel.

Many years ago, Monsignor James Shea, President of the University of Mary, asked me on a job interview: "What do you think about the Enlightenment?" I cannot remember exactly what I said, but I got hired. This book is a more thorough answer.

Many colleagues at the University of Mary helped with this project. Thank you especially to Donald Bungum, Chris Collins, Michon Matthiesen, Julie Jacobson, and Jordan Grant. I am grateful to the staff at Welder Library — especially Nicole Eckroth — who managed to secure hundreds of books and articles for my use. Patrick McCloskey of the *360 Review* helped me develop a more readable writing style. Students have given valuable feedback, especially those in the Catholicism and the Modern World class (spring 2019) and the Enlightenment and Eighteenth Century class (fall 2019). Thank you especially to Stephen Tan, Annie Roufs, Jonathan Hagen, Merry Blomquist, Nicholas Hoffarth, Cray Kennedy, John MacLeod, and Kyle Reynolds.

Rethinking the Enlightenment

I have not tried to break new ground in this book but to bring together the incredible work of other scholars. Without their penetrating research and wise judgments, I could never have accomplished my aim. They are acknowledged in the footnotes.

I am so grateful to Fae Presley, Heidi Pohl, and Ray Gruby for their comments on various drafts. Sister Agatha Muggli and Father Benedict Fischer helped me understand more deeply the Benedictine spirit. Christopher Blum offered critical comments. Floy Hampshire and Richard P. Heitzenrater helped me with John Wesley. It has been a joy to work with everyone at Sophia Institute Press on this book.

Having the good fortune to have grown up near Piety Hill in Michigan, I am grateful for many years spent there with Annette Kirk and the formal dinners and salon conversations she hosted with scholars, businesspeople, and politicians. Experiences there shaped my appreciation for "Catholic Enlightenment" and for events such as "Dining at Ferney" in chapter 3.

I offer thanks to Laura and Jim Frank, my mother-in-law and father-in-law. Their practical know-how in the daily affairs of life often made it possible for me to focus on writing. My two little daughters, Ann Marie and Rose, prayed that "Daddy can finish his book soon"; thank you.

Truly, it takes a community to write a book, and at the heart of mine is my wife, Barbara. She believed in this project from the start. Barbara's keen eye for clarity, grammar, and truth regularly challenged me and inspired me. I dedicate this work to you, my bride.

Introduction

The Enlightenment was a powerful and diverse cultural movement of the eighteenth century, trumpeting the merits of science, practical improvements, and polite interaction in the burgeoning public sphere of coffeehouses and cheap print media. It was an exciting time of increasing networks of communication, with information spreading through individuals interacting in ways resembling our digital age. The Enlightenment changed conceptions of time, space, and sociability—even in Christian churches and monasteries. It supported a culture of conversation and publicity both dangerous and enriching. While some thinkers attacked the churches, many leaders saw religion as the basis of society and virtue, which made the 1700s the "Age of Benevolence" as much as the "Age of Reason," the "Age of the Holy Spirit" as much as the "Age of Revolution."

Because the Enlightenment is often ignored as a source of religious inspiration, it needs to be remembered differently. To do that, we must rethink how it has often been portrayed as the root of secular modernity. Seen as opposing faith to reason, the Enlightenment is blamed (or praised) for putting religion into terminal decline. Despite creating serious challenges and direct attacks on faith, however, the Enlightenment also opened new avenues for faith to flourish—Christian faith in particular.

That paradox is the subject of this book. It is not enough simply to investigate the relationship between Christianity and the Enlightenment as two systems of thought. Rather, it is necessary to trace the interaction of two cultures, two lived realities and two overlapping ways of life.

A cultural approach in this book makes it possible to take up the challenge of Joseph Ratzinger (Pope Benedict XVI). He wrote that the Second Vatican Council (1962–1964) "incorporated the collective efforts of theologians and philosophers from the previous two hundred years to open the gates that had divided the faith from the learning of the Enlightenment and embark on a fertile exchange between the two."[1] Historians can help too. By advancing this exchange between faith and the Enlightenment, we will see how early modernity not only *combated* Christianity, it also *enabled* it. For example, Enlightenment-era Christians learned to appreciate "rational devotion." They better distinguished between the natural and the supernatural to combat superstition while supporting both science and faith. Christians appealed to individual minds and hearts by utilizing improvements of the "Practical Enlightenment" in transportation and communication. They had *faith in the age of reason*, often sharing its hopes and taking up its solutions to problems.

I argue that Christians interacted with the Enlightenment in three ways during the eighteenth century: through conflict, engagement, and retreat. The "Conflictual Enlightenment" in part 1 was centered in France and collided with basic Christian beliefs about divine revelation and human nature. It resulted in conflict, confrontation, and even martyrdom, as in the fate of the Carmelites of Compiègne. The sins of Catholics, however, and their own internal conflicts, proved as dangerous to Catholics as the attacks of famous writers such as Rousseau and Voltaire.

The "Catholic Enlightenment" in part 2, based in Italy and Germany, sought to embrace human reason as a powerful tool for reforming the Church and society. It elicited an optimistic strategy of sophisticated cultural engagement, as in the work of Maria Agnesi, Pope Benedict XIV, and the Benedictines.

---

[1]   Joseph Cardinal Ratzinger, "Letter to Marcello Pera," in *Without Roots: The West, Relativism, Christianity, Islam* (New York: Basic Books, 2006), 116.

The "Practical Enlightenment" in part 3, focused on the English-speaking world, denotes the Enlightenment of the practical people who profoundly shaped modern history through innovations in industry, business, and politics. Amid this new material world, the Christian strategy of retreat (in a spiritual sense) was not one of direct conflict or engagement. It had a different emphasis: to build up the household of faith from within Christian culture and to reach out to others in the "New Evangelization" of the day. This movement utilized certain achievements of the Practical Enlightenment, such as mass publishing and better roads, to touch the hearts of thousands with the gospel. Religious revival worked a moral revolution that affected basic assumptions about political authority in the United States and human dignity in the British campaign against African slavery.

The three Christian strategies of conflict, engagement, and retreat emerged in different times and places and in different ways. They involved various emphases and different strengths and weaknesses. Christians discerned the need for each of these three strategies depending on their circumstances. I argue that it is ultimately necessary to integrate all three strategies for a fruitful relationship between religion and culture. When different parts of the Kingdom of God work together according to diverse vocations and talents, the relationship between faith and reason rests on a solid foundation. This happened in the Age of the Enlightenment, which has important implications for our times.

In order to understand this argument, a few terms need clarifying. I use the term "Enlightener" instead of *philosophe* to refer to protagonists of the Enlightenment, Christian or otherwise. The concept "modern history" refers to the entire period since Columbus until today, roughly 1500 onward. "Early modern" refers to the first part of this period to 1789—the beginning of the French Revolution. The modern world has partly resulted from "modernity," a mindset or atmosphere of ideas that, to some extent, one can choose to accept or not. The mentality of modernity emerged as a cultural force during the Enlightenment, involving individual autonomy and critical evaluation of tradition and custom. The term "Catholic Restoration" signals those early modern efforts by

Catholics not only to meet challenges stemming from the Age of Reformations (1500–1650) but also to renew and build up a more vibrant Catholic culture into the eighteenth century. The word "culture" itself means a common way of life of a people. Every culture is influenced by multiple traditions that interweave with other cultures through complex channels of interaction. This book is about some of those interactions in the Age of the Enlightenment.

Part 1

Conflict and the Conflictual Enlightenment

Crush the infamous!
—Voltaire

Do not be conformed to this world.
—Romans 12:2

Do you think that I have come to give peace on earth?
No, I tell you, but rather division.
—Luke 12:51

1

Obedience unto Death

After her election as Carmelite prioress in 1786, thirty-four-year-old Mother Teresa of St. Augustine learned of a mysterious document in the monastery's archive. The document dated from the previous century. It recorded the strange mystical dream of a partially paralyzed young woman who had lived at the Compiègne monastery, north of Paris, for years as a paying guest. In 1694, this woman entered the monastery as a nun. In the dream, she saw herself and the Compiègne community receive the embrace of Christ and a special call to "follow the Lamb" who offered himself up in sacrifice for the good of others.

When Mother Teresa of St. Augustine discovered this record, she did not know it would eventually lead her community to offer their lives as a sacrifice to God to end the worst stage of the French Revolution, the Reign of Terror. Yet, as she read it, her heart and her soul thrilled with the premonition of a great calling, a high vocation to "follow the Lamb" by resisting the spirit of the age. The document inspired in her the re-alization that Christ might be calling her community to a particularly dangerous kind of witness.[2]

A few years after Mother Teresa of St. Augustine read this document, and one century after the mysterious dream, the National Assembly of Revolutionary France ordered all monasteries to close. This forced the

[2]   William Bush, *To Quell the Terror* (Washington, DC: Institute of Carmelite Studies, 1999), 39–42.

Carmelite nuns out in the streets. All they had to wear were dresses so low-cut that they had to cover their bosoms with scarves. More than 140 Carmelite monasteries collapsed; many of the monks and nuns fled the country. The days of suffering had come, as prophesied.

The previous fusion of French culture and Christianity had ended, and the expulsion of these Carmelite women signaled a radical conflict of cultures. A new way of life had emerged in eighteenth-century France, inspired by what could be called the "Conflictual Enlightenment." This was a powerful strand of the Enlightenment movement in conflict with basic Christian truth claims. Though it did not constitute the whole story of the Enlightenment, this Conflictual Enlightenment attacked Christianity in direct and subtly seductive ways — not least by infiltration. Many well-intentioned priests and bishops, enthusiastic for social reform, deceived themselves about the seemingly benign spirit of the age. They not only forwarded the Conflictual Enlightenment but also helped ignite the Revolution in 1789. Some ended up marrying and forsaking their priesthood. Others took an oath agreeing that the French nation possessed authority over all religious matters, putting them in schism with Rome.

After confiscating Church property, making the Church dependent on government largesse, the authorities sought to remove completely the centuries of Christian influence woven into the culture. They eliminated the Christian calendar, replacing the seven-day week with a ten-day week called a "decade." They based the year number on the birth of the Republic rather than on the birth of Christ. In Year II of the French Republic, the government closed churches or turned them into "temples of Reason." The Committee of Public Salvation, with masterful art and propaganda, organized huge festivals in honor of the Republic and of the Supreme Being — most notably on June 8, 1794, the old Christian feast of Pentecost and the birthday of the Christian church. A new, secular religion and its "church" of the state was emerging, and it strove mightily to efface Christ. Presided over by the revolutionary leader Maximilien Robespierre, the new religion demanded daily blood sacrifice. For the sake of group advancement, it executed individuals deemed "public enemies" on the altar of the guillotine. Robespierre also popularized its new motto: Liberty, equality, fraternity. Those words appeared on buildings all over Paris (and still do). The Catholic and Royal Army, made up of thousands of peasants from western France, rose up to resist this new paganism in 1793. Within a year, they had fallen in defeat, and the government's troops crushed them in mass executions.

During these attacks, the Carmelites of Compiègne refused to leave their vocations or their mission. "We are victims of our century," penned one of them, "and we must sacrifice ourselves that it be reconciled to God." As the moon and the planets follow obediently the trajectories laid out for them by God's laws of nature, so these Carmelites would keep to their way of living out God's divine law revealed in their consciences. They would swim against the current.[3]

Their story reveals the conflict between the holy logic of the Christian way of life and the worldly logic of the Enlightenment way of life. The nuns' witness provides a touchstone against which to view, in the later chapters of part 1, the stories of two great Enlighteners who passionately attacked Christianity, Jean-Jacques Rousseau and Voltaire, as well as the sad legacies of Catholic sin. But first, one must understand the lives of these nuns.

Liberty, Fraternity, Equality — the Carmelite Way

After their expulsion from their monastery in 1792, the Carmelites lived secretly in four separate groups. They met together for Mass and for their daily act of consecration, offering themselves to Christ for peace in the Church and in France and for a lessening of the numbers going to the guillotine. They strove to maintain as best they could their rule of life, which derived from St. Teresa of Avila in the sixteenth century.

---

[3] Madame Crérien de Neuville, July 1794, quoted in ibid., 38.

According to their Rule, they were a community of women governed by women. They lived out their Christian liberty through electing their own leaders. No male superior could force them to vote for a candidate—"for the Nuns are always at full liberty to elect any other whom they may think best qualified," the Rule stated.

They only admitted new members truly seeking to live a life of prayer, holiness, and detachment from the world—even from "carpets, curtains, or cushions," as their Rule put it. Their ascetic purpose was to submit themselves to their true end: God. Their vocation was not of their own choosing, in the sense that each woman felt called to the community by God. Novices who aspired to become new members, however, had to give their full consent to join: "for the Nuns should not in any way wish to keep them in the Convent against their will but only with their full consent." The Rule was regularly read aloud to the nuns so they would know it well. Respect for persons permeated it: "Consequently, when it appears that they [the novices] do not wish to persevere in the Order, ample opportunity is to be given them of opening their minds to proper persons, and of clearly manifesting their will." In addition, the Rule required the discreet presence of multiple nuns when guests or male confessors visited the community. This helped guard the community from abuses of authority and misunderstandings.[4]

Before their expulsion from the monastery, the parents of one Sister Constance sought to bring her home, with force, if necessary. She had not yet made her final vows. Her family believed that due to the current political situation, she had no future with the community. Confronted by her brother and the police, Sister Constance remained firm: she refused to leave her community. She expressed love and respect for her parents and her brother but declared resolutely that—led by her

---

4 *Rule and Constitutions of the Discalced Nuns of the Order of Our Blessed Lady of Mount Carmel* (Dublin: Cahill, 1928), 24, 27.

conscience—nothing but death could separate her from her companions. Convinced of her free will in the matter, the police (at that time) did not force her to leave.[5]

On another occasion, with armed guards posted throughout the monastery, local authorities questioned the women to see how many of the nuns secretly yearned to leave and resume life as normal French citizens. The written responses of the women still exist. Each believed she was vowed to God until death and wanted to remain in the cloister. The novice mistress explicitly told the authorities she had turned away from the world's cares, its judgments, and its so-called freedom. She preferred the sweet chains binding her to God, knowing that all the world could offer was of little worth, as one historian summarized her testimony.[6]

In these ways, the Rule respected the nuns' liberty. It also encouraged their "fraternity"—another value of the French Revolution—by inculcating mutual love and correction, common ownership of property, and service to one another. Individual nuns had specific responsibilities to care for certain elderly or ill sisters. During times of recreation, the nuns "should endeavor to be affable and agreeable to one another, and their mirth and conversation should be moderate and discreet," the Rule noted.[7] Resentment and antipathy sometimes entered their community too, but the nuns were called to forgive and bear with one another's faults.

In addition to liberty and fraternity, the nuns lived out the value of equality too. "The Prioress and senior Religious should not be treated with greater attention or care than the rest of the Community, but all alike." The nuns should not address each other with titles peculiar to worldly rank, such as "Lady" or "Madam," but in humble terms such as "Mother" or "Sister."[8] While the Compiègne community included a

---

[5]   Bush, *To Quell the Terror*, 70.
[6]   Ibid., 83–84.
[7]   *Rule and Constitutions*, 34.
[8]   Ibid., 45.

diversity of women from the illiterate to the aristocratic, they strove to regard each other with equal respect.

Together, they created a path through the difficulty and goodness of shared communal life. "Where two or three are gathered in my name, there am I in the midst of them," Christ told his followers (Matt. 18:20). Based on their participation in Christian community and the practice of virtue, the nuns knew the simplicity of God's saving truth as accessible even to the most uneducated person. Yet this sort of knowledge—what can be called "participative knowledge"—was difficult to live out, to practice, and therefore to know well. The more they strove for it with Christ, however, the better they could understand the holy wisdom of the saints.[9] This wisdom strengthened these Carmelite women internally for the challenges they would face ahead. Naturally, the new regime did not acknowledge that its liberal ideals—liberty, fraternity, and equality—had any Christian roots or that the Carmelites already lived those ideals in their own way.

The Enlightenment

The wider context of these women's lives was the Enlightenment. This powerful cultural movement of the eighteenth century was energized by globalized trade and knowledge production. Inspired by the possibilities of rationalism, empiricism, and technology, and angered by abuses of power, the protagonists of the Enlightenment (whom I call "Enlighteners") affected many aspects of life—from agriculture to worship, education, and the practice of medicine and the arts. They often opposed what they viewed as irrational traditions, ignorance, and barriers to individual liberty. Usually clustering in cities, Enlighteners adopted a code of public civility that restrained passions, moderated tempers, and refined tastes. They believed in the possibilities of human action, church reform, and the

---

[9]   Brad S. Gregory, *The Unintended Reformation: How a Religious Revolution Secularized Society* (Cambridge: Belknap/Harvard University Press, 2012), 308.

power of useful knowledge to improve life. They often sought to influence wider society through persuasion and through popularizing knowledge in vernacular languages (rather than the more scholarly Latin). Enlighteners — Christian and otherwise — tried to reform the world around them by applying new practices in data storage and media: dictionaries, encyclopedias, newspapers, pamphlets, learned journals, letters, and books. In addition, enlightened entrepreneurs, inventors, and businesspeople amplified a culture of innovation, institutional change, and freer markets, which launched modern economic growth.

This new Enlightenment culture was not value neutral, as it might present itself. It was not inherently anti-Christian either. For example, the culture of polite sociability that Enlighteners promoted in salons, coffee shops, bookstores, theaters, Benedictine monasteries, and masonic lodges disseminated information and news in the "paper public sphere," open to all, much like the "digital public sphere" (the Internet) today. "It was said of Socrates that he brought Philosophy down from Heaven, to inhabit among Men; and I shall be ambitious to have it said of me, that I have brought Philosophy out of Closets and Libraries, Schools and Colleges, to dwell in Clubs and Assemblies, at Tea-tables, and in Coffee-houses," wrote Joseph Addison in his famous daily publication *The Spectator.*[10] Since one could make truth claims in novel ways, both challenges and new opportunities presented themselves to Christians (and everyone else). With increasing wealth and literacy in the 1700s, the pursuit of truth — and the spreading of lies — more and more involved communication and exchange between larger numbers of people.

Regarding the Enlightenment as a cultural movement from the Christian point of view, there were three strategies of interaction possible: conflict, engagement, and retreat. This means that Enlightenment culture and Christian culture sometimes butted heads, so to speak, as in the case of the Carmelites. At other times they got along well, and at still others, they

---

[10] Joseph Addison, *Spectator*, March 12, 1711, https://www.gutenberg.org/files/12030/12030-h/SV1/Spectator1.html#section10.

largely ignored each other. This is the main argument of the present book. Since various strands of the Conflictual Enlightenment fed into the French Revolution and the situation facing the Carmelites of Compiègne, the first five chapters examine how such an extreme divide between Christian culture and the Enlightenment came about and its significance.

Conflict

Some leading figures of the day — call them "Conflictual Enlighteners" — associated scientific development with the overthrow of religion. Atheist philosophers such as Baron d'Holbach (1723–1789) thought that "religion is a mere castle in the air" and that "theology is ignorance of natural causes." Religious enthusiasts of a "barbarous God" have cut each other's throats in their religious disputes, he wrote. Away with it all! "Instructors have long enough fixed men's eyes upon heaven; let them now turn them upon earth."[11]

Conflictual Enlighteners denied original sin and the human being's need of divine redemption. Instead, they proclaimed human salvation through wealth, power, individual liberty, reason, and science: all these would create a happy future. "No bounds have been fixed to the improvement of the human faculties," the French philosopher and mathematician Nicolas de Condorcet (1743–1794) wrote.[12] The perfectibility of man is limitless. In addition, Condorcet and others substituted for the hope of Heaven the hope of living in the memory of future generations through their own fame.

They believed the world will get better and better through human effort. This was the idea of "Progress" created by the Enlightenment. Interestingly, as historian Christopher Dawson pointed out, Progress

---

[11] Baron d'Holbach, author's preface to *Good Sense without God: Or Freethoughts Opposed to Supernatural Ideas* (1772; London: W. Steward, ca. 1900), https://www.gutenberg.org/files/7319/7319-h/7319-h.htm.

[12] M. de Condorcet, *Outlines of an Historical View of the Progress of the Human Mind* (1795; Philadelphia: Lang and Ustick, 1796), 11.

represented a secularization of the Christian teleological conception of life (i.e., the belief that time has an ultimate purpose and end in God). Dawson wrote that the belief in the moral perfectibility and the limitless progress of the human race "took the place of the Christian faith in the life of the world to come, as the final goal of human effort."[13] This meant that two soteriologies (visions of salvation) competed for dominance in the eighteenth century: salvation by man and salvation by God. They collided in the French Revolution and drove the drama surrounding the Carmelites.

Another important theme of the Conflictual Enlightenment concerned the way humans come to know truth. Scandalized by two centuries of Christian infighting, confused theology, and abuses of power, Conflictual Enlighteners viewed the Christian God as capricious and irrational. God's law and church hierarchy seemed to restrict human liberty. Cast off the guardians, the pastors, and the authoritative witnesses around you, and "have courage to use your own reason!" proclaimed Immanuel Kant in his 1784 essay "What Is Enlightenment?" He promoted individual rational autonomy as the highest ideal. Submit even religious doctrine to the tribunal of individual reason. Along this line of thinking, Thomas Paine wrote in his 1794 *Age of Reason*, "My own mind is my own church."[14]

Such individualism separated reason more and more from the kind of participatory knowledge found among the Carmelites and in any genuine human community. It overlooked the problem of whether questions of ultimate meaning in human life really can be answered by individual minds on their own, without tradition and community. This move would eventually secularize knowledge and create the modern myth of value-neutral rationality as the only basis for shared, public life.

---

[13] Christopher Dawson, *Progress and Religion: An Historical Enquiry* (1929; Washington, DC: Catholic University of America Press, 2001), 149.

[14] Immanuel Kant, "What Is Enlightenment?," in *The Portable Enlightenment Reader*, ed. Isaac Kramnick (1784; New York: Penguin Books, 1995), 1; Thomas Paine, *The Age of Reason* (1794; London: Freethought, 1880), 2.

By way of contrast to this methodological individualism of the Conflictual Enlightenment, the Carmelite sisters prayed the psalms together every day. "Sacrifice and offering you do not want," the psalmist intones in Psalm 40, "but ears open to obedience you gave me." This was the touchstone not only of the Carmelites but of Christian culture as a whole, linking it back to God's historical revelation through obedience. Obedience required trust.

Ordinary human knowledge, too, requires trust. Even accomplished scholars who know a great deal in their own fields choose to trust each other. Trusting other witnesses who have seen and verified is necessary to making progress in knowledge. Analogously, like natural faith, supernatural faith has the character of nonautonomous knowledge by which one participates in the knowledge of others, as Ratzinger wrote. By means of an act of faith, the human person passes beyond the limited perspective of the individual to share in the "wealth of a communal reflection."[15]

If natural theology proved the reasonability of believing in God, natural reason also suggested that if God existed, he might reveal himself. The Carmelite sisters held that a transcendent and loving God had indeed made himself known. His authority guaranteed the credibility of what he revealed through his people as a historically continuous community making specific theological truth claims.

Whereas Conflictual Enlighteners took natural reason solely as their guide in religious matters, imagining themselves as their own highest authority, Christians were obliged to take their ultimate principles from outside themselves. But they did not accept from others blindly. They verified the truth claims of that historical community (the church) by their own participative knowledge inside their communities. In that sense, Kant's dictum to use one's own understanding is sound: God's law

---

[15] Joseph Cardinal Ratzinger, *Christianity and the Crisis of Cultures*, trans. Brian McNeil (San Francisco: Ignatius Press, 2006), 101–102; Pope John Paul II, *Fides et Ratio: On the Relationship between Faith and Reason* (Boston: Pauline Books & Media, 1998), no. 101.

and his mercy, passed down through tradition, internalized and lived out, really *are* the true sources of liberty, fraternity, and equality. From the Christian point of view, true liberty could never involve rejecting God, for how could an authentic use of human liberty involve rejecting the very source of human realization?

In effect, however, the arguments of the Conflictual Enlighteners worked to undermine communities of faith by sowing the seeds of distrust. Their attacks contributed to a mounting spiritual crisis that swept across the eighteenth century like a wave until it enveloped the whole of modern history.

In response to that crisis, the prioress Mother Teresa of St. Augustine carefully guarded her community. The other nuns possessed the duty of obedience to her authority, but on her lay the responsibility to exercise her authority for the true spiritual and temporal good of her sisters. The bond of obedience would preserve the roots of faith in communal, participatory knowledge. Mother Teresa had to guard the decorum and the enclosure of the monastery with discernment, because the spirits of distrust tempted with compromise following on compromise until they might breach the walls of the enclosure altogether. She was also concerned that none of her sisters went to martyrdom against her will or the will of God. She would not impose her private interpretation of the mystical dream on the others, as if it were inevitable. Rather, she would vigorously defend her community after their arrest against the false charges put forward by the Public Prosecutor.[16]

Through the Silent Streets of Paris

It was on June 22, 1794, that local authorities arrested the Carmelites of Compiègne and sent them to Paris for trial with an explanatory letter. The Revolutionary Surveillance Committee had found evidence in their apartments that the nuns were still trying to live their Carmelite lives,

---

[16] Bush, *To Quell the Terror*, 179.

which was illegal. "Always in pursuit of traitors, we constantly focus our attention on those perfidious persons who dare plot against the Republic," the letter read, "or who express wishes for freedom's destruction."[17]

In Paris, Public Prosecutor Fouquier de Tinville dated the formal accusation against the nuns July 16, 1794—which happened to be the feast of Our Lady of Mount Carmel, patroness of the Carmelite order. In the "Courtroom of Liberty" the next day, he charged them with fanaticism. One of the sisters challenged Fouquier de Tinville, asking him what he meant by labeling them "fanatics." He replied that their attachment to their Christian religion qualified them as such. That made them enemies of the people. There was no doubt now they would suffer because of Christ. Ironically, the three judges who presided sat beneath posters proclaiming human rights. Charged with conspiring against the Republic, officials loaded the nuns into the tumbrels (wagons) that would take them to the guillotine.

As they rode to the place of execution, faces radiant, they began to sing all together the Miserere — "Have mercy upon me, O God, after thy great goodness." Usually the crowds mocked and yelled at the condemned, but those who saw what happened that day testified to the silence of everyone. Historian William Bush speculated that perhaps for some of the spectators, the singing conjured up for them "holy memories" of their Christian past, now effaced for years by the new regime.[18]

Through the silent streets of Paris, with crowds holding their breath, the Carmelites sang Vespers, Compline, the Office of the Dead, and the Salve Regina, sacred words welling up from their hearts as much as from the depths of Christian culture. Those words announced the transcendence of God against the arrogance of the age.

---

[17] The Revolutionary Surveillance Committee of Compiègne to the People's Representatives of the National Convention Constituting the Committees of Public Salvation and of Public Security, June 25, 1794, quoted in ibid., 165.

[18] Bush, *To Quell the Terror*, 201.

As the scaffold came into sight at the Place du Trône, on the road to Vincennes leading out of Paris, the nuns chanted the Te Deum—"It is Thee we praise, O God!" They probably did not know that as they moved along, they drew nearer the place where a deep tremor had once occurred beneath the surface of time, subtle but powerful, inside a human soul that changed the tone of the age. Years before, the great Conflictual Enlightener Jean-Jacques Rousseau had fallen by the side of that very road—the road to Vincennes—in a kind of ecstatic vision. His moment of revelation had inspired the impassioned writing of his many books. Rousseau's words helped fuel the engine of revolution that now bore down on the nuns.

The Carmelites of Compiègne at the guillotine.

2

The Road to Vincennes

Rousseau's Tears

It was a sweltering day in 1749. Thirty-seven-year-old Jean-Jacques Rousseau scanned the pages of a literary magazine as he walked along the road, heading east out of Paris. The trees planted along the roadside, shorn of most of their branches as per local custom, did not offer much shade. The amateur musician had recently returned to Paris from Venice, where he had worked as secretary to a French ambassador. In Paris, he met the chambermaid Marie-Thérèse Levasseur, an illiterate young woman from a family that had fallen on hard times. They lived together as lovers, and she gave birth to their children. Rousseau dropped them off one by one at the foundling hospital, convincing Thérèse that this would preserve her "honor." Without little ones to care for, he was free to pay regular visits to his philosopher friend Denis Diderot, who was imprisoned just outside the city in the town of Vincennes.

As he walked along reading, his eye fell on an advertisement for an essay competition. "Has the progress of the sciences and arts contributed to corrupt or purify morals?" it read. The question suddenly ignited his mind and overwhelmed his soul. Perhaps humans are naturally good? Perhaps evil proceeds not from the heart of man but from the constraint and competition of an artificial civilization? Maybe we need to return to our natural simplicity in order to be whole? From the moment he read those words in the magazine, Rousseau wrote, "I beheld another world and became another man." Dazzled by a thousand sparkling lights as crowds of lively ideas thronged his mind, he felt giddy and intoxicated. With difficulty breathing and violent palpitation of the heart, he threw himself down under a tree and "there passed a half hour in such agitation that on rising I found the whole front of my shirt wet with tears, without having been conscious that I had shed them." He noted that if he could have written down what he saw in those moments of clarity, he would have brought out all the contradictions of society and simply demonstrated that man is naturally good—only by institutions is he made bad. There is no such thing as sin. Rather, an artificial society causes evil and misfortune. Goodness means following the impulses of nature; virtue is not obedience to an unchanging truth but simply restraining one's impulses from hurting others. In a flash of inspiration, in a moment of what the ancients called "poetic fury," Rousseau's inverted conversion experience led him to believe he finally understood what it is to be human.[19]

Rousseau's experience that day elucidates the side of the Enlightenment in conflict with Christianity. His collapse in ecstasy before a vision of man's original goodness subtly denied the need for a personal redeemer. Human beings can save themselves, his best-selling books would imply, because the enemy is not sin but competition, unjust social structures, and the guilt-provoking "other." Rearranging society and politics would lead to true freedom and happiness. Though different versions of that seductive, utopian vision existed among Conflictual Enlighteners, their belief in ultimate worldly happiness deeply inspired the French revolutionaries and propelled the most acute stage of the eighteenth-century cultural conflict. Rousseau's tears and his many books inaugurated a moral revolution *before* the later political revolution that would seek to destroy

---

[19] Jean-Jacques Rousseau, Second Letter to Malesherbes, January 12, 1762, in Jean-Jacques Rousseau, *The Confessions, and Correspondence, Including the Letters to Malesherbes*, ed. Roger D. Masters, Christopher Kelly, and Peter G. Stillman, trans. Christopher Kelly, vol. 5, *The Collected Writings of Rousseau* (Hanover: Dartmouth College, 1995), 575; Jean-Jacques Rousseau, *The Confessions* (1782; New York: Modern Library, n.d.), 361.

Christianity and the Carmelites forty-five years later, on the very same road to Vincennes Rousseau strolled that fateful day in 1749.

Taking Up a Mission

When Rousseau arrived at his destination in Vincennes, his friend Diderot wondered why he seemed so agitated. Diderot (1713–1784) would become one of the lead characters of the Conflictual Enlightenment in France, serving as chief editor of that great compendium of Enlightenment thought called the *Encyclopédie*, published between 1751 and 1772. Not long before Rousseau's visit, Diderot had published his *Letter on the Blind*, about the science of visual perception and about how a doctor had performed a surgery on cataracts. Diderot's letter drew attention to the plight of the blind and helped overcome long-standing contemporary prejudices against them. He also revealed his atheism, however, and his belief that one can explain everything in terms of matter and motion. This landed him in prison.

Rousseau told him what had happened by the side of the road. Diderot encouraged his friend to give full play to his ideas. "With inconceivable rapidity, my feelings became elevated to the tone of my ideas. All my petty passions were stifled by the enthusiasm of truth, liberty and virtue."[20] Rousseau dashed off his essay and entered the contest.

He won. The news of his victory transformed him. It awoke again all the ideas that had been born on that day on the road to Vincennes. It animated him with fresh vigor, stirred up his heart, and broke loose a latent power deep inside that gave him the words to express his meaning in a language the people of his age would understand.[21] He secretly believed that what had happened to him was the revelation of a divine mission to spread natural religion of the heart. For the first time, after repeated experiences of failure in his life, he gained a sense of purpose. Rousseau's

[20] Rousseau, *The Confessions*, 361–362.
[21] Ibid., 362, 366.

friends and acquaintances no longer recognized him. Audacious, proud, and undaunted, he carried with him everywhere a newfound confidence.[22]

Rousseau's sudden and overwhelming moment of revelation changed the direction of his life. The energy released on that day started a chain reaction that propelled the creation of his major writings for more than a decade: *Discourse on the Arts and Sciences* (1750), *Discourse on the Origin and Basis of Inequality among Men* (1754), *Julie, or the New Heloise* (1761), *Emile, or On Education* (1762), and *The Social Contract* (1762), among others. These works caused a revolution in Western literature, morality, social relationships, education, and politics.

After publishing his major works by 1762, Rousseau fled France as a fugitive due to resistance to his ideas. Even in exile, people stoned his residence in Switzerland and the local pastor denounced him as the Antichrist. Rousseau would escape this personal distress by heading out into nature on solitary walks. He would flee into a wild spot in the forest, some deserted place without tiresome people demanding things of him. He loved humanity in general, and he loved the idea of people, but real people he found burdensome. They came between him and his natural self, and thus between him and happiness.

In his wild place, Rousseau would deliver himself up to the world of his imagination. He peopled it with worthy men — imaginary and perfect people in his mind who made no demands. Rousseau recorded that in order to fill the "inexplicable void" he found in himself that nothing could fill, he would give himself over to sentiment. From there he would try to lose himself in contemplation of all the beings of nature, the universal system of things, and the incomprehensible being who embraces all things. With his mind lost in the immensity of it all, he would abandon himself to the confusion of these great ideas. Melting into nature, he found himself "smothered in the universe" with the desire to throw himself into the infinite. Those times of "stupefying

---

[22] Ibid., 430.

ecstasy" outdoors were truly the days that gave him the most happiness in life, he wrote.[23]

Here Rousseau entered the worldview of pantheism, and an "emotional pantheism" at that. This is the belief that the world is divine. God is not transcendent over his creation; he *is* creation. Nature and supernature collapse into one. There is no real distinction between the secular and the sacred. When this view intersected with politics in his writings, Rousseau essentially collapsed church and state into one, powerful "sacred state"—as actually emerged during the French Revolution.

Developing the Doctrines of Emotional Pantheism

Rousseau was born in 1712 in Geneva, a city infamous for its regime of strict Calvinist morality that suppressed human sinfulness. The Reformer John Calvin (1509–1564) had turned it into a "Protestant Rome" in the sixteenth century, a model city on a hill that sent out missionaries across Europe. Those missionaries deeply affected France, where a puritanical form of Catholicism called Jansenism took root. Because Calvin believed in the total depravity of human nature, one could not trust people to act virtuously on their own. So they had to be forced. Calvin set up the Consistory in Geneva as moral police that pushed good behavior through surveillance of conduct and punishment of misbehavior. Rousseau's ancestors had fallen under its scrutiny at various times. Law was an external, oppressive force rather than a life-giving one, and Rousseau spent his days fleeing it.

By Rousseau's time, the old Calvinist doctrines of predestination and depraved human nature had gone into decline—though the mental habits and culture they created remained. In early-eighteenth-century Geneva, Christianity was about morality: living an austere, virtuous life

---

[23] Jean-Jacques Rousseau, Third Letter to Malesherbes, January 26, 1762, in Rousseau, *The Confessions, and Correspondence, Including the Letters to Malesherbes*, 5, 578–579.

that avoided worldly enjoyment. Godliness consisted of denying oneself pleasure. While the puritanical restrictions on pleasure had relaxed somewhat during the previous generation, the city still banned the theater in Rousseau's time.

Despite Rousseau's hatred of restraint, Calvin and the patterns of Genevan culture retained a certain hold over him. In fact, Rousseau inverted Calvin: Calvin's idea of depraved human nature prompted reaction through Rousseau's vision of purely good human nature. Calvin thought he could arrive at ultimate truth by going to God directly through the Bible, and Rousseau mirrored this unmediated individualism by going to nature directly through his emotions. In addition, Rousseau always thought of himself as the citizen of a state founded by a philosopher (Calvin). Rousseau would sign the title pages of his books as, "J. J. Rousseau, Citizen of Geneva," signifying his attachment to his city as a kind of ideal. Calvin was actually a lawyer and a theologian, not a philosopher, but no matter. Rousseau imagined him founding the city of Geneva and that impressive accomplishment seems to have shaped his utopian approach to politics. Politics was not the art of the possible in Rousseau. It was the art of forming a community in the same opinions and virtuous behavior through the action of the state. The ideological possibilities latent in this vision would fire the imagination of Robespierre and other leaders of the French Revolution.[24]

Rousseau's mother died at his birth. His weak father, who did not send Rousseau to school but "educated" him at home, lived a dissolute life, reading romance adventures to his young son all night. In the early morning, hearing the birds begin to sing, his father would say, "Let us go to bed; I am more of a child than yourself." Rousseau recalled in his immensely popular autobiography, *The Confessions*, that these childhood experiences with his father instilled in him a romantic notion of human

---

[24] Maurice Cranston, *Jean-Jacques: The Early Life and World of Jean-Jacques Rousseau, 1712–1754* (New York: W. W. Norton, 1982), 15, 17, 20–21, 27.

life and passion.[25] Rousseau's father got into a quarrel and fled Geneva, leaving his son with relatives. Young Rousseau ended up as an apprentice to an engraver. He hated his new master and restraint of any kind. He developed the habit of justifying his actions no matter what. Even years later, he believed there was nothing wrong about his lying and stealing as an adolescent.

Finding himself unhappy and locked outside the city gates one night, he fled Geneva and fell in with a Catholic priest. The priest, in turn, gave him to the care of twenty-nine-year-old Françoise-Louise de Warens (1699–1762), living south of Geneva. This was his real education. Madame de Warens was a noblewoman of Protestant background who had separated from her husband and converted to Catholicism. She loved music and entertaining educated members of the clergy. Rousseau was not quite sixteen. She took care of him in every way. Rousseau idolized her as his "mommy."

As a convert and professional lay proselytizer, Madame de Warens received money from the King of Piedmont (northwest Italy) to help bring Protestants to Catholicism. Thus, Rousseau converted to her religion, which he practiced for a time. Madame de Warens was attracted to Catholicism's more optimistic view of human nature, beauty, and pleasure. Rousseau followed her in rejecting stark Calvinist doctrine on these matters. He would, though, revert to Calvinism later in life so he could reinstate his Genevan citizenship.

Madame de Warens believed only in the Catholic doctrines that appealed to her, however. Nothing was bad. Impulse seemed always to move her. She was influenced by the mystical movement Quietism that

---

[25] Rousseau, *The Confessions*, 6, 7. Rousseau's *Confessions* effectively flipped the theme of St. Augustine's autobiography of the same title by replacing original sin and the human need for repentance with his own vision of the original goodness of human nature without need of repentance. His "conversion" was away from God and toward Self. Rousseau's *Confessions* would influence modern autobiographies and the modern novel that developed after it, due to its shockingly frank portrayal of feelings and personal faults.

arose in the region during the 1680s (and was condemned by the pope as a heresy). Quietism prioritized passive interiority and good intentions over virtuous action. Quietism longed for unmediated relationship to the divine and absorption into it—a pantheistic impulse. A pure inner life made external actions irrelevant. Thus, Madame de Warens initiated Rousseau not only into Catholicism and the life of the mind but also into the intimacies of sex. The sexual aspect of their relationship confused him, but he always considered her the greatest love of his life. "She guided me," he wrote, "and always guided me well."[26]

Madame de Warens's influence laid the foundation for Rousseau's way of life during his twenties. The beliefs inspiring that way of life, coming into focus after 1749, negated original sin and closely aligned virtue with interior sincerity. Those two ideas would greatly shape his lifework.

In his book *Emile* (1762) on the education of children, Rousseau wrote, "Let us lay it down as an incontrovertible rule that the first impulses of nature are always right; there is no original sin in the human heart."[27] Obviously, Rousseau had never experienced raising real children! (After all, he abandoned his own.) Holiness, he thought, consists in loving one's own goodness without comparison and in fostering sincere intentions—the Quietist impulse. While he admitted to mistakes, Rousseau believed he never committed evil because he was always well intentioned. He trained his conscience to shift guilt to someone or something else, undermining the language of apology needed in any genuine human relationship. He fell out with those around him and found himself increasingly isolated.

When alone and troubled, Rousseau would sometimes create his own society in his imagination, made up of emanations of himself who could interact. These fantasies would hold court, find Rousseau good, and then melt back into himself. He valorized the autonomous individual and believed that unhappiness began when humans learned to depend on one another. Seeking pleasure in himself through autoeroticism, which he

---

[26] Ibid., 126.

[27] Jean-Jacques Rousseau, *Emile, or On Education*, trans. Allan Bloom (1762; New York: Basic Books, 1979), 92

nevertheless considered a bad habit, became the pattern for his seeking forgiveness in himself.[28] Presumably from much experience, he wrote a play called *Narcissus, or the Self-Admirer*. Unable to deal with his own guilt, he constantly sought to explain it away and excuse it, failing to see his real need for confession and humble reception of the mercy of God.

The archbishop of Paris, Christophe de Beaumont (1703–1781), wrote a pastoral letter against Rousseau's book *Emile*. That work on education would influence French revolutionaries during the 1790s as they pushed educational revolution as the best way to sustain political revolution over the long term. The archbishop condemned Rousseau's denial of original sin. Such a denial leads to the very destruction of the Christian religion. The archbishop and Rousseau agreed on the goodness of human nature, but the churchman insisted that one cannot understand both the greatness and the baseness of human actions in history without the truth that original sin had *damaged* man's good nature and made it prone to sin. Original sin involves the tendency to prefer self to God by rebelling against the insurmountable limits of man's creaturely status. The current *Catechism of the Catholic Church* states: "Without the knowledge Revelation gives of God we cannot recognize sin clearly and are tempted to explain it as merely a developmental flaw, a psychological weakness, a mistake, or the necessary consequence of an inadequate social structure, etc." — the very temptation that ensnared Rousseau.[29]

Rousseau's beliefs about human nature made him a powerful threat to Christianity, not least because he sought to reinterpret Christianity as the natural religion of the heart and Jesus as a moral philosopher. Through a famous, imaginary dialogue between — of all characters! — a Catholic priest and a young man walking together in the foothills of the Alps, Rousseau argued that revelation is not needed. God directly speaks to

---

28 Carol Blum, *Rousseau and the Republic of Virtue: The Language of Politics in the French Revolution* (Ithaca: Cornell University Press, 1986), 97; Jacques Maritain, *Three Reformers: Luther, Descartes, Rousseau* (London: Sheed & Ward, 1928), 108, 128.

29 *Catechism of the Catholic Church*, no. 387.

the mind and the heart. Witnesses to an ancient deposit of faith should not be believed; rely instead only on one's own reasoning. Why listen to others when one can open the book of nature for oneself and know God directly? People have within themselves a witness that enables them to do without the witness of others. Therefore, formal religion is superfluous. Besides, religious diversity around the world proves that no religion is true, Rousseau thought.[30]

One of France's best Catholic apologists responded to these ideas of Rousseau because he believed they were more dangerous than outright denial of God. Nicholas Bergier (1718–1790) — a real priest — argued against Rousseau's imaginary priest in *Deism Refuted by Itself* (1765). Religion is not merely a private affair between God and the soul. Christian revelation is a fact of history. In addition, it is not a private revelation but a revelation to all persons. It is an alliance between God and people. That alliance is made known through a body of witnesses, the Apostles, and the continuity of the Church since their time. God certified their witness through miracles, martyrdoms, and sanctity. One cannot be a Christian without accepting their testimony. Bergier challenged Rousseau's line of reasoning as absurd, based on uncritical faith in the omniscience of the individual (himself). The apologist also denied the rationalist assumption that if people simply used their reason in religion, they would all agree on a few simple truths. Appeal to mere reason leads not to religious unity but to fragmentation. Rather, faith and reason are needed together. That is because communication from an infinite God to finite creatures must necessarily surpass their comprehension.[31]

Besides denial of original sin, a second major doctrine of Rousseau's emotional pantheism involved a novel approach to virtue. In the

---

[30] Rousseau, *Emile*, 295–313. The ideas in this paragraph come from the section of *Emile* called "Profession of Faith of the Savoyard Vicar," which was admired by Voltaire.

[31] R. R. Palmer, *Catholics and Unbelievers in Eighteenth Century France*, 2nd ed. (New York: Cooper Square, 1939), 97–98.

Christian and classical traditions, virtue is the habitual tendency to do good through prudence, justice, fortitude, and temperance. In this view, the virtuous person, assisted by grace, consistently chooses the good in concrete actions. One becomes good by practicing good among other people (as did the Carmelites in their monastery), which can be difficult and humbling. This is the only way to become an integrated person. Even mainstream Conflictual Enlighteners such as Diderot and Voltaire agreed that virtue involved *doing* good.

But Rousseau had never belonged to a genuine human community —not even a family. No one had ever taught him how to practice virtue as a young man. He thought of it as an inner feeling of goodness, a state of being one can enter on one's own through cultivating sincere affections for "truth" and "justice" and "freedom" and "equality." As long as one refrains from hurting others, if one is well intentioned, one is virtuous, Rousseau believed.

Feelings and intentions inhabit the autonomous world of mind and imagination, not the world of action that links one to other people and to reality. Constantly dogged by an inability to engage uncomfortable reality, Rousseau lived in a dream world by his own admission. He created for himself an imagined reality without the cross. This way, his "free thinking" could continue to justify the gratification of his emotional and physical desires unhindered, redefining virtue to match his actions rather than vice versa. Without systematic intellectual discipline as a young man, Rousseau's random readings in philosophy only furnished him with weapons against religious dogma and convinced him of the practical insignificance of all speculation as a guide to reality and to life, the scholar Norman Wilde commented.[32]

Rousseau's doctrine of virtue tended to disassociate thought and action, man's inner and outer world. He could let loose his virtuous imagination "with the quieting consciousness ... that its cost had not

---

[32] Maritain, *Three Reformers*, 96, 100; Norman Wilde, "On the Conversion of Rousseau," *International Journal of Ethics* 26, no. 1 (October 1915): 61.

to be reckoned in deeds." His sexual affairs and his abandonment of his children may have been faults. But because he was essentially good, those faults did not make him a bad man because he deeply felt enthusiasm for justice and virtue. When it came to the moment of action to put his virtuous ideas into practice, however, he usually shrank back in escape from reality. He was weak but he was good. Thus, he separated the abstract from the concrete, as Madame de Warens had done; he excused himself when specific actions betrayed his high ideals.[33] This is the virtue of the celebrity who, caught up in his own eloquence or beauty, tries to overawe others and create a cult following around an appearance of goodness. It encouraged followers to live in their heads in the company of beautiful ideas — even while tracking footprints of blood, pooling from the guillotine, through the streets of Paris.

Rousseau discovered after that day in 1749 on the road to Vincennes that he had the power to put these doctrines on original goodness and virtue into words that thousands would read and absorb. Yet his tears were no sign of an altered life. His experience was not one of conversion so much as of clarification. It was a change not of personal morality but of the *expression* of morality. Rousseau became an expert at moral posing.

Rousseau Feels Good

Rousseau eventually fled Paris and his growing fame. He landed in an intense affair with an aristocratic woman. She had taken shelter in his modest cabin after her coachman made a wrong turn, trapping her vehicle in the mud. She was, in part, the inspiration for Rousseau's 1761 epistolary novel *Julie, or the New Heloise*, one of the best sellers of the eighteenth century. Here Rousseau created a society of perfect beings, full of desire for one another, melting and flowing into one another. The adorable seventeen-year-old Julie (his ideal woman) is filled with sentimental virtue and hypnotizes everyone around her. She falls in love with her

---

[33] Maritain, *Three Reformers*, 64, 69, 70.

tutor, Saint-Preux (Rousseau's projection of himself, and pronounced "San-Pruh"). Filled with guilt, she confesses to her parents. The father beats her in anger because Julie has fallen in love with a man of the lower class, causing the pregnant Julie to miscarry. Julie forgives her father, and she obediently marries an older, honorable man she does not love. Her husband forgives her earlier transgression with Saint-Preux and even invites him to become the tutor of their children, trusting the sincerity of both Saint-Preux and Julie. They do not betray that trust, and as she is dying from illness, Julie writes to Saint-Preux that he is the only man she ever truly loved. During this love story, Rousseau demonstrated his ideas not only on the goodness of natural human desires and the virtue of sincerity, but also on the need for toleration, education, and opposition to authority and tradition.

Although Rousseau wrote the work as a novel, a philosophical theory pervades it. Autonomy and authenticity, not rational principles, should serve as the foundation of moral decisions. One should conform to society only if such conformity agrees with the deepest feelings that make up one's core identity. Inauthentic behavior leads to self-destruction.

In an age when adultery and casual sex were as common as marrying for status rather than for love, readers found this new morality revolutionary. True love is natural and involves intense romantic and well-intentioned feelings. What distorts this love are social prejudices that smother the human heart.[34]

Demand for Rousseau's book outran supply so much that readers rented it out by the hour. Robert Darnton, an American historian of the French Enlightenment, writes about how Enlighteners such as Voltaire disliked the book but ordinary readers from all ranks of society were swept off their feet—even those who disapproved of novels. "They wept, they suffocated, they raved, they looked deep into their lives and resolved

---

[34] Claudia Durst Johnson and Vernon Johnson, *The Social Impact of the Novel: A Reference Guide* (Westport: Greenwood, 2002), 129–130; Blum, *Rousseau and the Republic of Virtue*, 63–64.

to live better, then they poured their hearts out in more tears — and in letters to Rousseau, who collected their testimonials in a huge bundle, which has survived for the inspection of posterity." The sound of sobbing permeated the letters. One fan read the same passages out loud to his friends at least ten times, each time with bursts of fresh tears all around, Darnton recorded. So overcome by emotion while reading the novel, droves of readers from all over Europe wrote to Rousseau wondering if the characters were real and telling him about the profound effects of the book on them. Women especially became so intoxicated that many offered themselves to Rousseau, the man who "truly" knew how to love. Much pleased with his success, he became one of the first celebrity intellectuals.[35]

The book incited love of "virtue" in its readers — they constantly mentioned this in their letters. Julie "never ceased to be a model of all virtues even when she lost her virtue," one fan wrote, declaring she wanted to kiss Julie's portrait. What kind of a world do we live in where virtue is but an idea? wondered another. "Happy mortal, perhaps you alone know it and practice it," she wrote to Rousseau, imagining that he must be the ideally integrated human person. One detects a longing for the figure of the *saint* in the letters, and Rousseau, many thought, was that saint who understood the human heart so well. A certain C. J. Pancourcke wrote in February 1761 to Rousseau that his words were "divine," an "all consuming fire." In Pancourke's search for happiness, they penetrated his soul, fortified his heart, and enlightened his mind. After reading other modern authors, he had become a thorough scoundrel. "I needed a god, and a mighty god, to pull me away from that precipice, and you, Monsieur, are the god who has performed the miracle." How many tears did he shed over Julie! "How often I saw my guilt. Ever since I read your blessed book, I have burned with the love

---

[35] Robert Darnton, *The Great Cat Massacre, and Other Episodes in French Cultural History* (New York: Vintage Books, 1984), 242, 245–247.

of virtue, and my heart, which I had thought extinguished, beats harder than ever." Rousseau helped readers see deeper into the meaning of their lives, Darnton noted.[36]

Rousseau even affected the *way* people read. "Rousseauistic reading" would break down the barriers between author and reader. Rousseau presented *Julie* as the unmediated communication of souls, Darnton noted. One reader concluded, "Who else can wield a pen so forcefully as to make his soul pass into theirs?" Rousseau taught readers to digest books so thoroughly that they would absorb literature into their daily lives. Reading a novel became a moral preparation for life, as was the old religious literature of the bygone age. In those times, especially in intense Calvinist religiosity, one read in order to absorb the unmediated Word of God into one's soul, Darnton wrote. One learned to apply religious books such as Scripture or catechisms to one's daily living. Rousseau encouraged his readers to apply the old style of religious reading to new material, the novel, transferring their sacred allegiance to it — and to him. "Rousseau demanded to be read as if he were a prophet of divine truth," Darnton commented. "What set Rousseauistic reading apart from its religious antecedents ... was the summons to read the most suspect form of literature, the novel, as if it were the Bible." In this way, Rousseau hoped to regenerate the world according to his vision.[37]

The letters of Jean Ranson, a wealthy merchant from La Rochelle in western France, demonstrate how Rousseau's intense hold over his readers lasted for decades. The letters were written to a friend who worked for a Swiss publisher of French books from 1774 to 1785. They reveal the same kind of response readers had in 1761 when *Julie* first appeared. Ranson received a solid Calvinist education and, as an adult, ordered many religious books, including the Bible, devotionals, a catechism, and collections of sermons from the publisher. He also ordered Rousseau's books — all of them and multiple copies of the same book. He called

---

[36] Ibid., 244–247.
[37] Ibid., 232, 233, 245, 251.

Rousseau his "friend." Ranson was very concerned to have accurate editions of Rousseau's works and longed to hear stories from the publisher about the person of Rousseau. He wanted to raise his children according to Rousseau's advice. The deist Voltaire provoked Ranson's indignation, but Rousseau! He wanted to know every word. Ranson, Darnton wrote, "wanted above all to possess the complete Rousseau, to absorb it into his inner world, and to express it in his daily life." Rousseau, who later in life saw himself as a Christlike figure, a victim for humanity due to constant (often self-created) sufferings, became Ranson's principle for a new way of life.

Thus, the Conflictual Enlightenment clashed with Christianity at the deepest level. The Carmelite sisters (on their way to the guillotine) sang the Miserere: "Have mercy upon me, O God, after thy great goodness." Not Rousseau. Man can save man, his substitute religion held, because the enemy is not sin but the guilt-provoking other.[38]

The Shrine

Rousseau died in 1778, lonely and isolated from everyone. His persona and his cult continued to grow, however, inspiring an inexhaustible market in portraits, prints, statuettes, and busts of his image. His tomb was in a beautiful park on the Isle of Poplars near Ermenonville, northeast of Paris. One of Rousseau's disciples who drew his inspiration from the master's idealization of nature designed the romantic-style garden. It resembled a natural environment untouched by human intervention. The monument itself was in neoclassical style and inscribed with the words "Here rests the man of Nature and of Truth." There were busts of Socrates and Virgil and a Temple of Philosophy. Columns celebrating Voltaire and Newton made Rousseau their equal.

People came from everywhere to visit and weep on the grave of this secular saint. "If some day I should travel near Ermenonville, I shall

---

[38] Ibid., 239; Blum, *Rousseau and the Republic of Virtue*, 104.

Tomb of Jean-Jacques Rousseau, *by Jean Michel Moreau the Younger (1778).*

not fail to visit his grave and perhaps to shed some tears on it," Ranson wrote to his friend the publisher. A certain Gabriel Brizard, an admirer of Voltaire and Rousseau and future supporter of the French Revolution, made a pilgrimage to the tomb in 1783 with a friend. On the first day, he recorded seeing relics of Rousseau in his nearby cabin. Touching Rousseau's snuffbox made his heart thrill and his soul purer, he recalled. Brizard and his friend admired the shoes of the simple man who always walked in the path of virtue. On day two, they went to the lake and addressed prayers to "St. Julie." They saw various Englishmen swimming across to the island to visit the tomb. The next day, still not daring to cross over themselves, they sang hymns in honor of Rousseau. Finally, they crossed on the fourth day to kiss the stone of the monument. "I shall not have made this pilgrimage to no purpose," Brizard wrote later, "it was with the object of getting better acquainted with virtue."[39]

[39] Darnton, *The Great Cat Massacre*, 239; Maritain, *Three Reformers*, 107.

Leading figures of the age also paid homage. Benjamin Franklin, Thomas Jefferson, King Louis XVI, Marie Antoinette, and revolutionary leaders such as Saint-Just and Robespierre all made pilgrimages there at one time or another. This secular shrine signaled the ways that Rousseau's pantheistic celebration of nature commanded respect even if it did not win over all the elites of the age.

Rousseau's revelatory experience on the road to Vincennes inaugurated a moral revolution. He became the prophet of a new gospel. "It is impossible to exaggerate the effect of Rousseau's teaching on his generation," historian Christopher Dawson wrote. "It came into the brilliant artificial world of the Enlightenment like a warm west wind from the fields into a lighted salon, extinguishing the tapers and filling the air with the scent of damp earth and rain-soaked vegetation." The natural man, free from the fetters of abstract reason, is the good man. The simple peasant, simply because he is simple, is better than the educated man. In a rationalist world of strict etiquette and tight corsets, of urbanized elites cut off from natural ways of life by their posturing and their striving for money, Rousseau inspired people to live differently, even to the point of dressing up as peasants and watering artificial flowers in pavement gardens. Go back to the goodness of nature and of human emotion, was his message. Voltaire gnashed his teeth in anger, for Rousseau—not himself—was to be the spiritual father of a new generation mesmerized by the idea of the Common Man, of the People. As we will see, Rousseau's political thought fired men's minds with the ideal of democracy as a new way of life and as the Kingdom of God on earth.[40]

Making the State Holy

On October 15, 1794, the people of Paris transferred the body of Rousseau to the Panthéon, underscoring the link they saw between him and

---

[40] Thomas P. Neill, *Makers of the Modern Mind* (Milwaukee: Bruce, 1949), 164; Christopher Dawson, *The Gods of Revolution* (1972; Washington, D.C.: Catholic University of America Press, 2015), 32–33.

the French Revolution. Enthusiasts delivered lectures and prepared plays, poems, and songs in his honor. They even created an artificial replica of his shrine on the Isle of Poplars. The president of the Convention gave a speech on the occasion. "It is to Rousseau," he said, "that we owe this salutary regeneration which has caused such fortunate changes in our morals, in our customs, in our laws, in our minds, and in our habits." The literary cult of Rousseau had turned into the political cult of Rousseau.[41]

Historians debate how much the ideas of the Conflictual Enlighteners—and of Rousseau in particular—influenced the French Revolution. While contemporaries saw Rousseau as a father of the Revolution, it seems that his political cult was more a result than a cause of the event. Rousseau's political ideas made more sense in the fervent years after 1789 than before, and all major political factions of the Revolution adopted them at one time or another to justify their various ideologies.[42]

In Rousseau's political writings, "virtue" meant putting what he called the "general will" above one's own individual will and even conscience. Self-interest is bad, and "partial associations" of citizens mar the harmony of the whole. As mystics seek ultimate fulfillment in giving themselves completely to God, so Rousseau counseled giving oneself unreservedly to the community, thus forming a union "as perfect as possible." Embodying this general will of the community, the state could change human nature (redeem it) through legislation, making its members unselfish and concerned for the whole. In this way, it would create citizens who would choose only what the general will decides. The always "politically correct" general will would thus create a perfectly unified democracy, incorporating citizens into the mystical body of the state. Citizens would

---

[41] Blum, *Rousseau and the Republic of Virtue*, 280.

[42] Gordon H. McNeil, "The Cult of Rousseau and the French Revolution," *Journal of the History of Ideas* 6, no. 2 (April 1945): 201–202; Alexis de Tocqueville, *The Ancien Régime and the Revolution* (1856; New York: Penguin Books, 2008), 142, 143, 146, 147.

retain the natural freedom of individuals because they would desire only what the general will decided.[43]

In linking the principle of popular sovereignty to the general will, historian Jacob Talmon noted, Rousseau became the prophet of "totalitarian democracy" — the tyranny of a majority enthused by one absolute and perfect political truth. Rousseau rejected any attempt to divide political authority, implying that the separation and balance of powers were impossible routes to social harmony. The very clashes between factions that Rousseau condemned as paralyzing "partial associations" were celebrated by James Madison (1751–1836) in the United States. Rival factions, the American wrote in *Federalist Paper 10* (1787), would help preserve freedom. Madisonian constitutionalism *limited* democracy. It attempted to institutionalize the constraints of justice and the rule of law on majority rule, one political scientist wrote. This American approach was more in line with that of the medieval theologian Thomas Aquinas: law proceeds from reason, not will. In Rousseau, however, whatever the people *will* is law. This view was enshrined in the Declaration of the Rights of Man and Citizen (1789) at the very outset of the French Revolution, in article 6: "Law is the expression of the general will." The people are god. Limited democracy in the United States recognized the prerogatives of God, churches, and culture; Rousseau's kind of democracy recognized no such limits.[44]

In fact, Rousseau's desire to rid the body politics of contradictions meant he deplored the effect of Christianity in separating Caesar and God. Divided allegiances interrupted true communion of persons, he felt. In the ancient world of paganism, and in Muhammad's religion, Rousseau

---

[43] Jean-Jacques Rousseau, "On the Social Contract," in *The Basic Political Writings*, ed. Donald A. Cress (1762; Indianapolis: Hackett, 2011), 164, 173.

[44] J. L. Talmon, *The Origins of Totalitarian Democracy* (New York: Frederick A. Praeger, 1965), 2, 4, 5, 43, 45, 46; Paul R. DeHart, "Madisonian Thomism," *Public Discourse* (January 23, 2017), https://www.thepublicdiscourse.com/2017/01/18427/.

wrote admiringly, state and church constituted one powerful unity. He advocated a return to this ideal, to a kind of state not unlike Geneva, which would determine the articles of faith for the citizens of the city.

As Joseph Ratzinger wrote, "When the Christian faith falls into ruins and faith in mankind's greater hope is lost, the myth of the divine state rises again, because man cannot do without the totality of hope." Rousseau's political thought fulfilled those words perfectly. To serve the state was to serve God. There were no other priests than magistrates, no other pontiff than the one who embodies the pure and unified democratic people. This left the state *as* the church and created a coercive political religion in the service of messianic purposes. But such exalted salvific goals can in reality be realized only *beyond* the sphere of political action, Ratzinger noted. That is why Rousseau's "mythological politics" made *reasonable* politics difficult or impossible.[45]

The most radical group of the French Revolution, called the Jacobins, strove to bring Rousseau's political ideas to bear on all of France. Rousseau "was read in chorus at Jacobin meetings," one historian wrote; "he was quoted reverently and authoritatively in national assemblies."[46]

The most famous leader of the Jacobins was Maximilien Robespierre. He drank deeply of the works of Rousseau and became enamored with the idea of the "virtuous self." When Robespierre was only six years old, his mother had died in childbirth and his grieving father left his children in the care of others. Recommended by the bishop, Robespierre studied law at the University of Paris, where he read the works of Rousseau. The goodness of human nature fired his imagination with possibilities. Unmarried and completely focused on his mission, he was a man of immaculate dress and manners. During the Revolution, he was known as

---

[45] Jean-Jacques Rousseau, *The Social Contract and Discourse on Inequality*, ed. Lester G. Crocker (New York: Pocket Books, 1967), xiii–xviii, 141, 145; Joseph Cardinal Ratzinger, *Church, Ecumenism, and Politics: New Endeavors in Ecclesiology*, trans. Michael J. Miller et al. (San Francisco: Ignatius Press, 2008), 144–145.

[46] Neill, *Makers of the Modern Mind*, 189.

"the Incorruptible." He thought of himself as embodying the general will of the pure French people.

On February 5, 1794, while facing war with enemies both inside and outside France, Robespierre addressed the National Convention with his speech "On the Moral and Political Principles of Domestic Policy." He made the pursuit of virtue the justification for the Reign of Terror: "We want to substitute morality for egotism," he proclaimed, and the virtues of the republic for the absurdities of the monarchy. Virtue is the soul of the republic. "In the system of the French revolution, what is immoral is impolitic, what is corruptive is counter-revolutionary." He said:

> If the spring of popular government in time of peace is virtue, the springs of popular government in revolution are at once virtue and terror: virtue, without which terror is fatal; terror, without which virtue is powerless. Terror is nothing other than justice, prompt, severe, inflexible; it is therefore an emanation of virtue; it is not so much a special principle as it is a consequence of the general principle of democracy applied to our country's most urgent needs.[47]

The Reign of Terror emanated from virtue! There was no political compromise possible here — the hallmark of ideological politics. Under military pressure from France's enemies, Robespierre justified eliminating those who he perceived as threats to the general will and to the new state religion.

On June 8, 1794, about a month before the death of the Carmelites, Robespierre presided over the Festival of the Supreme Being in Paris. This neo-pagan celebration inaugurated the new state religion of the Cult of Reason in place of Catholicism. The festival brought together much of the city of Paris around a huge papier-mâché mountain that Robespierre

---

[47] Maximilien Robespierre, "On the Moral and Political Principles of Domestic Policy," Milestone Documents, https://www.milestonedocuments.com/documents/view/maximilien-robespierre-on-the-moral-and-political-principles-of-domestic-po/text.

ascended in godlike fashion, hoping to realize in practice the pantheistic natural religion of his idolized Rousseau.

Singing on the Road — 1794

As the Carmelite sisters of Compiègne came within sight of the guillotine on the road to Vincennes just outside Paris, they started singing the Te Deum, a prayer dating back to the time of Augustine's Baptism by his spiritual mentor, Ambrose. "We praise Thee, O God: we acknowledge Thee to be the Lord." As the stench of the putrefying blood around the scaffold reached their noses, with one voice they chanted, "All the earth doth worship Thee: the Father everlasting. To Thee all Angels cry aloud: the Heavens, and all the Powers therein." One could usually detect a visible movement of revulsion on the faces of prisoners upon first sight of the guillotine. This song of salutation by the nuns, however, shocked the spectators into a profound silence as the drama unfolded in front of their eyes. "Holy, Holy, Holy: Lord God of Hosts; Heaven and earth are full of Thy Majesty, of Thy glory," their voices sang.

The carts moved up close to the guillotine, and the evening sun cast the shadow of the blade across the road. "The glorious company of the Apostles praises Thee. The goodly fellowship of the Prophets praises Thee. The noble army of Martyrs praises Thee." They climbed out, and the executioner allowed Mother Teresa of St. Augustine time to finish community devotions before beginning his work. "The holy Church throughout all the world doth acknowledge Thee; . . . Thou art the King of Glory, O Christ." They finished the Te Deum with the words "Vouchsafe, O Lord, to keep us this day without sin. O Lord, have mercy upon us, have mercy upon us. O Lord, let Thy mercy lighten upon us, as our trust is in Thee. O Lord, in Thee have I trusted, let me never be confounded." Aware of their own sins — their previous fears and jealousies and hesitations — the nuns brought them to God and laid them at the feet of his mercy. Their faces at peace, they spun no webs of excuses for their faults. They shifted no blame for their uncomfortable predicament, as Rousseau had always done. Their composure and communal sense of purpose contrasted with his lifelong restless walking, fear, and isolation. In some way, they had *chosen together* this suffering; they had embraced this cross in their daily offering of themselves to Christ. It seemed that their God broke through those enlightened webs of self-justification and rationalization, those wounds of the Enlightenment on the souls of modern people that blind them to personal responsibility—and gave the nuns his mercy and thereby his peace. He freed them from resentment: they made no protest against the new government of France, no denunciation of their impending and disgusting death, no complaint about violation of their most basic human rights.

After singing the Te Deum, and at the very foot of the guillotine, Mother Teresa led the usual devotions for a dying Carmelite, starting with the Veni Creator Spiritus: "Come, Holy Ghost, Creator, come from Thy bright heav'nly throne; come, take possession of our souls, and make them all Thine own." As a counterpoint to the cold steel of reason poised above them, they prayed to the Holy Spirit, "O guide our minds with Thy blest light, with love our hearts inflame; and with Thy strength, which ne'er decays, confirm our mortal frame." They renewed their vows of poverty, chastity, and obedience. Then, a witness recorded, one nun burst out, praying, "Only too happy, O my God, if this little sacrifice can calm your wrath and reduce the number of victims!" The Carmelites believed their invocation of the Holy Spirit at that putrid place of death would release spiritual power into the world to bring about good, Bush wrote in his eloquent account of what happened that day.

Mother Teresa of St. Augustine moved to the foot of the scaffold. She would preside over the sacrifice, Bush commented, and die last. Sister Henriette of the Divine Providence stepped up to stand by Mother Teresa and help each sister climb the steps. The crowd watched as the executioner put on his well-worn, blood-stained leather apron. Mother Teresa summoned Sister Constance, the youngest member of the community, who had refused to leave upon demand by her family. She had just pronounced her vows for the first time at the foot of the guillotine and knew she was to die a Carmelite. Her face was radiant as she knelt before the prioress and kissed a statue of the Virgin and Child cupped in Mother Teresa's hand. Still kneeling, and with her head humbly bowed, Sister Constance asked in her clear, young voice, "Permission to die, Mother?"[48]

---

[48] Bush, *To Quell the Terror*, 15, 207, 209, 212.

3

Dining at Ferney

Arrival

Visitors to the country estate at Ferney in eastern France usually approached it from nearby Geneva, just across the French border. Evening sunlight sparkled on the great lake there and lighted the Alps behind the city. The owner of the manor chose Ferney because he had enemies. He could easily escape to Switzerland if they gave him trouble. Drawing near in their carriages, callers and tourists noticed new additions to the three-story château, with its mansard roof, its classical façade, and its fine setting amid fields, trees, and gardens. The round turrets gave it the air of a castle. Visitors also noticed the theater house and the chapel with a sign on it that read, "Erected to God by Voltaire, 1761."

They had arrived at the home of the great French Enlightener, the "patriarch of Ferney," François-Marie Arouet—better known as "Voltaire." If the visitors were lucky, he might meet them on the steps. For some, like the young Scotsman James Boswell, their hearts raced as they surveyed his elderly and dignified form, eager to meet the most famous and controversial man of the eighteenth century. Voltaire's celebrity—like that of Rousseau—and his wit fascinated everyone. He mastered many forms of communication: travel narrative, pamphlets, poetry, histories, plays, popular science, novellas, and widespread correspondence in nearly twenty-thousand letters to people across Europe. Everyone wanted to know what he thought and what he said on everything, even if only to refute it.

Voltaire did not start out life looking for trouble. He just wanted to succeed as a playwright and poet who could move people to tears. He came into conflict with political and ecclesiastical authorities not as a strategic choice but as a result of his desire to write what he wanted.[49]

Later in life, from the safety of his estate at Ferney, he openly challenged abuses of power he saw in these authorities. He emerged as the icon of the Conflictual Enlightenment, famous for his criticism of the Catholic Church and for his defense of freedom of speech and separating religion and politics — ideas many at the time considered threatening. If Rousseau's utopian pantheism unintentionally helped fuel the Revolution that bore down on the Carmelites of Compiègne in 1794, Voltaire's legacy of deism and negative criticism did too — at least as interpreted by the revolutionary generation. When revolutionaries brought Voltaire's body to Paris for burial in the Panthéon in 1791, three years before they brought Rousseau's body there, a sign on Voltaire's casket read: "He prepared us to become free."

What kind of freedom? That was one of the questions driving the conflict of cultures during the eighteenth century. A key place to gain a view of this conflict was Voltaire's estate at Ferney — "ground zero" of the Conflictual Enlightenment in many ways. Joining dinner-party guests at Ferney through their surviving letters and memoirs will reveal from within the culture of the eighteenth century. What kinds of ideas did people talk about? How did they characterize science and religion? How did they interact at the dinner table when they disagreed with each other? The following chapters will examine where the Conflictual Enlightenment came from and to what extent "Catholic sin" helped create it.

Making Introductions

Voltaire addressed English-speaking visitors in their own tongue as he led them into the house. He took pains to articulate his words carefully and

---

[49] Ian Davidson, *Voltaire: A Life* (New York: Pegasus Books, 2010), xvii.

accent them fully, not having lived in England since 1728. Neverthe-less, he spoke English well. Voltaire possessed an air of the world with a sagacious and comical look. Despite his seventy years or so, he was very lively in his actions and accompanied his emphatic words with equally emphatic movements that animated his whole person.

The master of the house ushered his guests into a beautiful *salon*[50] and made introductions. When the Americans John Morgan and Samuel Powel visited, he offered them coffee in a shallow dish, which was how people drank it back then. He then complimented them on fighting against the French so well in the Seven Years' War, just concluded in 1763, smoothing over a potentially awkward situation. "We must now look upon them [the Americans] as our brave friends, since we are now at peace," Voltaire declared to the rest of the household and guests, which included a French military officer recently returned from fight-ing the Americans. "To this we replied," wrote Morgan, "that we hoped this peace might be lasting, that we might always regard one another in the same light of Friendship. Then Mons'r Voltaire introduc'd us more particularly by Name; we received & return'd Compliments with mutual respect."

Morgan surveyed the people positioned around the salon, elegantly adorned with paintings of classical figures. Voltaire himself wore a wig and often a slate-blue greatcoat that served as his uniform at Ferney. On Sundays he donned a bronze-colored suit with wide skirts, gold braiding, and embroidery, with lace cuffs down to the fingertips — a style much out of date. Besides the military officer, several others were present, includ-ing a middle-aged French lady, "well-painted" in cosmetics, who "seem'd

---

[50] This was a reception hall characteristic of aristocratic homes, where men and women of different social classes could freely mingle. In the English-speaking world, salons became *parlors*. During the Enlightenment, salons often served as centers of literary, philosophical, and scientific discussion, governed by strict rules of refinement and politeness. They could involve a shared meal too.

Voltaire Welcoming His Guests, *by Jean Huber.*

one of the family" (probably Voltaire's mistress), and a young woman of about twenty. She was Voltaire's adopted daughter, Marie-Françoise Corneille, a descendent of the famous French dramatist Pierre Corneille. Marie-Françoise had been living in poverty, and Voltaire decided to take her into his family and personally educate her. She was lovely and delighted Voltaire. "I call her my Daughter & have marri'd her to that Young Man," he said, indicating another figure in the company. "Their Children I look on as if they were my own, & take care of them all as of my own family," Voltaire said to his guests. There were also several servants about the house, including the sturdy Swiss woman Barbara, very hard-working and possessed of a bold scorn for her master's reputed cleverness. She openly ridiculed his belief that he possessed common sense, to Voltaire's amusement. "These were the personages & such the arrangement of our goodly Company," Morgan concluded.[51]

Sometimes dozens of elite guests stayed at Voltaire's home since there was no village inn. Voltaire invited specific people to come visit, too, such as Rousseau, though he never came. The two men fell into great dislike for each other. Voltaire mocked Rousseau's "back to nature" ideal of man (it "makes one long to go on all fours" like a beast, Voltaire scorned him in a letter). He exposed to the public the secret that Rousseau had abandoned his children. While Rousseau licked his wounds and stayed away, many others came to Ferney, armed with letters of introduction. Casual passersby stopped too, expecting to be fed and entertained. These Voltaire sometimes received rudely, especially if he did not feel well that day or they interrupted him in his study. Increasingly, great men and women on the Grand Tour of Europe made Ferney a destination. "I happen to live in a part of the country situated right in the middle of Europe," he wrote to one correspondent. "All the passers-by come to my house, I have to deal with Germans, with Englishmen, with Italians, even with Frenchmen, whom I shall never see again." Voltaire bore the expense and the strain of all this, for he loved society, conversation, and pomp.[52]

Voltaire's mistress (and niece), Madame Denis (1712–1790), helped entertain guests. Voltaire took her in after her husband died, and she acted as his housekeeper and hostess. Gay and sociable, Madame Denis loved music and theatre and spending Voltaire's money. It was illegal for Voltaire to marry her without a papal dispensation since they were related by blood. So they lived together in a quasi-marital relationship.

---

[51] John Morgan, *The Journal of Dr. John Morgan of Philadelphia from the City of Rome to the City of London*, September 16, 1764, Voltaire Society of America, https://www.whitman.edu/VSA/visitors/Morgan.1.html.

[52] Voltaire to Rousseau, August 30, 1755, Voltaire Society of America, https://www.whitman.edu/VSA/letters/8.30.1755.html; Voltaire to Madam du Deffand, June 4, 1764, quoted in Davidson, *Voltaire: A Life*, 337; Jean Orieux, *Voltaire*, trans. Barbara Bray and Helen R. Lane (New York: Doubleday, 1979), 372.

Together, Voltaire and Madame Denis organized amateur theater performances. Voltaire had built a theater seating three hundred spectators and regularly performed in his own plays. They might run for hours, long into the evening. The English historian Edward Gibbon visited Ferney in 1763 and recorded that the old man performed in a very ranting and unnatural way. "I was too much struck by the ridiculous figure of Voltaire at seventy acting a Tartar Conquerer with a hollow broken voice, and making love to a very ugly niece of about fifty." Nevertheless, it was all extraordinary. Gibbon recorded that after the performance the whole company sat down to a lovely dinner until two in the morning. Then they danced until four and rode back to Geneva in their carriages just as the gates opened at dawn. Extramarital sexual relationships, feasting, displays of wealth, and late-night merriment characterized the increasingly prosperous European elites and philosophers of Enlightenment culture.[53]

Voltaire worked during the day from his bed or in his study in the left wing of the estate. The study housed his working library of more than six thousand volumes. Voltaire interacted energetically with his books, making marginalia in many of them for the purposes of research and writing. He believed books ruled the world.

Here at Ferney, Voltaire wrote his *Philosophical Dictionary* (1764). The book came together as a series of short essays arranged alphabetically and intended to serve as a guide to Enlightenment thinking and attitudes. For example, the true and universal religion is simply belief in God and living justly, Voltaire wrote in the *Philosophical Dictionary*. One should believe in God but not in churches: "Every sect, of every kind, is a rallying-point for doubt and error," Voltaire noted. There are no sects in geometry. "The point in which [religious sects] all agree is therefore true, and the systems through which they differ are therefore false," he wrote.

Voltaire thus illustrated very well the anti-institutionalism and religious syncretism characterizing the conflictual side of the Enlightenment.

[53] Edward Gibbon to his stepmother, August 6, 1763, Voltaire Society of America, https://www.whitman.edu/VSA/visitors/gibbon.html.

These had partly resulted from exotic reports of many world religions in a newly globalized age and from the deep theological skepticism imposed on the European mind by Christian division since the Age of Reformations.

The *Philosophical Dictionary* offered a cheaper alternative to the greatest of all Enlightenment projects, the *Encyclopédie*. That weighty work had started appearing under the direction of Denis Diderot soon after he left the prison at Vincennes, where Rousseau visited him in 1749. Diderot's *Encyclopédie*, to which both Rousseau and Voltaire contributed, sought to spread the Enlightenment among social elites. From them it would naturally percolate down to the wider society, Diderot hoped. While it left room for "revealed facts," the work subjected revelation to reason. It promulgated a conflictual relationship between religion and science. The *Encyclopédie* ruled out of bounds any knowledge not derived from sensation and reflection. This would subtly cut orthodox religion off the map, consign it to the unknowable, and thus "exclude it from the modern world of learning," as historian Robert Darnton put it.

Voltaire later criticized the *Encyclopédie* because it was large and expensive; a pricey book never created a revolution. Hence the need for his *Philosophical Dictionary*, he believed. Both works severed the connections of knowledge to tradition and faith to put it solely in the hands of intellectuals committed to their version of the Enlightenment. Everyday life should be restructured according to abstract "rational" principles. As we have seen, the attempt by later revolutionary leaders such as Robespierre to enforce this project would create an avalanche sweeping away French Catholicism — including the Carmelites. As soon as the *Philosophical Dictionary* appeared, church and state condemned it, even as seemingly everyone read it.[54]

---

[54] Davidson, *Voltaire: A Life*, 306; Voltaire, "Philosophical Dictionary," in *The Portable Voltaire*, ed. Benn Ray Redman (1764; New York: Penguin Books, 1977), 195–196; Darnton, *The Great Cat Massacre*, 205, 209.

Rethinking the Enlightenment

Touring the Gardens

After introductions in the salon, if time and weather allowed, Voltaire sometimes conducted visitors on a tour outdoors in the fine gardens. From there, one could see Lake Geneva and the mountains beyond. They strolled through the bower of hornbeam trees, where Voltaire liked to rest and to write in the open during the summer. They walked together through the vineyard and down the gravel walks, passing green lawns and a carp pond. Voltaire talked as they moved along, passing the patches of herbs and the kitchen garden he liked to tend himself, gesturing around with animation and taking pinches of snuff. He told of going out among his fields to supervise the planting. "He prided himself in having ordered every thing himself, from the building [of] the Chateau to the Disposition of the Garden," Morgan reported.

Voltaire had brought in extra families from Switzerland to work his fields and operate the grape press. He purchased farm equipment and took an interest in horse breeding. He worked to create jobs for the people (he employed one hundred himself) and improve the economic life of the region by building small manufactories of silk, lace, and eventually watches. "I must look after my peasants and my cattle when they are ill, I must find husbands for the girls, and I must improve fields abandoned since the Flood. I see all round me the most frightful misery, in the midst of a smiling countryside." He wanted to remedy a bit of the evil accumulating over the centuries, he wrote to a friend. This was true philosophy, he believed: practical and devoted to improving the world. That was the Enlightenment in brief.

Voltaire even made sure to pay public respect to religion by attending Mass, for the sake of the local peasants; and he provided catechism lessons for the children of his servants. It would not do to deprive the common people of faith, for how otherwise would they remain moral? Protestant and Catholic villagers lived together in the village, which became a model of toleration and prosperity.

Voltaire told his visitor Edward Gibbon he had never enjoyed so much true happiness than in this simple, rustic life. Impressed, Gibbon wrote,

"He has got rid of most of his infirmities, and tho' very old and lean, enjoys a much better state of health than he did twenty years ago." The plunder and violence of kings could not compare with the happiness of a quiet and productive life, Voltaire declared; therefore, "let us cultivate our garden," he ended his novella *Candide* (1759). Seeing the grass grow in the fields and the abundant harvest ripen—"That is man's true life: all the rest is vanity," he wrote to a Paris correspondent. "I have never been less dead that I am at present," he wrote her a few weeks later. "The bulls, the cows, the sheep, the pastures, the buildings, the gardens, all take up my mornings; the afternoons are for study; and after supper, we rehearse the plays which we perform in my little gallery theater. This way of life makes me want to live."[55]

At Ferney, for the first time in his life, Voltaire existed in a relatively stable household with a family. He experienced a shared life together, oriented toward a common good through mutual rights and duties. The activities of the household, such as work and leisure, united one to another and thereby fostered natural human happiness—through participative knowledge—in ways he had never experienced before.

Voltaire was born as François-Marie Arouet in 1694. His mother died when he was six. His two surviving siblings were much older than he was, so he grew up essentially an only child with a professionally ambitious and authoritarian father. Voltaire's brother was a follower of the Catholic movement known as Jansenism, which stressed rigorous moralism to quash a depraved human nature. Jansenists were the "Puritans" of the Catholic Church, and Voltaire hated them and his brother. Perhaps to distance himself from his family, he changed his name from Arouet to Voltaire when he was twenty-four. It was not uncommon for writers of the time to change their names, though it is not clear why he chose Voltaire.

[55] Voltaire to Nicolas Thieriot, September 17, 1759, quoted in Davidson, *Voltaire: A Life*, 296; Edward Gibbon to his stepmother, August 6, 1763; Morgan, *Journal*; Voltaire to Madam de Deffand, April 12, 1760, in *The Portable Voltaire*, 501; Voltaire to Madam de Deffand, April 25, 1760, quoted in Davidson, *Voltaire: A Life*, 303.

Rejecting the Jansenist view of God as a largely unfeeling monarch, Voltaire devoted himself to achieving fame through theater and acquiring wealth through business acumen. He succeeded at both. Later in life, he realized that bad theology—making a tyrant out of God—was a superstition that invited men themselves to become tyrants. In plays such as *Alzire* (1736), performed many times at Ferney, he explored the tension between a religion of fear and a religion of mercy and forgiveness. Despite his deist tendencies, which posited a distant God, Voltaire portrayed God in this play as a *parent*, as the kind, loving father he himself never had.[56]

Also, for the first time in his life, Voltaire took an interest in common people. This worked a transformation in him. Before settling down at Ferney, he had lived in capital cities and royal courts, focused on his own comfort and networking with the powerful in the pursuit of his highly successful literary career. But at his country estate, the problem of evil came home to him. Just before purchasing it, he wrote in 1758 that "half the inhabitants [around Ferney] die of poverty, and the other half rot in prison cells. One's heart is torn when one witnesses so much misery." Voltaire worked for years to improve their lot, including protecting them from a violent local Catholic priest who tried to use the law courts to force tithe payments from his poor parishioners. Voltaire wrote to the local bishop about this: "You, Sir, know better than I, how the Popes in the early ages of the church were incensed against the Clergy who sacrificed to temporal affairs that time which should have been dedicated to the service of the altar." Voltaire himself paid off the large sum to keep the peasants from having their possessions seized or landing in jail. He excoriated such money-grubbing clerics: you have trampled us under your feet, he wrote, that "you might fatten on the substance of the unfortunate." He prophesied: "But tremble for fear that the day of reason will arrive!" Voltaire's new sense of social responsibility would stay with

---

[56] Dominic Erdozain, *The Soul of Doubt: The Religious Roots of Unbelief from Luther to Marx* (New York: Oxford University Press, 2016), 146, 148, 150, 157–158.

him until the end of his life, when he returned to Paris in 1778 and the common people cheered him in the streets.[57]

Table Talk

Back in the house, the servants had prepared a meal. Though Voltaire would not always join his guests, he kept an open table in a most hospitable manner. Quakers, Anabaptists, Lutherans, Presbyterians, Episcopalians, Methodists, Pietists, Mennonites, and Catholics—Voltaire welcomed all of them, "provided that you have no dagger in your pocket," he once wrote; "bow down together before the Supreme Being, thank him for having given you ... young chickens, venison, and good bread for your food, a mind to know them and a heart to love them; dine together merrily after having given him thanks."[58] Voltaire believed sitting together at table opened peoples' hearts and made them more sprightly and sociable, especially when good wine was served all around. He would proudly tell everyone that much of the food came from his own estates. Servants in waistcoats offered guests trout, hare, dates, oranges, pomegranates, and other delicious foods.

The Enlightener disliked small talk. He thought very few people possessed within themselves a fund of useful conversation, so sometimes he arranged to have edifying texts read from a lectern during dinner. Rather than talk with the greatest wit in Europe, disappointed guests would have to listen in silence—as in a monastery—to readings on the history of the Church or to the beautiful sermons of Jean-Baptiste Massillon (1663–1742), the French Catholic bishop, preacher, and respected intellectual much admired by Voltaire. In those sermons, Massillon stressed less dogmatic questions than morality and the secrets of the

[57] Voltaire letter, November 18, 1758, in Davidson, *Voltaire: A Life*, 296.; Voltaire to the Bishop of Annecy, 1759, in Jean Louise Wagniére, *Historical Memoirs of the Author of the Henriade* (Dublin: R. Moncrieffe, 1777), 61; Voltaire, *Philosophical Dictionary*, in *The Portable Voltaire*, 54.

[58] Voltaire, *God & Human Beings*, trans. Michael Shreve (1769; Amherst: Prometheus Books, 2010), 151.

human heart. Voltaire's respect for him underscored only one of the many paradoxes of his life: he heavily criticized religion while also practicing an idiosyncratic, but real, piety.[59]

Among those who could talk well, though, Voltaire thrived on real conversation about books, great authors, and theater. When he spoke of great actors, "his eyes have such a brilliancy in those moments, that you forget he is about seventy-two," recalled one guest.[60] He thought learning how to talk well required mastering other forms of communication: not just reading intelligently but also good writing that is clear, simple, and natural—not affected.

Voltaire had an excellent talent of adapting his conversation to his company. Once a little dog appeared, and Voltaire turned to his English guests and asked, "What think you of that little dog; has he any Soul or not, & what do the People in England now think of the Soul?" Voltaire continued: "These are four things w'ch I adore that the English boast of so greatly … Liberty, Property, Newton & Locke." (He had lived in England between 1726 and 1728.) This was an example of the Enlightenment ideal of "polite sociability." Polite sociability involved adaptation to others and rules of genteel conversation by which one should speak in witty and compelling ways without contradicting others. One joined in the conversation not so much to advance knowledge as to display social skills and contribute to collective entertainment. This Enlightenment ideal of polite sociability marked the age.[61]

With his English guests, Voltaire praised Newton for laying open the planetary system. He waxed eloquent about how Locke dissected the soul and discovered the powers of understanding. To him and to other Enlighteners, the English scientist Isaac Newton (1643–1727) and the English philosopher John Locke (1632–1704) were the heroic

---

[59] Erdozain, *The Soul of Doubt*, 170–171.

[60] Samuel Sharpe, August 18, 1765, Voltaire Society of America, https://www.whitman.edu/VSA/visitors/Sharpe.html.

[61] Morgan, *Journal*.

grandfathers of the Enlightenment. Thanks to his former lover Émilie du Châtelet (1706–1749), who translated Newton into French, Voltaire got to know the work of this founding father of modern science well enough to write a popularization called *Elements of the Philosophy of Newton* (1738).

Newton's great achievements in the laws of motion and the science of optics seemed to confirm the philosophy of *empiricism* Locke promulgated. Empiricism posited that all (or most) knowledge comes from the senses—called "empirical knowledge"—as opposed to traditions or the structure of the mind itself. Locke's attempts to base his understanding of human nature, limited government, and reasonable religion on empirical knowledge inspired many thinkers of the Enlightenment.

If knowledge simply comes from the senses and experience, as Locke thought, however, then where did that leave the soul? This was why Voltaire asked his guests, "What do the People in England now think of the Soul?" In his entry on "soul" in his *Philosophical Dictionary*, Voltaire asked, "When we wish to have a rude knowledge of a piece of metal, we put it on the fire in a crucible; but have we any crucible wherein to put the soul?" If one cannot see, weigh, or measure the soul, does it exist? What is its nature? The philosophical implications of an autonomous empiricism would haunt the modern world ever after. They would obscure the differentiated nature of reality and lead many to forget that knowledge of metal, in Voltaire's example, is of a different *kind* from knowledge of the soul. Thus, one needed a different method to understand it—not simply the empirical method upheld by a major strand of Enlightenment thought, but also *metaphysical* (beyond the physical) method. Unsurprisingly, without that, the soul remained a "vague and indeterminate term" (as Voltaire put it)—perfect for a lively and harmless discussion during dinner. After all, he smiled sardonically, *what harm can mere ideas do anyone?*

More Wine, Please

As visitors relaxed during the meal, enjoying the food and wine, they warmed up to Voltaire, asking him questions. Had he read the account of electricity by Dr. Franklin? What did he think about it? Benjamin Franklin was a man of genius, to be sure, Voltaire responded, a great natural philosopher (scientist). Had Voltaire read any David Hume or any of William Robertson's *History of Scotland?* one guest asked. Yes, both were "Men of Merit," Voltaire said, but he preferred Hume, who wrote more like a philosopher. The American guest John Morgan told Voltaire of recent travels in Italy and of the archaeological excavations moving forward at Herculaneum near Pompeii, destroyed by the same volcano in A.D. 79 and recently discovered. The Enlightener was interested in all manner of things.[62]

Some found Voltaire's conversation good-natured, complimentary, amusing, and constantly enlightening on most subjects. He is all brilliance! exclaimed Boswell during his visit. Voltaire had humor, boldness, and a forced oddity of style. He would introduce wit into the most ordinary conversation and found wit in others even when they may not have intended it. For example, he once asked a visitor what religion he practiced. The visitor replied, "My parents brought me up Catholic." Voltaire said back to him, "A good answer. He doesn't say he is one." On another occasion, when the hawks that Voltaire allowed to fly around his house attacked a pigeon in front of his guests, he would quip that they were kings who tear innocent subjects to pieces—even though he was not an anti-monarchist.[63]

Others found his conversation blasphemous and lewd. "With ladies, he is rather indecent; as with the church, he is but too apt to be ludicrous," one visitor recorded. On one occasion, when the eyes of one important guest kept wandering away from Voltaire to the cleavage of the buxom Swiss maids serving cream, Voltaire, angry over losing his attention in conversation, jumped up, laid hands on the snowy curves of the nearest

---

[62] Morgan, *Journal*.
[63] James Boswell to William J. Temple, December 28, 1764, in *Boswell on the Grand Tour: Germany and Switzerland*, ed. Frederick A. Pottle (New York: McGraw-Hill, 1953), 293; Orieux, *Voltaire*, 375–376.

maid, and cried, "Nothing but bosoms, bosoms, all over the place! Clear out of here!" Then he calmly sat back down to converse with the man, whose startled attention turned back to Voltaire.[64]

Nevertheless, "those who are invited to supper, have an opportunity of seeing him in the most advantageous point of view," one guest wrote. Voltaire exerted himself to entertain the company, often making intelligent and funny comments. He was equally delighted by well-placed words coming from others. "When surrounded by his friends, and animated by the presence of women, he seems to enjoy life with all the sensibility of youth. His genius then surmounts the restraints of age and infirmity, and flows along in a fine strain of pleasing, spirited observation, and delicate irony."[65] Undoubtedly, the crates of wine that arrived regularly at the Ferney estate aided the flow of genius.

Evening Salon

After the meal, guests sat snugly around the burning fireplace in the salon, chatted in small groups, sang, or played music and games—a typical scene in great country houses of the eighteenth century. Some would sidle up next to Voltaire to engage in talk. On one occasion, the conversation happening to turn on the genius of Shakespeare, "Voltaire expatiated on the impropriety and absurdity of introducing low characters and vulgar dialogue into Tragedy; and gave many instances of the English bard's having offended in that particular," one guest recorded—a certain Scottish physician named John Moore. "A gentleman of the company," Moore continued, "who is a great admirer of Shakespear[e], observed ... that though those characters were low, yet they were natural." Voltaire retorted, "Excuse me Sir, but my ass is also very natural, so I put on

---

[64] John Conyers, 1765, Voltaire Society of America, https://www.whitman. edu/VSA/visitors/Conyer.html; Orieux, *Voltaire*, 375.

[65] John Moore, A *View of Society and Manners in France, Switzerland, and Germany*, 2nd ed., vol. 1 (London: W. Strahan, 1779), 267–268.

underwear." Voltaire's criticisms of Shakespeare really did him no honor, Moore concluded, as it betrayed his national prejudices and his ignorance of the finer points of English.[66]

Young James Boswell reported that when Voltaire came to the subject of religion — "then did he rage." On that particular evening, the others left the salon and Boswell remained alone with Voltaire, a great Bible before them — a book the Enlightener frequently studied, quoted, attacked, undermined, and sometimes admired. Even while he tried to explain the Bible simply in human terms, he felt its power. Boswell looked over the Bible between them at Voltaire: "and if ever two mortal men disputed with vehemence, we did," he recorded.

Boswell (1740–1795) was a seeker, constantly asking questions about religion of those he met and regularly falling into doubts and dread over annihilation at death. Boswell had only recently fled the hellfire Calvinism of his youth into Catholicism, even as he constantly slept with different women. He then fell away from the Catholic faith into a philosophy of libertinism and irreligion that was inspired by the atheist philosopher Hume. However, in May of 1763, a year and a half before speaking with Voltaire on this particular evening, he had met the great Anglican man of letters Samuel Johnson (1709–1784) in London. Boswell later wrote one of the great literary biographies of the English language about this man. Johnson anchored Boswell in Christianity for the rest of his days, even while he continued to doubt and question.[67]

"For a certain portion of time there was a fair opposition between Voltaire and Boswell," Boswell wrote about himself in the third person. However, "the daring bursts of his ridicule confounded my understanding. He stood like an orator of ancient Rome," much agitated. "His aged frame trembled beneath him," and he let himself fall upon an easy

---

[66] Ibid., 275–276.
[67] Boswell to Temple, December 28, 1764, in *Boswell on the Grand Tour*, 293; Dixon Wecter, "The Soul of James Boswell," *Virginia Quarterly Review* 12, no. 2 (Spring 1936), https://www.vqronline.org/essay/soul-james-boswell.

chair. He recovered, and Boswell resumed the conversation, in a different tone. "I talked to him serious and earnest," the Scotsman wrote. "I demanded of him an honest confession of his real sentiments." Voltaire consented to give them "with a candour and with a mild eloquence which touched my heart. I did not believe him capable of thinking in the manner that he declared to me was 'from the bottom of his heart.' He expressed his veneration — his love — of the Supreme Being, and his entire resignation to the will of Him who is All-wise. He expressed his desire to resemble the Author of Goodness by being good himself. His sentiments go no farther. He does not inflame his mind with grand hopes of the immortality of his soul. He says it may be, but he knows nothing of it." After listening to Voltaire's profession of faith, Boswell wrote, "I called to him with emotion, 'Are you sincere? Are you really sincere?' He answered, 'Before God, I am.' Then with the fire of him whose tragedies have so often shone on the theatre of Paris, he said, "I suffer much. But I suffer with patience and resignation; not as a Christian — but as a man.'"[68]

Coffee and Chess

While visitors sat in groups around the salon, Voltaire drank coffee late into the night. First coming to Europe from the Turks, the hot drink spread rapidly among the populace during the eighteenth century — even in monasteries. Coffee was associated with free conversation. Safer to drink than water from the rivers, the liquid stimulant powered the Enlightenment

[68] Boswell to Temple, December 28, 1764, in *Boswell on the Grand Tour*, 293–294; Voltaire, *God & Human Beings*, 135, 149. Voltaire believed the ordered geometry of the heavens proved their creation by an eternal Geometer, and that whether one worships the Supreme Being through Confucius, Marcus Aurelius, Jesus, or someone else, what does it matter? Religion consists of morality and belief in God, who created the universe and governs it according to the laws of nature, with which he does not interfere.

through coffeehouses proliferating in cities such as London, Amsterdam, and Paris. Smoky, candlelit coffeehouses were the information and social hubs of the eighteenth century. People increasingly utilized them as neutral spaces to read newspapers, talk openly about literature and politics, listen to scientific lectures, strike business deals, share news, and gossip. Enlighteners met up in coffeehouses because they felt free there to express themselves. Rousseau had first met his friend Diderot, for example, at the Café de la Régence in Paris, amid the busy chess tables. Some people would stay all day in the new coffeehouses, just as some of their descendants would stay online all day. These institutions—and the drink, coffee—had a significant impact on Parisian social and cultural life by fostering a culture of conversation, and Voltaire adopted the fad at his château.[69]

He then rang a bell—a signal for the Jesuit Father Antoine Adam to join him for chess. Father Adam was a professor from Dijon whom Voltaire had taken in after the Jesuits had been expelled from France in 1762. He enjoyed teasing the priest. When introducing him to the company, Voltaire said, "He may be Father Adam, but is far from being the first of men." "I have a Jesuit in my house," he wrote in a letter, "who says Mass most properly, and who plays chess very well; he's called Adam, and though he is not the First Man, he has merit."[70] Father Adam lived at Ferney as a member of the household for many years, saying Mass (Voltaire would often attend), playing chess, and conversing with the Enlightener.

Chess spread all through France during the eighteenth century. Voltaire loved playing it with Father Adam. The Enlightener pretended not to mind that the priest was better at the game than himself. In truth,

---

[69] Fernand Braudel, *The Structures of Everyday Life: The Limits of the Possible*, vol. 1, *Civilization and Capitalism, 15th–18th Century* (New York: Harper & Row, 1981), 260.

[70] John Conyers, *Annual Register for the Year 1767*, Voltaire Society of America, https://www.whitman.edu/VSA/visitors/Conyer.html; Davidson, *Voltaire: A Life*, 304.

Voltaire Playing Chess, *by Jean Huber.*

however, he hated losing. "But I love chess, I love it passionately, and Father Adam, who is a fool, beats me at it all the time, without mercy!" As Father Adam's pieces moved in on Voltaire's king, the Enlightener started to hum a little tune. The Jesuit started fidgeting nervously. More than once, Father Adam took flight, a biographer wrote, "pelted with chessmen that stuck in his wig, and sometimes took refuge in a closet to escape a hail of blows from Voltaire's cane." Anger would quickly pass, and Voltaire would call out, "*Adam, ubi es?*" parodying Genesis 3:9. Adam would come out, and all would be forgiven.

This was a Jesuit that a philosopher could get along with—he even helped Voltaire by writing to the confessor of someone who owed Voltaire money, a fellow Jesuit. Father Adam asked the confessor to remind his charge that it was his Catholic duty to pay his debt. Voltaire got his money back.[71]

Madame Denis once complained that Voltaire spent too much time with Father Adam. When the Enlightener eventually ended up in a dispute with the local bishop, however, the priest could no longer say Mass for him or hear confession. Voltaire immediately found some local Franciscans who would come from time to time to say Mass and hear confession at Ferney. Did he fear dying without the availability of confession? Or did he simply request they come for the sake of others? One cannot know. What is certain is that Voltaire took a genuine interest in the friars, even helping them financially. He received a letter of thanks from the head of the order in Rome conferring on him the title of benefactor to the order of St. Francis. Voltaire began signing off in his letters as "Friar Francis." Biographers often interpret scenes such as this as playacting at religion on Voltaire's part, which it was, but there was also "substance beneath the theater," wrote one commentator.[72]

At the end of the evening, servants prepared rooms with fires and candles for those settling in for the night at Ferney. If not staying, guests needed to return to Geneva before the city closed its gates. "We thanked [Voltaire] in the politest terms for the Honor he had done us," wrote Morgan. Voltaire returned the compliments, and, as if pleased with their conversation and the freedom they had taken with him, turned to the rest of the company and praised Morgan and his companion aloud, "Behold two Amiable Young Men Lovers of Truth & Inquirers into Nature." He continued, crying out, "I command You Gentlemen — go on [to] love Truth & search diligently after it." Then, almost as a party slogan in the theatrical show of his life, Voltaire advised, "Hate Hypocrisy Hate Masses & above all hate the Priests." Compliments being over, they left the party, and Voltaire accompanied them to the door. He told them to

---

[71] Orieux, *Voltaire*, 369–370.
[72] Erdozain, *The Soul of Doubt*, 170–171.

come again to dine with him. They who endeavor to make themselves agreeable would never want for company at his house, he said. "We return'd our Thanks once more in the warmest terms, & gett'g into the Chariot drove off."[73]

[73] Morgan, *Journal.*

4

Fleeing Catholic Dragons

Anxiety Overshadows Voltaire

One day, a visitor arrived at Ferney with a story that would change Voltaire's life. He told the Enlightener about a recent execution in March of 1762 at Toulouse, a city in southern France. The judges there had condemned the Protestant cloth merchant Jean Calas for allegedly killing his son Marc-Antoine to prevent him from becoming Catholic. The visitor assured Voltaire of Jean Calas's innocence. "I answered him that the crime was not a probable one," Voltaire remembered. But he believed it even more improbable that Calas's judges should, without any motive, condemn an innocent man. Voltaire dismissed the story of the supposedly unjust execution; it did not concern him. Who was Jean Calas, anyway? Who cared? He was an obscure Protestant, and Voltaire abhorred French Protestants even more than Catholics because they preached against playacting.

However, Voltaire's disdainful and uninvolved tone suddenly changed. Within days of hearing the visitor's story, Voltaire's biographers remark, his attitude passed from condescension to "anxious, emotional, uncertain and quivering on the edge of horror and indignation." He wrote in a letter to his friend Cardinal Pierre de Bernis: "May I beg your eminence to tell me what I should think of the frightful adventure of this Calas?" Eventually Bernis wrote back as a man of the world, taking sides with neither the judges nor the condemned man. Why be concerned about this? What does this have to do with you, Voltaire? The judges will stand together anyway, protecting their decision behind their veil of secrecy. If you confront them, Voltaire, they will be formidable opponents.

But Voltaire could not let the story go. It "grips my heart; it casts sadness over my pleasures and corrupts them." It is not known for sure what changed Voltaire's mind so suddenly, but his attention dramatically shifted from theater drama to a real tragedy. He set out to challenge the verdict in the Calas case and launch himself on a new vocation as a campaigner against injustice caused in part by Catholic sin. He hated the persecutory regime enforced by "Catholic dragons" earlier in French history whose legacies reached into his own day. Examining this background story will reveal how, in part, the Conflictual Enlightenment arose in reaction to problems Christians themselves created through their antagonism toward each other during the Age of Reformations.[74]

By chance, right after hearing the visitor's story, Voltaire heard that one of the sons of Jean Calas, twenty-two-year-old Donat Calas, happened to be in Geneva seeking refuge. "His flight made me presume the guilt of the family," Voltaire wrote. However, he wondered, how could a sixty-nine-year-old father kill his twenty-nine-year-old son? "I never remember to have read of any old man being possessed by so horrible a fanaticism." Voltaire invited the young Calas over to his house. "I expected to find him a religious enthusiast [fanatic]," the Enlightener wrote. However, "I found a simple and ingenuous youth, with a gentle and very interesting countenance, who, as he talked to me, made vain efforts to restrain his tears."[75] Donat told Voltaire the following story.

A Tragic Death

On the evening of October 13, 1761, the Calas family ate dinner together in their home above their shop, located on a busy commercial

---

[74] Davidson, *Voltaire: A Life*, 317, 320, 333; Orieux, *Voltaire*, 355–356.
[75] Voltaire to M. Damilaville, March 1, 1765, Voltaire Society of America, https://www.whitman.edu/VSA/letters/3.1.1765.html.

street in Toulouse. They were Huguenots — French Protestants — one family among two hundred others of their faith in a city of fifty thousand Catholics. Jean Calas and his wife had six children, of whom only the two eldest (Marc-Antoine and Pierre) lived at home and worked in the father's business. One son had converted to Catholicism and lived in Toulouse, away from the family. Another son (Donat) was an apprentice in another city. Two daughters were not present that evening because they were away visiting in the country.

Those present on October 13 included Jean and his wife, Marc-Antoine and Pierre, a servant, and the twenty-year-old Protestant Gaubert Lavaisse, son of a prominent lawyer and friend of the two sons. They ate together until about 8:00 p.m., when Marc Antoine went downstairs; the family assumed he was going to the café and pool hall, where he liked to spend his evenings. By 9:30 p.m., Lavaisse made ready to leave. Pierre went downstairs before him with a candle. When they reached the main floor, they noticed that the door leading into the shop was open. There they found Marc-Antoine's body (on the floor, they first claimed; hanging from a doorway, they later stated). They cried out in grief, and Pierre called for his father, who immediately sent word for the doctor and legal authorities.

The Calas Affair in Toulouse

To this day, the cause of Marc-Antoine's death is unknown. At the time, it seemed a clear case of murder. The family told the initial story about the discovery of the body on the floor only to protect themselves from the dishonor of suicide, they said. Within twenty-four hours, however, authorities arrested all five people present that evening. The general assumption among the Catholic populace spread quickly that this Protestant family killed Marc-Antoine because he secretly wanted to become a Catholic. Driven by hatred of the faith, these Calvinists committed murder. This assumption imputed a purely religious motive for the deed.

The defendants presented a convincing case against this indictment, however. All five persons remained together upstairs after Marc-Antoine went below. They separated only moments before discovering the body, already cold. Lavaisse was merely a visitor, and the servant was a Catholic. Furthermore, Marc-Antoine's coat and shirt were found on a counter neatly folded after the manner of a suicide. The time of day made no sense for a murder: Why kill someone at 8:00 p.m., with the streets full of people who could have heard a struggle inside? Witnesses who entered the house attested to the tears of the parents, and the accused had promptly sent for help. It was not a case of murder, at least not by the family, they argued.

The question of motivation lay at the heart of the case. The prosecution rested its argument on the popular presumption that Marc-Antoine died because of his intention to convert. The defense, however, showed that there was no evidence suggesting that the young man intended to convert. No priest admitted to hearing Marc in confession, and since the other brother had already converted without violence from his family, the religious motivation made no sense. It was true that people had often seen Marc in Catholic churches, but that, the defense claimed, attested to no more than an interest in music and did not prove his intent to convert. Rather, the evidence pointed toward suicide because Marc had run up against some seemingly insurmountable obstacles in his life. He had studied law at the University of Toulouse and needed only official approval to be called to the bar. The law, however, required that a law candidate have a certificate of Catholicism. Marc asked for such a certificate of a local priest, but the priest would not grant it until he received Catholic sacraments. Marc could not fulfill that condition, so his legal ambitions were blocked in a city where that profession set the tone for the whole community. He worked at his father's store, but he was nothing more than a clerk with few prospects for his future. The Seven Years' War was hurting business, and his father would not or could not make him a partner in the business. Frustrated at every turn, the defense argued, Marc decided to take his own life.

Few took these arguments seriously. The zealous city magistrate and prosecutor David de Beaudrigue led the investigation, and he believed immediately in the family's guilt. In fact, he looked for evidence based on that presupposition. He attempted to prove that Marc-Antoine had died for his new Catholic religious beliefs at the hands of his fanatical Calvinist family.

This presumption of religious motive then powered the development of the case. Posted in public, the authorities approved an official *Monitoire*, a public notice calling for more testimony in a court case. Traditionally, the authorities of church and state threatened excommunication and prosecution if any witnesses withheld information. The notice read: "Calling to testify under general subpoena: 1. All those who know by hearsay or otherwise that Marc-Antoine Calas had renounced the so-called Reformed Church in which he was raised, that he attended celebrations of the Catholic Church, that he presented himself to the sacrament of penitence, and that he was to have made public abjuration of Calvinism on October 13; all those to whom Marc-Antoine Calas communicated this decision." The document was designed to produce evidence indicting the Calas family. In fact, the document went on to imply that the wider Protestant community had met and planned Marc's death to prevent his conversion. This document was read during Catholic Masses throughout the city.[76]

Even while the trial continued, the authorities ordered the burial of Marc's body in a Catholic cemetery, prejudging one of the main contested facts of the case: Marc died a Catholic. The populace of the city felt he had died a martyr. Marc's funeral took place in a Catholic church and was attended by more than forty ecclesiastics. The White Penitents, a confraternity organized around the practice of penance and public good works, preceded the body of what they assumed was a new convert. They praised God for having opened the young man's eyes to the holy religion before he died; yet there was little evidence to suggest he had even intended to convert, let alone actually done so.

Many Catholics in Toulouse believed that simply being Protestant inclined one toward fanaticism. "Fanaticism," the same charge that would

---

[76] David D. Bien, *The Calas Affair: Persecution, Toleration, and Heresy in Eighteenth-Century Toulouse* (Princeton: Princeton University Press, 1960), 15–16.

condemn the Carmelite sisters in Paris thirty-two years later, involved putting principles into practice in a dangerous and unreasoning sort of way. The Jesuits were fanatics too, many Catholics believed, just like the Protestants: they shared a rashness that threatened social order (the Jesuits owed loyalty directly to the pope, and many Catholics of the time viewed this as fanatical, which is why they suppressed the Jesuits in France in 1764). Fanaticism constituted the core of what it meant to be Calvinist, as the court saw it in 1762. Protestant fanaticism, many Toulousians believed, usually took the form of political resistance and rebellion, but it could also reveal itself in killing family members inclined (supposedly) to Catholicism. The "murder for religion was quite understandable to the judges who were sure they knew the innermost nature of the antisocial Huguenot," one historian of the Calas affair commented.[77]

Many at the time believed that the religion of the *other* (the Protestants) made them violent, just as Protestants in other countries believed that the religion of the Catholics made *them* violent. Thus, the belief that religion causes violence is not a recent creation of twenty-first-century New Atheists but an idea that emerged from Christian infighting. Christians used it as a weapon against each other, accusing the other of holding principles automatically leading to violence. That justified forcible exclusion from their confessional regimes. (One might almost be tempted to say these people needed an Enlightenment.)

Meanwhile, Jean Calas was tortured to reveal more information—somewhat standard practice at the time. Presided over by David de Beaudrigue, Jean was stretched on the rack and then forced to swallow many pitchers of water. Jean did not waver in his refusal to admit guilt. Early modern criminal law proceeded on the assumption that determining guilt could be private and secret, even to the condemned; punishment was rigorously public to instill social obedience. This was the exact opposite of more recent practice, where determination is public and punishment largely private. Within two years of the Calas case,

[77] Ibid., 115.

the Enlightener Cesare Beccaria (1738–1794) published his *On Crimes and Punishments*, condemning torture. By what right did a judge inflict pain before knowing whether someone is guilty? he wrote.[78] Appealing to rational principles allowed Beccaria to challenge errors that had accumulated over many centuries in the area of European criminal law.

The judges arrived at a verdict on March 9, 1762: Jean Calas was guilty of murdering his son. He would go to the cathedral to make a public apology for his crime and then proceed to a scaffold to be tied to a large wheel. His limbs would be broken, and he would remain facing up toward the heavens for as long as God would give him life. Actually, after two hours of suffering, he was strangled and his body was burned. The crowd marveled at Jean's perseverance, and a certain unintended sympathy for him arose.

Partly due to that sympathy and to the divided nature of the panel of judges, none of the rest of the accused were executed. Pierre and Lavaisse went through the forms of conversion to Catholicism while in prison to secure their release. Lavaisse returned to his family, and the authorities picked up the Calas daughters and locked them in separate convents in Toulouse. The judges sent Pierre into permanent exile from France, his property confiscated. They released Madame Calas and the servant without declaring them innocent.

These decisions suggested that a lack of evidence prevented further punishment. Jean had been executed based on the same evidence, however, so the family's release surprised many in the populace who criticized the court for its leniency. The other family members should have been punished too, if Jean was guilty.[79]

Donat Calas fled to Geneva, whence he made his way to Ferney to tell the story of his scattered family to Voltaire. As he did so, the Enlightener's blood began to boil.

---

[78] Cesare Beccaria, *On Crimes and Punishments, and Other Writings* (1764; Toronto: University of Toronto Press, 2008), 32.

[79] Bien, *The Calas Affair*, 23–24.

Living the Christian Faith in Toulouse

What factors led to the Calas affair? The answer has much to do with how early modern *sacral culture* kept alive certain prejudices about Protestants. The sacral culture of the time tried to fuse faith and society. It attempted to link all aspects of life to the sacred, to religion — even one's civil status. People simply assumed government should play a decisive role in the religious life of the individual.

Tradition in sacral cultures enculturated people from birth into sacred language, customs, and truths that they believed almost instinctively. Reinforced through communal processions, feast days, and even rules about who could enter certain professions, tradition formed the basis of continuity and identity in such a culture.

Tevye in the musical *Fiddler on the Roof*, speaking from the perspective of early twentieth-century Jewish sacral culture, said, "Because of our traditions, we've kept our balance for many, many years.... Because of our traditions, everyone knows who he is and what God expects him to do."[80] Tradition could help one make wise decisions by supporting nonautonomous knowledge. Since no one person's reason accessed all the truth or always avoided mistakes, tradition linked the individual to a wider and deeper rationality of the generations. It could give direction and a feeling of hope.

Some traditions, however, could make one *less* human. They might inculcate superstition. Sometimes one needed to cast doubt on them and evaluate them through critical inquiry. Many Catholic citizens of Toulouse had consciously and unconsciously absorbed the idea of the sacral state, the holy state (a bit like Rousseau, ironically), in their efforts to create a confessional regime ever since the Age of Reformations. They believed the Church should buttress the authority of the state through preaching obedience as a religious duty, while the state should maintain the authority of the Church. In this sort of sacral culture, diverse religious

---

[80] Jerry Bock, "Tradition," *Fiddler on the Roof* (1964), prologue, https://genius.com/Jerry-bock-prologue-tradition-main-title-lyrics.

ideas and values seemed to threaten the stability of the common way of life. Many held that Protestants were fanatics by nature. They forgot the humanity of their neighbors. They accepted as normal that the sacral state would defend the faith by enforcing religious unity. Success would be measured by behavioral modification in accord with law. This would lead to a more stable and prosperous society, or so they thought.

As one historian pointed out, however, obedience to rules cannot replace the practice of virtue. "The *mere* securing of social control by coercive laws and practices worked *against* the kingdom of God, because grudging conformity simply is not a joyful life of shared faith, hope, and love," he noted. The resulting web of religious legalism darkened the lives of French Huguenots, as it did in the experience of Marc-Antoine Calas. In this way, certain traditions worked against human flourishing in Toulouse and beyond during the eighteenth century. As the Catholic philosopher Charles Taylor noted, "There can never be a total fusion of the faith and any particular society; and the attempt to achieve it is dangerous for the faith."[81] The Christians of Toulouse failed to live up to their own principles. This happens in any human community, but it had long-reaching consequences—through the action of Voltaire—for Christian culture far beyond just Toulouse.

The problem was not only a failure of faith, hope, and love but also a malfunction of practical reason. The French man of letters Charles-Louis de Secondat, baron de Montesquieu, put it this way in his 1748 book *The Spirit of the Laws*: "The most true and holy doctrines may be attended with the very worst consequences when they are not connected with the principles of society." In other words, without practical reason mediating between "holy doctrines" and the "principles of society," piety easily degenerates into fanaticism and superstition. This happens "when insufficient attention is given to the purifying and structuring role of

---

[81] Gregory, *The Unintended Reformation*, 161; Charles Taylor, *A Catholic Modernity?* (Dayton: University of Dayton, 1996), 12, http://ecommons. udayton.edu/uscc_marianist_award/10/.

reason within religion." These last words were not uttered by Voltaire, though they may well have been; they are the words of Pope Benedict XVI.[82] Faith and reason need mutual correction from each other. It is true that the sacral culture of Restoration Catholicism gloried in its art, architecture, and spirituality as responses to the Protestant Reformations. It is also true, however, that Catholics of this era sometimes confused the proper boundaries of faith and reason, and of the natural and the supernatural. This derailed charity.

The derailment became severe enough to eventually generate desire for a new kind of culture then emerging in the eighteenth century — not sacral but *civic* culture. Appealing to freedom of conscience using both Enlightenment and Christian values, civic culture decoupled religion from one's civil status, undermining the sacral ideal. The new model held that political and social stability do not require everyone to share the same conception of the sacred. More than one church can occupy the same territory of a society. Proponents of the civic cultural model defended the emerging "public sphere" from direct control of governing authorities — church or state. In the new social space of coffeehouses, clubs, and print media, Enlightenment ideas became a culture, a civic way of life uniting diverse people around worldly projects. The new civic culture of toleration and polite sociability fostered cooperation, wealth creation, and new opportunities for religious minorities.

While solving some problems, Enlightened civic culture eventually created new ones. Spiritual fragmentation and lack of common vision would open space for new sacral projects, as during the French Revolution. Civic culture proved not to be quite the neutral ground Enlighteners imagined, even as its methods of reconciling various factions proved fruitful, especially in the United States.

---

[82] Pope Benedict XVI, Address in Westminster Hall" (September 17, 2010), http://www.vatican.va/content/benedict-xvi/en/speeches/2010/september/documents/hf_ben-xvi_spe_20100917_societa-civile.html; Montesquieu, *The Spirit of the Laws* (Chicago: Encyclopedia Britannica, 1952), 205.

At the time of the Enlightenment, however, sacral and civic cultures conflicted. To have reached an understanding, Church leaders and Enlighteners would have been obliged to acknowledge that "religious and political societies, being in essence different by nature, could not be governed by similar principles," as Alexis de Tocqueville wrote. Few could imagine such a possibility then, and so it seemed necessary for Conflictual Enlighteners to attack the Church when arguing for political and social reform.[83]

One of the great festivals of Toulouse illustrates the ambiguous and problematic tendencies of sacral Christian culture and why Enlighteners attacked it. The festival occurred each year on May 17 and included a religious procession celebrating victory over the Huguenots back in 1562 during the "Religious Wars" of the Age of Reformations. Through this festival, the Catholic people of Toulouse held on to the memory of their bitter struggle with the Protestants. Thousands of people flooded into the city, where a carnival atmosphere took hold. In May of 1762, just two months after the execution of Jean Calas, the city celebrated the two hundredth anniversary of the event with great fanfare. Bonfires lit the route of the procession when, early that morning, dozens of guilds of tradesmen marched along, escorting relic shrines of different saints. Then came various monastic orders, representatives of parishes, town hall officials, the Blessed Sacrament, judges, and university officials.

Rain delayed the second half of the celebrations for two weeks. Finally, in anticipation of the fireworks display, people pressed into the large square before the City Hall, decorated with flowers and lit by lanterns. Over

---

[83] Tocqueville, *The Ancien Régime*, 152. A good example of the civic cultural model appeared in Benjamin Franklin's efforts to start a subscription library in Philadelphia in 1731 along with other members of the Leather-Apron Club, an association of tradesmen: "tho' 'tis composed of so many Persons of different Sects, Parties and Ways of Thinking, yet no Differences relating to the Affairs of the Library have arisen among us; but every Thing has been conducted with great Harmony, and to general Satisfaction." See Benjamin Franklin, *The Autobiography and Other Writings* (1791; New York: Signet Classics, 2001), 180.

the doorways, signs praised those ancestors who had made "heresy feel the strength of the Almighty" (referring to the events of 1562). In the center of the square rose an artificial mountain of scaffolding, sixty feet in height, representing a "temple of religion." At the top, two ten-foot figures struggled—one, Religion, held a chalice and a cross with which it pinned down the other—Calvin, who struggled to free himself. Religion conquered. (Thirty-one years later in Paris, a similar artificial mountain rose inside Notre Dame Cathedral upon which not Religion but Reason conquered, personified by a shapely actress.) At midnight, fireworks lit up the sky, and the pleased crowd dispersed.[84]

In a Dominican church in Toulouse just down the street from the fireworks rested the body of Thomas Aquinas (1225–1274). Though the Dominican had died in Italy, the pope had permitted the transfer of his remains to the French city, the birthplace of his order in the early thirteenth century. Aquinas believed that governments rightly tolerate certain evils lest other goods be lost. This meant allowing the religious rites of Jews, pagans, and sometimes even heretics—when they are very numerous—to continue. Unbelievers who have not received the faith should never be compelled into the Church, Aquinas thought, "because to believe depends on the will"—unless they pose a grave threat. Then unbelievers may be resisted with force, not to compel them to believe but to defend the faith of Christ. In the case of heretics, however, the Church should admonish them, for they fall under her authority as those who have been baptized. Only after multiple warnings should the Church turn heretics over to the state for punishment. Aquinas defended the possibility of putting heretics to death as criminals and threats to the common good, though the state possessed no independent competence to do this.

In the days of Aquinas, members of his order preached to the Cathars in southern France near Toulouse, who believed that two powers, good and evil, dominated the universe, and the evil power made material reality. The Dominicans spread the Rosary to combat the heresy. The tradition

---

[84] Bien, *The Calas Affair*, 49–52.

of praying the Rosary originated around Toulouse and would enter deeply into Christian cultures far and wide. In addition to preaching and prayer, local authorities acted militarily against the Cathars. Precedent existed at Toulouse, then, for the cooperation of church and state against heresy.[85]

However, Christian leaders had worked out an idea of religious freedom long before the time of Calas or Aquinas during the Roman persecutions of the early Church. Tertullian wrote in the early third century: "It is no part of religion to coerce religious practice, for it is by free choice not coercion that we should be led to religion." Later in the first millennium, Christian leaders condemned the use of torture and the death penalty for heretics. These practices returned to Christendom, however, with the rediscovery of Roman law just before the time of Aquinas. Aquinas himself dodged the ethical status of torture. Church leaders never claimed that the practices were consistent with the gospel or part of Catholic doctrine. Today, Church teaching has clearly reaffirmed the *older* Christian tradition against torture and coercion that was sadly lost for nearly one thousand years.[86]

When Voltaire heard about the May 17 festival at Toulouse, he condemned it as a superstitious and barbarous celebration of four thousand murders. That was a simplistic judgment, for the festival also filled an important civic and religious function. But it is true that the traditional celebration reinforced in Catholics the belief that Calvinists were fanatics who could not be trusted. Those prejudices partly shaped the trial and execution of Jean Calas.

Catholic Absolutism

Catholic silence about those prejudices—and about the laws and festivals that reinforced them—kept alive a certain popular conception

---

[85] Thomas Aquinas, *Summa Theologiae*, prologue, q. 10, arts. 8, 11; q. 11, art. 3.

[86] Robert Louis Wilken, *The Christian Roots of Religious Liberty* (Milwaukee: Marquette University Press, 2014), 16.

of Protestants as the very icons of social disorder. Many believed those who attempted to live out their Protestant faith represented a security threat. Catholics felt Protestants were not trustworthy because they bore a heavy historical responsibility for bloodshed in the days of the "Wars of Religion," when they had sought to build a state within a state. "We must do everything to stop the seditious undertakings of those who seek to sow trouble and division in the state under the pretext of Religion," summarized a document of the judicial court of Toulouse about Protestants. If all Frenchmen are not Catholics, disorder will envelop the country, people assumed. It was not so much divergence from Catholic theology but the danger to the state that bothered them.[87]

Where did this body of laws against the Protestants and this Catholic acquiescence to the resulting police state come from? They emerged out of the memory of the French "Wars of Religion" (they were about politics, too) in the sixteenth century. Voltaire had called those conflicts "the fatal consequence of that dogmatic turn, which had for so long a time been introduced among all ranks of people" due to the Reformations.[88] (He did not live long enough, however, to see the fatal consequences of the dogmatic turn of Reason during the French Revolution.) The Edict of Nantes (1598), promulgated by King Henry IV, inaugurated peace in France by giving the Huguenots the right to practice their religion without persecution by the state. At a time when England pressed severe penal laws against its Catholics, the French regime protected freedom of conscience, and, in effect, distinguished between civil and religious unity. Civil rights did not depend on being Catholic. Voltaire later lionized Henry IV for this achievement in toleration. Many French Catholic leaders, however, condemned Henry in his time for abandoning the Christian-state ideal.

Toleration of Protestants in France slowly eroded in the 1600s due to the way King Louis XIV (reigned 1643–1715) interpreted the Catholic

---

[87] Bien, *The Calas Affair*, 57–58.
[88] Voltaire, *The Works of Voltaire*, vol. 12, *The Age of Louis XIV* (1751; New York: St. Hubert Guild, 1901), 16.

Restoration—the attempt to restore and reform the Church in response to the Protestant Reformations. A pompous man with a Jesuit confessor, Louis regularly visited both his beautiful royal chapel and his beautiful mistresses. He built up the French monarchy to unprecedented heights of absolute authority. Louis was the "most Christian king," governor of the Church in France, and he appointed bishops and abbots. He believed in the divine right of kings to rule and worked to eliminate any resistance to the crown through centralization of authority around his court, eventually based at the vast and sumptuous Palace of Versailles. Formal rules governed speech codes and dress codes inside the palace, just as formal gardens governed the landscape outside, through symmetry and geometric shapes to represent harmony, order, and the ideals of the Renaissance and ancient Rome. The palace was a symbol of an all-embracing power over culture, religion, and the state; it was a model for European courts for a hundred years.

The presence of the Huguenots in France did not sit well with Louis's conception of himself or his absolute reign over state and church. By the 1680s, the government had already employed various strategies to encourage Protestant conversion: missionaries, bribes, destruction of Calvinist temples, barring certain professions, overburdening Protestant schools, banning mixed marriages, transferring Protestant hospitals to Catholics, and limiting professional advancement for Protestants. The last of these would block the career of Marc-Antoine Calas in the Toulouse of Voltaire's time.

John Locke (1632–1704), the Protestant English Enlightener, traveled in France during the 1670s and keenly observed the worsening conditions of the Huguenots. On January 31, 1676, Locke recorded, the Protestants living in a town near Montpellier had just received an order that week from the king forbidding them to choose Calvinist governors and ordering the destruction of their Protestant temple. "The pretence given is that their Temple being too near the papist church, their singing of psalms disturbed the service." Locke observed firsthand, by lodging and worshipping with French Protestants, the ways that absolutism undermined local government by means of religious intolerance. In this,

Catholic-inspired religious oppression fueled the growth of the modern state. In response, Locke would later author books on separation of power, the right of revolution, consent of the governed, and religious toleration (that would eventually influence the formation of the United States). For no man can, if he would, conform his faith to the dictates of another," he wrote in his *Letter Concerning Toleration* (1689). "All the life and power of true religion consists in the inward and full persuasion of the mind; and faith is not faith without believing."[89]

While this was all going on, reports of mass conversions reached the French monarchy. The king came to believe that all Protestants would soon enter the Church. Therefore, France no longer needed the old Edict of Nantes granting religious toleration. In his mind, the Catholic Restoration had (nearly) succeeded. The goal of eliminating heresy was within reach. People around the king encouraged him to revoke the Edict of Nantes. One of these was probably his devoutly Catholic second wife, Madame de Maintenon, by whose influence the king had recently become more personally devout. Another who likely encouraged him to revoke the Edict was his Jesuit spiritual adviser. Certainly, his secretary of state for war encouraged him. So, too, did the archbishop of Paris, who met regularly with the king and pushed the revocation that would end toleration. That seemed the best way forward.

The king ordered a debate on the proposal to revoke the Edict of Nantes. Opinion was divided. Some advocated moderation, "claiming that consciences could never be governed by a raised cudgel," the diplomat Choisy recorded. But others, carried away by zeal, claimed that the handful of Protestants in France (there were in reality hundreds of thousands) would lose heart without their leaders and abandon their cause. If the king would speak up directly and firmly, the Huguenots would all

---

[89] John Locke, journal entry for January 31, 1676, in *Travels in France, 1675–1679*, ed. John Lough (Cambridge: Cambridge University Press, 1953), 22–23; John Locke, "A Letter Concerning Toleration," in *The Works of John Locke*, vol. 5 (London: G. & J. Rivington, 1824), 11.

follow him like sheep. Many believed that the Huguenots corrupted the soul of the nation through their inclinations to fanaticism and political subversion. Members of the clergy counseled the king to use his power to eliminate heresy because freedom of conscience constituted a dangerous precipice. The public presence of people of other faiths weakens faith as the bond of the community. Many believed toleration leads to disorder, religious indifference, and scandal. As a mother and as the true church of Jesus Christ, the Catholic Church possessed the right to discipline her wayward and rebellious children (the Protestants) in order to bring them home. These arguments justified the theory of righteous persecution, which won over the debate.[90]

Louis promulgated what is known as the Revocation of the Edict of Nantes on October 22, 1685 (nine years before the birth of Voltaire). It ordered the closure of Protestant schools, exile of their pastors, and mandatory Baptism and education in the Catholic faith of all Protestant children. Subsequent laws enforced participation in the Catholic sacraments of Eucharist, marriage, and extreme unction. When Rousseau desired to marry his mistress later in the eighteenth century, for example, he was prevented by law because he had reverted to Calvinism. Only Catholic marriage was valid. The Revocation permitted private worship in homes, stopping just short of legislating conscience: one could believe as a Protestant but could not act upon such beliefs. One retained private freedom of conscience without the public free exercise of worship.[91]

---

[90] Owen Chadwick, *The Popes and European Revolution* (New York: Oxford University Press, 1981), 433; Geoffrey Adams, *The Huguenots and French Opinion, 1685–1787: The Enlightenment Debate on Toleration* (Waterloo, Ontario: Wilfrid Laurier University Press, 1991), 9; Gilette Ziegler, *At the Court of Versailles: Eyewitness Reports from the Reign of Louis XIV* (New York: E. P. Dutton, 1966), 226; H. Daniel-Rops, *The Church in the Seventeenth Century* (London: J. M. Dent & Sons, 1963), 207.

[91] Christie Sample Wilson, *Beyond Belief: Surviving the Revocation of the Edict of Nantes in France* (Bethlehem, PA: Lehigh University Press, 2011), 68–69, 76.

This was not unlike Protestant treatment of Catholics in Ireland under the Penal Laws, established during the 1690s to ban the Mass, ordination, and the presence of bishops. The Penal Laws also closed Catholic schools in Ireland and led to violent torture and persecution in an attempt to force Catholics to join the Irish state church (Anglican). In France, provincial and ecclesiastical authorities would share the responsibility of enforcing similar laws against the Protestants in the 1685 Revocation.

The French intelligentsia, including Catholic bishops, explained why the Revocation was a good idea and praised the king for his piety. They had been conditioned for generations to respect order, hierarchy, and unity in politics as much as in religion and art. The French Academy offered prizes for works celebrating the eradication of heresy, and leading painters incorporated this theme.

Louis even put pressure on the papacy to approve the Revocation. Naturally, the king had not consulted the pope about the matter, and as head of the Church in France, he rarely listened to the successor of St. Peter. Deliberately misled by the envoy at the French embassy in Rome (among others), Pope Innocent XI (reigned 1676–1689) did not know about the use of force associated with the Revocation. So he ordered celebrations in Rome to mark the occasion. Bells pealed across the city and cannon fired from Sant'Angelo. Processions, bonfires, and fountains running with wine made for three joyous days of Catholic celebration.

Naturally, Pope Innocent XI supported the overall goals of the Catholic Restoration launched by leaders of the Church at the Council of Trent (1545–1563) in response to the Protestant Reformations. The Restoration had really started to achieve major results by the late seventeenth century. Clergy were better educated because of the spread of seminaries, and they became increasingly committed to teaching their parishioners the catechism and helping them achieve the basic requirements of the Catholic faith: Baptism and Easter duties of Confession, penance, and Eucharist.

At the heart of this movement, however, lay a desire by Church leaders to project an image to the world of uniformity and order against Protestant variety and disorder. Catholic reform took on a centralized, defensive, and aggressively apologetic approach. This easily justified whatever means were necessary to achieve the noble end of a "Christian state." Innocent XI, like most Christians of his day, held to this conception of the state as the bulwark of orthodoxy. Through mutual acceptance of the principle of "whose realm, his religion," Christian states, both Protestant and Catholic, sought to enforce internal religious conformity with severe criminal codes—except in a few places, such as Catholic Maryland, Quaker Pennsylvania, and the Calvinist Dutch Republic. In France, some Catholics did resist the political and religious centralization of the time; however, they were attracted to Jansenism, which was condemned by the pope in 1713. Thus, little room remained for Catholics there to take a different position on church and state.[92]

It seemed natural to many that the state should compel Protestants to convert in France because, in the end, this would be good for them. The king simply wanted to secure the triumph of the Catholic faith, and so, unsurprisingly, many Catholics went along with a politically correct religious zeal. They reassured themselves that preaching would bring the Protestants around as willing converts anyway. In addition, efforts to teach the faith to the new converts spilled over into the general Catholic community, intensifying its devotion. In this way, the Revocation actively forwarded the goals of the Catholic Restoration. Protestant children would be baptized Catholic, they further reasoned, so eventually they would not know the difference between the faiths and would simply accept their Catholicism. All would be as one in the kingdom.

Because many church and state leaders believed this myth, they cooperated in their efforts to bring it about. They mutually reinforced each other in theory and in practice. The great theologian Robert Bellarmine (1542–1621) had written in his treatise on the pope's temporal power, "That government is best which is most ordered; and it can be

---

[92] Louis O'Brien, *Innocent XI and the Revocation of the Edict of Nantes* (Ph.D. diss., University of California, Berkeley, 1930), 193–194.

demonstrated that monarchy is more ordered than aristocracy or democracy. All order consists in this, that some should command and others should be subjugated. And order may be discerned not among equals but among those who are superior and inferior." This kind of political thinking, efficient for reaching certain goals, nevertheless obscured other truths about the nature of the human person and of politics and contributed to the persecution of the Protestants in France.[93]

"Compel Them to Come In"

The mutual reinforcement of church and state in Catholic France can be seen in the actions of the great French bishop and theologian Jacques-Bénigne Bossuet (1627–1704). He was renowned for his intellectual virtues, beautiful sermons, and devotion to his diocese. As court preacher to Louis XIV, however, he unfortunately provided theological rationalization for the Revocation of the Edict of Nantes. Despite his efforts toward mutual theological understanding with Protestants and gentle means of persuasion, Bossuet was somewhat obsessed with the idea of authority. He strongly advocated political absolutism and the divine right of kings.

On the day before the king would promulgate the Revocation, Bossuet officiated at a royal Mass at Fontainebleau—in full panoply, including crozier and miter—and preached on the text of the day: Jesus' parable about a king preparing a wedding banquet for his son. When the invited guests did not come, the king sent his army to destroy them and their city. Bossuet also preached on the *compelle intrare* passage of Luke 14:23: "The master said to the servant, 'Go out to the highways and hedges, and compel people to come in, that my house may be filled.'" Bossuet's secretary recorded that tears were in the eyes of all those present, their hearts pounding as they considered over the significance of what the king was about to do: secure the full Catholicity of the kingdom.

---

[93] Dom Paschal Scotti, *Galileo Revisited* (San Francisco: Ignatius Press, 2017), 51.

Bossuet's sermon enchanted the monarch, especially the reference to St. Augustine's interpretation of the "compel them to come in" passage. In his letter to Vincentius (A.D. 409), Augustine wrote that he had originally opposed coercion because "we must act only by words, fight only by arguments, and prevail by force of reason." Augustine changed his mind, however, when he saw how effectively imperial edicts brought his own town over to Catholic unity. "How many, believing that it mattered not to which party a Christian might belong, remained in the schism of Donatus only because they had been born in it, and no one was compelling them to forsake it and pass over into the Catholic Church!" Bossuet implied in his sermon that by revoking the Edict of Nantes, Louis would faithfully follow the example of Augustine—despite the fact that at other times Augustine stated faith could not be coerced. The overall implication of the sermon, however, was clear: the state has the duty to control and correct religion. Heresy is a public crime because it threatens the true good of all. The king's power is from God, so he needs to take action against those who refuse God's Church. "The sermon affected the whole Court most deeply," the secretary wrote, "and Madame la Dauphine [wife of the heir apparent, Louis's eldest son] was so carried away with fervor that she talked about nothing else throughout dinner."[94]

The political correctness of Bossuet's cultural context shaped the way he read Scripture and which truths he chose to highlight. While the original sermon is lost (and so Bossuet cannot speak for himself), the record of his secretary makes it seem as though the great bishop said on that occasion what the king wanted to hear, which contributed to disastrous consequences.

Unfortunately, the king's decision to revoke the Edict of Nantes, backed up by Bossuet's literal interpretation of Luke 14:23, accomplished

[94] Augustine, Letter 93, to Vincentius, pars. 16–17, trans. J. G. Cunningham, in *Nicene and Post-Nicene Fathers*, First Series, vol. 1, ed. Philip Schaff (Buffalo, NY: Christian Literature Publishing, 1887), revised and edited for New Advent by Kevin Knight, New Advent, http://www.newadvent.org/fathers/1102093.htm; Ziegler, *At the Court of Versailles*, 227.

in the political sphere what the Inquisition's 1616 decision against Galileo, also backed up by literal biblical interpretation, had done in the scientific sphere: both decisions confused the natural and the supernatural and contributed to an abuse of authority. For all the Baroque glory of Restoration Catholicism, it had lost some of the medieval sensitivity to the four senses of Scripture[95] in its sparring with Protestants. In their theological controversies after the Reformations, biblical literalism shored up certain teachings but also narrowed Catholic interaction with Scripture, in these cases causing major blunders in their engagement with science and politics. That tragically put Church leaders and theologians on the wrong foot in those important arenas just as the modern age emerged.

Eventually, Christians started to shake some of their biblical literalism and regain more multilayered interpretations. The Spanish priest Josemaría Escrivá (1902–1975) interpreted the *compelle intrare* passage very differently than Bossuet. If one understands that Christ gently invites people to follow him, then readers will not mistake Luke 14:23 as a command to coerce, Escrivá wrote. Christ's "*compelle intrare* implies no violence, either physical or moral. Rather, it reflects the power of attraction of Christian example, which shows in its way of acting the power of God." Christian apologist C. S. Lewis wrote about the verse from Luke in the context of his reluctant conversion. He recounted how he kicked and screamed against God's relentless pursuit of him, his eyes darting in

---

[95] The *literal sense* is the meaning conveyed by the words of Scripture. It is the basis for all other understandings of Scripture. The medieval Church, however, also utilized three other *spiritual senses* referring to further significations of the literal meaning of the words. The *allegorical sense* sought to understand the hidden meaning behind the surface of the text. An author might write one thing but intend another. The *moral* sense paid attention to the moral lessons for guiding one's life found in Scripture. The *future sense* considered what Scripture tells us about our final end, the goal of our journey of life as we are led toward Heaven. See Pauline A. Viviano, "The Senses of Scripture," United Stated Conference of Catholic Bishops (2015), http://www.usccb.org/bible/national-bible-week/upload/viviano-senses-scripture.pdf.

every direction, looking for a chance to escape. Based on this experience, Lewis offered a profound moral interpretation of Luke 14:23: "The words *compelle intrare*, compel them to come in, have been so abused by wicked men that we shudder at them; but, properly understood, they plumb the depth of Divine mercy. The hardness of God is kinder than the softness of men, and His compulsion is our liberation."[96]

In Bossuet's age, however, the close alliance of church and state obscured certain biblical truths. Though that alliance caused some advantages for both faith and politics, it also caused numerous abuses. This became increasingly obvious in the eighteenth century. It was at Ferney that Voltaire started signing his letters with the shadowy phrase *écrasez l'infâme*—"crush the infamous"! Did he mean the Catholic Church? Not exactly. Scholars believe the phrase referred more to the church-state connection that Voltaire believed fostered intolerance, abuse of power, and persecution.

Not only Voltaire made that criticism. The Duke of Saint-Simon (1675–1755) wrote a lively account of King Louis XIV's court of Versailles. This pious but critical French diplomat stated it was a terrible mistake to suffer the clergy in affairs of the state. They encouraged the king to believe revoking the Edict of Nantes glorified God. The king believed that the Protestants had already genuinely converted. "Those responsible took great care to persuade and beatify him in advance," the diplomat noted sardonically.

After approving the Revocation, the king congratulated himself on his power and piety. Saint-Simon interpreted the king as believing the use of state power to enforce Catholicism would repair before God the sins and scandal of his life. "He thought he was back in the time of the Apostles, and took all the credit. The bishops wrote him panegyrics, some

---

[96] Josemaría Escrivá, *Friends of God* (Dublin: Four Courts, 1981), no. 37, Josemaría Escrivá, http://www.escrivaworks.org/book/friends_of_god-point-37.htm; C. S. Lewis, *Surprised by Joy: The Shape of My Early Life* (London: Collins/Fontana Books, 1955), 183.

called Louis a new Charlemagne, and the Jesuits made their pulpits and monasteries reverberate with praise." All France was full of horror and confusion (due to the persecution of Protestants), Saint-Simon wrote, but never had there been such a triumph, joy, and praise of the monarch.

Saint-Simon believed repealing the Edict of Nantes was the worst blunder Louis XIV ever made. It forced people to sacrifice their conscience and commit perjury and sacrilege. Good and true Catholics and holy bishops bemoaned with all their heart what was happening throughout France, the keen observer wrote. They saw that Catholic leaders were acting against the heretics as pagan tyrants had once acted against the martyrs in the early Church. "They wept bitterly over the irremediable and odious results these hateful methods would have on true religion."[97] They were correct: the Revocation and its enforcement would create so much resentment in France that the Conflictual Enlightenment would take strong root during the course of the eighteenth century. It would seek revenge on what it perceived Catholicism to be, and the Carmelites of Compiègne would pay the price.

Fleeing Catholic Dragons

Meanwhile, the French dragons (or *dragoons*) fanned out across the country to enforce the laws against the Protestants. They were mounted infantrymen nicknamed after their short guns known as "dragons" — perhaps because they belched a lot of sparks when fired. A certain devout Huguenot named James Fontaine (1658–1728) fled the dragons on his swift horse in his escape from France to England and then Ireland. Several of his children would emigrate to the American colonies. His epic story illustrates why the abuse of authority by both church and state in the late 1600s generated much of the anger behind the Conflictual Enlightenment and Voltaire's later attacks on the Church.

---

[97] Duc de Saint-Simon, *The Age of Magnificence: The Memoirs of the Duc de Saint-Simon* (1788; New York: Capricorn Books, 1964), 273, 281–283.

Cartoon of a French dragon intimidating a Huguenot,
by Godefroy Engelmann, after a design of 1686.

Fontaine started writing his *Memoirs of a Huguenot Family* in 1722 in order to leave his family a record of the mercies of God to himself and his descendants. He recalled as a young, virile man watching helplessly as the dragons roamed the countryside of western France near the Atlantic coast, converting Huguenots to Catholicism through force and fear. Even rumors of approaching dragons brought whole villages over to Catholicism. One dragon commander joked that Protestant leaders were so eager to follow orders they would convert to Islam if told to do so. The mounted soldiers lodged with Protestant families and harassed them until they converted. When caught trying to flee the country, authorities told one group of Huguenots, "Mass or the galleys" (which meant, convert or forcibly serve as a galley slave in the French navy). Each dragon was a sovereign judge and executioner, Fontaine noted. They inflicted thousands of robberies, tortures, and rapes on the Huguenots. They coordinated a religious reign of terror. "Oh! my God! to what a horrid pitch of barbarity can mankind be borne by the blind zeal of superstition and idolatry," Fontaine wrote in a passage sounding like Voltaire.[98]

The Catholic political correctness of the age, born out of a mutated conflict mentality, acted as a kind of superstition. Under its influence, many French Catholics looked the other way. They did not gaze into the faces of their Huguenots neighbors to see their dignity as men and women.

This superstition twisted faith. It obscured truths that human reason could perceive from its own inquiry, independent of faith. Thus, it created scandal: some men and women of reason could see the dignity of the Huguenots as people, while many people of faith did not. It created a double scandal when Catholics went along with the reigning political correctness. If believers do not even hold to the truths of reason, how can anyone ever respect their faith?

Some Catholics *did* look at their Protestant neighbors as people. They took them into their homes to protect them. For example, in the town of Loriol in southeast France, the significant Protestant population was not forced or threatened into conversion. Though the Calvinist temple was destroyed by order of the bishop, the Catholic people of Loriol, including town leaders and the local priest, did not use their power to force Protestants to conform. They adapted to the new situation by giving the appearance of obedience to royal commands and church expectations. The priest looked the other way when Protestants did not show up to receive the sacraments. The appearance of the town as an ideal Catholic community meant it did not attract attention from higher authorities, which protected the peace of the community.[99]

---

[98] Daniel-Rops, *The Church in the Seventeenth Century*, 208; James Fontaine, *Memoirs of a Huguenot Family* (New York: George P. Putnam, 1853), chaps. 4 and 8.

[99] Wilson, *Beyond Belief*, 1, 6–8, 64–65, 82.

Some French bishops refused to allow dragons in their diocese. Bishop Étienne Le Camus of Grenoble, for example, approved of the Revocation but not of the use of force. French authorities denounced him to Rome for diluting Catholic doctrine. Sensing foul play in France, Pope Innocent XI snubbed these authorities by making Le Camus a cardinal. In a pastoral letter to the priests of his diocese, the new cardinal forbade the use of force: "God wishes the service rendered him to be voluntary.... Remember that the maladies of the soul are not cured in a moment, nor by constraint nor violence, but rather by the fervor of prayer and the gentle promptings of truth and charity."[100]

Other bishops, however, actively invited dragons to their dioceses to help push thousands toward conversion, measuring success by numbers. New converts, especially their children, would be watched to make sure they were active participants in the Catholic faith.

Pope Innocent XI heard reports from other parts of Europe about French Huguenots fleeing violence in their home country. Church leaders in Rome started to fear retribution against Catholic populations in Protestant states. The pope himself, a kindly, generous, and charitable old man, detested cruelty and did not believe force constituted a wise conversion strategy. In a 1688 letter to Holy Roman Emperor Leopold, Pope Innocent XI bemoaned the tactics of the French king: "The horrible thought of so many sacrileges which have been committed will cause me to shudder for the rest of my days." He feared for Louis's salvation and for the souls of the Huguenots. Would it not have been better for the glory of Jesus and the salvation of souls to have left the Huguenots at liberty rather than putting them in such straits?[101]

For his part, "my blood boiled under the sense of injury," Fontaine wrote. "I desired earnestly that the Protestants should take up arms in a body and offer resistance, instead of waiting quietly to be slain like beasts."

---

[100] Étienne Le Camus, diocesan letter, April 28, 1687, quoted in O'Brien, *Innocent XI*, 131.

[101] Ibid., 147–148, 193.

He met with a group of Huguenots leaders to determine a course of action. They counseled patience and long-suffering. Fontaine dissented totally from them; obedience to one edict only paved the way to the next. He argued that their lives and property did not simply belong to the king. As men as well as Christians, they should defend the agreement with their fathers, the Edict of Nantes, that had protected religious liberty. "I made a solemn appeal to them," he wrote, that unless they resisted, thousands of their people would abjure their faith, unable to take the strain of persecution. If we could put arms in their hands, Fontaine said, "they would willingly shed their blood, and sacrifice their lives, in defense of the truth." The leaders Fontaine met with rejected the "carnal spirit" behind his words and declared it contrary to the gospel. (Some Protestants—called Camisards—eventually did revolt some years later.) Instead, they drafted a letter declaring they would obey the king in all things consistent with their duty to God and that nothing would induce them to change their religion.

Fontaine gave up trying to convince them and fled. As the dragons swept into his region of western France, most of the Protestant leaders rushed to the Catholic churches to recant their faith, as the contumacious young man had predicted. The poor country people showed more determination, fleeing to the forests to conceal themselves or to the seacoast to try to escape the country by sea. "I left the home of my childhood, never to return to it, about midnight," Fontaine wrote. The dragons took possession of it two hours later. He brought a few belongings and left by horseback, "well armed, and I had resolved, if I should encounter *dragoons*, to sell my life as dearly as possible." He knew the country well and avoided the main roads on his great Arabian horse he believed could outpace any dragon. At one point, soldiers approached him. Disguised with a great wig as a country gentleman, he rode directly toward them, saluting as they rode past on their quest for converts. Fontaine moved by night, staying with family members and friends, encouraging them to resist at least spiritually in such difficult times. Nevertheless, he wrote, "It was distressing in the extreme to see the vast numbers who had made shipwreck of their faith," moved by the argument that God commanded obedience to political authorities (Rom. 13:1–2). They thus participated in the Catholic sacraments without believing, just as Pope Innocent XI feared. Fontaine struggled to keep up his courage. His peril and the collapse of faith in so many caused in him extreme distress.

At one point, Fontaine bumped into the local Catholic priest from Royan, a "respectable man," who urged him to do as many others had done: to "appear to change." That would answer every purpose. Fontaine replied that his conscience did not permit him to take that course of action. "He [the priest] then told me in confidence," Fontaine wrote, "that he was himself overwhelmed with grief at the state of things. He feared the just judgments of God would overtake the Catholics for forcing the Protestants to approach the altar without faith, and to partake of that Holy Sacrament which should only be received by the sincere in heart." The priest feared that God would chastise France for this sin. Fontaine concluded that the priest spoke with great force on the subject, "and he really appeared to have the gift of prophecy." Indeed, he did. God's punishment, it seems, would partly take the form of Voltaire and later the Reign of Terror. The violence unleashed against French Catholics in 1793 and 1794 was not unlike what they unleashed against Protestants in 1685.

Fontaine resolved to escape France. He collected his fiancée and several others and made for the coast, where he arranged for an English sea captain to smuggle them out. The coast was strictly guarded by sea and by land to prevent emigration and the resulting loss of talent and wealth from France. Harsh penalties fell on those attempting to flee the country. Catholic clergymen and neighbors would tip off local authorities if they saw suspicious activity, such as Huguenots trying to sell livestock or furniture. Perhaps they planned to emigrate? France turned into a giant prison for the Huguenots, enforced by cooperation between church and state at all levels of society.

The English captain finally sent word to Fontaine that his ship would pass between the island of Oléron and the mainland. They should then come out in a small boat to board his ship. Fontaine waited on the remote section of coastline opposite Oléron. When the captain did not appear, detained by suspicious authorities, they all knelt upon the shore and prayed. Ironically, in 1794, even as the Carmelites of Compiègne suffered, hundreds of Catholic priests starving in marooned prison ships would also gaze out in misery on those same waste sands of Oléron, just as Fontaine and his party did on that frightening day over a century earlier. The tables had turned by 1794, though, and the local priest of Royan, who bemoaned Catholic sins to Fontaine, spoke true prophesy: the persecuted Catholics took the place of the persecuted Huguenots on the very site where Fontaine's little party awaited rescue.

Finally, they saw the ship and embarked at dusk in a small boat through the waves. Darkness shrouded them from those guarding the approaches to the sea. Armed and ready, Fontaine resolved to defend those in his care to the death. Making their way laboriously and hopefully toward the captain's ship, they suddenly saw one of the king's frigates on patrol for Protestants. It turned toward them. If captured, Fontaine would be sent to the galleys, the women to convents. The frigate shifted toward the captain's ship instead, however, and the king's men searched the ship thoroughly. Not finding any Protestants, they ordered the English captain to make for sea immediately. Desperate, Fontaine thought of a plan: just as he had boldly ridden into danger on his Arabian horse, saluting the soldiers as they passed him, he told the boatman to sail straight for the king's frigate while the rest of them hid under a sail. This he did, terrified. Those aboard the frigate questioned the boatman and waved him onward. After putting enough distance between themselves and the frigate, Fontaine and his company signaled the English captain, who slowed so they could overtake his ship. They boarded with the French frigate still in sight.

"I bless God for the multitude of his mercies," Fontaine wrote. "He allowed me to bring to England the dear one whom I loved better than myself, and she willingly gave up relations, friends and wealth to be the sharer of my poverty in a strange land, where we could worship God according to the dictates of conscience." Fontaine married his fiancée and immediately tried to set up a business in England to support them both. "I here testify that we have fully experienced the truth of that promise of our Blessed Savior, to give an hundred fold more, even in this present life, to those who leave all and follow him."[102]

In all, tens of thousands of Protestants successfully fled France during these years, by sea and by mountain pass. They settled in England, America, Geneva, and the Dutch Republic, adding financial, intellectual, and military capital to France's enemies and bitterness to Protestant anti-Catholicism.

Rebelling against Authority

Enforcing the Revocation of the Edict of Nantes associated widespread abuse of authority with political and ecclesiastical leaders. Over the following decades, this instilled so much resentment in France and beyond that it created a powerful reactionary anticlerical movement. Perhaps Enlightenment-era doubt about Christianity resulted more from Christian failure to live up to their own ideals than from new philosophical or scientific ideas. Deeply embedded Christian moral principles generated moral outrage and critique when the gap between theory and practice gaped wider and wider. Christian culture spawns its own critique, one scholar observed: modern assaults on religion have, paradoxically, often proceeded from consciences deeply infused by Christian principles.[103] Abuse of authority in the late 1600s severely damaged the handing on of the faith. It created one of the important launching pads of the Conflictual Enlightenment.

Sadly, American Catholics today can empathize with how abuse of authority by churchmen can have these effects. Sex abuse scandals have revealed not only thousands of victims but also attempts by members of the hierarchy to cover up the problem behind a culture of secrecy.

---

[102] Fontaine, *Memoirs of a Huguenot Family*, ch. 4, 8, 9.
[103] Erdozain, *The Soul of Doubt*, 5, 7.

Studies have shown that victims can suffer lifelong trauma. That trauma not only affects their ability to have faith but also fosters a negative perception of the Church and of authority figures. Father Joseph Guido met with one of these victims, named "Danny." Danny wanted to speak once again with a Catholic priest, decades after his abuse. They met at a coffee shop—"neutral turf," as Danny called it, outside political or ecclesiastical influence. Danny, once a pious Catholic, had left the Church twenty years before when he was sexually abused by his parish priest. He took up running as a sport and a diversion; it helped him flee his memories. He became a morally determined man, like Voltaire after hearing about Calas: Tell people my story, Danny urged Father Guido. Tell them what that priest took away from me: "not just my innocence but my faith. I'm like a spiritual orphan, betrayed by what I loved, and I feel lost and alone." Danny lost not just his faith but also his sense of the sacred. What Innocent XI feared for the persecuted Huguenots became true for Danny as he ran as far away from the Church as he could.[104]

Something like this happened after the Revocation of the Edict of Nantes. The Conflictual Enlightenment began in the 1680s among Huguenot exiles as a religious reaction against Catholic sin. The enforcement of religious unity and the accompanying abuse of authority left no room for freedom of opinion in France. The energies of controversy seething beneath the surface eventually expressed themselves in terms of utopian idealism (Rousseau) and negative criticism (Voltaire). Both cursed the past.

"Thus it is no accident," historian Christopher Dawson wrote, "that the age which saw the end of French Protestantism was followed by the

---

[104] Joseph J. Guido, "A Clergy Sex Abuse Survivor's Story and Its Lessons for Restoring Faith," *America*, August 31, 2018, https://www.americamagazine.org/faith/2018/08/31/clergy-sex-abuse-survivors-story-and-its-lessons-restoring-faith; Diane Shea, "Effects of Sexual Abuse by Catholic Priests on Adults Victimized as Children," *Sexual Addiction & Compulsivity* 15 (2008): 251, 257, 261.

age of the philosophic enlightenment; indeed the latter may be regarded as a second Reformation that carried the revolt against authority and tradition from the sphere of theology to that of secular culture." He continued: "Every institution and every accepted belief was submitted to the test of criticism and was summarily dismissed if deemed unreasonable or devoid of social utility." The time had come, the Conflictual Enlighteners believed, to build a new civilization based on simple rational principles that would meet the needs of an enlightened age.[105]

John Locke and Pierre Bayle

Some of the Huguenots exiles who fled France in the name of conscience, like Fontaine, became the first ones to enunciate principles that would animate the Conflictual Enlightenment. They became leaders of an international movement of angry, critical, and anti-Catholic sentiment based in the Dutch Republic, England, and northern Germany, where they settled. They created an organized campaign of public propaganda against the Church. The most radical of them even relativized religion altogether, explaining the multiple religions of the world as simply different cultural systems without any reference to truth. Angry Huguenots smuggled radical tracts back into France, where they added fuel to the fires of resentment.

An example of how religious persecution led to Enlightenment reaction is found in two major figures: John Locke (the English Protestant philosopher already introduced) and Pierre Bayle (1647–1706), a French Huguenot writer in exile. Locke had to leave England for the Dutch Republic in 1683 to escape allegations that he supported a plot to eliminate the English king and his heir, who increasingly sympathized with Catholicism. Although probably not directly involved, Locke found himself in exile just as other Protestants from France arrived in the Dutch Republic. There he fell under their influence. Together they began to

---

[105] Dawson, *The Gods of Revolution*, 14, 20–21.

speculate about political and religious toleration as well as separation of church and state. Afraid that an absolutist form of Catholicism might take over England, Locke wrote his famous *Letter concerning Toleration* during the winter of 1685–1686 and published it a few years later. "I esteem it above all things necessary to distinguish exactly the business of civil government from that of religion," Locke wrote. At the same time, Pierre Bayle, a refugee from France, was writing his work on the same subject. It is possible that they influenced each other. Together, these two figures would exert an immense influence on the Enlightenment as a whole and the Conflictual Enlightenment in particular.

Bayle was a highly erudite Huguenot. He was born in southern France, and he died in 1706 in Rotterdam (the Dutch Republic), where tens of thousands of his coreligionists had sought refuge from French persecution. Many of them were literate and skilled workers, printers, booksellers, writers, and journalists, making the Dutch printing sector the "store of the universe," as Voltaire put it. This became the publishing and cultural transmission center of the early Enlightenment, fueled by skeptical anti-clericalism. These French refugees connected with the most important information hub of the age at the very moment when the French language was replacing Latin as the common language of Europe.

Bayle was born to a Calvinist minister, but after attending a Jesuit school in Toulouse, he converted to Catholicism. He was disaffected by the practice of his new faith that he witnessed around him. He soon returned to Calvinism, making him a target of persecution. Bayle fled France as Fontaine did. Angered at Bayle's escape, authorities went after his brother who was still in France. They put the brother in prison, where he died. Bayle eventually settled in the Dutch Republic, where he developed a highly skeptical writing program doggedly attacking superstition, intolerance, various philosophical and theological systems, and historical inaccuracies in other writers.

In 1686, one year after Louis XIV's court preacher, Bossuet, had used Luke 14:23 to justify the Revocation of the Edict of Nantes in front of the French royal family, Bayle wrote *A Philosophical Commentary on*

These Words of the Gospel, Luke 14.23, "Compel Them to Come In, That My House May Be Full." Bayle argued that the word "compel" in Luke 14:23 cannot mean "force," or else all believers who consider their beliefs orthodox would have a duty to persecute. That would create mutual slaughter, which God does not desire.

The lack of reason in those who used Scripture to justify the theory of righteous persecution compelled Bayle to make the opposite argument: reason should serve as the rule of all interpretation of Scripture. He did not intend by this to stretch reason so far as to eliminate mysteries such as the Trinity or the Incarnation, however. But without bringing their reading of Scripture to the "Throne of Reason," people tend to impose their own prejudices and national customs on divine revelation, distorting it, Bayle believed. Instead, the light of reason is the very light of God. This truth leads to the principle Bayle developed in his *Philosophical Commentary*: *"That all literal Construction, which carries an Obligation of committing Iniquity, is false."* Nothing is more contrary to the spirit of the gospel, Bayle wrote, than "Dungeons, Dragoons, Banishment, Pillage, Gallys, Inflictions, and Torture. Therefore this literal Sense [of the *compelle intrare*—'compel them to come in'] is false." Literal interpretation cannot lead one to actions against nature, the Ten Commandments, or gospel morality.

Bayle called for Christians to have an enlightened faith. "Our greatest need in the present historical moment is people who make God credible in this world by means of the enlightened faith they live." Those words came not from the pen of Bayle however, but from that of Joseph Ratzinger. "The negative testimony of Christians who spoke of God but lived in a manner contrary to him has obscured the image of God and has opened the doors to disbelief," Ratzinger continued. This is exactly what happened at the time of Bayle. In fact, Bayle observed that people around him were amazed that so many "Free-Thinkers and Deists" gained prominence at the time. He said, rather, "I'm amaz'd that we have not more of this sort among us, considering the havock which Religion has made in the World, and the Extinction, by an almost unavoidable

Consequence, of all Vertue." Bayle witnessed and aided the very birth of the Enlightenment in its conflictual mode.[106]

In the end, the Revocation of the Edict of Nantes failed to eliminate Protestantism from France. The religion survived in the homes and daily lives of those thousands who practiced passive resistance. When Louis XIV died in 1715, Protestant leaders were already reorganizing across the country. Legislating Catholicism did not create true religious unity. Catholic adulation of the state and its political solution to problems failed. Instead, their efforts created confessional coercion and legalistic moralism that deeply wounded the Kingdom of God.

Catholics believe that the Church's Magisterium has been tasked with guarding the deposit of faith since the time of the Apostles. Bayle's Protestant background did not include this conception. So he appealed to reason alone as the arbiter of conflicting scriptural interpretations. Ironically, many Catholics of the time did not appreciate the Magisterium either, especially in France, where many of them thought of the French Catholic Church as largely independent of Rome. Isolated from the wider Church by their own Gallican ecclesiology, they accepted the politically correct theory of righteous persecution based on literal interpretation of Scripture. There was little that could check them once they started moving toward that superstition. It led to abuse of authority. Seeing this, and the divisive problems of *sola Scriptura* (only Scripture) stemming from the Age of Reformations, Protestant thinkers such as Bayle increasingly turned to *sola ratio* (only reason) as an alternative final authority. This solution of turning to reason to solve the social and existential problems associated with Christian division would profoundly influence the Enlightenment and the entire trajectory of modern history. It marginalized faith from real human questions of ultimate meaning. Though reason has

---

[106] Pierre Bayle, *A Philosophical Commentary on These Words of the Gospel, Luke 14.23, "Compel Them to Come In, That My House May Be Full"* (1686; Indianapolis: Liberty Fund, 2005), 64–67, 84; Ratzinger, *Christianity and the Crisis of Cultures*, 52.

provided many worthy answers to scientific and social problems since the time of Bayle, *sola ratio* created new problems. It denuded the world of meaning, broke down bonds between people, and created clashing ideologies throughout the twentieth century, spilling much blood. *Sola ratio* also created persecutory regimes.

Bayle published his *Historical and Critical Dictionary* in 1697. It became one of the most widely read books of the eighteenth century. Its critical spirit deeply affected Voltaire, who thought of Bayle as a great master of reasoning. Bayle's hypercritical stance, however, did not lead him to deism, as Voltaire's did. Bayle retained his Calvinist faith, for which he had suffered. He struggled, however, to relate it to reason and so tended toward fideism. Many of his contemporaries and later followers assumed he meant to attack religion as a whole. They saw him as preparing the way for the Age of Reason. Bayle's work exerted an immense influence on Thomas Jefferson and Benjamin Franklin in the American colonies; Montesquieu, Rousseau, and Voltaire in France; Hume in Scotland; and important German thinkers too. Bayle died with his pen in hand, harbinger of the critical spirit emerging in the European-wide Republic of Letters that Voltaire would deeply influence as its leading citizen. Many intellectual elites have remained deeply critical of religion and tradition ever since.

5

Brothers in Sin

Voltaire, Whistleblower

When Donat Calas finished telling the story of his family to Voltaire at Ferney in 1762, the Enlightener quizzed him. He asked the young man if his parents were of a violent character. No, Donat answered: never were parents more tender and indulgent. "I confess," Voltaire wrote after the interview, "that no more was needed to give me a strong presumption in favor of the innocence of the family." Such a case of injustice in our days! he exclaimed, "at a time when philosophy has made so much progress! and when a hundred academies are writing for the improvement of our way of life!" Far from believing the Calas family to be fanatics, he wrote, "I thought I saw that it was the fanatics who had accused and ruined them." Voltaire would blow the whistle.[107]

From that moment on, Voltaire became obsessed with the Calas case. Seeing it as a miscarriage of justice, he resolved to get the verdict overturned and indict the culture of secrecy surrounding the French justice system. He also came to see the case as an example of religious fanaticism at work. Toulouse and the Calas affair represented to him the typical results of traditional Christian superstition. He articulated his "Voltaire

---

[107] Voltaire to M. Damilaville, March 1, 1765, Voltaire Society of America, https://www.whitman.edu/VSA/letters/3.1.1765.html; Voltaire, *Treatise on Tolerance* (1763), 3, Early Modern Texts, https://www.earlymoderntexts.com/assets/pdfs/voltaire1763.pdf.

thesis": belief in objective religious dogma leads necessarily to persecution. This is what the Calas case seemed to prove.

Voltaire's campaign on behalf of Calas would serve as a touchstone of a major Enlightenment agenda to bring about legal and intellectual change in France and beyond. The Enlightener would be hailed as a hero of the common man and of individual rights long after his death, not least during the French Revolution. But the circumstances of his death, in contrast with the deaths of the Carmelites of Compiègne, would reveal fundamental weaknesses of his critical stance toward human institutions. He would die as he had lived: an autonomous individual.

The purpose of this chapter is to show how the Christian conflictual attitude toward the Enlightenment, revealed so heroically by the Carmelites, was not always a simple struggle of good versus evil. Conflict between Catholics and Enlighteners sometimes benefited the Church. It could serve as an engine of doctrinal development and Church reform because it revealed areas of the faith not well articulated and not well lived. Conflict between Voltaire and the Catholics forced the latter to confront their own failures — not least those of the Catholic dragons. The Carmelites suffered for more than they knew: not only for the sins of their revolutionary killers but for those of their fellow, persecuting Catholics.

Voltaire's strategy at first involved writing more than one hundred letters about the Calas case, seeking more information to confirm his instinctive presumption of innocence. The Toulouse authorities guarded the information about the procedures of the case, and others discouraged Voltaire. Why are you stirring up controversy? they wondered. Let the dead bury the dead. But the Enlightener would not give up. He admired Jesus' story of the Good Samaritan. It showed a "heretic" Samaritan making up for the failures of the orthodox priests. Voltaire responded to his critics: "I found an Israelite in the desert — an Israelite covered in blood; suffer me to pour a little wine and oil into his wounds. You are the Levite, leave me to play the Samaritan."[108]

---

[108] Erdozain, *The Soul of Doubt*, 164.

Voltaire realized that publicity would be the most powerful weapon to force the French authorities to act. His three-pronged strategy involved securing the facts of the trial as best he might, contacting influential people, and mobilizing public outcry. He sought a public audience because he predicted that his efforts to help the Calas family through official bureaucratic channels would take too long: they would suffer much in the meantime and give up even trying to seek redress.

So he started a publicity campaign to put pressure on the authorities. Like Siobhan O'Connor in 2018, the Catholic whistleblower who responded to the toxic silence and chronic inaction of her bishop on behalf of victims of sexual abuse, Voltaire would turn to the "media" of his day to pressure authorities. O'Connor, former executive director of the Diocese of Buffalo, New York, had noticed that when a certain investigative journalist would contact her bishop, the churchman would on occasion act. Taking this as a cue, she leaked documents in the hope of effecting further and immediate change. It worked, and her story went national through *60 Minutes*. Something like this happened when Voltaire "leaked documents" he himself had written to compel public opinion across Europe to see the case from the Calas point of view. Just as in the O'Connor example, "fear of negative publicity played a role in motivating those in positions of power and authority to respond to the Calas campaign," one historian remarked. Voltaire's campaign for justice marked an important moment not just during the Enlightenment but for our own time as well: Voltaire broke new ground in the use of public opinion as a source of authority independent of the political and ecclesiastical authorities of the day.[109]

---

[109] Siobhan M. O'Connor, "Confessions of a Catholic Whistleblower," *First Things* (November 22, 2018): 156–157, https://www.firstthings.com/web-exclusives/2018/11/confessions-of-a-catholic-whistleblower; James Hanrahan, "Creating the 'Cri Public': Voltaire and Public Opinion in the Early 1760s," in *Voltaire and the 1760s: Essays for John Renwick*, ed. Nicholas Cronk (Oxford: Voltaire Foundation, 2008). O'Connor credited her love of history and exposure to historical examples of injustice with giving her the courage to act.

Rethinking the Enlightenment

The Voltaire Thesis

From the safety of his estate at Ferney, near the French border, Voltaire broadened his attack. He wrote his famous *Treatise on Tolerance* (1763) as part of his publicity campaign on behalf of Jean Calas and to combat religious fanaticism. It quickly became an enormous popular success and a landmark of the age of Enlightenment. "The murder of Calas ... is one of the most singular events that deserve the attention of our own and of later ages," he penned in the first paragraph. The Revocation of the Edict of Nantes had led to a disastrous loss of money and talent as thousands of Huguenots fled France, Voltaire noted, using an economic argument for toleration. The Revocation also boosted Catholic fanaticism through the practice of intolerance. Ever since the Age of Reformations, Voltaire believed, Christians had flooded the streets with blood over various dogmas. Fewer dogmas equals fewer disputes and violence, he claimed. In this way, he developed a line of argumentation that would eventually grip the modern mind: belief in religious truth is incompatible with tolerance in a modern, pluralistic society. As he wrote elsewhere, criticizing the French maxim "one faith, one king, one law," "An Englishman, being a free man, goes to Heaven by whatever path he chooses.... Were there only one religion in England, despotism would be a threat; were there two, they would be at each other's throats; but there are thirty, and they live happily and at peace with one another."[110] Belief in one true religion is dangerous.

This thesis represented skilled rhetoric but weak history. By it, Voltaire supported the historical narrative constructed by the Conflictual Enlightenment that tolerance arose in the modern world only after the light of reason banished the darkness of faith. Many have simply assumed this view of modern history ever since. It is true that elite intellectuals deserve some of the credit for greater awareness of the importance of toleration in the eighteenth century. Social and cultural historians have shown, however, how common people practiced toleration long before

[110] Voltaire, *Philosophical Letters* (1733; Indianapolis: Hackett, 2007), 15, 20.

Voltaire enunciated the idea of it. Since the early days of the Reformations, ordinary people who believed in religious truth also had to face religious difference in their daily lives. Tolerance for them was not so much a concept as a form of behavior: peaceful coexistence with others of a different faith at the local level, in villages, cities, and regions across early-modern Europe. Sometimes violence broke out, but not usually.[111]

An example of this practical toleration is found—ironically—in Toulouse, of all places, where peaceful relations between religions was actually normal. Though it was true that authorities there occasionally took vigorous action against Huguenots before the Jean Calas case, one could freely discuss Protestantism and practice it in private. The Calas family gathered every evening for prayers and every Sunday to hear Marc-Antoine read chapters of the New Testament, psalms, and the sermon for the week. Catholic townspeople traded with the Huguenots on a wide scale. Those Protestants with special "certificates" of Catholicism could rise to positions of influence and wealth in the city.

Catholics also befriended Protestants. Marc-Antoine had numerous Catholic friends with whom he would talk intimately about normal personal and family problems. He did this on the day he died, in fact, mentioning how happy he was to be receiving a blue suit his father had promised him. Marc freely spoke about religion with his Catholic friends, maintaining his Calvinism among them without hesitation. He enjoyed visiting the Catholic churches in Toulouse to enjoy the culture there through art, music, and sermons. Though Marc was not seen attending Mass, he did kneel in the streets when the Holy Eucharist passed by in procession, as required by law. His Catholic friends told him he did not need to do this. It was not expected of a Protestant. Out of respect for the other, neither Marc nor his Catholic friends wanted to impose their practices.

---

[111] Benjamin J. Kaplan, *Divided by Faith: Religious Conflict and the Practice of Toleration in Early Modern Europe* (Cambridge: Harvard University Press, 2007), 2, 4, 8.

Therefore, historian David Bien argued, Voltaire's idea that Christians normally practice violent persecution is unfounded. "The anti-Protestant excitement, the intolerance, which found expression in the official and popular condemnation of Calas, was *not* typical of Catholic attitudes and behavior. It was, on the contrary, unique," caused by latent prejudices that rose to the surface due to particular circumstances of the time, such as the hardships of the Seven Years' War then raging between Catholic France and Protestant England. This war was understood by many in religious terms (Catholic versus Protestant), which cast suspicion on French Protestant loyalty. Furthermore, out of exaggerated concern for good order, the French judicial system generally operated on the assumption of guilt rather than on the assumption of innocence. With the murder of young Calas, these factors activated deep cultural prejudices against the Huguenots that then affected the trial.[112]

In this way, communities such as Toulouse practiced a kind of toleration *even without modern, "enlightened" values*, a fact that somewhat challenged the Voltairean narrative of historical progress from darkness to light. In fact, the idea of religious freedom has a deep Christian history. It was born not of indifference or skepticism or secular open-mindedness, but of Christian faith. Nevertheless, the example of Toulouse shows how peaceful coexistence is a precarious achievement. It requires an elaborate set of accommodations and practical compromises that sometimes fail, in the twenty-first century too. Can people who hold irreconcilable religious beliefs live together peacefully? That is one of the most important questions of modern history. Voltaire's admirers ever since have tended to say no, not without privatizing and relativizing religion. Yet ordinary people, long before Voltaire, did just that: live together (usually) in peace. They believed that conflict is a normal part of social life and that peaceful coexistence is achieved not by eliminating conflict but by regulating and containing it. In fact, their ordinary practice of limited tolerance created

---

[112] Bien, *The Calas Affair*, 32–33, 35–36, 38, 42.

an environment that would eventually absorb the idea of toleration. In other words, people lived tolerance before they theorized it.[113]

Toleration in Toulouse: The Rest of the Story

Nevertheless, Voltaire's efforts made a difference. As already described, the unique circumstances of war and economic downturn combined with Catholic prejudices about Huguenots as inherently dangerous to create an outburst of anti-Protestant sentiment in Toulouse in 1761 and 1762. Jean Calas died as a result. Within ten years, the situation had changed entirely, however. The city moved from toleration by indifference to toleration in principle. Enlightenment ideas and altered religious values made anti-Protestant views unfashionable. Voltaire's influence increased in Toulouse, as seen in a letter to him from Joseph Audra, a churchman and controversial history professor: "You could not believe how much the zeal of honest people, and their love and respect of you, is increasing in this city." Young judges and lawyers are "full of zeal and *lumières* [light], and learned men are not lacking among the highly placed.... You could not believe how much everything has changed since the unhappy adventure of the innocent Calas."[114]

A dramatic group put on Voltaire's plays. Historians ridiculed the superstition and persecution of the past in ways that encouraged acceptance of new ideals. One of the magistrates most responsible for the Calas case, David de Beaudrigue, was stripped of his position. The annual May 17 procession celebrating the massacre of the Huguenots declined and died out. Audra wrote to Voltaire that even the archbishop of Toulouse disseminated Enlightenment ideas, "and I hope that it will cause a great explosion in several years." Audra may have hoped for more than he bargained for.

---

[113] Kaplan, *Divided by Faith*, 9–10, 12, 358; Robert Louis Wilken, *Liberty in the Things of God: The Christian Origins of Religious Freedom* (New Haven: Yale University Press, 2019), 6.

[114] Bien, *The Calas Affair*, 148–149, 153–154.

Interestingly, Enlightenment ideas in Toulouse did not automatically conflict with Catholicism. Writers and poets adapted the ideas of the Enlightenment to their Christian culture, forming a tentative civil religion of common values. Madame du Bourg, for example, was married to a leader in the court, and her dinners and salon marked the heights of Toulousian society. When not tending to her twenty children, she read the latest writers, including Voltaire. Yet she remained a Catholic who loved Christ, as evidenced in her letters to her son studying theology in Paris. Religion must never serve as a pretext for persecuting those who do not think as Catholics do, she wrote to him. "Jesus Christ has given us examples for everything in his Bible: the one who looks for a strayed lamb does not bring it back by the whip; he carries it on his back, caresses it, and tries to attach it to himself by his benevolence." Madame du Bourg interpreted her religion in terms of the new ethos of tolerance.

Catholic leaders in Toulouse developed a sophisticated distinction between theological and civil toleration. Archbishop Loménie de Brienne took the lead in this. Theological toleration was an impossibility because Catholicism was the one, true religion, which the Church must uphold no matter what. Civil tolerance, however, meant that the king needed to permit his subjects to believe what they choose in religion. One can believe in theological truth, in other words, without feeling the need to impose it on others through governmental power. Brienne thereby opposed both the Voltaire thesis and the Catholic argument at the time of the Revocation of the Edict of Nantes in support of righteous persecution: that theological truth should be enforced across society for the sake of political unity. Brienne argued, rather, that the king is merely an individual Christian like any other, and so, by attempting to compel consciences, he usurped the Church. The monarch should advise and exhort his subjects to Catholic belief; he should never force them. This implied a social realism that accepted the fact of diverse religious belief within human communities.

In this way, Toulousians adapted to modern values of the day without feeling as if they rejected their Catholic faith. Movement toward the reality of civic culture and away from the ideal of sacral culture happened quickly after the Calas affair because it came within the framework of traditional Catholicism. "For the Catholic, and most continued to be Catholics, it was not the victory of the Enlightenment at the expense of Christianity, but a development consistent with Christian principles properly understood," one historian remarked.[115] Unfortunately, the French Revolution would soon end this development by imposing its own dogmas by force. That would polarize memories of "Catholic" and "Enlightenment" for generations.

Rehabilitating Calas

Voltaire's efforts to contact influential people and mobilize public outcry over the Calas affair finally caught the attention of Parisian elites. Madame de Pompadour (the king's mistress and an ally of the Enlighteners) wrote in a letter how the Calas case made her tremble. "The people of Toulouse are excitable and have far more of their kind of religion than they need for being good Christians. May it please God to convert them, and make them more human."[116] The whole of France cried out for revenge for the unjust death of Calas.

Others besides Voltaire also helped bring the case to the attention of the political elites. Nanette, one of the Calas girls, met a kind nun in her convent confinement. After questioning and observing her, the nun also came to believe in the innocence of the family. She wrote to a government official about the whole matter, and that letter ended up in the hands of Voltaire. After reading it, he wrote, "The virtuous simplicity and candor of this nun of the Order of the Visitation seems a terrible condemnation of the bloodthirsty fanaticism of the murderous magistrates of Toulouse." However, when Nanette wanted to express thanks to Voltaire for helping her family, the nun said, revealing the fault line of the culture wars

---

[115] Ibid., 157, 165, 167, 170–173.
[116] Davidson, *Voltaire: A Life*, 325.

of the time: "Can there be anything great in a man who sets himself up against the author of his being?" Perhaps she underestimated Voltaire.[117]

Nevertheless, it seems that this nun's intervention, combined with Voltaire's influence, secured the review of the case in Paris—a major legal success. When Jean Calas's widow arrived in the city for the review, Voltaire made sure she was warmly welcomed, and her expenses paid. Others soon helped financially too. The judicial court in Toulouse resisted Parisian interference at every step.

Paris authorities annulled the verdict against Jean. When news reached Voltaire at Ferney, Pierre Calas happened to be present. The old man and the young man embraced and wept. In March 1765, the legal review process resulted in the exoneration and rehabilitation of Jean Calas. The king granted financial remuneration to the widow Calas and to each family member. A commemorative print of the family was created and sold for their benefit. Voltaire hung a copy by his bed.

Eventually, partly due to Voltaire's efforts in the Calas case, laws on religious toleration would change in Europe and the American colonies, including ones that benefitted Catholics. In Ireland, for example, the first crack in the Penal Laws against Catholics there came in 1778. Voltaire's name was invoked during the debates. His influence inspired legal reform in the United States to exclude the kind of hearsay evidence that had condemned Jean Calas, to distinguish better between public law and religious doctrine, and to prohibit cruel and unusual punishment. The French legal system revived the long-obscured principle "innocent until proven guilty" that authorities in Toulouse had so neglected.

Because attitudes in Toulouse began to change after the Calas affair, laws changed there during the 1770s. The key issue was whether a marriage conducted by a Protestant pastor constituted a legal marriage. The Toulousian court answered yes, it does, and by doing so broke down the requirement that made Catholic religious belief and practice the test of citizenship. Protestants gained civil standing in their country without

---

[117] Orieux, *Voltaire*, 360; Palmer, *Catholics and Unbelievers*, 16.

regard to religion, effectively undermining the Revocation of the Edict of Nantes and the sacral culture ideal.

In France at large, the collaboration of Enlighteners and Christian leaders coalesced in the Edict of Versailles (1787). This edict officially revoked the Revocation of 1685. It granted non-Catholics in France the ability to practice their religion openly as well as civil status, which included the right to contract marriages without having to convert to Catholicism. To some Catholics, this decline of sacral culture looked like secularization. To others, it seemed a better expression of Christian principles through the new civic culture ideal. Sometimes secularization exists only in the eye of the beholder. However that may be, this law came about partly through the joint efforts of the Catholic economist Jacques Turgot and the Protestant leader Rabaut de Saint-Étienne. Turgot had once written that the maxim "one land, one faith" had brought disaster; religion must not be compelled. "Whoever will make religion a persecutor abuses it, because the characteristics of Christ's religion are gentleness and charity."[118] The ecumenical alliance of Turgot and Saint-Étienne prevailed.

Conflict and the Development of Doctrine

We have seen how the conflict between the Enlightenment and Christianity was rooted significantly in conflict between Christians. Catholics in France even used up valuable time, energy, and good will struggling to vanquish other Catholics. This happened in the Jansenist controversy, for example, about the extent of human depravity and free will, and again in the French suppression of the Jesuits in 1764. These internal struggles seriously damaged Catholic unity and cultural authority in France, allowing the Conflictual Enlightenment to gain the upper hand.

---

[118] Gaston Bonet-Maury, "The Edict of Tolerance of Louis XVI (1787) and Its American Promoters," *American Journal of Theology* 3 no. 3 (July 1899): 559.

This was not all negative, however. The Conflictual Enlightenment contributed to helpful self-criticism among Christians, forcing them to rethink their approaches to faith. Attacks such as Voltaire made in his *Treatise on Tolerance* even appealed to forgotten Christian principles. Catholics should tolerate Protestants at least minimally by protecting their basic rights because they are brothers, children of the same Father, Voltaire wrote. Jesus himself exemplified gentleness, patience, and indulgence. Voltaire mentioned specific parables and actions of Jesus: the prodigal son, the workers in the vineyard who received equal pay, the Good Samaritan, forgiveness of sinners. Expressing ideas similar to those of Pierre Bayle, the Huguenot refugee thinker who lost his brother to the Catholic dragons in the last chapter, Voltaire asked his readers: Does the divine origin of Catholicism imply that it should be ruled by fury, exile, confiscation of goods, imprisonment, and torture? "Would you sustain by executioners the religion of a God who died at the hands of executioners, and who preached only gentleness and patience?"[119]

Curiously, Voltaire's appeals to the example of Christ would echo in the Second Vatican Council's Declaration on Religious Freedom (1965). The document noted that Jesus refused to come as a political Messiah. He sought to rouse faith in his hearers, not coerce them into it. It is one of the major tenets of Catholic doctrine, as seen in the Church Fathers, that the human response of faith to God must be free, the document declared, recovering an ancient tradition on such matters. A civil community may offer special recognition to one religion, as in the "Christian state" ideal, but it still must respect the right of all citizens, equal before the law, to religious liberty. Provided that just public order is observed, people should have the freedom to internal and external religious acts in self-governing communities. No one should be compelled into the Church.[120]

---

[119] Voltaire, *Treatise on Tolerance* (1763), 6, 25, 35, 43–44.

[120] "Declaration on Religious Freedom," in *The Teachings of the Second Vatican Council* (Westminster, MD: Newman Press, 1966), 369–370, 373, 375, 377.

The document would leave in place, however, the view of the Church as an independent institution capable of enforcing her teachings against her own members, the baptized, who have an obligation of fidelity. The Church has the responsibility to guard the spiritual common good, such as by excommunication or by banning books or certain practices that threaten to lead souls astray with heresy, apostasy, and schism. She may request the state's aid in meeting this responsibility. The declaration changed none of this, for the use of the rod can be a service of love. "Today we can see that it has nothing to do with love when conduct unworthy of the priestly life is tolerated," Pope Benedict XVI remarked. "Nor does it have to do with love if heresy is allowed to spread and the faith twisted and chipped away, as if it were something that we ourselves had invented. As if it were no longer God's gift, the precious pearl which we cannot let be taken from us."[121] Religious freedom is not an excuse to pass by on the other side of the road.

Nevertheless, the greater emphasis on religious freedom by the Catholic Church in the twentieth century came as the result of painful experience in modern history. That experience included totalitarian regimes but also the Enlightenment and conflict with the whistleblowing Voltaire. The efforts of Voltaire on behalf of the Calas family to raise public awareness of prejudice constituted an important turning point not only in the history of modern legal justice but also in the recovery of the idea of religious freedom. As John Henry Newman would perceive in his *Development of Christian Doctrine* (1845), an idea such as religious freedom develops its mature form from the original deposit of faith that comes into

---

[121] Joseph T. Stuart, "*Dignitatis Humanae* and the New Evangelization," *Newman Rambler* 10, no. 1 (Fall 2013): 11; Thomas Pink, "Conscience and Coercion: Vaticans II's Teaching on Religious Freedom Changed Policy, Not Doctrine," *First Things* (August 2012), https://www.firstthings.com/article/2012/08/conscience-and-coercion; Pope Benedict XVI, "Papal Homily at the End of the Year for Priests" (June 11, 2010), http://www.vatican.va/content/benedict-xvi/en/homilies/2010/documents/hf_ben-xvi_hom_20100611_concl-anno-sac.html.

conflict with the messiness of social life around it. Even opposing forces like Voltaire could forward its growth. As Pope John Paul II wrote in *Fides et Ratio*, even those philosophers whose work drove faith and reason further apart can speak precious insights which aid in discovering truth. Out of the conflict of Christianity with the Enlightenment during the eighteenth century emerged a greater appreciation for religious freedom.[122]

Two Ways to Die in Paris

Voltaire planned to die at Ferney, building a pyramidal tomb—significantly—half inside his chapel and half outside it. But he would not pass away there. At eighty-four years of age, he finished two new plays and traveled to Paris to see them performed during the spring of 1778.

Paris provided the scene of his death, as it would that of the Carmelites sixteen years later. The most dramatic stories of the conflict of cultures happened in that city—one, the culture of the Conflictual Enlightenment, the other of Catholicism. The deaths of Voltaire and the Carmelites captured in vignettes the conflict of two radically divergent visions of human happiness: one of temporal happiness on Earth, the other of happiness in communion with God in the next life.

Voltaire perhaps held the achievement of fame as the key to happiness. It would secure his place in the memory of posterity, and in that way he would live "forever." Fame would allow him to escape the annihilation caused by death. He was fortunate, then, that despite his growing weakness, his spring 1778 trip to Paris sealed his position as icon of the Enlightenment. When he arrived to watch his play, a tumult of applause welcomed him and delayed the commencement by twenty minutes. He was crowned with a laurel wreath. Uproarious cheering followed the end of the play. The curtains opened to reveal a bust of Voltaire, and the actors placed wreaths upon it. Exhausted, pale, teary-eyed, Voltaire

---

[122] John Henry Newman, *An Essay on the Development of Christian Doctrine* (London: Longmans, Green, 1906), 38; John Paul II, *Fides et Ratio*, 64.

waved and took his leave. An enormous crowd met him, hailing Voltaire as the defender of the poor and the defender of Calas. People climbed onto his carriage, hoping to shake his hand. He was a hero, "and he was here fulfilling the role usually played by the monarch," one biographer wrote. "Yet the King and Queen were conspicuous by their absence." The Enlightenment was making wonderful progress.[123]

At the height of his fame, as his health rapidly declined, did an inner conflict break out in Voltaire's soul? The elites of the Conflictual Enlightenment tended to posit happiness in this life as the ultimate end. As one historian noted, they substituted the love of humanity for the love of God, the perfectibility of man through his own efforts for the redemption of Christ, and the hope of living in the memory of future generations for the hope of immortality in another world. This hope of living forever in the memory of posterity after one's death justified the sacrifices and hard work necessary to live a good human life. Yet Voltaire clearly believed in God, even picturing God as a loving Father in some of his plays. Had he not written in *Alzire*, "The true God ... the God of Christians is a God of mercy"?[124]

◌

By May 1778, Voltaire was dying. He had hoped to make it back to Ferney from Paris, but it was no longer possible to do so. The Enlightener received a dignified and modest letter from a priest, the Abbé Gaultier, who was a Jesuit before the suppression.[125] It seemed there was always a Jesuit about Voltaire, a biographer remarked, from his earliest school

---

[123] Roger Pearson, *Voltaire Almighty: A Life in Pursuit of Freedom* (New York: Bloomsbury, 2005), 379–380.

[124] Carl L. Becker, *The Heavenly City of the Eighteenth-Century Philosophers* (New Haven: Yale University Press, 1932), 129–130; Voltaire, "Alzire," in *The Works of Voltaire*, vol. 9 (New York: E. R. Dumont, 1901), 9.

[125] The Jesuits were suppressed in France in 1764 and throughout Catholic countries by Pope Clement XIV in 1773.

days to playing chess at Ferney. "When Voltaire heard the word 'Jesuit' it stirred some fiber in him: the child who had not known his mother or loved his father or brother had loved his teachers and been loved by them. He had rebelled against them, but he had remained their most sensitive and adroit as well as their proudest pupil." Gaultier made it clear in his letter that he wanted to help Voltaire save his soul.[126]

☞

"Permission to die, Mother?" Sister Constance asked Mother Teresa of St. Augustine, kneeling before her at the foot of the guillotine. It was July 17, 1794, sixteen years after Voltaire's death. Leaders of the Revolution passionately believed their movement represented a century of Enlightenment and progress, the true hope of humanity. That was why their dogmas of reason turned persecutory. They had to eliminate anyone who stood in the way of human emancipation. So the dragons of the Conflictual Enlightenment pounced on the Carmelites of Compiègne.

Sister Constance's request for permission to die linked her, through obedience, to her community. It joined her, through them, to the witness of faith reaching all the way back to the Apostles. She had given up her autonomy for the sake of communion with others through her vows of poverty, chastity, and obedience. In doing so, she found her true self, as evidenced by her peace at the end. She sought *permission* to die because, contrary to the individualistic Conflictual Enlightenment, she lived not by her own judgment but by the nonautonomous and participative knowledge of faith. She sought to be faithful to love and therein find her happiness in communion with others and, ultimately, with God.

"Permission to die, Mother?"

"Go, my daughter!" Mother Teresa of St. Augustine answered. Witnesses recorded that as Sister Constance turned to face the guillotine

---

[126] Orieux, *Voltaire*, 469.

Kneeling Carmelite Nun, *attributed to*
Jean-Baptiste de Champaigne.

and start up the steps, she intoned the first line of Psalm 117: "Praise the
Lord, all ye nations! Praise Him all ye people!" She climbed the steps
toward her Lover, singing.

☞

Would Voltaire admit the priest Gaultier to his chamber? Would he confess?
Voltaire had often posed as a Catholic during his lifetime. Once he had
taken Easter Communion at Ferney from a visiting monk who first gave him
absolution. The local bishop heard about it and wrote Voltaire a dignified
and temperate letter: "Your communion was made without repentance,

without the amends made necessary by your past writings and conduct, and you should not approach the holy table without giving pledges of your sincerity, and without due reflection no priest will authorize you to do so." Voltaire assured the churchman of his good faith and asked for prayers. The bishop wrote back that faith consists in acts, not words. He forbade his priests from hearing Voltaire's confession or giving him the Eucharist.

Angry, the Enlightener tried to spite the bishop. Just before the following Easter, he lured a visiting friar up to his bedroom, where he lay putting on his best deathbed act, one biographer recounted: eyes glazed, hollow voice, skinny hands playing with the lace coverlet. He requested the friar to hear his confession and placed money in his hand. The petrified monk hurried off without yielding to his request. Voltaire persisted in his act, trying to convince everyone he was dying so a priest would come. He promised to make any declaration the Church required. Still the bishop refused to give permission for a priest to hear his confession. Voltaire then threated a lawsuit, because it was illegal at that time in France to deny the sacraments to someone dying. Finally, the bishop sent two priests. Voltaire recited the Apostles' Creed *and* made a verbal profession of deist faith: "I adore God in my own room. I do evil to no one." The priest had another profession of faith in his pocket and insisted Voltaire needed to sign it. The Enlightener retorted that the Apostles' Creed was enough and said — slyly — that this other profession of faith might introduce unorthodox innovations. When the priest kept insisting, Voltaire dropped his pretended illness and demanded absolution, which the priest gave. Voltaire lay back on the pillow, smiling. He felt he had triumphed over the bishop. After the priest left, Voltaire leaped out of bed. "I've had a little trouble with that dreary monk," he said to his secretary, "but it's all been most amusing and done me good. Let's take a walk around the garden."

One biographer remarked that all of Europe talked about Voltaire's blasphemous pranks, his playacting at religion. But was it simply a prank? One can be sure of nothing with Voltaire, for his ideas were subtle and fluctuating. One can only be sure, one biographer remarked, that he possessed a sincere passion for justice, truth — and drama. Was Voltaire simply acting a part? Could he have made an authentic confession even if he had wanted to? Was he so caught up in drama and pretending to be other than he was, that he could no longer access his real self? What if he really *did* want to confess?[127]

☞

"For His mercy is confirmed upon us, and the truth of the Lord endureth forever! Praise the Lord!" sang Sister Constance as she neared the vertical balance plank of the death-dealing machine. The others joined her in their final song (Psalm 117), sung by their great foundress, St. Teresa of Avila, at the foundation of a new Carmel.

Sister Constance waved aside the executioner and the valet who normally helped prisoners into position. Her radiance, dignity, and sense of purpose impressed those watching. Her feet left the scaffold as the plank tipped forward into horizontal position. The valet adjusted it so that her neck appeared directly in the yoke beneath the triangular blade. "For His mercy is confirmed upon us."

☞

Voltaire responded to Gaultier's letter with a brief one of his own: "Your letter, sir, seems to me to be that of an honest man: that is sufficient to determine me to receive the honor of a visit from you on the day and at the hour most convenient to you. I shall say to you exactly what I said when I gave my blessing to the grandson of the wise and famous Franklin," Voltaire wrote, "the most honored of American citizens:[128]

---

127 Ibid., 356, 419, 422.

128 Benjamin Franklin was then in Paris securing a treaty of commerce and friendship (signed February 6, 1778). He appeared as the humble philosopher from the New World, wearing a fur cap, and thus representing both Rousseau's ideal of the man close to nature and Voltaire's ideal of scientific reason. Franklin used his immense popularity among the French of all classes to achieve the Thirteen United States of America's first great diplomatic victory, an alliance against the British.

I spoke only these words, '*God and liberty.*'" Voltaire continued: "I am eighty-four years of age: I am about to appear before God, the Creator of all the universe. If you have anything to say to me, it will be my duty and privilege to receive you, despite the sufferings which overwhelm me." Gaultier came. He was frank with Voltaire, and that pleased the dying man. The priest told him he would give a report of their meeting to his superior. Voltaire's attendants—his mistress and secretary, as well as a friend—interrupted their meeting. "Pray leave me with my friend the abbé—he does not flatter me," Voltaire said. The presence of the priest made the others uneasy. The Enlightener's reputation rested on his *not* recanting anything. However, his desire for a decent burial rested on reconciling himself at least to some degree with the Church.

Gaultier presented Voltaire with a prepared text, presumably a declaration of Christian faith and some kind of recantation of his anti-Christian writings. But the Enlightener brushed them aside and wrote in a shaky hand his own declaration: "I have said my confession to [Gaultier]; and that if God disposes of me, I shall die in the holy Catholic religion into which I was born, hoping that God in His divine mercy will deign to forgive me all my errors; and that if I have offended the Church I beg forgiveness of God and of it." Two witnesses signed it. Gaultier gave Voltaire absolution. Voltaire declined taking Communion, however, because of his health. Gaultier left.[129]

The executioner pulled the cord, and the blade fell. The head of Sister Constance tumbled into a blood-stiffened leather bag. The rest of the nuns continued to sing.

Voltaire wrote to his secretary, who had returned to Ferney, that he was dying. "I am really punished for your departure, for having left Ferney,

---

[129] Orieux, *Voltaire,* 469; Pearson, *Voltaire Almighty,* 376.

and for having taken a house in Paris. I embrace you tenderly, my dear friend, and with sadness."[130]

☞

Each nun knelt before Mother Teresa of St. Augustine. "Permission to die, Mother?" "Go, my daughter!" the prioress commanded. Each climbed to the guillotine as the others continued to sing. The silent crowd listened and heard the bump of the balance plank swing down into horizontal position, the click of the neckyoke closing, the swish of the blade falling, and then one less voice singing. One by one, the voices fell silent.

The execution of a whole community like this was unprecedented. "The women's implacable acceptance of everything happening to them, their simple joy as they sang, awaiting certain death, pointed toward a dimension beyond [ordinary experience]," one historian wrote. Love is communion with the divine Lover and with others, the actions of the nuns implied. They did not fear death because Heaven already resided in their souls. The communal witness of the nuns seemed a manifestation of God at work. "For through the inexplicable, self-imposed, and unprecedented silence that accompanied their long procession and continued throughout their ceremonial sacrifice, it was [God], through them, who was revealing something of his presence and power in the world at that hour," Bush wrote. Schoolboys from a nearby boarding school watched from the walls, fascinated. One of them inquired about the identity of these women. "They are daughters of St. Teresa" he was told. The young boy, the Count de Malet, took to heart a mysterious sympathy for that unknown saint who could so inspire her daughters. Later in life he always carried a biography of St. Teresa and after a military career and the death of his wife, he became a priest.[131]

---

[130] Davidson, *Voltaire: A Life*, 460.
[131] Bush, *To Quell the Terror*, 214, 220, 230.

⌒

Gaultier returned. Local church authorities did not consider Voltaire's earlier recantation enough and still threatened not to permit a Christian burial. The former Jesuit arrived with another priest to see what he could do. Someone shouted into Voltaire's ear that his confessor had come. "My confessor? Then be sure to give him my compliments," the dying man said, to everyone's surprise. The second priest asked Voltaire, "Do you recognize the divinity of Jesus Christ?" The Enlightener reached out and shoved the cleric away. "Let me die in peace," he said, and turned on his other side away from his visitors.[132]

⌒

"We are victims of our century," one of the Carmelites of Compiègne had scribbled in prison, "and we must sacrifice ourselves that it be reconciled to God."[133] The brides of Christ suffered for more than they knew, however. The Conflictual Enlightenment and the French Revolution had partly resulted from Catholic sin. That made revolutionaries and Catholics brothers in sin. They both persecuted the innocent. Just as at the Crucifixion, it would be Christ's sisters who would offer themselves to God—in union with him—as recompense.

⌒

Voltaire suffered in great pain, so his doctor prescribed a painkiller. "Now that Voltaire is near his end," the doctor wrote in a letter, some "people are beginning to talk, to evaluate all the damage he has done to society, which even those who are not infinitely severe are comparing to the wars, plagues and famines which for the past several thousand years have desolated the earth."[134]

---

[132] Pearson, *Voltaire Almighty*, 387.
[133] Bush, *To Quell the Terror*, 38.
[134] Davidson, *Voltaire: A Life*, 459.

Accounts of Voltaire's death are confusing because rumors circulated and different groups vied to control the narrative of his physical demise. Later Catholic propagandists used the doctor's letters to claim that Voltaire had been punished by dying in agony and the fear of Hell. Written by an unsympathetic observer, the doctor's account must be used with caution. Madame Denis said that though he did suffer, he died quietly.

According to one of Voltaire's French biographers, however, the man lay dying in a dark cottage removed from the main house, where Madame Denis — Voltaire's mistress — continued to receive guests. She worried Voltaire might revoke the will that made her his heir; the owner of the house worried about the furor that would accompany Voltaire's death. Preoccupied with their own concerns, they avoided the unpleasantness of Voltaire's suffering, a reminder, as it was, of their own mortality. Madame Denis did not stay with him; instead, she chose two women to watch over him. He writhed in pain on his bed; they chatted, laughed, and drank. He insulted them and threw a vase at them when he could muster the strength. Their nursing left much to be desired, it seems, for Voltaire lay in filth, hating those around him. The icon of the Enlightenment, who had based his ideas on independence and self-sufficiency, died as he had lived: an autonomous individual.

Voltaire had once written about "love" in a way that reduced it to sexual intercourse: love's perfection is cleanliness and care of oneself, thereby rendering the organs of pleasure more sensitive. For the old man, "The externals no longer remain the same. The wrinkles horrify, the white eyebrows shock, the lost teeth disgust, the infirmities estrange. All that one can do is to enjoy the virtue of playing nurse, and of tolerating what one once loved. It is burying a dead man." Those words came to fulfillment as he lay dying in agony. When told of his condition, Madame Denis, who hoped to possess Voltaire's vast riches soon, said, "What! Monsieur de Voltaire, the cleanest of men, who changed his linen three times a day rather than tolerate the slightest mark on it — what vile level is he reduced to? What revolutionary change does this represent?" It represented no revolution: only human mortality and her own abandonment of him.

One Catholic commentator on death wrote that no argument can be made for the salvation or damnation of the soul simply from the appearance of the body when passing away, whether calm or disturbed. Oftentimes, agitations of the dying come solely from physical causes. Good men, too, "are subject, by the will of God, to those agitations, in order to purify the soul, and lead the bystanders to the practice of true penance." Midmorning on May 30, 1778, Voltaire uttered a long and terrible cry that struck terror into his nurses. With that, he died.[135]

⌒

Only Mother Teresa of St. Augustine remained. "Let thy blade cut, completing all my offering!" she had written in a Christmas carol composed for her persecuted community a year or so earlier. The carol remained unknown until discovered by a historian in 1985. "For nothing but Thy will for me is sweet!" She crossed herself, kissed the statue of Virgin and Child, and then gave it to a pious woman standing nearby. As Mother Teresa climbed the steps to the scaffold, the last of her community, she could see the fifteen bloodied bodies of her sisters stacked in the cart. All eyes were fixed on the forty-one-year-old prioress as the executioners strapped her to the balance plank. They lowered her face down into the same prostrate position she had taken years earlier on the floor of the monastery church when she had first made her profession of vows, arms extended in a living cross. Now, once again, she lay face down, offering herself to Christ. "I thus yield up my reasoning and my seeing," she had penned in her Christmas carol. She gave up her autonomy to God. Mother Teresa opened not her mouth but entered silently into the mystery of the Lamb slain for

---

[135] Orieux, *Voltaire*, 487–90; Voltaire, "Philosophical Dictionary," in *The Portable Voltaire*, 156, 158; Pope Benedict XIV, *Heroic Virtue: A Portion of the Treatise of Benedict XIV on the Beatification and Canonization of the Servants of God*, 3 vols. (1734-1738; London: Thomas Richardson and Son, 1851-1852), vol. 2, 369.

the entire world. She offered her life as a witness amid the darkness that had engulfed France and the Church.[136]

⁓

In 1791, Voltaire's body was brought to Paris for burial in the Panthéon, where Rousseau's would also come three years later. The solemn procession carried his collected works (ninety-two volumes). Twelve white horses pulled Voltaire's casket with inscriptions on it. One said, "He avenged Calas." The other read: "Poet, philosopher, historian, he made a great step forward in the human spirit. He prepared us to become free." Voltaire's name lent itself afterward to those who sought to reform society and politics based on individual autonomy.[137]

⁓

Workers transported the bodies of the Carmelites to a huge pit full of putrefying bodies. They stripped them naked and threw them into the nameless grave, into the community of the dead.

⁓

The English traveler and writer Marianna Baillie visited Ferney in 1818. "Voltaire's sitting-room, and bed-chamber, have been scrupulously preserved in the same state in which they were left at the time of his death," she noted. Though the furniture was "dropping to pieces with age and decay," the beautiful gardens still looked out upon the glaciers of the Alps. Then she noted that Voltaire was mistaken and fatally deceived about the glorious truths of revealed religion. "Living in an age when the pure doctrines and benignant spirit of Christianity were so atrociously misconstrued and misrepresented ... it is less to be wondered at than regretted, that Voltaire's vigorous understanding should have disdained their disgraceful shackles; and that in his just ridicule and detestation

---

[136] Bush, *To Quell the Terror*, 119.
[137] Davidson, *Voltaire: A Life*, 461.

of the conduct of some followers of Christianity, he should have been unfortunately induced to mistake and vilify Christianity itself."[138]

⌒

It was July 17, 1794, when the guillotine silenced the last Carmelite voice. Ironically, Maximilien Robespierre — the Rousseau-inspired revolutionary leader responsible for the mass executions — toppled from power just ten days later. The blade of the guillotine fell on him just as it had fallen on the Carmelites. It seemed their sacrifice had indeed been accepted by God to end the Reign of Terror.

Since these events, it has appeared to many secular historians and Catholics that the religious antagonism of the age signaled a decisive break between Christianity and the Enlightenment. The uncompromising stance of figures such as the Carmelites of Compiègne seemed to prove that the conflict of the eighteenth century separated Christ from the Enlightenment, faith from enlightened reason, and religion from modernity as decisively as the guillotine had once separated heads from bodies.

But there is another way to tell the story of Christianity and the Enlightenment.

---

[138] Marianne Baillie, *First Impressions on a Tour upon the Continent in the Summer of 1818, through parts of France, Italy, Switzerland, the Borders of Germany, and a part of French Flanders* (London: John Murray, 1819), 249–250.

Part 2

Engagement and the Catholic Enlightenment

Enlightened reform should work to the "benefit of the
Roman Catholic religion . . . and public and private profit."

—Lodovico Muratori

The true light that enlightens every man
was coming into the world.

—John 1:9

6

Not an Ordinary Salon Girl

Captivating

A beautiful twenty-year-old woman calmly faced her audience. The quiet room of the Palazzo Agnesi in Milan was richly furnished with a harpsichord, mirrors, and gilded candleholders. Forty modern paintings in identical frames decorated the walls with landscapes, seascapes, and scenes from the life of Christ and the New Testament. The largest of all pictured the Resurrection.

Those gathered waited eagerly to hear her speak. They had heard rumors of her exceptional intellectual abilities. The host (Carlo Belloni) rose and dramatically called everyone's attention in Latin so the international audience could understand. As one of the woman's tutors, he was a man of brilliant manners and vast culture. He began by talking about various scientific phenomena, including controversial subjects such as the nature of tides and the origin of spring waters. Then the young woman began to respond to his arguments, debating boldly in Latin. She keenly defended the scientific views of Isaac Newton and other modern thinkers. The men among the audience included magistrates, senators, writers, professors, ecclesiastics, and foreign travelers. They were captivated by her performance, and perhaps even a bit unsettled, as they brought up other topics of interest. They tested her. They asked philosophical questions about the nature of the soul and its relationship to the body, and further scientific quandaries concerning light, colors, and geometrical curves. She spoke like an angel, one guest recorded; she was "more stupendous than the cathedral of Milan."[139]

As the night descended, uniformed servants lit candles and brought ice creams and sorbets for the guests as they continued to listen. The summer evening in 1739 was hot, but the young woman's combination of academic bravery, skill in debate, and virtuous modesty fascinated them. When she was finished, her talented sister played the harpsicord in the background and sang songs of her own composition.

As the salon conversation ended, everyone rose from his seat, and talk became general. Some moved in to speak with the academic performer informally, and she could communicate in French, German, Italian, or Greek, depending on the person's request. She joked gracefully with one of the visitors that she was sorry their first meeting had to take place at a disputation in a large group. For every interested person, twenty were probably bored, she said self-deprecatingly. Some topics were better discussed with a few like-minded friends. The guest nodded in agreement, admiring her common sense alongside her academic brilliance.

The woman's name was Maria Gaetana Agnesi (1718–1799). She became a minor celebrity in northern Italy and beyond for her intellect and her charity. She was the first woman in history to publish a book of mathematics in her own name. It was called *Analytical Institutions* (1748) and explained the new techniques of differential and integral calculus to general readers. Her work was so brilliant, the Bologna Academy of Sciences made her a member. This was almost unprecedented for a woman of that time. Her book was translated into French and English. It was considered the best introduction to its subject for decades afterward. In addition, the University of Bologna, then under papal control, offered

---

[139] Massimo Mazzotti, "Maria Gaetana Agnesi: Mathematics and the Making of the Catholic Enlightenment," *Isis* 92, no. 4 (December 2001): 670; Massimo Mazzotti, *The World of Maria Gaetana Agnesi, Mathematician of God* (Baltimore: Johns Hopkins University Press, 2007), 4–6, 21.

Agnesi an honorary lectureship in mathematics. Agnesi was hailed across Europe.

Agnesi's story introduces a different sort of interaction with the Enlightenment than conflict, for only a small number of Catholic writers in the eighteenth century combated the Enlightenment as a whole. Instead, many Catholics (and other Christians) *engaged* the Enlightenment. These Catholic Enlighteners, such as Maria Agnesi, shared the optimism of the age about human effort toward improving life. They engaged and broadcast modern knowledge and advanced the education of women. The story of what has been called by recent historians the "Catholic Enlightenment" ranges from Agnesi's Milan to the enlightened papacy of Benedict XIV in Rome, from the Academy of Sciences in Bologna to the monasteries of enlightened Benedictine monks in Germany. The Catholic Enlightenment demonstrated both a sophisticated strategy of cultural engagement in the eighteenth century and certain dangers inherent in that engagement.

Salon Conversation

Salon conversations like Agensi's in 1739 originated in Renaissance Italy but spread widely from there. They became key events of the Enlightenment, most notably in Paris. Rules of polite sociability governed the conversations of men and women mixing not only with each other but also with different social classes. Self-educated aristocratic women[140] played central roles in the Paris salons. They hosted, selected topics and guests, and regulated interactions. Salons prized talent and wit. They connected Enlighteners around science, literature, and culture.

---

[140] Like Madame Geoffrin—one of the leading women of the Enlightenment in France. From 1750 to 1777, she hosted many of the most influential Enlighteners of her time. This gained her international recognition. She modeled Enlightenment sociability and provided guidance, gifts, and connections to advance the careers of various Enlighteners.

This 1956 painting by Fray Pedro Subercaseaux Errázuriz, in the Instituto Nacional Sanmartiniano, portrays a salon gathering. Note the Dominican friar present on the far right.

The salon conversations put on by Agnesi's father in Milan resembled the famous Parisian salons. His, however, showcased academic disputation rather than witty conversation and literary readings. The salon conversations at Palazzo Agnesi differed in another important way too. In Paris, the best-known salon women were praised for their social skills, not so much their intellectual achievements. Agnesi strove for both.

Catholic Feminism

Agnesi was born in Milan. Her father, Pietro Agnesi, descended from a family of wealthy textile traders. She was the eldest of twenty-one children born to Pietro and his three successive wives. Pietro desired to raise his family's social standing into the aristocracy not only by purchasing fancy carriages and properties but also by sponsoring literary and scientific culture. He resolved to give his eldest daughter the best education money could buy. He built up a library in the family palace and hired tutors. This showy strategy eventually led to financial ruin. However, it also profoundly shaped the life of Maria Agnesi and created one of the great stories of the Catholic Enlightenment.

Few eighteenth-century women could participate in the intellectual sphere of their day. Universities and academies remained closed to them. Deeply ingrained assumptions about the weakness of female minds prevailed across Europe. Women were barred from institutions of higher learning. Some of these barriers gave way for a time in the early 1700s. This was not due to the efforts of anti-Christian or Protestant activists, as one might expect from the history of later women's movements.

Maria Gaetana Agnesi, Italian mathematician.

Assumptions about women first changed in Catholic countries, especially in Italy, where early modern feminism began. Why? Why in Italy did some women such as Maria Agnesi achieve high positions of intellectual achievement?

Recent scholarship points in a clear direction: the culture of the Catholic Enlightenment created space for them. At a time when Rousseau and others depreciated women, the Catholic Enlightenment — especially in Italy — pushed a reformist religiosity that valued the education of women and their intellectual achievements. Through examples of strong female heroines in classical mythology, determined women saints, and René Descartes's philosophical dualism of soul and body, the Catholic Enlightenment of the eighteenth century made the intellectual equality of women more than simply an idea. It made it a sociological reality in its time. The Catholic Enlightenment made it possible for some talented women to excel as *filosofessa* — female "philosophers" or Enlighteners in some academies, salons, and in Bologna in particular in the Papal States. "The Enlightenment Pope," Benedict XIV, promoted women's careers in Bologna — including that of Agnesi.[141]

What was the Catholic Enlightenment? Through what channels did it influence Agnesi in Milan? How did it form her spiritually and intellectually? How did she engage the powerful Enlightenment movement that fed into the creation of the modern world?

---

[141] Other women of the Catholic Enlightenment did appear outside Italy; they did not, however, receive the same institutional recognition. See Ulrich L. Lehner, ed., *Women, Enlightenment and Catholicism: A Transnational Biographical History* (New York: Routledge, 2018). Scholars from around the world detail in this book, for example, the remarkable contributions of Polish writer and art collector Izabela Czartoryska (1746–1835), the English writer Jane Barker (1652–1732), the German princess and home-schooling mother Adelheid Amalie Gallitzin (1748–1806), the French author of the best-known version of *Beauty and the Beast*, Jeanne-Marie Leprince de Beaumont (1711–1780), and the Spanish writer and feminist Josefa Amar y Borbón (1749–1833).

The Catholic Enlightenment

For years, historians have characterized the Enlightenment as a largely secular movement in conflict with Christianity. That was how Peter Gay portrayed it in his famous 1966 book *The Enlightenment: The Rise of Modern Paganism*. Much evidence for the conflict between Christianity and the Enlightenment does exist, especially in France, and this is where Gay chose to focus. Defining only nonreligious thinkers as "enlightened," Gay quoted those from the Age of Reason who believed in the irreconcilability of Christian faith and human reason.[142] His work implied that no Catholic Enlightenment existed. It *could not* have existed. Modernity is, by implication, a secular project to be celebrated.

Ironically, for many years, Catholics accepted this separation of Christianity from the Enlightenment. They merely inverted interpretations like Gay's: instead of "Christianity bad" and "modernity good," they held "Christianity good" and "modernity bad." They thought of the Enlightenment as the enemy responsible for the secularization of the modern world. Enlightenment principles led to the French Revolution, which destroyed the Catholic Church in France and killed thousands of faithful, including the Carmelites of Compiègne. Many Catholics became embarrassed by any evidence of positive Catholic participation in the Enlightenment.[143] Just as in the case of later secular historians, their frame of reference limited their view of the eighteenth century. A "Catholic Enlightenment" did not happen. It *could not* have happened, they thought. Modernity is, by implication, a secular project to be opposed.

Since the early 2000s, however, historians have created an entirely new interpretation of the Enlightenment and the eighteenth century. Looking both more widely and more deeply for evidence, they have found many examples of Catholics who contributed much to the Enlightenment.

---

[142] Peter Gay, *The Enlightenment: The Rise of Modern Paganism* (New York: Vintage Books, 1966), 3, 212.

[143] Ulrich L. Lehner, *The Catholic Enlightenment: The Forgotten History of a Global Movement* (New York: Oxford University Press, 2016), 3, 11.

Rethinking the Enlightenment

Like Agnesi, they have been largely written out of the secular narrative about the past that many people today have absorbed. In reality, only a small percentage of Enlighteners adopted anti-religious views. Most sought to reconcile faith and reason in one way or another. Religious Enlighteners (Catholics, Protestants, Jews) shared the conviction that new discoveries in science and philosophy could help renew their faith. The Enlightenment could be "reverent as well as irreverent," one historian wrote, and it made possible new expressions of faith.[144] Modernity has secular *and* religious roots.

As part of the wider religious Enlightenment, the Catholic Enlightenment lasted from around 1700 until 1803, when Napoleon's armies enabled the German princes to dissolve monasteries—centers of Catholic Enlightenment—and secularize Catholic institutions of higher learning. Before that tragic time, priests, bishops, laypeople such as Maria Agnesi, Benedictine monks, and even a pope—Benedict XIV, "the Enlightenment Pope"—constituted a flourishing Catholic Enlightenment.

Catholic Enlighteners engaged the "information revolution" of the time by exchanging manuscripts, trading controversial books, reading about new scientific discoveries in the burgeoning periodical press, socializing in salons and clubs and coffeehouses, and working in places such as seminaries, monasteries, schools, homes, hospitals, and even gardens. Catholic Enlighteners promoted social charity over mysticism, critical thought over blind obedience, rational devotion over emotional exuberance, local church governance over papal centralization, the modern Newton over the ancient Aristotle in physical science, and freedom of scholarship over suppression of new ideas. Their views revealed an optimism about human nature, reason, and improvement of life in this world. The Catholic Enlightenment was a vital participant in the overall Enlightenment movement, not simply a less developed precursor. The

---

[144] David Sorkin, *The Religious Enlightenment: Protestants, Jews, and Catholics from London to Vienna* (Princeton: Princeton University Press, 2008), xiv, 3, 5.

Enlightenment must be viewed as a whole and on its own terms, not simply as a cause of the French Revolution or modern secularism.

The Catholic Enlightenment generally adopted a temperate attitude toward change. It did not promote an ideology of political revolution. It did not look for cultural conflict. Rather, the Catholic Enlightenment's major characteristics included compromise, conciliation, and moderation. It desired to absorb as much as possible the intellectual and social energy of the eighteenth century to secure reform *ad intra* (inside) the Church and *ad extra* (outside) in the wider society.

The weak political position of the papacy and most Italian states in the eighteenth century fostered a favorable environment for these Catholic Enlightenment values. The papacy deemed it wise to remain neutral in the various political struggles between Catholic princes across Europe. Thus, "an attitude of appeasement and accommodation necessarily carried the day," wrote one historian.[145] The Catholic Enlightenment sought to bring about reform by working in collaboration with secular power rather than confronting it.

This meant that the papacy and some Catholic Enlighteners tended to favor a cultural strategy over a political one. They did not seek so much to respond to Protestant challenges (as earlier generations had done) as to engage the emerging modern world on its own terms through history, art, and culture. The Catholic Enlightenment was a religious movement with cultural goals resembling some of those of the New Evangelization as urged by Pope John Paul II in the late twentieth century. The Catholic Enlightenment varied by national culture. Wherever it spread — Italy, Portugal, Spain, Poland, Malta, Habsburg lands in Austria and beyond — Catholic Enlighteners related faith and reason. They took seriously divine revelation and "modern" ways of life and thought of their time.

Several influences combined to form the Catholic Enlightenment in the eighteenth century: the Christian humanism of the Renaissance;

---

[145] Christopher M. S. Johns, *The Visual Culture of Catholic Enlightenment* (University Park, PA: Pennsylvania State University Press, 2015), 3.

the breakthroughs of the Scientific Revolution in the 1600s by Galileo, Descartes, Newton, and others; and the Council of Trent. This council met between 1545 and 1563. It responded to the challenges of the Protestant Reformations. Major Protestant teachings about the depravity of human nature and predestination—the idea that God chooses who is saved and humans have little (or nothing) to do with it—were refuted by the council. Catholicism stresses the goodness of human nature, which is flawed but not destroyed by Original Sin. That one can perform good deeds without explicitly Christian faith was the basis for the idea of natural virtue in the Enlightenment period.

Human freedom remains intact and essential for the life of faith. One can freely accept or reject God's grace. At a time when families sometimes forced their daughters into marriages (or convents), the council insisted people have the right to choose freely their own spouse. No one can force another to marry someone—a radical position threatening the desire of kings to form marriage alliances. This spirit of liberty connected to the council, together with the achievements of Christian humanism and the Scientific Revolution, would influence the atmosphere of Catholic feminism in early modern Europe, the Catholic Enlightenment, and Maria Agnesi. She walked a fine line between honoring her father's authority and choosing her own vocation, for example.

The Council of Trent bore immediate fruit for Catholic culture, especially in the reforming efforts of Archbishop Charles Borromeo (1538–1584) in Milan during the late 1500s. Twentieth-century research on Borromeo's example of pastoral sanctity and reform so inspired Pope John XXIII (a church historian), he called the Second Vatican Council in 1962. He desired another Trent to reformulate truth in contemporary terms in order to renew the life of the Church.

It was not until the Catholic Enlightenment of the eighteenth century that the fruits of Trent fully ripened. Catholic Enlighteners sought to increase the number and quality of seminaries, deploy the arts to promote piety and provide examples of sanctity, and reform Church bureaucracy, as called for by Trent. Catholic Enlighteners extended the spirit of reform into other areas, too, such as ending the nepotism[146] that ran rampant in the baroque-era Church of the 1600s and promoting social over strictly theological issues.

Catholic Enlighteners opposed prejudice, blind obedience, emotional spirituality, philosophical dogmatism, and abuses of power by popes and bishops. Without attacking doctrine (usually) or hierarchy per se, Catholic Enlighteners sought a more collaborative idea of the Church. They often opposed the Jesuits because the latter controlled educational institutions with outmoded curricula, they believed. Also, Jesuits increased popular overemphasis on rites and ceremonies, leading people to neglect Christ. Naturally, Jesuits disagreed with that assessment. Eventually, an alliance of anti-Jesuit forces among Catholic Enlighteners, Jansenists, and political rulers pressured Pope Clement XIV to suppress the Jesuits in 1773.

Catholic Enlighteners sought to eliminate common superstition surrounding witches, curses, and hauntings. Superstition is defined as an excess of religion, a deviation of religious feeling. It attributes magical power to mere external performance of ritual practices that might otherwise be lawful or necessary — such as ringing church bells to bring good weather or saying certain prayers to bring good health. Superstitious people tended to blame every misfortune on diabolical agency, confusing supernatural and natural causality. In response, Catholic Enlighteners insisted that one should clearly distinguish between the two different kinds of causes. They proposed a sober, rational, and internal piety in support of this goal.

Catholic Enlighteners also opposed "baroque spirituality," which they thought ostentatious. "Baroque" refers to the beautiful and triumphalist art and culture of seventeenth-century Catholicism, such as the gilded paintings full of naked angel babies and saints gazing Heavenward. Baroque

---

[146] Nepotism is the practice of those in power favoring their relatives and friends; popes would often elevate their relatives to the position of cardinal in the sixteenth and seventeenth centuries, allowing certain families to dominate the papacy through political intrigue. Catholic Enlighteners worked against such practices.

artists and writers typically desired to promote frequent encounters with the supernatural through physical reality. Mixing material and spiritual reality, and taking their theological impulse from the Council of Trent about the goodness of human nature, the creators of Baroque culture believed even human emotions and senses could be enlisted in the service of God.[147] Baroque-era Catholics promoted plays, art, architecture, sculpture, theatrical styles of preaching, rituals, relic festivals, flamboyant church music that might even include trumpets, popular practices such as decorating images, celebrating alleged miracles and feast days, burning candles, and processions of public flagellation. Their triumphalist (sacral) Catholic culture produced incredible art, a powerful global missionary impulse, great saints—and confusion about the boundaries of the natural and the supernatural. This confusion contributed to problems ranging from the Galileo affair to the Revocation of the Edict of Nantes and the subsequent persecution of Protestants as seen in chapter 3.

Baroque spirituality flourished well into the eighteenth century, but Catholic Enlighteners believed its excesses promoted superstition and superficiality. They believed that moral integrity, practicality, and simplicity in worship are more conducive to godliness than elaborate communal rituals. The Mass and the Eucharist needed to take clear precedence over saints, relics, and processions.

One of the most widely read books of the Catholic Enlightenment promoted these anti-baroque views. It was *The Science of Rational Devotion* (1747) by the Italian priest, historian, and archivist Lodovico Antonio Muratori (1672–1750). His influence extended throughout Catholic Europe and even into the Agnesi library. He was concerned with "boundary thinking." He distinguished between the boundaries of the natural and the supernatural. He did not like them mixed, as when angels suddenly interrupt a natural, human scene in a baroque painting. Muratori likely would have

---

[147] Elizabeth Lev, *How Catholic Art Saved the Faith: The Triumph of Beauty and Truth in Counter-Reformation Art* (Manchester: Sophia Institute Press, 2018), 4–5.

advised leaving the angels out, letting the scene speak for itself. In *Rational Devotion*, he sought to combat as unreasonable the externalized, excessive, superficial, and superstitious forms of devotion he had observed in many Catholics of the time. Faith and reason need to cooperate to purify each other. In order to regulate one's devotion properly, the Christian must be aware of the proper bounds of external devotion, of what merely *appears* as devotion. "It is a well known Principle, that the essential Substance of Devotion should be truly internal, that is, it should reside in a Heart well affected to God, and our Neighbour for the Love of God," Muratori advised his readers. External devotion should be in accord with internal devotion, for "the Modesty and decent Propriety of our appearance should accord with a reverential Mind." Any devotion that does not tend to correct one's vices or regulate one's affections of the heart, making them obedient to the law of God, is superficial and merely externalized piety.

Unlike baroque-era mixing of spiritual and physical reality, or the Conflictual Enlightenment's denigration of spiritual reality, Muratori and other Catholic Enlighteners sought to distinguish clearly the dual nature of reality. For example, in *Rational Devotion*, Muratori wrote of the importance of material objects such as pictures of saints and rituals that awaken devotion. However, religious veneration and thoughts should not, by any means, fix upon material objects in and of themselves. Minds should rise to God or to the saint who is represented to the imagination by an image. Relics of saints, considered in themselves, are simply material things; pictures an aggregation of colors; images an assembly of wood or marble. "What is therein of *Matter* so considered, is certainly worthy of no sort at all of Respect or Veneration, and whoever would exhibit it to *Matter*, as such, would commit Idolatry." When kneeling before an image, one must remember the saint himself is "not at all there.... His Soul is in Heaven." One's thoughts should ascend to Heaven, then, and not "fix themselves upon the mere *Matter* before our Eyes."[148]

---

[148] Lodovico Antonio Muratori, *The Science of Rational Devotion*, trans. Alexander Kenny (1747; Dublin: James Byrn, 1789), 10, 215–217, 234, 237–238.

Rethinking the Enlightenment

Muratori and Catholic Enlighteners believed such boundary think-ing would help people to cooperate with God and to live a more fully human—and holy—life. For example, it would help them understand how natural diseases differ from spiritual afflictions in order to seek the appropriate remedy. This was an important consideration not just for ex-orcism but also to protect people from medical quacks trying to sell their various forms of "faith healing." Education in medicine and empirical sciences such as physics or anatomy dispels superstition and purifies reli-gion, freeing people to improve their lives, in this world—*and* the next.

The Catholic Enlightenment in Milan

Milan is an old Roman city in the wide valley of the Po River in north-ern Italy. Constantine proclaimed his famous edict there in A.D. 313, granting religious toleration in the empire. In Agnesi's time, the city still looked to Rome for cultural influence and (spiritual) governance, but also to Vienna. That was because Milan was controlled politically by Austria throughout most of the 1700s. The Austrian empress Maria Theresa (reigned 1740–1780) was one of the great female rulers of her age who rejected certain Enlightenment ideas while implementing others in her educational and ecclesiastical reforms. Agnesi dedicated her book on calculus to her. Rome and Vienna represented the remote channels by which the Catholic Enlightenment filtered into Milan to affect Agnesi.

The proximate channels included Agnesi's father's aristocratic con-nections, her tutors, salon conversations, the up-to-date palace library, and her spiritual formation in the context of Milanese Catholicism. Her tutors were mostly well-connected, sophisticated, and rising ecclesias-tics who educated her according to the Catholic intellectual tradition, Renaissance humanism, and modern knowledge. They recognized her prodigious memory and astonishing talent for languages. By age eleven, she knew Greek so well that she could speak it and instantly translate Greek passages into Latin. She became used to saying her daily prayers to the Virgin Mary in Greek and continued that practice throughout her life. As Agnesi matured, she acquired etiquette and practiced music (the cello). She studied ballistics (the science of projectiles and firearms), trigonometry, hydraulics, globes, solar clocks, anatomy, and rhetoric — by which she learned the techniques of disputation for public defense of knowledge normally reserved to men.

Records generated after her father's death reveal the contents of the Agnesi family library.[149] There were books for the study of languages and self-help manuals for writing, polite conversation, and good manners — all Enlightenment themes. One could find the *Journal of Italian Literature* in her family's library, an example of the new print media associated with the Enlightenment. The most successful Italian journal of the age, this publication helped form a sense of national identity. It reflected concern for economic, administrative, and religious reform associated with Muratori's "rational devotion" and the wider Catholic Enlightenment in Italy. Its editors and writers believed in disseminating up-to-date science as the best means to promote social reform — a typical Enlightenment perspective.

The library also contained poetry, works of contemporary playwrights, and a French translation of *Robinson Crusoe* — but few novels or those books of the time explicitly targeting women. There were works by ancient Greeks and Romans and works on history and politics. Moral, dogmatic, and spiritual theology were all represented. One found works of early Church Fathers and biblical exegesis. Books about witchcraft, possession, and heresy appeared on the shelves.

The rest were contemporary books in mathematics and physical science. Descartes and those working to relate his mathematically inspired methods and ideas (called "Cartesian rationalism") with the empirical methods (sense-based) of experimental science (empiricism) figured prominently: Gottfried Wilhelm Leibniz, Christian Wolff, Locke, Newton, Nicolas Malebranche, Jean-Antoine Nollet, and Antonio Vallisneri.

---

[149] Mazzotti, *The World of Maria Gaetana Agnesi*, 93–104.

The Agnesi family surrounded itself with a wide range of resources in the Catholic intellectual tradition and modern thinkers.

Agnesi's Formation, Spiritually and Intellectually

The Catholic Enlightenment formed Agnesi in a lay spirituality oriented toward inner devotion, outward social charity, and upward intellectual development. This happened largely through the thriving Catholic culture in Milan during her formative years. Trent and the pastoral model of Archbishop Charles Borromeo emphasizing Catholic education inspired renewal in early eighteenth-century Milan. Agnesi directly benefitted. Milanese church leaders such as Archbishop Giuseppe Pozzobonelli (1696–1783), a friend of Pope Benedict XIV and one of Agnesi's patrons, encouraged people to connect their spiritual and intellectual lives with social action. He specifically promoted the education of women.

Milanese Catholic culture supported a lay spirituality oriented toward the world — not just safe spaces such as convents, churches, and households. Leaders believed that the highest spiritual achievement is open to the most ordinary person, one historian wrote.[150] Along with Muratori, they believed one should practice a moderate civil devotion tending to bring one outside oneself by practical charity. Through serving others, one supports society. This Milanese spirituality inculcated a positive view of human effort to achieve good in this world — a central tenet of the Catholic Enlightenment overall.

Agnesi's association with the Theatines reinforced Catholic Enlightenment lay spirituality. This religious order, cofounded by St. Gaetano Tiene (1480–1547), encouraged clergy and laity to live out their faith by seeking personal holiness in service to others. Maria's middle name, Gaetana, reflects her family's devotion to this saint. The Theatines administered a church down the street from the Agnesi palace and often attended the young woman's salon conversations. As Agnesi matured

[150] Ibid., 69.

under their guidance, she learned to be wary of disorderly devotions and theatrical piety. She came to believe that reason plays an essential role in the spiritual life. She believed that baroque piety—emphasizing the senses as avenues to spiritual realities—tended toward superstitious devotions, as the wider Catholic Enlightenment held. She thought baroque communal religious practice tended to stimulate fantasy, credulity, and fatalism rather than the intellect and clear understanding of religious duty. In this way, through her *religious* formation, she absorbed the Age of Reason around her—an example of how the Enlightenment filtered into eighteenth-century Catholicism.[151]

Agnesi lived out these ideals of the Catholic Enlightenment both inside and outside her family's palace. When not studying or debating, she educated her siblings and taught the catechism to the family servants. The historian Antonio Francesco Frisi knew Maria Agnesi personally and relied on her friends, manuscripts, and correspondence to write a short work about her life. Frisi recounted that by working to improve the lives of others around her, Agnesi tried to give a good example to the servants. They respected her for it. "It was quite a sight," Frisi wrote, "to see the lazy servants in the chambers of the [Agnesi] home instantly compose themselves, when they were surprised by her accidental passage in the rooms, and tell each other in a low voice: *Behave brothers! Here is the Philosopher.*"[152]

Passing by the servants, Agnesi often made her way to her private chapel and study, adjacent to each other. Sheltered by a series of quiet corridors in the palace was the prayer room with a walnut prie-dieu facing an ivory crucifix. From there, a door opened into Maria's sparse study,

---

[151] Ibid., 73–74.

[152] Antonio Francesco Frisi, *Historical Praise of the Woman Maria Gaetana Agnesi* (Milan, 1799), found in Antonella Cupillari, *A Biography of Maria Gaetana Agnesi, an Eighteenth-Century Woman Mathematician, With Translations of Some of Her Work from Italian into English* (Lewiston: Edwin Mellen, 2007), 73.

just as her faith opened a door into her mind. A visitor would have immediately noticed four large globes, three armillary spheres,[153] and various instruments for the study of mathematics. A desk held piles of books and maps. The walnut bookcases of her library were fully accessible only with the help of a ladder. Here she worked and met with tutors.

Outside the palace, she volunteered for local confraternities — voluntary associations of laypeople devoted to a specific religious cause. The Congregation of the Schools of Christian Doctrine was a federation of local, parish-based groups that led more than two hundred catechism schools for boys and girls in Milan. Through the Congregation, Agnesi taught in parishes and encountered many young people from the working class and the poor. She combined her catechism lessons with reading lessons. In these ways, her formation in Catholic Enlightenment spirituality spilled out into the local neighborhood to reach even the poor people of the streets.

Mathematics and Holiness

Agnesi loved mathematics. The Milanese Catholic Enlightenment encouraged high development of intellect for the benefit of the spiritual life. The study of mathematics aided holiness, she believed, and was to be part of any education of young people. Christian minds needed math.

For those of us today in the twenty-first century who reside among the lower levels of mathematical talent, Agnesi's enthusiasm about the subject and its connection to the spiritual life might seem odd or intimidating. It is difficult for those not versed in the language of mathematics to appreciate how beautiful and compelling it is. As contemporary theoretical physicist Terry Pilling wrote, the equations describing nature are often stunningly elegant and beautiful. Einstein's equation for gravity, for example, may look unintelligible to many. To the educated, however, Pilling continued,

---

[153] An armillary sphere was a model of objects in outer space consisting of a spherical framework of rings centered on the earth or the sun.

it "contains pictures of galaxies and nebulae, wormholes and timewarps, comets, black holes, and even the big bang and the subsequent expansion of the universe." Pilling described such equations as "ethereal," meaning "delicate," "heavenly," and "unworldly." They lack material substance and are therefore "pure." Mathematics conveys an ethereal light to the human mind. When one understands the language of mathematics in this way—"the world opens up in glory before you like one emerging from Plato's cave," Pilling penned.[154]

Sometimes when pondering a mathematical problem, Agnesi's mind would enter that ethereal realm of beauty and begin to operate in a way seemingly independent of her body. Her relatives reported that on occasion she would awake from sleep, jump out of bed in her nightgown, and hurry through the hallways to her study to write down the solution to a mathematical problem she had been working on earlier. She would return to bed, and the next morning, she would find the solution on her desk—without remembering having awakened in the night!

Agnesi believed that mathematics is the only field in which the human mind can achieve certainty on its own; hence its importance for education. Experiencing the harmony of deep and profound truth gives one the *feeling* of certainty. That feeling can ignite the desire to live one's life out of a place of certainty and confidence, a willingness to correspond to great truths compelling the mind. The wheel of fortune does not affect these truths. They are permanent things. In an age of intellectual confusion and skepticism in the wake of the Age of Reformations, mathematical certainty appealed to Agnesi, just as it had appealed to earlier thinkers such as Descartes. Mathematics helped anchor her to those truths that moved her whole life. Intellectual and spiritual certainty grounded her commitment to her Catholic faith and to engaging Enlightenment culture.

---

[154] Terry Pilling, "Ethereal Delights," *Engineering Quarterly* (Spring 2019): 7. *Engineering Quarterly* is a publication of the University of Mary, Bismarck, North Dakota.

Rethinking the Enlightenment

Metaphysical Modesty

The Catholic Enlightenment shaped the way Agnesi engaged Enlightenment approaches to knowledge. The Enlightenment prioritized natural and human sciences over theology, which until then had dominated the sacral culture model. This implied the humbling of theology, but not necessarily its irrelevance. The Enlightenment reprioritization represented a "metaphysically modest" approach to public knowledge that Agnesi adopted.

"Modesty" makes one think of restraint in presenting one's physical person to the world rather more than a strategy for approaching knowledge. And indeed, Agnesi was conscious of wearing appropriate clothing in different contexts, from salon to study to street. In the eighteenth century, however, the ideal of modesty also applied to the intellect. It encouraged veiling not just bodies but also knowledge. That was one reason even men sometimes published anonymously: to avoid showing off. "Immodest words admit but this defense,/ That want of modesty is want of sense," penned Benjamin Franklin.[155] Modesty, in this sense, opposed the exhibition of intimate things and helped one to resist the allurements of fashion, praise, and prevailing ideologies.

While Agnesi practiced this kind of personal modesty, she also stretched it in her spectacular salon conversations. Preachers of the time warned about mixed conversations of men and women in the salons. Some people frowned at new forms of Enlightenment sociability and at seeing learned women out in society. That seemed "immodest." Agnesi, however, was not afraid to mix with men, to put herself forward as an individual, and eventually to publish under her own name. She was a modern woman.

"Metaphysical modesty," a phrase borrowed from Agnesi's biographer,[156] refers here to a specific kind of modesty different from the physical and intellectual kinds described above. It involved nondogmatic ways of

[155] Franklin, *The Autobiography and Other Writings*, 20.
[156] Mazzotti, *The World of Maria Gaetana Agnesi, Mathematician of God*, 110.

154

presenting truth. Ever since Martin Luther (1483–1546), European think-ers faced new struggles about truth; specifically, if different churches all claimed to be Christian but taught vastly different doctrines, what is the truth? This was deeply, existentially disturbing. Catholics main-tained that only the authoritative Church, linked back to the Apostles through Tradition and Scripture, could guarantee authentic knowledge of divine revelation. Others, however, appealed to Scripture alone. Some turned to direct inspiration from the Holy Spirit; some to reason alone. While Christian division narrowed and divided the paths to the highest theological and *metaphysical* truths (those beyond physical, empirical data), other European thinkers widened and united the avenues to lower, physical truths. Galileo, Descartes, Newton, and hosts of others in the seventeenth century—the "Age of Genius"—solidified the scientific method and the use of mathematics to understand what they called "the laws of nature." If people cannot agree on the highest truths, then maybe at least they can on the lower ones. This insight electrified the Enlightenment with excitement.

It energized the reprioritization of knowledge, putting controversial theology and higher truths on the back burner in order to focus on the physical sciences and their implications for human life. Metaphysical modesty accompanied this rearrangement as a new social strategy. It advised discretion and veiling one's highest and most intimate beliefs concerning the nature of reality. These intimate parts are not necessar-ily shameful, but out of a healthy sense of modesty one should not bring them into public. They belong in the inner sanctum of religious colleges.

In the new public spaces of salons, coffeehouses, and print media, rules of genteel conversation de-emphasized dogmatic questions such as the attributes of God and the nature of the church. It was more appropriate to discuss open-ended scientific and social questions in these public places because their "inferior epistemological status made them metaphysically safe" topics.[157] In other words, questions answerable through empirical

---

[157] Ibid., 57.

knowledge were more suitable for polite conversation because they did not necessarily threaten someone's highest allegiances or deepest fears.

One can see how Agnesi absorbed a metaphysically modest reprioritization of knowledge by contrasting her modern education with the education generally available in the traditionally minded Jesuit colleges of the day. Students in those colleges studied a traditional curriculum emphasizing logic, metaphysics, and general physics. Teachers would dictate large amounts of material from Aristotle because he had been held in such high regard for centuries.[158] Modern, empirical disciplines were "tacked on" to this body of knowledge. In other words, their education prioritized metaphysics over experimental disciplines, traditional knowledge over modern knowledge.

Agnesi's tutors reversed that. They were freer than those in the colleges to focus on experimental disciplines over metaphysics. It was not that the highest truths held no importance; Agnesi studied theology at a high level later in life. Rather, her faithful and reform-minded clerical tutors did not hold Scholasticism essential to the defense of religion. They held that updated, metaphysically modest approaches to knowledge were not only legitimate but could even better serve faith in certain ways. Agnesi and her tutors focused their efforts on the new knowledge gained in the physical sciences. They wanted to engage the world and its ideas.

Agnesi's student notes survive and illustrate this. She skipped long sections from her traditional textbook on syllogistic logic and the metaphysics

---

[158] Agnesi appreciated Aristotelian metaphysics but—rightly—followed the lead of the Scientific Revolution on empirical (scientific) questions *as surpassing Aristotle*. This in no way implied discontinuity, however, or irrelevance of the Greek thinker. In fact, as Edward Feser argued recently, Aristotle's philosophy of nature (as distinct from his science) is not only compatible with modern science but is implicitly presupposed by it. See Edward Feser, *Aristotle's Revenge: The Metaphysical Foundations of Physical and Biological Science* (Neunkirchen-Seelscheid, Germany: Editiones Scholasticae, 2019), 1. The wider Enlightenment movement, despite its hostility to Scholasticism, nevertheless did draw inspiration from Aristotle in its approach to morality, natural law, and politics.

of God and the angels. Her notes minimized metaphysics to focus on physical science and mathematics. She contrasted Descartes and Newton on optics and magnetism (generally preferring Newton). Her notes delved into earth science, the structure of plants, and what sort of souls animals have—an important topic in Aristotle's philosophy of nature. Agnesi believed in the *advancement* of knowledge, in the possibility of discovering new truths unknown before, even by the Greeks. This characteristically modern idea spread widely during the Enlightenment.

It is true that Enlightenment-era metaphysical modesty also created new dangers in modern culture, from the Christian point of view. Motivated by *acedia* (spiritual sloth), it could contribute to a false modesty toward truth. Some people might be content with partial truths, "no longer seeking to ask radical questions about the meaning and ultimate foundation of human, personal and social existence," as Pope John Paul II wrote.

On the positive side, however, metaphysical modesty mitigated the dangers of brazen theological and political monopolies in sacral cultures like Louis XIV's France. It affirmed the dignity and fitting autonomy of the temporal order. The human world should be studied and governed according to the norms proper to it, and theology should not determine those norms. Pope Benedict XVI once called this "positive secularity": the secular, worldly sphere enjoys a proper autonomy from religion and thereby should be studied on its own terms.[159] This was the central insight of the

---

[159] Zenit Staff, "Benedict XVI Favors a 'Positive Secularity,'" Zenit, October 17, 2005, https://zenit.org/articles/benedict-xvi-favors-a-positive-secularity/; John Paul II, *Fides et Ratio*, no. 5. Benedict's idea of "positive secularity" was ultimately grounded in the Second Vatican Council document *Gaudium et spes*, and in this way the Catholic Enlightenment clearly connects—midway between—both major councils of modern history, Trent and Vatican II. *Gaudium et spes* says, "If by the autonomy of earthly affairs we mean that created things and societies themselves enjoy their own laws and values which must be gradually deciphered, put to use, and regulated by men, then it is entirely right to demand that autonomy.... Man must respect these [temporal realities] as he isolates them by the

Catholic Enlightenment: medical problems, for example, are medical, not spiritual, just as historical questions are historical, not pious stories. This makes a great deal of difference. The distinction of faith and reason was already present in Thomas Aquinas. But in the eighteenth century, this split unleashed tremendous creative energy through the Catholic Enlightenment. One major source of this nuclear fission was Descartes.

Catholic Rationalism

Besides metaphysical modesty, the second way Agnesi engaged Enlightenment knowledge concerned the legacy of French philosopher René Descartes (1596–1650). He was the father of modern rationalism, one of the major strands of thought present in the eighteenth century (the other being empiricism). Together, those two strands of thought created the scientific method,[160] which fed into the Scientific Revolution and the Enlightenment. If empiricism draws from the senses, physical facts, and experimentation for knowledge, rationalism looks to the mind's reasoning powers themselves to deduce new truths from ones already held. Euclid did this in his *Elements*: if one accepts his definition of a point, a line, and a circle, one can reason one's way to numerous geometrical truths that follow without relying on any experiments or additional facts. Those truths are beautiful, clear, and certain. And anyone with reason can discover them.

---

appropriate methods of the individual sciences or arts" (36). To the extent that human beings have a religious duty to appreciate and know God's creation, one could even say they have a *duty to be secular*.

[160] One way to think of the scientific method is like an arch. At the left foot of the arch lie empirical facts painstakingly assembled. The left leg itself represents the inductive reasoning taking one upward from the evidence to a general conclusion (the apex of the arch). The right leg is the deductive reasoning from a general conclusion down to specific empirical predictions lying at the right foot. See Feser, *Aristotle's Revenge*, 66–67.

This proved to be incredibly exciting to people like Descartes. The twentieth-century mathematician and philosopher Bertrand Russell wrote: "At the age of eleven, I began Euclid, with my brother as my tutor.... I had not imagined that there was anything so delicious in the world."[161] Descartes felt that too. He read Euclid in his Jesuit education. Mathematics became his passion, and therein lay his true genius. His algebraic notation is still used today. The "Cartesian coordinate system" is named after him. Accordingly, all things can be located in physical space by referencing x, y, and z coordinates to an assumed origin, the background of the Global Positioning System (GPS) today. From his mathematical background, Descartes perhaps did more than any other to create the modern idea of the "laws of nature" as the central object of study in science.

His broader interest, however, was philosophical revolution. He believed that mathematics provided a model for all reasoning. Because mathematics could be potentially independent of concrete things, it might be applied to any subject. In fact, it could be the master science, Descartes dreamed, the key to unlocking the secrets of the world and advancing knowledge. This seemed the perfect answer to the skepticism, theological bickering, and religious violence disturbing Europe since the Age of Reformations. The world could be remade according to unaided reason through the mathematically inspired "Cartesian method," named after him. The possibilities implicit in this method of rationalism have electrified imaginations ever since, especially in the Age of Reason.

Cartesian rationalism inculcated methodological doubt. By this, one discards uncertainties and builds up knowledge one piece of certainty at a time. This method has formed generations of thinkers and academics ever since in the ideal of "objectivity," by which one seeks to transcend personal views and cultural traditions in order to map reality objectively and scientifically, with Cartesian coordinates, so to speak.

---

[161] Bertrand Russell, *Autobiography* (New York: Routledge, 2009), 25.

The power of Cartesian rationalism is its ability to *cut*, to separate one thing or idea from another, like a scalpel in anatomical dissection: this muscle is not that bone; that kind of truth is distinct from this one; the soul is different from the body. Cartesian rationalism makes distinctions. To understand is to split, to break down, to analyze from all possible directions (even outside the field of mathematics). This in no way automatically excluded belief in God. Descartes was a believing Catholic. Rationalism in the eighteenth century was simply a deductive system of truth, analogous to a mathematical system, as one historian of philosophy put it.[162] One could use it within a theistic or an atheistic worldview. It made a profound impression on the entire age.

Cartesian rationalism directly and indirectly inspired Catholic Enlighteners to make careful distinctions between spirit and matter. This boundary thinking could be inculcated in students by training them in analytical fields such as algebra and geometry, Agnesi's tutors believed. Adopting Descartes's dualism and his methodical doubt even outside mathematics could not only unmask superstition but also separate false from true claims to miracles and diabolical influence, for example. This latter topic greatly interested Agnesi, as evidenced by her interest in the famous case of "the woman from Cremona," which well illustrates the importance Catholic Enlighteners put on Cartesian-like distinctions.

Cremona was a city not far from Milan. In 1746, reports told of how a thirty-three-year-old woman there discharged stones, metal, and glass from her body, even in the presence of respected physicians. She had a history of hysterical convulsions and hallucinations. Many in Cremona considered this a supernatural phenomenon caused by a demon. Others wondered if it was the result of disease. What was the role of medicine here? What was the role of the Church? Could stones, for example, develop in the stomach, as they could in the bladder or the kidney? Could they be ejected? What was the best cure?

---

[162] Frederick Copleston, *Descartes to Leibniz*, vol. 4, *A History of Philosophy* (Garden City, NY: Image Books, 1960), 29.

The woman's spiritual director, backed by some Jesuit theologians, declared a diabolical cause and performed an exorcism. They represented a baroque devotional style predicated on frequent encounters with the supernatural. Opposing this solution with Cartesian-like methodical doubt was another theologian who claimed that the woman from Cremona faked her condition. She was an impostor. Various physicians represented the empirical viewpoint of scientific medicine. They thought the condition was possibly caused by the woman's imagination and hysteria. One of them (Paolo Valcarenghi), distinguishing between spirit and matter, did not exclude in principle the possibility of possession or diabolical forces, one historian remarked. But Valcarenghi was "inclined to consider their presence in everyday experience extremely remote"—a summary of the Catholic Enlightenment position overall.[163] The local bishop tried to cover all bases and favored combining religious and medical solutions to apply to her condition. While it is unknown what eventually happened to the woman, the debate between medical, scientific, and ecclesiastical authorities eventually resulted in acceptance of the medical explanation and the pursuit of a medical cure.

The Cremona phenomenon attracted attention from around Europe, including Maria Agnesi's. She collected books on it. In fact, it was a frequent topic of debate at the salon conversations at her home. The case underscored the importance Catholic Enlighteners placed on making the kinds of natural and supernatural distinctions they believed baroque Catholicism sometimes failed to make. Spiritual and medical problems are two distinct things. The boundaries of dogmatic theology had been illegitimately broadened in the past. By utilizing Descartes's method to "cut," they could work to reconcile faith and reason, dogma and analysis. Clearly understanding the limits of different fields would prevent conflicts between various kinds of truths and forward an overall strategy of engaging the Enlightenment.

---

[163] Mazzotti, *The World of Maria Gaetana Agnesi*, 100.

A striking example of how Agnesi practiced this boundary thinking is found in her interaction with Archbishop Giuseppe Pozzobonelli. They met shortly after his selection as archbishop of Milan in 1744 at a meeting of the Trasformati—a group of thinkers, artists, and ecclesiastics who gathered in Milan to converse about ideas and culture from a Catholic Enlightenment point of view. By then, Agnesi had pursued advanced theological studies in addition to her mathematical work for several years. A Catholic Enlightener himself, Pozzobonelli recognized Agnesi's exceptional mind and asked for her analysis of a controversial book just published called *Politics, Law, and Religion in Order to Reason Correctly and to Distinguish Truth from Falsehood*, by Giuseppe Gorini Corio. It drew from Cartesian rationalism and other modern philosophies and touched on many themes Catholic Enlighteners supported, such as denouncing false miracles. It also argued for clearer distinctions between church and state. The book vigorously pushed the boundaries of engagement with modern thought. Pozzobonelli worried how it might affect Roman and Viennese perceptions of his reform efforts. He would need great discretion to respond well to the book. So he requested Agnesi's help.

In her notes for the archbishop, as analyzed by one historian, Agnesi said there were serious problems with the book, though the author explained many truths of the Catholic faith well. Corio tended to reduce explanations of all spheres of human life to *"mettere sotto i sensi"* (to investigate through our senses") and *"sottoporre a calcolo"* (to reduce to calculation). In other words, he simplified all areas of life, even religion, to problems of empiricism or rationalism. Agnesi wrote that this tendency invalidated his treatment of several issues. Under the guise of condemning false miracles and superstition, for example, he contradicted both the Fathers of the Church and the *Catechism of the Council of Trent*. Defending a sober cult of relics as authentically Catholic, Agnesi stated that the author made unreasonable demands for "proofs" of the authenticity of relics. In such historical matters, she argued, "moral certainty" is all one can ask for.[164]

---

[164] Ibid., 89–90.

Though Descartes tended toward simplifying all problems to mathematics, his legacy of rationalism supported efforts in the early eighteenth century to distinguish between spiritual and material realities and thus different kinds of knowledge. Relying on her own authority and her own study of the Catholic intellectual tradition, Agnesi made those distinctions in her notes to the archbishop regarding Corio's book.

Agnesi and the "Woman Question"

Besides making metaphysical modesty and Cartesian rationalism her own, Agnesi engaged several practical Enlightenment programs, including women's education and the popularization of knowledge for a general audience. All women should "serve the glory of their gender," Agnesi noted in the dedication of her book on calculus to Empress Maria Theresa.[165] Agnesi pursued that goal throughout her entire life in several ways.

The "woman question"—the question of the cognitive and moral equality of women to men—had emerged as a popular theme in Milan during Agnesi's youth. The local church supported its discussion. Some Catholic Enlighteners expressed moderately favorable views on female education and the possibility of careers as academicians, professors, and artists. Naturally, Agnesi strongly supported that position. She believed in the modernization of education to better integrate the sciences into Catholic pedagogy for the young, the poor, and the female.

Agnesi engaged the woman question from a young age. When she was nine, in 1727, she stood before an audience of family and local elites in the palace garden to give an oration on the importance of female education. Some people of the time thought women were not fully human. They should practice docility and limit themselves to the domestic sphere. Others argued that women are fully human, should receive an education, and should even have an opportunity to excel in institutions

---

[165] Maria Agnesi, *Analytical Institutions*, dedication, in Cupillari, A *Biography of Maria Gaetana Agnesi*, 240.

of higher learning. Agnesi's father had carefully orchestrated this garden event to put his Milanese salon at the center of the debate.

Maria had already been publicly celebrated for her fluency in French by age five. Now—just four years later—in a Latin oration delivered from memory, she defended women's rights to study the arts and sciences. It was probably composed mainly by her tutor, but young Agnesi may have contributed to its composition because—one commentator suggested—it is vague on a few points more accomplished orators would have specified. She translated her talk, "Oration in Which it is Demonstrated that the Studies of the Liberal Arts by the Female Sex are by No Means Inappropriate," from Italian into Latin and then memorized it as part of her studies. It was highly unusual for someone so young to give an oration or take up publicly such a controversial subject.

"It will perhaps seem strange and unusual that I, not yet at the end of my childhood and having scarcely completed my youthful training in Latin," Agnesi began, "dare to speak in the presence of very distinguished men who are most well versed in every kind of knowledge." She hoped, she said, her audience would not discount what she had to say as the frivolous opinion of a clever girl. While she made no case for women to speak in church or civic affairs, Agnesi stated, she resolved to argue against those men who forbid women cultivation of knowledge. "I will have done my job if, however many things my adversaries are able to force upon me, I may weaken and destroy them to such an extent that the deceit of empty gildings is removed and a plain and genuine version of the truth at last appears." She summarized the threefold strategy of her opponents who argued against female education due to custom, supposed female bodily weakness, and the idea that educating women introduces disturbance into civil and domestic affairs.

These arguments are contrary to the truth, Agnesi said. She highlighted the presence of learned women in the ancient and early Christian world. Intelligence is more related to learning than to gender, the girl told her audience. Some men believe the softness of women, their attraction to mirrors, curling irons, earrings, boxes of ointment, bracelets, and "womanly things," proved their inaptitude for serious study. This is not so. Physical strength does not imply intellectual strength, even in men. Women can work out in the "literary gym" just as well as men because physical differentiation of bodies does not imply differentiation of rational souls, she said. What man of sound mind does not doubt that women have been "divinely conceived with an equal soul?"

In addition, Agnesi argued that women's studies are very useful in both private and public affairs: "Who, therefore, does not envy the most fortunate condition of certain families," the girl said, "where the learning of the parents fosters their children's studies, and in which the girls and boys are consumed by a certain most noble rivalry in their studious eagerness? What can be more pleasing, what can be sweeter for parents than to see their hopes so well positioned, which will not only be useful for them but also will benefit others at some future point?" In addition, she continued, men do not really want to struggle with a stubborn and unlearned wife. Rather, nothing is more blessed than to hear repeatedly her most cultivated conversation. Her learning is the best part of conjugal happiness, she said. Must the republic of women grow old in domestic idleness? No, let us open the academies and the schools to them.[166] Agnesi concluded her oration with an appeal to great women in history, including the devout Venetian Elena Piscopia (1646–1684). She was the first woman in the history of the world to receive a university degree — in 1678, from Padua. Interestingly, she was a Benedictine oblate — a laywoman dedicated to God's service.

With that, young Agnesi finished her oration. Her performance so impressed the audience that they decided to publish the oration in her honor. It appeared in print that year and then again in 1729 as part

---

[166] Maria Agnesi, "Oration in Which it is Demonstrated that the Studies of the Liberal Arts by the Female Sex are by No Means Inappropriate," in *The Contest for Knowledge: Debates over Women's Learning in Eighteenth-Century Italy*, ed. Rebecca Messbarger and Paula Findlen (Chicago: University of Chicago Press, 2005), 128–140.

of the proceedings of a major national debate on the woman question titled *Academic Discourses by Various Living Authors on the Education of Women, the Majority Recited in the Academy of the Ricovrati in Padua*. The Agnesi family—and their friends among local Milanese elites, including professors, senators, and ecclesiastics—adopted a clear position on the woman question.

The Soul Has No Sex

Agnesi's arguments in her oration for the equality of male and female souls connected to wider early modern debates over the nature of the human person. Descartes and the Scientific Revolution had caused a crisis in this area. If the entire world is like a machine operating by intricate wheels and interdependent powers, what happens to humans? To their moral freedom? Are they simply part of a vast clock that determines their fate? Or do they somehow transcend the material world? Descartes answered these questions by asserting that human beings are both spiritual minds and physical bodies. As distinct, the body falls under the laws of science, but the mind is spiritual and retains freedom and transcendence over the system of mechanical causality in nature.

Hence, Descartes's famous dualism. "I think, therefore I am" is the phrase most associated with him. He wrote that the "self—that is, the soul by which I am what I am—is completely distinct from the body." Reality consists of two types of substances: spiritual and material. He believed that God is the source of both material and spiritual reality. In that sense, Descartes's dualism preserved the tradition of medieval metaphysics. He was *not* a dualist in the sense of believing in two powers, one good and one evil, at war in the world, as a Manichaean or Cathar heretic would.[167]

---

[167] René Descartes, *Discourse on Method, and Related Writings*, trans. Desmond M. Clarke (1637; New York: Penguin Books, 1999), 25; Copleston, *Descartes to Leibniz*, 4:33.

If soul and body are separate, then it follows that "the mind has no sex." This was a common phrase among early Catholic feminist writers of the seventeenth century, often influenced by Descartes. In fact, these "Cartesian women" spelled out the implications of Descartes's analytical distinction between mind and body. That distinction could help free women from the obligations and prejudices attached to their female bodies. "A dualism that emphasized the separability of soul and body lent dignity to the intellectual enterprise of the salon and validated women as thinking subjects," as one historian summarized. Dualism meant that bodily differences in no way implied weaker female minds. The body did not "taint the dignity of the rational soul," as Agnesi put it in her oration.[168]

If Cartesian dualism defended the thinking woman, it also seemed to drain her of all feeling and emotion connected to the body. This reduced her body — and the human body in general — to the status of a mere machine disconnected from her. The Cartesian women of the seventeenth century were aware of that problem, and this explains their simultaneous attraction and resistance to such dualism.

Nevertheless, the idea of sexless souls influenced early modern Catholic women to reinterpret the Bible and understand themselves differently than in the premodern past. They began to read Genesis and St. Paul in ways divergent from various misogynist interpretations floating around that seemed to give theological justification for women's lower status. Souls created in the image of God — who is spirit — have no sex and are therefore equal. This reinterpretation of Scripture found its way into the 1726 work *Defense of Women*. This was by the great Benedictine monk and skeptical Enlightener Benito Feijoo (1676–1764), who virtually led the Spanish Enlightenment by writing in the vernacular. Hundreds of thousands of copies of his books appeared in multiple languages across Europe. Authorities were divided on whether Adam or Eve committed the

---

[168] Agnesi, "Oration," 133; Erica Harth, "Cartesian Women," *Yale French Studies* 80 (1991): 150.

graver sin, he noted, but it took a superior being to deceive the woman. This was not the case with the man. The sexes are equal, he argued. In effect, he showed how poor science had led to an impoverished theology of woman. Feijoo's work provided a catalyst for government-sponsored women's education in Spain decades later.

The fact that Descartes himself dedicated one of his books to a learned woman (Princess Elizabeth of Bohemia) and spent the final months of his life under the patronage of highly intelligent Queen Christina of Sweden encouraged feminist interpretations of his work. For example, the priest Giovanni Nicola Bandiera, who wrote his *Treatise on Women's Studies* in 1740, underscored the fundamental equality of pure intellect characterizing both men and women. No anatomist had found any significant differences between male and female brains, he wrote. The spirit has no sex. This did not imply sameness of gender roles or irrelevance of biological differences. It did imply, however, that men and women can both study the arts and sciences, just as both men and women can both strive for salvation. One historian wrote: "The defense of an essentially Cartesian and antimaterialist image of the mind lies indeed at the core of the explicit defenses of the right of women to study the sublime sciences that were produced within [Catholic Enlightenment] culture."[169] This fostered an environment favorable to female education, furthered in Milan by organizations such as the Confraternities of the Schools of Christian Doctrine, of which Agnesi was a member, and the Ursuline nuns.

Cartesian dualism trickled down to Agnesi through her books, tutors, and even spirituality. For the Theatines, who deeply shaped her religious sensibilities, life was a struggle between "two wills," one higher and spiritual, the other lower and sensual. Dualism did not mean the physical was

---

[169] Massimo Mazzotti, "Maria Gaetana Agnesi (1718–1799): Science and Mysticism," in *Enlightenment and Catholicism in Europe: A Transnational History*, ed. Jeffrey D. Burson and Ulrich L. Lehner (Notre Dame: University of Notre Dame Press, 2014), 304; Mazzotti, *The World of Maria Gaetana Agnesi*, 136.

unimportant. Quite the contrary. It simply meant that spirituality was more primary than materiality, and they should not be confused. Disorder easily led to superstition and false claims to miracles. The highest end of human life is union with God. To achieve that end, one must train the intellect and the will—such as by the study of geometry, as Descartes himself had done—against the deception of the passions and the senses. The intellect is the "eye of the soul," and only a clear intellect can truly guide the will. Thus, there is a need to purify the intellect of the senses so it can understand more clearly. In this way, Cartesian dualism, which had resulted from Descartes's choice to "assume that nothing was the way the senses made us imagine it," as he wrote in his *Discourse on Method*, supported Catholic Enlighteners in their overall suspicion of baroque spirituality and its frequent encounters—through the senses—with the supernatural.[170]

In addition to her Cartesian-inspired spiritual conception of the female mind, Agnesi drew a healthy sense of self-esteem from the example of the Virgin Mary. Teaching orders in northern Italy regularly commissioned paintings representing the education of the Virgin in the first half of the eighteenth century. Giuseppe Antonio Petrini painted an altarpiece in 1744 depicting Mary's mother teaching her to read. Catholic feminists even before Agnesi's time had emphasized the feminine glory of Mary as balancing the masculinity of Christ to make their arguments. Defending devotion to Mary as consonant with love of God, Agnesi wrote: "The love that we have for his great lady is not at all in contrast with the love of God, because all the love we have for her goes to God, who placed in her so many graces and gifts and the strength to protect them."[171] If God placed "so many graces and gifts" in Mary, why not in other women too? The Catholic Enlightenment—drawing inspiration from Descartes and the Virgin Mary—opened space for women to develop their talents.

---

[170] Mazzotti, *The World of Maria Gaetana Agnesi*, 33–37; Descartes, *Discourse on Method*, 24.

[171] Cupillari, *A Biography of Maria Gaetana Agnesi*, 221.

Agnesi's example in this area had a great influence on others, including educated men. Before interacting with her through correspondence, one scholar (the great Venetian mathematician Jacopo Riccati, 1676–1754) wrote privately to one of her tutors. In his letter, he exemplified the typical prejudice of the day about how the "weaker sex" is prone to fantasy: "in which realm women better men as much as they are bettered in the realm of intellect." Sixteen years later, however, after reviewing Agnesi's manuscript of her great mathematical treatise, Riccati wrote to her directly: "I was amazed when casting my eye over an accomplished treatise on Cartesian analysis that a young lady could reach these heights in such delicate and abstruse matters." Her example made a difference.[172]

Nevertheless, loss of a spiritual conception of the human mind amid the greater materialism of the later eighteenth century undermined the status of the Cartesian Catholic woman. The image of "man the machine"—without a soul—reignited assumptions about women's weakness. A new, more pseudo-scientific misogyny spread, igniting the second wave of Enlightenment feminist writers in Protestant and deist circles, such as the Englishwoman Mary Wollstonecraft in her *Vindication of the Rights of Woman* (1792). Wollstonecraft has captured the attention of historians of the Enlightenment ever since, and rightly so. Strangely, however, her Catholic predecessors—Agnesi, Feijoo, Bandiera—have been forgotten. Agnesi lived the "rights of woman" long before Wollstonecraft's book appeared. In reality, Catholic culture provided a key site of debate over women's status—contrary to standard views of the Enlightenment. "Taking religion seriously, as all enlightened minds did, requires us to reformulate some of our too-easy alignments of the secular

---

[172] Jacopo Riccati to Ramiro Rampinelli, August 16, 1729; Jacopo Riccati to Maria Agnesi, August 18, 1745, in Clara Silvia Roero, "M. G. Agnesi, R. Rampinelli and the Riccati Family: A Cultural Fellowship Formed for an Important Scientific Purpose, the *Instituzioni analitiche*," *Historia Mathematica* 42 (2015): 301, 302.

with the progressive, and to rethink our views on what constitutes a properly feminist mentality," wrote two scholars in the field of historical gender studies.[173]

Achieving Mathematical Fame

Agnesi's engagement with Enlightenment culture helped to put Catholicism at the cutting edge of modern thought in Milan and encouraged the education of women. It also made her famous. In 1748, one year before Rousseau walked along the road to Vincennes to visit Diderot, Maria Agnesi published her great mathematical text *Analytical Institutions for the Use of Italian Youth*, about "rules of analysis" in algebra and calculus. It was the first mathematical book in history by a woman under her own name.

Calculus is the mathematical study of continuous change that has widespread applications in science, engineering, and economics. At Agnesi's time, there was great interest in calculus for applications to the "science of waters" and how to control flooding and irrigation in the Po River valley of northern Italy. Agnesi was well aware of these engineering problems, but she wrote her book as a work in pure mathematics — that is, leaving out practical considerations. She did this partly out of respect for others already writing about practical applications of calculus, but also out of her Cartesian proclivity toward theoretical clarity and untainted, ethereal mathematical thought.

Agnesi desired to write her *Analytical Institutions* as a work of synthesis for Italian youth, bringing together highly specialized and disparate knowledge. This goal of writing for the general reader rather than for specialized scholars shared a characteristic Enlightenment concern for the widespread dissemination of knowledge — as in Voltaire's *Philosophical Dictionary*, mentioned in chapter 2. Agnesi's desire to do this dawned on her slowly as a teacher of her younger siblings and street girls with

[173] Sarah Knott and Barbara Taylor, eds., *Women, Gender and Enlightenment* (New York: Palgrave Macmillan, 2005), xviii.

learning disabilities. She had a gift for identifying obstacles to learning and overcoming them. She wrote her book in Italian, the language of the common people. In fact, in her preface she excused herself from the custom of translating her work into Latin, as most scholars would normally do, because she had originally intended it for the instruction of her younger brothers in mathematics. It became the first vernacular treatise on calculus in Italy and helped establish Italian as a serious scientific language.

Yet the work appealed to great scholars as well.[174] Some dedicated their own works to her. Steadily, *Analytical Institutions* gained a European reputation. This was due not only to positive reviews and translations but also to the way Agnesi integrated mathematical insights from both discoverers of calculus, Leibniz (German) and Newton (English). Ecclesiastics around Italy praised the book, and Agnesi joined the prestigious Academy of Sciences of Bologna. A professor at Padua wrote to her and praised the work's clarity, concluding that she had provided the most convincing argument for women's equal capacity to men in the sciences. The renowned French Academy of Science cited her book as the "most clear, methodical, and complete" presentation of calculus to date.[175] She

---

[174] It is known that the following scholars, among others, read Agnesi's book — showing its widespread dissemination in the highest circles: French geophysicist and astronomer Jean-Jacques d'Ortous de Mairan (1678–1771); French mathematician and editor with Diderot of the *Encyclopédie* Jean le Rond d'Alembert (1717–1783); French mathematician and leading light of the rationalist Enlightenment, the Marquis of Condorcet (1743–1794); French mathematician Alexandre-Théophile Vandermonde (1735–1796); English clergyman and Cambridge professor of mathematics John Colson (1680–1760; he translated her book into English); and Italian mathematicians Joseph-Louis Lagrange (1736–1813), Ramiro Rampinelli (1697–1759); Jacopo Riccati (1676–1754); and Vincenzo Riccati (1707–1775; he was one of the sons of Jacopo). See Roero, "M. G. Agnesi, R. Rampinelli and the Riccati Family," 312.

[175] Mazzotti, *The World of Maria Gaetana Agnesi*, 121–122.

was compared to the great French woman of science, Émilie du Châtelet, Voltaire's lover during the 1730s who translated Newton into French. After Châtelet's tragic death while giving birth in 1749, some French commentators on Agnesi's book rejoiced that Châtelet's spirit lived on in the woman from Milan.

Agnesi consciously promoted the widespread dissemination of her work. Nevertheless, she did not seek fame as an end in itself. "I do not intend to collect praise, because I am content with having enjoyed myself in a sound and real way, and having provided help for others," she wrote in the preface. She did not immodestly seek to bring attention to herself.

In addition, she was different from many of the fashionable ladies in the Paris salons — some of them mistresses to Enlighteners — who sometimes discussed scientific and philosophical topics with verve and wit but who were not themselves scholars. Agnesi "aspired to a deeper level of understanding that ostensibly distinguished the serious philosopher from the philosophical dilettante," one historian remarked. The Milanese *filosofessa* was no casual consumer of knowledge, or easy lover. She was not an ordinary salon girl.[176]

Agnesi's achievement gained Rome's attention. Pope Benedict XIV was so impressed that he wrote her a letter: "You are without a doubt numbered among the leading Professors of Analysis."[177] He hoped she would accept an honorary lectureship in mathematics at the University of Bologna — in the Papal States — which he secured for her behind the scenes. Maybe she would at least come for a ceremonial visit and public celebration of her book? Bologna was known as the "paradise of women" because a handful of talented ladies — sponsored by the pope — had managed to secure degrees and teaching positions there. Such institutional

---

[176] Paula Findlen, "Calculations of Faith: Mathematics, Philosophy, and Sanctity in 18th-Century Italy," *Historia Mathematica* 38, no. 1 (2011): 256, 265; quotation on 254.

[177] Pope Benedict XIV to Maria Agnesi, June 21, 1749, in ibid., 264.

recognition for learned women was unheard of in the rest of Europe at the time. Acceptance of the invitation would connect her to one of the greatest pontificates—and one of the greatest sites (Bologna), of the eighteenth-century Catholic Enlightenment. Would Agnesi go there?

7

Benedict Brain

_____

Morality Play

The human dissection in Bologna was about to begin. The anatomist made a vertical cut down the front of the corpse. A horizontal incision followed on either side of the navel. Pulling back skin, fat, and muscle, he revealed to the large audience the stomach, the liver, and the intestines. Candles and torches emitted smoke and a light that glimmered off the wood-paneled walls. The flickering light did little to warm up the cold but noble room. (The low temperature helped preserve the body.) Near the marble dissection table rested the necessary tools: razors, hooks, drills, paring knives, bowls, and sponges to soak up blood. Musical accompaniment added to the somber mood. Nearby, a Catholic Mass was said for the soul of the criminal whose body lay open on the table—the Mass stipend paid for by the anatomy professor. Meanwhile, piece by piece, the professor presented parts of the body to the gaze of the onlookers seated in a circle all around, as in a theater. He showed them the brain—*the* organ of the Age of Reason, viewed as the seat of the soul, the source of the self, and the symbol of rationalized religious devotion.

Many of those gathered had seen the public notices advertising the dissection event and bought tickets. They wore masks because it was carnival season, just before Lent—a time of raucous festivities and bodily indulgence. They could get rowdy and taunt the academics present, dressed in their formal robes, who debated anatomical matters. Foreigners had come from far away to see this renowned spectacle unfold in Bologna, second largest city in the Papal States. Many enjoyed the excitement of transgressing taboo; some were curious, and others repulsed, to witness the insides of a human being. The dissection made them conscious of their own bodies—and their own mortality—in uncomfortable ways.

In the audience sat the archbishop of Bologna, Prospero Lambertini (1675–1758). He would become Pope Benedict XIV in 1740—the greatest pope of the eighteenth century, "the Enlightenment Pope." He corresponded with Maria Agnesi about her work and cultivated the public persona of a science patron. As archbishop of the city of his birth, he often accompanied to the scaffold criminals condemned to a double punishment: execution *and* dissection. He heard their confession and prayed with them. The dissection usually began after sunset on the same day.

Anatomy is the science concerned with the bodily structures of organisms, especially as revealed through separating parts for analysis. Unlike today, when the practice of anatomy might seem marginal or elementary to some, during Lambertini's time it was the master scientific discipline for the study of life. Its practitioners represented the most cutting-edge research in medicine and set the agenda for other disciplines. Bologna was one of the great sites for the study of anatomy in the eighteenth century. Its archbishop was often present at the public anatomy events popularly called "Carnival Dissections" all during the 1730s.

Historians have shown how the Carnival Dissections of early modern Europe, which first started at Bologna in 1316 but spread widely, functioned as three-act morality plays co-produced by church and state. They did not serve science primarily. Students who really wanted to learn anatomy attended private dissections, where they could move in close to watch and participate. Instead, these events employed theatricality and the prestige of science to teach moral truths.

Act 1 commenced with public execution. Act 2, the dissection, could last several days. In terms of social psychology, it partly functioned as a punishment against the body of the criminal who had violated the body politic. Beyond that, viewing a dissection allowed one to marvel at God's creation. God is good, and man is his highest work, evident in the wonderful functioning of the body. For example, the motto of the Amsterdam anatomical theater, completed in 1691, was: "God's power is evident even in the smallest part of the body." The study of anatomy was a way of knowing God and knowing oneself.

Act 3 began with a celebratory banquet after the completed dissection. Scientists, civic leaders, and churchmen all attended. Christian burial of the criminal's body marked the restoration of social order, one historian wrote. By giving up their bodies to death and dissection, lawbreakers could offer retribution for their deeds. Justice had prevailed.[178]

Lambertini's strong support for the Bologna public anatomy events revealed the intimate relationship between religion and science in his age. Contrary to the view of American historian Andrew Dickson White, who famously helped create the science-versus-religion myth in his book *A History of the Warfare of Science with Theology in Christendom* (1896), Catholics did not ever oppose the practice of anatomy. White said the medieval Church prohibited dissection, which crippled medicine and surgery for centuries. This "impressed upon the mind of the Church the belief that all dissection is sacrilege."[179] These claims, however, are false. The contemporary historian of anatomy, Andrew Cunningham, who described himself as an atheist, wrote: "The fact is that the Catholic Church has never been opposed to the practice of anatomy.... Never, ever, anywhere."[180] There were *no* prohibitions on the dissection of dead humans or animals. Popes sponsored anatomists. Even a saint's body—Ignatius of Loyola—was dissected. The anatomizing of the dead papal physician Marcello Malpighi took place *in a church*! White was wrong.

---

[178] Rebecca Messbarger, *The Lady Anatomist: The Life and Work of Anna Morandi Manzolini* (Chicago: University of Chicago Press, 2010), 27; Andrew Cunningham, *The Anatomist Anatomis'd: An Experimental Discipline in Enlightenment Europe* (Farnham Ashgate, 2010), 48–50.

[179] Andrew Dickson White, *A History of the Warfare of Science with Theology in Christendom*, vol. 2 (1896; New York: D. Appleton, 1910), 32.

[180] Cunningham, *The Anatomist Anatomis'd*, 14.

Pope Benedict XIV (also known as Lambertini) saw supporting this field — and several other empirically based research areas — as central to his cultural engagement strategy with the Enlightenment.

Lambertini's strong support for the public anatomy events demonstrated the type of Catholic Enlightenment agenda he had in mind. He created the first chair of surgery in Bologna in 1742 and donated surgical tools to its occupant. One of the requirements was to perform forty lessons per year in human anatomy in Bologna's two main hospitals. Thus, he called on Bologna's pastors to persuade their parishioners to donate their bodies for dissection after death. He created the first chair of obstetrics in the city, concerned with childbirth and the care of women giving birth. As stipulated in the appointment, this person would regularly give hands-on lessons to midwives and surgeons using both teaching texts and three-dimensional obstetric models. Lambertini aimed to raise surgery and obstetrics to a higher position of honor in medicine. These fields were traditionally looked down upon at the time because they involved the "mechanical arts" of hands-on technique. But in the spirit of the Enlightenment, Benedict desired to join the theoretical to the practical for the sake of public health and disseminating knowledge. He pursued medical modernization as both archbishop in Bologna and as pope in Rome.

As Pope Benedict XIV, Lambertini desired to engage the modern world not so much through politics as through science and culture. Pursued at a time when it was obvious that the glory days of papal temporal power had passed, this strategy made sense. While some might say Lambertini had limited success in directing the papacy away from power politics to a cultural agenda, he believed that employing art, science, and history for the public good would help make Christian faith relevant to the people of his age. Through direct experience of the power of material *things* (both anatomical and antiquarian) — a very different approach to truth from traditional Scholastic reliance on *texts* — this was made possible. Historical and empirical evidence embodied in objects could undergird the modern credibility of the Church, he thought. By believing in the ability of the physical first to attract the eye and then to stimulate reason and faith, he achieved significant success in creating art museums and in supporting science.

This modern approach to faith led to his greatest work, *On the Beatification and Canonization of Saints* (1734–1738). This four-volume book was based on his years of work as promoter of the faith for the Congregation of Rites, disputing hundreds of claims to sainthood and miracles. He wrote it as archbishop of Bologna in consultation with the scientific and medical community of that city. Reviewed in major literary journals, the work sought to establish firm boundaries between the natural functions of the body and supernatural healing. One nineteenth-century commentator compared it to Thomas Aquinas's *Summa theologica*: "He has done with the practice of the Church what S. Thomas and the Schoolmen did with reference to the Faith."[181] It was a *Summa* of rationalized saint-making and procedures for busting fake miracles. Indeed, the book guided beatifications and canonizations for two hundred years and continues to exert influence today.

What exactly was the overall cultural program of Pope Benedict XIV (Lambertini)? And why did he consider anatomy, history, and medicine so important to his goals? In trying to answer these questions, one will see how the Roman pontiff engaged the second major strand of thought (besides rationalism, discussed in chapter 6) that influenced the Enlightenment. This was empiricism, a theory of knowledge committed to obtaining new understanding through the senses, factual research, and scientific experimentation.

Lambertini linked empiricism to the Catholic Enlightenment. He did this first by developing a rigorous and influential "science of the saints" to refute both Catholic credulity on the one hand and Enlightenment-era doubt over miracles on the other. Second, he utilized the "science of the past" to create and augment new institutions for studying and preserving history. Two important fruits of this movement, which Lambertini

---

[181] Benedict XIV, *Heroic Virtue: A Portion of the Treatise of Benedict XIV on the Beatification and Canonization of the Servants of God*, vol. 1, xxiii, xxiv.

supported, included the first public museum in the world (the Capitoline in Rome) and the Vatican Museums. Third, he patronized his home city of Bologna, making it into one of the great sites of the Catholic Enlightenment. He built up Bologna's Academy of Sciences as a center for advanced research, bringing the arts and the sciences into conversation. In addition, he created a renowned museum of anatomy there and forwarded the careers of learned women.

The Enlightenment Pope

Lambertini liked coffee, as did Voltaire and many others in the Age of Reason. This is the first point to make about him as a person. Conversation and the informal spirit of coffeehouse culture characterized his temperament, his administration style, and the way he interacted with people. Imported into Europe through expanding global trade and colonization, coffee deeply influenced the changing nature of human interactions in the eighteenth century. Lambertini exemplified Enlightenment sociability not only by attending salon conversations in Bologna and Rome but also by interacting with his friends in coffeehouses. As pope, he even built one himself!

The stimulant caffeine powered Enlightenment networking and energy. It was considered good for general health because coffee lessened intake of alcohol (a depressant), thereby promoting moderation. Freer and more egalitarian ways of relating and conversing with others characterized coffeehouses — including between men and women, at least in Italy (elsewhere coffeehouses were only for men). These houses spread through European cities in the early eighteenth century. One could learn the news there and enjoy the casual and spontaneous mood. One could freely speak according to the norms of civility. Less violent than taverns, coffeehouses thus embodied in microcosm the idealized liberty and order of the emerging civic cultural model. Perhaps human society really can operate largely on its own without political and religious authorities hovering nearby?

Pope Benedict XIV (1741), by Pierre Subleyras.

After his election as successor of St. Peter, Lambertini built a coffeehouse, the Caffeaus, in the garden of the Quirinale Palace[182] in 1744.
The Caffeaus did not *look* like a coffeehouse; it was built as a neoclassical
garden pavilion. But its purpose was to promote the coffeehouse culture
of discussion, exchange, and informality. The pope went there nearly

---

[182] This palace, located east of the Vatican across the Tiber River, was the
papal administrative center and preferred residence of the pontiffs in the
eighteenth century. Today it is one of the three official residences of the
president of the Italian Republic. Pope Benedict's coffeehouse still stands
in the gardens and tourists can see it.

every day. He received friends and important visitors, discussed news, and drank coffee—all in an atmosphere of joking and laughter. "He was able to achieve much," one biographer wrote, "by making people laugh." Laughter involved a certain detachment from emotional issues and a flash of common feeling between those amused together.[183] As such, the Caffeaus became a key site of Catholic Enlightenment discussions about modern ideas and administrative reform in the Papal States.

Lambertini desired to interact with others as equals. Accordingly, he talked in a very direct way. This sometimes involved swearing. He tried very hard to curb his use of four-letter words. He even put a giant crucifix in his audience chamber as a reminder to take care when speaking. That did not work, so he asked a friend to stand by him and pull on his cassock if he used any offensive language.

When King Charles VII (then ruling Naples) arrived at the Caffeaus in the year it opened, pope and monarch sat in identical—hence, equal—armchairs. Benedict put visitors at ease to discuss items of interest, with relaxed protocol and court etiquette, at least by eighteenth-century standards. Lambertini could almost forget he was Pope Benedict XIV for a while and appear more human to others.

According to this informal style, even as pope he would walk casually around Rome instead of riding in sedans or carriages. He visited churches, oratories, hospitals, convents, and monasteries, "making himself visible to the city's inhabitants and generating enormous esteem and good will in the process," one historian wrote. Sometimes he wandered into the slums of Trastevere, chatting with anyone. He liked to see for himself what was happening. Besides trying to better relations between the papacy and the people, he sought to set an example for bishops and cardinals. Pope Benedict XIV was convinced that "only reform and a return to clerical pastoralism could keep the Church relevant in the modern world."[184]

---

[183] Renée Haynes, *Philosopher King: The Humanist Pope Benedict XIV* (London: Weidenfeld and Nicolson, 1970), 193.

[184] Johns, *The Visual Culture of Catholic Enlightenment*, 42.

Lambertini's moderately progressive vision in many areas was rooted in his belief that true and creative reform of church and society emerges from faith and reason together, in continuity with authentic tradition. The beautiful Caffeaus reinforced this middle-ground mentality. It included both sacred and profane objects and imagery that drew together innovation and tradition, one art historian noted.[185] "Modern" things such as fine porcelain (used in serving coffee) and French furniture were surrounded by beautiful wall and ceiling paintings on traditional subjects from Scripture.

Lambertini viewed art as an important means of communicating the ideals of the Catholic Enlightenment. So the painting *Landscape with the Good Samaritan* in the papal coffeehouse, for example, was almost certainly Benedict's idea. It highlighted practical charity given by a "heretic" to a total stranger. God's grace works through all kinds of people, even those outside the visible Church. The mission of the Church is not to lord it over others but to serve them. These were key premises of "rational religion," according to Muratori and other Catholic Enlighteners, as well as deists such as Voltaire or Franklin. Thus, Lambertini (as temporal ruler of the Papal States) took seriously outside criticism of the Church, including by Protestants. He tolerated reproach against papal government and even himself.

Lambertini's coffeehouse mentality gave him wide publicity in progressive European circles and contributed to his good reputation even among Protestants. Despite Voltaire's anticlericalism, he called Pope Benedict XIV "the ornament of Rome and the Father of the world." Voltaire wrote a letter asking the pope to accept the dedication of a play critiquing religious fanaticism. "Your Holiness will pardon the liberty taken by one of the lowest of the faithful, though a zealous admirer of virtue, of submitting to the head of the true religion this performance." As seen in an earlier chapter, Voltaire is difficult to interpret and often indulged in witty mockery of exalted figures. However, there may have been a certain authenticity to

[185] Ibid., 211.

his words asking for protection of his play (from censorship) and for a benediction — "in hopes of which, with the most profound reverence, I kiss your sacred feet." The pope wrote back carefully to Voltaire praising his literary talents. Traditionalists criticized him for even communicating with the Frenchman. The pope explained to them, "As we did not find it evident that the author was outside our communion we thought it well to reply."[186] Nevertheless, many of Voltaire's works were judged dangerous and eventually ended up on the 1757 Index of Prohibited Books. The interaction of Pope Benedict XIV and Voltaire, however, suggests that intellectual opinion in the early eighteenth century did not neatly divide faith and reason, religion and philosophical literature.

In addition, the Protestant writer and politician Sir Horace Walpole (1717–1797) wrote a famous dedication to the pontiff: "Beloved by Papists/ esteemed by Protestants:/ a priest without insolence or interest;/ a Prince without favourites,/ a Pope without nepotism;/ an author without vanity;/ in short a Man/ whom neither Wit nor Power/ could spoil."[187] This gives some indication of Pope Benedict's international reputation for wit, charm, and genius. His moderate temper, his stand against nepotism and playing favorites, and his remarkable breadth of intellectual interests greatly impressed elites across Europe.

The Caffaeus also symbolized Lambertini's enlightened administrative and diplomatic decisions. Though he made mistakes as an administrator,[188]

---

[186] Voltaire to Pope Benedict XIV, August 17, 1745, in *Benedict XIV and the Enlightenment: Art, Science, and Spirituality*, ed. Rebecca Messbarger, Christopher M. S. Johns, and Philip Gavitt (Toronto: University of Toronto Press, 2016), 5; Haynes, *Philosopher King*, 182.

[187] Messbarger, Johns, and Gavitt, *Benedict XIV and the Enlightenment*, 6.

[188] Historians generally agree that he wrongly decided in the Chinese rites controversy, for example. The Jesuit missionaries in China had been working long and hard to reconcile Christian belief with Confucianism and ritual practices such as ancestor worship. The Dominicans and Franciscans disagreed with Jesuit methods and reported them to Rome. Knowing little about China, and lacking sympathy for the Jesuits in general, Benedict reaffirmed the ban on Jesuit accommodation and prohibited debating

he typically asked for the advice of others and sought to gain his purposes through moderation instead of pushing to extremes according to his own agenda. In this, he was much like his great namesake St. Benedict (ca. 480–ca. 543), who wrote in his ancient Rule: "All things are to be done with moderation on account of the fainthearted" (chapter 48). The pope sought to use compromise to achieve his ends in political negotiations—even if that meant sacrificing temporal interests of the Church for the sake of spiritual concerns. For example, he gave permission for taxation of ecclesiastical entities in Bologna and made some compromises over clerical immunity from the jurisdiction of civil courts. He refused all nepotism and promoted talent—an important concern to Catholic Enlighteners. During the War of the Austrian Succession (1740–1748), involving Catholic countries on both sides, Lambertini took no position. Austrian troops ravaged Bologna and even his own house and garden, yet he worked for peace without favoritism, choosing to suffer the "martyrdom of neutrality" instead, as one historian put it.[189]

Despite Lambertini's love for books, as reader, caretaker, and author, he privileged practicality over theoretical speculation when it came to social concerns—much like Voltaire and other Enlighteners. That was true philosophy, Voltaire believed: practical and devoted to improving the world, as at his Ferney estate. Lambertini largely agreed. When he arrived as the new archbishop of Bologna, he "began at once deliberately and methodically to inform himself about the state of his new diocese," a biographer wrote. "He had no ready-made ideas as to what needed to be done, no pet patterns of reorganization to impose. The first necessity was to discover the facts."[190] Accordingly, as a pope influenced by Muratori's economic thinking, he lessened the number of feast days for Catholics. Catholic political rulers had complained that the many days

---

the question. This crippled the Catholic mission there. See Messbarger, Johns, and Gavitt, *Benedict XIV and the Enlightenment*, 13.

[189] Haynes, *Philosopher King*, 226.

[190] Ibid., 57.

set aside from work hurt their economies; Catholic peasants struggled to make enough to live. The pope agreed and reduced the number of feast days while also building granaries throughout the Papal States.

Pope Benedict XIV was wary of power, finding it an "ever increasing and intolerable burden," one biographer wrote. He knew he was not immune to the temptations of power. "I don't know myself any more, I am so overwhelmed with business," he wrote in a letter to another bishop. "They suffocate me with praise, and I am forever rowing against the current of lies they try to make me believe, against the pride with which they try to make me drunk, and against importunities of every kind." The pontiff did not believe in using censorship as a weapon to silence opponents. He reproached by letter the Grand Inquisitor of Spain for banning a book under pressure from the Jesuits. "How many times have we ourselves found here or there in Muratori and other respectable writers opinions that are certainly condemnable; but, in the interest of peace and scholarship, we have done nothing about it!" Serious Catholic scholars should enjoy maximum freedom. In that spirit, Pope Benedict XIV personally helped revise the Index of Prohibited Books in a way that would better respect the importance of open discussion and the role of books in stimulating such discussion. Accordingly, authors in his 1758 Index appeared in alphabetical order for the first time — just as Diderot organized his *Encyclopédie*, also appearing during the 1750s and discussed in chapter 3. Enlightenment methods of organizing knowledge penetrated even the Vatican. Benedict told a group of churchmen who urged him to make more rigorous judgments: "I like to leave the Vatican lightnings asleep.... The Sovereign Lawgiver, whose interpreter and vicar I am, never once made fire fall from heaven, and He lived surrounded by heretics and unbelievers."[191]

This was the Enlightenment Pope.

---

[191] John L. Heilbron, "Benedict XIV and the Natural Sciences," in Messbarger, Johns, and Gavitt, *Benedict XIV and the Enlightenment*, 189; Haynes, *Philosopher King*, 159, 221.

Catholic Empiricism

How did Lambertini absorb so much of the empirical (scientific) mindset of the Enlightenment era? He was born in Bologna, and that made all the difference. The city boasted the oldest university in the world, founded in 1088. The University of Bologna still ranks as one of the leading institutions of higher learning in Europe. By the time of Lambertini, great teachers and natural philosophers (what we call "scientists" today) had created influential scientific legacies there.

During Lambertini's youth, for example, Marcello Malpighi (1628–1694), an anatomist and physician, pioneered microscopic anatomy in Bologna. Interested in new kinds of questions, Malpighi reoriented his earlier Scholastic methods of disputation (learning about nature through argumentation and classical texts) toward new experimental methods. "Do not stop to question whether these ideas are new or old," Malpighi advised his readers, "but ask, more properly, whether they harmonize with Nature. And be assured of this one thing, that I never reached my idea of the structure of the kidneys by the aid of books, but by the long, patient, and varied use of the microscope."[192] Such scientific empiricism — or "mechanical philosophy," as it could also be called at the time — treated natural organisms as machines one could take apart in order to understand them. One gains scientific knowledge through the senses and through experiment. This empiricism, together with the rationalism of the previous chapter, gave birth to modern physical science, and Lambertini paid attention.

---

[192] Marcello Malpighi, *Concerning the Structure of the Kidneys* (1666), in *Source Book of Medical History*, ed. Logan Clendening (New York: Dover, 1942), 214. Malpighi ended his life as papal physician. He offered his body for dissection after his death — a private event that took place in a church. Malpighi's name is attached to several physiological features related to the biological excretory system, such as the Malpighian corpuscles and Malpighian pyramids of the kidneys and the Malpighian tubule system of insects. He was also the first person to discover the link between arteries and veins — something that had eluded William Harvey when he published the first complete description of blood circulation in 1628.

Some churchmen and scientists viewed Scholasticism and mechanical philosophy (empiricism) as conflicting with each other. In realty, however, they did not conflict — as philosopher Edward Feser has recently shown. They only appeared to clash because their practitioners often confused different kinds of questions: those answerable through philosophical reasoning and those answerable through empirical research. To blur them was simply to commit a category mistake.

Aware of these issues, Lambertini as pope steered a delicate path between these two philosophies of nature. He appreciated the importance of Scholasticism on one hand *and* mechanical philosophy on the other. One could ask wide-angle synthetic questions about the larger structure and nature of physical reality as Scholastics did *and* analytic questions about parts of that reality as scientists. Lambertini set his entire cultural program on that premise. His background in "Galilean Catholicism," which had formed in the late 1600s among elites in the region around Bologna, helped him navigate this path.

Galilean Catholics took inspiration from Galileo Galilei (1564–1642), the Italian physicist and "Father of Modern Science," during the decades on either side of 1700. They were mostly churchmen enjoying close relationships with men of science. The Inquisition in Rome had convicted Galileo — a believing Catholic — as "vehemently suspect of heresy" in 1633 for asserting as fact — in apparent contradiction to Scripture — that the sun, not the earth, is the center of the universe. Historians agree today that Galileo had not actually proved his scientific claim with the evidence available to him at the time. We also know that while the sun is the center of our solar system, it is certainly not the center of the universe, as Galileo claimed. Nevertheless, poor decisions were certainly made in the Galileo case, including by Galileo. Myths about him — that he was imprisoned and that his eyes were gouged out — were created by eighteenth-century writers, including not only Voltaire but even churchmen who should have checked their facts. In reality, Galileo was put under house arrest in good conditions. The pope sent copies of Galileo's condemnation around Europe. Most Catholic states outside Italy, however, tended to see it as an abuse of power and refused to cooperate in enforcing it.[193]

Despite the condemnation, Galilean Catholics inside Italy took inspiration from Galileo, especially his legacy of faith and reason. Galileo wrote that Scripture and nature both "equally derive from the divine Word." Moreover, for Scripture to adapt itself to the "understanding of all people," it was appropriate for it to say many things about nature that are different from absolute truth in appearance, he wrote. Thus, in the Scripture, the intention of the Holy Spirit "is to teach us how one goes to heaven and not how heaven goes," Galileo noted.[194] This vision inspired later Catholic Enlighteners.

Lodovico Muratori—introduced in the last chapter as one of the greatest figures of the Catholic Enlightenment—was one such Galilean Catholic. He was from Modena, not far from Bologna (Lambertini's hometown). His overall view was anti-Scholastic, anti-baroque, and mechanistic in regard to nature. Correspondence between Lambertini and Muratori reveals mutual admiration, trust, and friendship. As one historian wrote, Muratori staunchly defended Galileo's distinction between theological dogma and empirical knowledge. Through this dichotomy, not unlike Cartesian dualism, he could preserve the realm of faith while employing legitimate experimental methodologies to understand the world. Scholastic metaphysics—heavily indebted to Aristotle—could retain its position in theology, while Aristotelian philosophy of nature yielded ground to the new mechanical philosophy for discovering how material things work. "Most distinguishing features of the scientific culture of Catholic Enlightenment derived precisely from this fundamental cognitive dualism," one historian wrote, insightfully.[195] Exactly: use sci-

---

[193] Scotti, *Galileo Revisited*, 259, 262.

[194] Galileo Galilei, "Letter to Castelli," in *The Essential Galileo*, ed. Maurice A. Finocchiaro (1613; Indianapolis: Hackett Publishing, 2008), 104; Galilei, "Letter to the Grand Duchess Christina," in *The Essential Galileo*, 119.

[195] Mazzotti, *The World of Maria Gaetana Agnesi*, 58.

ence to understand scientific things and Scholasticism to understand philosophical and theological things.

Thus, devout Catholic scientists—such as Antonio Vallisneri (1661–1730), a student of Malpighi in Bologna—could maintain their faith while eschewing biblical explanations of fossils or the age of the earth. Vallisneri and other Galilean Catholics "shared a strong dislike for metaphysical disputes and for all-pervasive philosophical systems," one historian wrote. This was the "metaphysical modesty" that Maria Agnesi practiced, an example of the reprioritization of knowledge happening during the Enlightenment. Agnesi, in turn, showed in her student notes how one could interpret Malpighi's and Vallisneri's scientific ideas as consistent with Scripture. In the case of Galileo's trial, Agnesi wrote, scientific study of the universe is not a question of dogma, and those who referred to the Scriptures to defend a particular theory were gravely mistaken. In this sense, Agnesi herself was a "Galilean Catholic."[196]

It is not surprising, then, that the position of Church authorities in Rome toward Galileo shifted somewhat during the Catholic Enlightenment. The Anglican priest James Bradley discovered the aberration of starlight in 1728, which was consistent with the heliocentric theory proposed by Galileo, that the earth moves around the sun. In 1737, Galileo's body was moved with much ceremony from behind the sacristy at Santa Croce in Florence to an impressive mausoleum in the main body of the church—nobility, religious leaders, and learned men all attending. Pressure to rehabilitate Galileo further came from Conflictual Enlighteners such as Jean d'Alembert (1717–1783), editor with Denis Diderot of the famous work of the Enlightenment the *Encyclopédie*. D'Alembert deplored the "theological despotism" he saw trying to dictate belief beyond the spiritual domain of faith and morals so apparent in the Galileo case. One must distinguish between the different kinds of questions addressed by the systems of religion and science, he thought, as Galileo himself had done.

[196] Ibid., 54, 59.

Many Catholic Enlighteners agreed with that. Reviewing the Galileo case, "would be worthy of the enlightened pontiff who governs the Church nowadays," d'Alembert wrote of Benedict XIV in 1754. "Friend of the sciences and himself a scholar, he [the pope] ought to legislate to the inquisitors on this subject." It turned out, Benedict did. And d'Alembert's words may have played a role in motivating him, one historian noted. As pope in 1757, Lambertini loosened restrictions on writers propounding heliocentrism and on Galileo's works themselves. In fact, during Lambertini's papacy, Galileo's *Dialogue Concerning the Two Chief World Systems*, the book that got Galileo into trouble, was republished for the first time. It included an explanatory essay (not by Benedict) arguing the Bible should not be regarded as a scientific authority, a point Galileo himself—and d'Alembert!—had made.[197]

Besides the influence of Bologna and Galilean Catholicism, Lambertini's "Catholic empiricism" also derived inspiration from Isaac Newton's ideas. Lambertini owned all his books. The profound influence of the Englishman's *Principia mathematica* (1687) impressed upon all Europe the power of the scientific method to discover the truths of the world. In fact, Lambertini's friends, such as Francesco Bianchini (1662–1729), the city's leading astronomical authority, first introduced Newton's work into Rome. On a mission from Rome, Bianchini visited Newton in 1713 and became a fellow of the Royal Society of London.

[197] Maurice A. Finocchiaro, *Retrying Galileo, 1633–1992* (Berkeley: University of California Press, 2005), 120, 123–125. After a thirteen-year investigation into the Galileo case inaugurated by the Pontifical Academy of Sciences, Pope John Paul II noted the following: "Thus the new science, with its methods and the freedom of research that they implied, obliged theologians to examine their own criteria of scriptural interpretation. Most of them did not know how to do so. Paradoxically, Galileo, a sincere believer, showed himself to be more perceptive in this regard than the theologians who opposed him." Therefore, the rise of modern science required all other disciplines to define more clearly "their own field, their approach, their methods." See Pope John Paul II, "Lessons of the Galileo Case," *Origins* 22, no. 22 (November 12, 1992): 372.

Finally, Lambertini's sympathies for science were deepened by his regular contact with physicians such as Giovanni Maria Lancisi (1654–1720) in Rome during the early 1700s. He worked together with Lancisi in many canonization proceedings for which Lambertini acted as promoter of the faith, or devil's advocate (1708–1728)—the one who argued against the canonization of a candidate by trying to uncover character flaws or misrepresentations of evidence about the life of the candidate. They were friends. Lambertini often deferred to Lancisi's opinion about whether a healing was miraculous. Lancisi was a learned and generous man, eager to help others. Lambertini quoted him perhaps more than any other medical authority in his treatise on saints (discussed below).

Lancisi practiced anatomy in Rome, trying to link symptoms and diagnosis to anatomical causes, and then to treatment. He recognized that mosquito-infested swamps bred malaria and recommended draining them, published on cardiovascular disease, and wrote the 1707 book *On Sudden Deaths*, reprinted four times in the early eighteenth century.

Pope Clement XI, who reigned from 1700 to 1721, commanded Lancisi write the latter book due to an unusual number of sudden deaths around the city of Rome. These deaths created a small scientific and religious crisis: What caused them? And what could be done to extend life long enough for the administration of the sacraments? Propelled by both scientific and religious motives, the resulting book *On Sudden Deaths* treated the subject in terms of the mechanical paradigm. It studied clinical signs for sudden death by correlating anatomy and pathology through systematically collecting observations. Lancisi explained what seemed to many an extraordinary event—sudden death—in terms of natural facts (what we would call brain aneurisms or heart attacks).

On Sudden Deaths was a manifesto to mechanical philosophy—one of the most accomplished of the time in Europe—openly inspired by Galileo, Descartes, and Malpighi (in papal Rome!). According to one historian, Lancisi largely abandoned classical medicine in his clinical stance and set aside Aristotelian natural philosophy in favor of empirical principles. He mentioned the soul only briefly and then as being inconsistent with a physician's research field. Lancisi sought only to explain the material causes of these events.[198] As physician for three popes, Lancisi enjoyed papal protection.

He secured analytical freedom by distinguishing the boundaries of his field — what it could and could not do. He did not pretend medicine possessed answers to all questions. He avoided philosophizing about the general nature of things. He sought to cure and give counsel — a practical aim. In the conclusion of one historian, Lancisi's book helped establish new boundaries between theology and science — boundaries implicitly acknowledged by Lancisi's papal supporters — in order to introduce modern medicine to Rome.[199] Engagement with contemporary scientific thought profoundly influenced Lambertini's patronage of saints, history, museums, research institutions, and anatomy.

The Science of the Saints

Christianity is a religion of empirical facts. Christians believe that Jesus Christ lived, died, and rose again. They believe he sees God and teaches us what he sees. That is how faith was first generated among his Apostles, first through seeing him and touching him. As described in chapter 1, later generations of Christians can also "see" Jesus in their own lives and through the heroic charity and suffering of witnesses, especially the saints. They depend on the "science of the saints," as Joseph Ratzinger wrote, on what the saints (canonized or not) have touched, heard, and seen. Faith is not the kind of knowledge that is a private achievement. It is a gift and a participation in a community. This is where the logic of faith unfolds, Ratzinger noted, which is why "faith is necessarily an

---

[198] Maria Pia Donato, "The Mechanical Medicine of a Pious Man of Science: G. M. Lancisi's *De subitaneis mortibus* (1707)," in *Conflicting Duties: Science, Medicine and Religion in Rome, 1550–1750*, ed. Maria Pia Donato and Jill Kraye (London: Warburg Institute, 2009), 321, 322.

[199] Ibid., 345.

ecclesial act." Faith has the character of "non-autonomous knowledge," he wrote, *contra* Rousseau, who rejected all mediation and sharing in the religious knowledge of others. Rousseau thought of himself as a religious individualist. However, faith—even natural faith in the scientific findings of other experts—involves a factor of mutual trust "whereby the knowledge of the other becomes my own knowledge," Ratzinger commented. Throughout our lives, this knowledge of faith is verified by my eyes, my mind, and the interior expectation of my heart. Ultimately, however, knowledge of God through Jesus is based on reciprocity with others; hence, it is a powerful basis for community.[200]

How do we know someone else has seen God? Conflictual Enlighteners denied the possibility. "Who are those who have seen God?" the atheist Baron d'Holbach asked in 1772. "They are either fanatics or rogues, or ambitious men, whom we cannot readily believe upon their word."[201] Possibly. Hence the need to *test* the words, heroic virtues, and supposed miracles of those popularly believed to have "seen" God—particularly candidates for sainthood.

In the canonization process, the Church does not "make" saints; rather, she recognizes sanctity through a process that takes years. A scholarly biography must be prepared with much documentation establishing the candidate's existence and heroic virtue. After that, miracles attributed to the person's intercession before God are normally required to recognize that person as a saint.

Did someone really live a virtuous life? For Rousseau, virtue involved sincere intentions and "authentic emotions." These are basically untestable, because they are internal. Virtue in the classical and Christian traditions, however, is the habit of choosing the good and of mastering

---

[200] Ratzinger, *Christianity and the Crisis of Cultures*, 101, 110, 114, 115. See Rousseau's "Profession of Faith of the Savoyard Vicar" in bk. 4 of his *Emile*.

[201] Baron d'Holbach, *Common Sense, or Natural Ideas Opposed to Supernatural* (1772), in *The Portable Enlightenment Reader*, ed. Isaac Kramnick (New York: Penguin Books, 1995), 146.

one's passions. It is something observable through external works and facts open to public viewing. Thus, the historical lives, deathbed scenes, and later veneration of candidates for sainthood hold great importance for deriving proofs—through public testimony—of virtue and miracles needed to verify sanctity.[202]

Did miracles really occur due to that person's intercession? After all, sometimes credulous Catholics appealed to highly suspect "miracles" to support their religious views and political agendas—as famously happened at the tomb of a Jansenist ascetic in Paris around 1730, much to the scandal of Voltaire and Hume. What is a fake miracle, and what is a real one?

As devil's advocate in Rome, Lambertini was to find reasons *not* to consider someone a saint. He and his team utilized methodical doubt, careful research into documents, testimonies, and records of experiments testing natural causality in medical conditions. These methods existed in the canonization process before Lambertini, but he drew them together and rationalized the process to a much higher degree in his work *On the Beatification and Canonization of Saints*, published between 1734 and 1738 before he became pope.

This text invited the Enlightenment spirit into one of the most intimate areas of Catholic life. The result was perhaps Lambertini's greatest contribution to the Catholic Enlightenment and to modern Catholicism. In 2006, Pope Benedict XVI recognized his predecessor and namesake as "the master" of the causes of saints.[203]

The treatise *On the Beatification and Canonization of Saints* addressed two major problems of the age: credulity and doubt. Catholic credulity too easily believed in miracles. They might see something unusual and allow their fantasy to carry them away either in false fear or in false belief.

---

[202] Pope Benedict XIV, *Heroic Virtue: A Portion of the Treatise of Benedict XIV on the Beatification and Canonization of the Servants of God*, vol. 2, 346–348.

[203] Pope Benedict XVI, Letter to the Participants of the Plenary Session of the Congregation for the Causes of Saints (April 24, 2006).

For example, in his treatise, Lambertini explained the automatic movements of corpses in natural terms that crowds might otherwise interpret spiritually—either diabolical or heavenly. "Around a corpse, many things may be observed that create not only the suspicion of a miracle, but certitude in the ignorant rabble," he wrote. In fact, corpses sometimes move naturally and remain warm for a long time after death. "These movements," he observed with scientific detachment and anatomical precision, are "but certain clumsy paroxysms brought forth by traces of living breath hiding and flickering among the recesses of the entrails."[204]

Superstitious beliefs generated by ignorance scandalized Protestants and deists. In the Age of Reformations, Protestant leaders had charged that some saints never even existed, and that sensationalism often accompanied claims to miracles. Thus, ever since the Council of Trent, Catholic leaders scrutinized the place of miracles and supernatural gifts in genuine sanctity. In the early 1700s, Catholic Enlighteners such as Lambertini believed the baroque era had given too much free play to visions and mysticism. This led to superstition in the Catholic population. Though the Carmelite nuns of Compiègne regarded the mystic St. Teresa of Avila as a model of sanctity, she and others like her were suspect to Catholic Enlighteners as models of sanctity. Instead, they believed one should focus more on practical charity and verifiable medical miracles, aspects more in line with the age of Enlightenment.

Besides credulity, the other problem Lambertini faced in writing his treatise on saints was doubt about the very possibility of miracles. At the extreme end of this tendency, the skeptical Scottish Enlightener David Hume published his *Enquiry concerning Human Understanding* in 1748. He wrote in section 10 that it is not reasonable to believe in religion unless validated by miracles. However, it is not reasonable to believe in miracles, especially when relying on the testimony of others, he thought.

---

[204] Rebecca Messbarger, "The Art and Science of Human Anatomy in Benedict's Vision of the Enlightenment Church," in Messbarger, Johns, and Gavitt, *Benedict XIV and the Enlightenment*, 107, 109.

(Unsurprisingly, his contemporaries viewed him as an atheist.) Rousseau agreed: "Who will dare to tell me how many eyewitnesses are needed in order to make a miracle worthy of faith?" he wrote in *Emile* (book 4). "If your miracles, which are performed to prove your doctrine, themselves need to be proved, of what use are they?" According to Hume, the testimonial evidence in favor of a miracle is less probable than the remote possibility that a miracle happened. We know for sure that dense objects sink in water, for example; that is a law of nature. Therefore, based on our experience of such laws, reports of someone walking on water are more likely false than true. Miracles break our sound experience of the laws of nature, so we can never really know if a miracle happened. Besides, miracle claims usually come from ignorant and barbarous nations (insinuation: as found in the credulous Catholic world); they are not part of a modern, rational age. That was Hume's view of the matter from Scotland.

Lambertini sympathized with such skepticism even while showing a way around Hume's critique. What if something new occurred, outside one's experience of nature? If one did not remain open to the possibility of mystery, to the experience of *other* people, science itself would cease to develop. Furthermore, who created the laws of nature on which the natural world operates? Lambertini and his colleagues found it unreasonable to exclude almost by definition the possibility that the Author of the laws of nature could choose to suspend those laws when he wills — as a parent who suspends the ordinary rules of the house for a particular child in a particular case. If God could do that, then one, in principle, should remain open to the possibility of miracles.

Lambertini remained open, even while looking for evidence against miracles as devil's advocate. This was necessary to prevent false saints from getting canonized and ending up as poor models for the faithful. The first step was to establish whether unusual events occurred connected to the candidate for sainthood, utilizing public evidence.

Speaking under oath to ecclesiastical authorities, witnesses (clerical, medical, and lay) testified to unusual events in canonization cases. As in a court of law, and especially if testimonies of multiple witnesses converged, there was no reason to doubt they told the truth. No court dismisses eyewitnesses just because they are eyewitnesses, wrote one philosopher, responding to Hume's dismissal of testimonies. The court does not *dismiss* them; it *evaluates* them. The behavior of eyewitnesses had its own laws and regularities allowing a court to assess it.[205] Investigators such as Lambertini verified the facts of the event by evaluating testimony, just as historians and lawyers verify the facts of any past event by comparing documents, detecting bias, and weighing records.

After establishing an unusual event as a matter of fact, the question turned to whether the cause of the event was natural, divine, or demonic. In the testimony-based epistemology at work here, witnesses provided the basis for making inferences from events to causes. So, as one historian of science wrote, the problem was no longer the reality but the *meaning* of the attested facts. Was the divine at work here? Could any hidden natural causes explain the supposed miracle? If so, then one cannot believe a miracle took place. Candidate dismissed. What about the imagination — "psychological processes" in our words today; could these explain a physical healing? Or hysteria? Or melancholy? If so, discount it. Candidate dismissed. Unless a medical cure is empirically verifiable, one cannot judge it a miracle (even if one really did take place).[206]

How does one verify empirically that a medical miracle took place? The first step is to know a lot about medicine. So, the pope assembled a vast medical library (including Jewish and Protestant authors) and maintained contacts with many physicians. In one historian's judgment, "Lambertini's medical erudition, as indicated by the amount and range of his quotations in the treatise, was extraordinary." The present-day atheist historian and hematologist (specialist in blood diseases) Jacalyn

---

[205] Anselm Ramelow, "Not a Miracle: Our Knowledge of God's Signs and Wonders," *Nova et Vetera* 14, no. 2 (2016): 671.

[206] Fernando Vidal, "Miracles, Science, and Testimony in Post-Tridentine Saint-Making," *Science in Context* 20, no. 3 (2007): 481.

Duffin also appreciated Lambertini. Duffin became interested in medical miracles after being asked to testify about a possible miracle in the canonization process for St. Marie Marguerite d'Youville (1701–1771) in the late 1980s. This experience alerted her to the presence of shelves of records about miracles in the Vatican Archive. Investigating them, she discovered Lambertini's work. Impressed at how he utilized medical knowledge in the canonization process, she wrote: "Without being a saint, he can surely be regarded as an honorary 'doctor' of the Church, in the medical, if not the theological, sense of the term."[207]

Lambertini established rules in his treatise for making sound judgments about an unexplained medical cure:

1. The disease must be severe and incurable by human means.
2. The disease must not be in a stage at which it is liable to disappear on its own soon.
3. No medical treatment must have been given; or, it must be certain that the treatment given did not affect the cure.
4. The cure must be instantaneous.
5. The cure must be complete.
6. The cure must be without relapse.[208]

If the cure passes these tests, Lambertini thought, there was a firm basis for declaring that a miracle had occurred. Today, Church leaders and medical experts still use these rules as guides, but they are considered impossible to apply fully.

Lambertini took pride in the strictness of these rules, as recorded by a biographer. One day a Protestant Englishman visited a member of

---

[207] Gianna Pomata, "The Devil's Advocate among the Physicians: What Prospero Lambertini Learned from Medical Sources," in Messbarger, Johns, and Gavitt, *Benedict XIV and the Enlightenment*, 127; Jacalyn Duffin, *Medical Miracles: Doctors, Saints, and Healing in the Modern World* (New York: Oxford University Press, 2009), 33.

[208] Bernard François, Esther M. Sternberg, and Elizabeth Fee, "The Lourdes Medical Cures Revisited," *Journal of the History of Medicine and Allies Sciences* 69, no. 1 (2012): 153.

the Congregation of Rites (where Lambertini worked). The member, who may have been Lambertini himself, showed his guest a dossier of evidence in support of a miracle in a canonization case. The visitor read the documents attentively, Lambertini recorded, and not without pleasure. The Protestant said that the "evidence set forth for believing in these events was remarkable and complete." He continued: "If everything proclaimed by the Church of Rome were as certainly true, and were based on such authentic and well-examined foundations we should see no reason why we should not assent to it all, thus exploding all those jokes and mockeries by which your miracles are called in question." The host replied to him: "But you must know that of all these miracles which seem to you to be so firmly established, not one has been approved by the Sacred Congregation of Rites, since the proofs were rejected as insufficient." Maybe even Hume would have been impressed.[209]

If the Enlightenment affected the way miracles were evaluated in the canonization process, it also influenced the kinds of candidates proposed. They were increasingly known not for their mysticism or feats of mortification but for their useful activities in teaching, nursing, relief for the poor, and plague assistance. This was the case with St. Camillus de Lellis (1550–1614), for example, whom Pope Benedict XIV canonized in 1746 after approving the miracles attributed to de Lellis's intercession. This violent man with a gambling addition eventually became a holy priest who founded a nursing religious order. His followers wore a red cross on their cassocks — the original red cross that has since become associated with charity and service. This canonization revealed the values Benedict wanted to emphasize, and a statue of de Lellis was erected in St. Peter's Basilica. The great 1746 painting by Pierre Subleyras of Camillus rescuing the sick from a flooded Santo Spirito hospital in Rome also emphasized Catholic Enlightenment values. The naturalism of the painting utterly rejected the theatricality

---

[209] Haynes, *Philosopher King*, 32.

St. Camillo de Lellis Saves the Patients at the Ospedale
S. Spirito in Rome during the Tiber River Flood in 1598,
*by Pierre Subleyras. This 1746 painting exemplifies the practical
ideal of sainthood celebrated by the Catholic Enlightenment.*

of the baroque style; here the supernatural was communicated through active charity, instead of angels or the obvious presence of the divine. In this way, the visual culture of the Catholic Enlightenment tended to emphasize religious interiority and the humanity of the saints more than dramatic experiences of the divine.

Museums

Lambertini's empiricism shaped not only the way he approached the canonization process but also his approach to cultural heritage. He built up public museums in Rome that laid the foundations for the modern Vatican Museums. Anyone who has visited them (the fourth most visited art museums in the world today) should thank the empirical impulse of the Catholic Enlightenment. The Vatican Museums trace their roots to the sixteenth century, but it was Catholic Enlightenment popes who transformed them into institutions serving the public good.

Museums arose out of the passion for collecting material things (of nature or of art) characteristic of the Renaissance. As knowledge of the world expanded in the sixteenth century through global exploration and early attempts at archeology,[210] people began to realize that knowledge could no longer be contained in a set of canonical texts. It would also have to be stored as objects—authentic witnesses to the past—in private collections and museums accessible to scholars. Collections were also important status symbols for elites, including churchmen. This new approach to knowledge, arising from engagement with material culture, spurred the rise of modern science, scientific history, and *public* museums. These museums were a sure sign of the Enlightenment era because of their concern to make the new knowledge available to a wider population than merely humanist and clerical elites.

With these ideas in the air, Pope Clement XII (reigned 1730–1740) was concerned about the loss of cultural artifacts from Rome through free-market forces. He decided papal government should purchase artifacts and place them in museums. So he opened the first public art museum in the world in 1734 in the heart of Rome. This would be a place where art could be enjoyed by all with unlimited access. It is now called the Capitoline Museum. This institution created the original idea of the public museum as a site for preserving European culture.

Through novel and innovative museum design, the Capitoline was created specifically for public edification. For the first time, one historian wrote, a major art collection was to be installed in a coherent

---

[210] For example, laborers accidentally rediscovered the Roman Catacombs in 1578. They found graves ornamented with Christian paintings, Greek and Latin inscriptions, and carved sarcophagi. This created a sensation. For the first time, people realized an entire city lay beneath their streets. It was like discovering another world, one connecting them visibly back to the early Church. Alas, much was lost or destroyed because Church leaders did not realize soon enough the importance of what had been found. See James Spencer Northcote, *The Roman Catacombs: A History of the Christian City beneath Pagan Rome* (1877; Manchester, NH: Sophia Institute Press, 2017), 51–52.

architectural space without competing functions. No models existed for such an undertaking.[211]

In turn, Benedict XIV, who followed Clement XII as pope in 1740, built up the Capitoline Museum into the "pride of Rome." He funded it largely through the papal lottery (ancestor to the modern Italian lottery!), which raised some eyebrows. Rome was the undisputed center of art in the eighteenth century, however, and Benedict wanted to keep it that way, especially to make up for the steady decline of papal temporal power.

So Pope Benedict desired to show the papacy as the responsible curator of a shared Western culture and tradition. He assisted in the restoration of the Colosseum, the Pantheon, the Triclinium of Leo III (one of the main halls of the Lateran Palace dating to the ninth century), and several ancient churches in Rome. He donated to the Capitoline artifacts found in papal-sponsored archaeological excavations. He purchased art to donate to the museum, such as the beautiful *Capitoline Venus* from a private family. This sculpture's public display helped form the canon of Western art.[212] As a result, the Capitoline indirectly inspired later public museums in London (1753) and Paris (1793).

Pope Benedict XIV also established the Capitoline Picture Gallery opposite the Capitoline Museum as a place to display great paintings. It was established in 1750 with the purchase of masterpieces by Titian, Caravaggio, and Rubens from private collections. This was perhaps the first public collection of paintings in history.

Underneath the Picture Gallery, Benedict established another cultural institution: the Academy of the Nude. Here, a paid male model posed nude for art students to practice drawing "from nature." Thus, one could both study great works and draw from the three-dimensional human body in the same place — essential training for academic artists well into the following century.

[211] Johns, *The Visual Culture of Catholic Enlightenment*, 140.
[212] Ibid., 160–162.

*The Capitoline Venus, purchased by Pope Benedict XIV
in 1752 and donated to the Capitoline Museum.*

Finally, Pope Benedict XIV established in 1757 the Museo Sacro (Sacred Museum) of Christian art in the Vatican Library. The idea was to display early Christian sculptures, funerary monuments, paintings, pontifical medals, coins, epistles, ivories, and other artifacts from the early Church. These physical objects would not only help artists visualize religious subjects with greater historical accuracy but would also offer empirical proof of the Catholic Church's divine origin. Thus, beside preservation, the Museo Sacro also had an apologetic goal: to help people visualize the truths of the faith and call them to emulate spiritual (not just aesthetic) perfection.

Later, Pope Clement XIII (reigned 1758–1769), separating pagan objects from Christian ones, created a Museo Profano (Profane Museum) at the other end of the Vatican library. It opened to the public in 1767. The Museo Sacro and the Museo Profano laid the basis for the Vatican Museums and amplified a revolution in how the public viewed art reaching back to the Renaissance. The museums separated the sacred from the *profane*, meaning "the worldly" or "the secular." The significance of this becomes clear when considering that the Museo Profano brought the nude idols of Greek religion *inside the Vatican*, dividing their religious meaning from their aesthetic qualities. One could view Greek religious sculpture—and even Christian religious painting—not necessarily as "idol" or "religious art" but as "fine art." This aestheticization represented a kind of secularization that reconceived religion categorically in a distinctly modern way, for better and for worse. The best religious art would migrate from sacred contexts to secular ones, such as museums. In 1815, after the return of art looted from Roman churches by Napoleon's troops, Pope Pius VII placed the stolen objects *not* back in churches, but in a museum gallery in the Vatican. They had now become "art." This change explains why the Western world was horrified when the Taliban destroyed the ancient Buddha statues of Bamyan in Afghanistan in 2001 because they were "idols," unable to distinguish between their religious and their artistic identities.[213]

The Academy of Sciences in Bologna

Besides canonization procedures and museums, Pope Benedict's empirically fueled cultural-engagement strategy included investing heavily in his native city of Bologna. In fact, unusually, he even retained his position as archbishop of the city after his election to the papacy. He probably did

[213] Ibid., 196; Louis A. Ruprecht, *Winckelmann and the Vatican's First Profane Museum* (New York: Palgrave Macmillan, 2011), 17. Pope Clement XIII's *motu proprio* of August 4, 1761, announced the creation of a "Museo Profano" inside the Vatican "entirely separate" from the Museo Sacro. See Ruprecht, *Winckelmann and the Vatican's First Profane Museum*, 149. This was, it seems, a significant moment in the Vatican's adjustment to modernity as public perception began to distinguish religion from other areas of life.

this to help bring to completion the renovation of Bologna's cathedral. Also, inspired by the great Charles Borromeo (archbishop of Milan) and his Tridentine zeal, Pope Benedict believed in the importance of bishops as mediators between faith and culture and as cornerstones of Catholic engagement with the modern world. In his capacity as bishop of Bologna and bishop of Rome, he sought to showcase Bologna as a center of modern inquiry and progress.

He did this by supporting its Academy of Sciences, creating an anatomy museum, and sponsoring learned women. The local university had declined in prestige during the late 1600s due to excessively theoretical teaching and inadequate practical training. So the Academy of Sciences was founded with considerable papal support in 1714. Its mission was to provide practical scientific education through observation, experiment, and research. In his treatise on canonization, Benedict alluded to the importance of the Academy in his own scientific education. His efforts to strengthen practical and empirical training revitalized Bologna as a major site of learning and culture known throughout Europe.

The Academy of Sciences occupied one of the finest palaces of the city. Pope Benedict donated twenty thousand books and manuscripts, telescopes, microscopes, maps, surgical tools, and various archaeological finds and natural-history specimens. He recruited renowned and well-paid professors in both the sciences and the arts—including painting and sculpture. Benedict believed in promoting the best intellectual and administrative talent available. Since Bolognese intellectual life characteristically related art and science to each other, the Academy of Sciences was supposed to be an "encyclopedia of the senses," as one visitor of the time called it. Another observer in 1758, the year of Benedict's death, judged it superior to all previous public foundations, ancient or modern. A third called it "the most remarkable thing in Bologna and indeed all of Italy regarding the sciences."[214]

---

[214] Jeffrey Collins, "Pedagogy in Plaster: Ercole Lelli and Benedict XIV's *Gipsoteca* at Bologna's Instituto delle Scienze e delle Arti," in Messbarger, Johns, and Gavitt, *Benedict XIV and the Enlightenment*, 393.

The design of the Academy of Sciences purposely located observatory, laboratories, libraries, art studios, museum galleries, and workspaces near one another to encourage discussion and exchange of ideas among scholars and researchers. The place brought together an assemblage of learned people, "zealous for their own sciences, and rivals of each other," to apply John Henry Newman's later words in *The Idea of a University* (discourse 5). By providing familiar intercourse with one another, and for the sake of intellectual peace, the layout of this Bolognese institution encouraged its scholars "to adjust together the claims and relations of their respective subjects of investigation" — to borrow more words from Newman. They learned to respect, to consult, to aid one another. "Thus is created" Newman wrote, "a pure and clear atmosphere of thought."

Two colorful characters of the Academy of Sciences, Francesco Algarotti (1712–1764) and Laura Bassi (1711–1778), illustrate these kinds of interactions. The many-talented Algarotti performed important experiments at the Academy in 1728, demonstrating the truth of Isaac Newton's optics. These were the most accurate and carefully recorded experiments of their kind performed to date on the Continent. Repeated numerous times, they convinced aristocrats, professors, and churchmen of the truth of Newton's system. Curiously, ecclesiastics were generally more open to Newton than some of the academics in Italian universities who viewed the Englishman's ideas as a threat to their man, Galileo.

The other character was Laura Bassi, the second woman in the world to receive a doctoral degree from a university (in 1732) — the first being Elena Piscopia (in 1678) mentioned in the previous chapter. Bassi moved from her earlier studies of Aristotle and Descartes to — like Algarotti — teaching and propagating Newtonian mechanics. She was one of the most remarkable women of the eighteenth century. Pious Catholic and mother of eight, she was the first woman in history to gain an academic chair in the sciences. Pope Benedict XIV intervened to protect her career from those who wanted to marginalize her. When a priest subtly mocked her in public using a Bible verse seeming to cast doubt on female intelligence, Archbishop Lambertini was so displeased by this misuse of Scripture that he referred to the man as "friar ass." In fact, Lambertini made Bassi part of an elite group of research professors at the Academy of Sciences. Voltaire even wrote to her in 1744: "There is no Bassi in London, and I would be much happier to be added to your Academy of Bologna than to that of the English, even though it has produced a Newton." Many traveled to Bologna to hear her lecture on physics at her home or watch her perform the annual public anatomy, described at the beginning of this chapter. In fact, one historian commented that few in the eighteenth century, except Newton and Voltaire, "enjoyed an equivalent degree of institutional recognition and public acclaim" as Bassi enjoyed. Three of her children pursued religious vocations, and Bassi taught young men preparing to enter religious orders, making faith and reason the foundation of her pedagogy. The pope saw in her, as he did in Agnesi, a way to advertise the new scientific learning that he believed could help revitalize the Catholic world.[215]

When the Newtonian experimenter Algarotti published his best-selling *Newtonianism for Ladies* (1737), he took Bassi for his inspiration. She likely would not have approved of the book, however. Algarotti had left Bologna for the Parisian salons and eventually ended up with Voltaire and his lover Emilie du Châtelet at their summer residence, reading parts of his manuscript to them aloud. He interpreted his Newtonian experiments as support for a subversive, libertine, and materialist philosophy of life. Ignoring the boundaries and limitations of different fields of knowledge, he indiscreetly applied empirical methods to metaphysics, morals, and politics. Thus, his was the only popularization of Newtonian physics to end up on the Index of Prohibited Books.

The Art and Science of Anatomy

At the very heart of Bologna's Academy of Sciences, Pope Benedict XIV established the first museum of anatomy in all the land. He commissioned

---

[215] Paula Findlen, "Science as a Career in Enlightenment Italy: The Strategies of Laura Bassi," *Isis* 84, no. 3 (1993): 441–442, 468.

the sculpting of eight life-size representations of the human body in colored wax. They showed the complete muscular and skeletal structures of the body in graphic high-resolution, so to speak. They were made based on body parts from dozens of cadavers through the efforts of master artist and anatomist Ercole Lelli (1702–1766). This took twenty years and no small expense. The resulting Camera della Notomia ("anatomy room") as a museum of anatomy signaled the resurgence of Bologna as a center of modern medicine and alliance between faith and empirical science sponsored by the Catholic Church.

The eight sculptures on display began with a male and female nude to illustrate "not only the symmetry but … the diverse sites and regions of the human body." The middle four figures revealed the layers of muscle and connecting tissue beneath the skin, and the last two, male and female skeletons, demonstrated "the difference that passes between the two sexes, even in the figure and disposition of various bones."[216]

The pope desired to portray sexual difference through his anatomy museum. Side-by-side anatomized bodies would allow for systematic comparison, broadening the "Science of Man" popular during the 1700s to include the "Science of Woman." Anatomical sex differences underlay the debates on the "woman question" in which Maria Agnesi participated. People were very interested in women's essential physical and mental composition. The pope wished to support the most cutting-edge science to provide context for these debates. In fact, the anatomy of sexual differences and his promotion of female scientists would foster international interest in his museum and the whole Academy of Sciences.

Interestingly, Pope Benedict did not primarily intend the anatomy museum to have a scientific purpose. The sculptures would not be used to train medical students. Authentic medical training, the pope insisted, required the dissection of real human bodies by experts in anatomy and renowned surgeons with "suitable instruments in the designated

[216] Messbarger, *The Lady Anatomist*, 38.

laboratories of the public hospitals," he wrote in 1747.[217] Rather, the pope intended to provide scientifically accurate models for artists and to enlighten the general public about the sacred dignity of male and female anatomy.

The eight sculptures displayed the mechanics of the human body within the context of a sacred narrative. The first two represented Adam and Eve in idealized neoclassical poses. The man looks imploringly up at the heavens, while the woman gazes down in shame, her long hair covering one breast. The figures represented not only the anatomy of the physical body but also — through their visible inner turmoil — the damage to the human being caused by the Fall. The last two skeletons in the series — again, male and female — hold scythe and a sickle, symbols of death. Mortality would ever after separate souls from bodies. Retributive justice upon the sinners is thereby rendered, as it was for the criminals in the Carnival Dissection. This was the anatomy of original sin — *contra* Rousseau, who hated the idea of original sin as much as he hated public anatomy. "What a dreadful apparatus is an anatomical room," Rousseau wrote. He preferred "glittering flowers" and "cooling shades, streams, groves" — his dreamworld — to the facts of life and death. By contrast, in Pope Benedict XIV's Enlightenment-era museum, faith and facts aligned. The spectacular result attracted tourists from all over Europe when the museum opened in 1752, just as the pope had hoped.[218]

The Lady Anatomist

Besides the museum of anatomy, the pope supported scientific anatomy, too, by forwarding the career of expert anatomist and artist Anna Morandi (1714–1774). Her husband had worked as chief assistant on the

---

[217] Ibid., 39.

[218] Jean-Jacques Rousseau, *The Confessions of J. J. Rousseau: With the Reveries of the Solitary Walker*, vol. 2 (London: J. Bew, 1783), Seventh Walk, 251; Messbarger, *The Lady Anatomist*, 40, 42, 46, 50–51.

museum of anatomy project but left after a disagreement with the director. Together, he and Anna set up their own anatomical sculpture studio in their home. Besides raising multiple children, they dissected more than one thousand bodies there in order to create wax models of parts of the body—from hands to the muscles of the eye and male genitals—for medical professionals, learned amateurs, science academies, and royal courts across Europe. They created models of the sensory organs for the Royal Society of London, the female reproductive system and pregnant uterus for Bologna's first school and museum of obstetrics, and anatomical models for Bologna's first chair of surgery appointed by Pope Benedict XIV. Experts and visitors frequently commented on Morandi's expert anatomical knowledge and the accuracy and lifelike qualities of her durable wax models.

This was art in the service of science, rather than the museum of anatomy's science in the service of art. Crowds gathered in their home while Anna (not her husband) presented the human body to them—in parts, especially the anatomy of sense perception, a topic of great interest to Enlightenment empiricists. Her records suggest that she interpreted human anatomy not so much in relation to God as in relation to the natural and purposeful design of the body toward the performance of its functions. She focused on natural causality alone. This implied no atheism—merely that she specialized in empirical study.

After Anna's husband died, she continued on alone, struggling financially yet resolving to distinguish herself in her field. Some actively opposed her in this. She was a menace to their own careers; her innately "inferior" female body and "immodest" interest in reproductive systems diminished her authority, they believed. Others defended Morandi. One observer argued that her femininity gave her certain *advantages* over male anatomists due to her maternity: "Through birthing her offspring and anatomizing cadavers, she achieves in both her synthetic and her analytic method a great understanding of the human species." The Lady Anatomist took bodies apart through dissection (a kind of analysis) and put them back together again (synthesis) not only through her art of wax modeling but also through pregnancy and childbirth. Her maternity gave her an unparalleled knowledge of the human body.[219]

Invitations came to her from around Europe to relocate her practice, but she did not want to leave Bologna. Pope Benedict XIV intervened with the civil authorities there to grant her a lifetime annual salary, which made it possible for her to stay. She was granted the title professor of anatomy by the Academy of Sciences.

Interestingly, Morandi created a bust of herself in wax, adorned in lavish feminine dress, dissecting a human brain (hair still attached to the scalp), the organ of the rational soul. One historian remarked, "The seat of knowledge that lies quite literally in her feminine grasp is a clear provocation to those who would doubt women's intellectual authority." Enlightenment thinkers from Descartes to William Harvey and John Locke increasingly viewed this organ as the physical location of the self. Harvey's discovery of the circulation of blood seemed to reduce the "heart" to a mere pump and to break its link to the soul. Enlightenment thinkers, therefore, tended to see the brain as the foundation even of emotions and will. Lambertini described the brain as the "most secure seat and domicile of the soul." Since he favored modern scientific explanations of the human body, this was one reason he rendered a negative judgment for the Congregation of Rites in 1727 on devotion to the Sacred Heart of Jesus, a relatively recent phenomenon rising in France. He thought it represented poor anatomical understanding of the body; the human heart is just a pump and not the seat of the person. Though it is unknown if Lambertini would have supported any "Sacred Brain of Jesus" devotion, his concern for a proper physiology of emotions backed up his Catholic Enlightenment suspicion of the kind of enthusiastic devotion practiced by Sacred Heart proselytes. Curiously, Morandi sculpted her husband's bust to show *him* dissecting a human heart—a subversion of the usual dichotomy of the day associating reason with men and emotion with women.[220]

---

[219] Messbarger, *The Lady Anatomist*, 94–95.
[220] Ibid., 101, 107.

Self-Portrait, *by Anna Morandi (wax, 1770s).*

Little evidence exists about Morandi's personal life. However, an art restorer found in 1999 a document tucked inside Morandi's self-portrait bust. It was a receipt showing Morandi's membership in a Catholic confraternity connected to the hospital in Bologna. This was possibly a subtle testimony to the religious faith at the center of her science.[221]

Morandi's work drew people from all over Europe to Bologna. Even the Holy Roman Emperor Joseph II, on his grand tour of Italy, stopped to talk extensively with her in 1769. The emperor toured the public-anatomy theater, too, and then the museum of anatomy established by Benedict. By that time, the museum also included an obstetrics collection of nearly two hundred models of the female reproductive system and the

---

[221] Rebecca Messbarger, "Faith, Science and the Modern Body: Anna Morandi's Studies of Human Anatomy in Wax," in Lehner, *Women, Enlightenment and Catholicism*, 110.

pregnant womb. The pope had ordered their inclusion for the instruction of surgeons and midwives. The emperor was so inspired that he eventually established the Josephinum surgical college in Vienna to train military doctors in anatomy and obstetrics by means of more than one thousand wax models. The pope's museum was also the chief inspiration behind Florence's new Museum of Physics and Natural History. All of this began in Benedict's Bologna, and Morandi played an important role.

Morandi's empirical study of anatomy, elbow deep in human cadavers, differed greatly from Maria Agnesi's (less messy!) rationalist methods of mathematics. Yet in that very difference, Morandi and Agnesi represented the two major philosophical traditions of rationalism (Descartes) and empiricism (Galileo, Newton) fueling the Enlightenment. Pope Benedict hoped to bring these strands of thought and practice together in Bologna as the ultimate site of the Catholic Enlightenment. Would Maria Agnesi of Milan accept the pope's invitation to go there? Would she join the first group of women in the world to hold high academic recognition?

8

The End of an Age

Making Decisions

For a long time after her death, historians and biographers looking back at Maria Agnesi's life failed to understand her decision. She was rich, well-educated, and well-connected. She starred in her father's central strategy for advancing the family and gaining acceptance with high society in Milan. Yet as she matured, she experienced discomfort at the salon conversations due to internal tensions. Requiring frequent rehearsal and staging, the events "spectacularized" her knowledge for large audiences fascinated by the rare phenomenon of a woman's intellectual power. She was grateful to her father but also weary of display. Publicity conflicted not only with the ideals of feminine modesty and seclusion prevalent during the day but also with her own growing sense of vocation.

Agnesi was not the only woman of the time feeling this inner conflict. Laura Bassi in Bologna did too. As news of her remarkable learning spread, she found herself more and more in demand to host receptions at her home, attend literary gatherings, and appear at Sunday evening academic debates. Bassi hesitated even as she chose to participate in this intense academic and social life. "All the gentlemen of Bologna make a great display of this girl, and depict her everywhere as the miracle of our age," wrote one enthusiast. Meanwhile, gossip circulated about her, an unmarried young woman, meeting with men of science to perform experiments at her home. She struggled to balance the cultural ideal of femininity with manifesting her knowledge publicly—the only way she could gain access to higher studies. She resisted calls for more appearances. Won over by "coaxing and prayers," however, she agreed to a public doctoral thesis defense at age twenty-one. This grand 1732 event — Archbishop Lambertini in attendance — generated so much interest, overflowing audiences fought among themselves for a place. Bassi won her degree. Civic and religious authorities saw supporting her career as promotion for their city. Their strategy worked: Bassi achieved European-wide renown, and foreign travelers put Bologna on their itinerary. Like Agnesi's father, however, they did not expect the young woman to have a will of her own.[222]

But she did. Bassi chose to marry, raise a family of eight children, *and* pursue her scientific career — an unheard of and shocking vocational decision. If a woman was to be learned, then she should at least join a convent or remain a virgin, most thought. Not Bassi. She explained in a letter, "I have chosen a [husband] who walks my path in the arts and who, through long experience, I was certain would not impede me from following mine." She saw marriage not simply oriented toward children or forming family alliances but also as the context in which she would *live vocationally* in a broad sense.

While Bassi was by far the more famous of the couple, husband and wife respected each other's gifts. By forming the habit of working together, they created one of the greatest scientific partnerships of the eighteenth century. In some areas, she held back in order to let him shine. Their marriage revealed an equality and reciprocity almost inconceivable in the day, especially among elites. "Remember ... the love I feel for my Children and to Yourself, who are the greatest wealth I possess on this Earth," her husband wrote to Bassi in 1746 when away on travels. She

---

[222] Findlen, "Science as a Career," 451; Marta Cavazza, "Between Modesty and Spectacle: Women and Science in Eighteenth-Century Italy," in *Italy's Eighteenth Century: Gender and Culture in the Age of the Grand Tour*, ed. Paula Findlen, Wendy Wassyng Roworth, and Catherine M. Sama (Stanford: Stanford University Press, 2009), 299.

arranged to teach university students in her home, which was conducive to her motherly duties. This domestic academy also freed her from the traditional Aristotelian curriculum at the university to pursue a more modern empirical curriculum of experiments in physics and electricity.[223]

Bassi refused to serve *only* as a civic ornament, as some would have preferred. She forged her own identity not by rejecting faith, marriage, or the institutional structures around her, but by embracing them. She worked within them patiently and gained immensely by giving and receiving. As she acceded to the needs and demands of her family, patrons, and supporters, she found herself in a position of strength, one historian noted. She could expect some degree of reciprocation. As her circle of patrons grew, Lambertini among them, they gave concessions to her requests for more responsibilities at the university and at the Academy of Sciences, as well as for more money to buy expensive scientific equipment.[224] As a result of her highly successful academic strategy, she became the first woman in history granted an academic chair in science. She even ended up with a higher salary than her male colleagues! At her burial in 1778, the same year Rousseau and Voltaire died, mourners filled the church of Corpus Domini in Bologna as for a beloved saint. Bolognese remembered her, one historian wrote, "as a woman [for whom] learning and fame never came at the expense of her devotion to family, personal modesty and willingness to perform acts of Christian charity." She was an enlightened Catholic who saw no conflict between faith and reason.[225]

---

[223] Gabriella Berti Logan, "The Desire to Contribute: An Eighteenth-Century Italian Woman of Science," *American Historical Review* 99, no. 3 (June 1994): 795; Marta Cavazza, "Laura Bassi and Giuseppe Veratti: An Electric Couple during the Enlightenment," *Contributions to Science* 5, no. 1 (2009): 117. The other great couple of the eighteenth century was John and Abigail Adams in the United States; their incomparable correspondence is a delight to read.

[224] Findlen, "Science as a Career in Enlightenment Italy," 457.

[225] Paula Findlen, "The Scientist and the Saint: Laura Bassi's Enlightened Catholicism," in Lehner, *Women, Enlightenment and Catholicism*, 114.

In contrast with Bassi's vocational choice, Agnesi suddenly announced during a public performance in 1739 her desire to become a nun. This fell like a lightning strike on her father. He entered into long discussions with her and proved remarkably understanding for a father of that time. Like Bassi, Agnesi did not view herself as an autonomous individual in rebellion with all authority around her. She respected her father by negotiating with him, even as she respected herself. Interestingly, she never became a nun. She may have used this "threat" merely to secure a different way of life from that which her father had planned. Regardless, historians have erroneously reported ever since how Agnesi experienced some kind of religious crisis, rejected mathematics, and became a nun. They have seen her as a "psychological enigma," split between reason (her young life) and faith (her later life). None of this bifocal image is true. It overlooks her deep piety, theological interests, and practical charity for others, present since her youth. It also fails to take seriously the creative tension at the center of her world between tradition and innovation, faith and reason. She made a lay vocational choice in deep continuity with her whole life.[226]

Agnesi and her father arrived at the following agreement by 1740: (1) she could dress simply, (2) she could visit Milan's churches whenever she wished, (3) she did not have to attend balls, theaters, and other worldly amusements, and (4) she could work as a volunteer at the Ospedale Maggiore (Major Hospital) of Milan, one of the oldest in Italy (founded 1456), to care for poor and infirm women. In return, she agreed to occasionally participate in her father's salon conversations. She promised to continue her studies and writing, although she would drop empirical science to concentrate on mathematics.

Thus, Maria Agnesi resolved to remain an unmarried laywoman. She embraced the Catholic Enlightenment culture of Milan and the new opportunities it opened for the pursuit of lay and active holiness for women. By separating herself from worldly amusements, she believed she

---

[226] Mazzotti, "Maria Gaetana Agnesi," 292–294.

could engage the world in a more meaningful way. So, at the prompting of her vocation, she decided not to go to Bologna, sacrificing any future academic honors she might have received there alongside Bassi, Morandi, and others.

Deeply moved by the poverty, illness, and prostitution she witnessed daily on the streets of Milan, Agnesi devoted her life to service and — while her father lived — to scholarship. On an average day, she attended Mass accompanied by a servant. She then met her spiritual adviser. Twice a week she confessed and received Communion. When not at work in her study, she spent much of the rest of her day at the hospital and paying visits to the sick who lived in the poor areas of her parish. For those needing a place to stay, she opened a few secluded rooms in her family palace. As more and more women moved in, her father limited their number and insisted she pay more attention to her appearance.

Agnesi upheld her side of the compromise deal with her father. A painting of her in 1748 (see page 139) shows a beautiful woman with pearl earrings and fur-lined dress, but also an unusually simple and practical hairstyle for a Milanese lady of the time. She continued to attend her father's salon conversations. Those who knew her, one historian wrote, were amazed at how she could effortlessly switch roles from hospital volunteer to academic debater, like a superhero changing costumes. She transformed herself just by passing through the door into the magnificent salon, leaving aside the humble work of the hospital to take up intricate questions, answers, and scientific riddles with grace. The number of her admirers only grew, and her withdrawal from the world and from celebrity only sealed her lasting fame.[227]

Agnesi and Bassi lived between two spiritual poles: affirming the goodness of human life and working to improve it, as did their enlightened contemporaries, and at the same time believing that human life and intellectual activity reached their fulfillment only in what is above and beyond them. They engaged the world and at the same time disconnected

[227] Mazzotti, *The World of Maria Gaetana Agnesi*, 78.

from it in order to attach themselves to their highest end: union with God. The tension found in their lives between fame and modesty, study and vocation, detachment from the world and engagement with the world defined the internal dynamic of the Catholic Enlightenment. They chose both-and, not either-or.

The Benedictines

This dynamic "in the world but not of the world" of the Catholic Enlightenment can be more fully understood by examining the Benedictines. This was probably the most important religious order for the Catholic Enlightenment. An ancient Roman with organizational genius — Benedict of Nursia — established the Benedictines in the 500s as the original institutional form of monastic life in the West. By their lives of prayer, manual work, and study, Benedict's followers have witnessed to the light of Christ for centuries. They also helped preserve the wisdom of both Jerusalem and Athens as foundations of Western civilization. Accordingly, Benedict is recognized as a patron saint of Europe.

The followers of St. Benedict thought of their monasteries as schools "for the service of the Lord," according to the Rule. Their whole existence was organized according to that principle — not the principle of "engaging culture." Yet in the eighteenth century, as at other times, they did engage culture through research, publishing, teaching, building, and communicating. This yielded impressive results. Ideally, all their activities — including study — proceeded from a spiritual motivation and detachment. As one Benedictine author expressed it: "studies undertaken, and then, not precisely scorned, but renounced and transcended, for the sake of the kingdom of God" is typical of the monks. Indeed, and not just for monks. Christians are meant to see their highest allegiance to God, who is divine reason, over their own, small minds. *Studies renounced* — as Agnesi renounced a promising academic career to turn her mind and energy in a different direction, out of faithfulness to vocation. Sadly, failure to pursue God first and enlightenment second would mark the decline of the Catholic Enlightenment and the end of an age. In combination with an earthquake, a famine, and the French Revolution, this failure had shaken Christian culture to its very foundations by the time Agnesi died in 1799.[228]

Why the Benedictines?

What explains the openness of many Benedictines to the Enlightenment? First, historians have studied some of the ways the surrounding atmosphere of the Age of Reason entered monastic enclosure through library acquisitions, personal letters, and visitors. "For the sake of visitors, but also for the sake of Christ, the door must not remain shut," one Benedictine commentator on the Rule wrote. Christ is found inside the monastery but also in those coming to the monastery from the outside. This meant that despite separation from the world, Benedictines remained open to the wider world through service to its needs by their very vocation.[229] They did not automatically take a hostile stance toward Enlightenment influences coming from outside.

Second, decentralized Benedictine organization contrasted with highly centralized orders such as the Jesuits. This was a legacy of the fragmented feudal age when Benedictine monasteries first spread across Europe. Later orders, however, followed patterns of centralization in church and state that appeared in the Middle Ages and the Age of Reformations. The independent governance among Benedictine monasteries allowed each abbot and community to choose whether to engage new ideas or not. Thus, the solution to the problem for monks of *what* to study and *how much* to study was not a simple one determined by a rule for the entire order. Rather, the "solution must be continually rediscovered, re-invented,

---

[228] Jean Leclercq, *The Love of Learning and the Desire for God: A Study of Monastic Culture* (New York: Fordham University Press, 1982), 12.

[229] Aquinata Böckmann, "Openness to the World and Separation from the World according to the *Rule* of Benedict," *American Benedictine Review* 37, no. 3 (1986): 322.

rejuvenated in a living and spontaneous manner, for each period and each milieu, for each monastery, and almost for each monk," wrote one of the great commentators on monastic intellectual life. Ideally, it was determined through personal vocation.[230]

Third, Benedict's Rule was a practical document. Unlike the *Ratio Studiorum* that universally guided Jesuit education according to Aristotle and Aquinas, the Rule did not specify what kind of studies Benedictines should undertake—other than meditative study of Scripture. Perhaps because they lived an integrated and stable way of life in their monasteries, their need for intellectual integration by means of Scholasticism was less. However that may be, a certain flexibility characterized Benedictine intellectual life in contrast to other orders that invested heavily in Scholasticism. Benedictines had thrived, after all, for centuries before Scholasticism ever came on the scene (though Benedictines helped create Scholasticism in the eleventh century).

This deep history gave them a different theological tradition from later orders. Scholastic theology among Jesuits and Dominicans, for example, allied itself with Aristotelian philosophy and sought clarity through logic, abstraction, and speculation. This intellectual tradition possessed many advantages, but it could also close in on itself. The historian Christopher Dawson thought Catholics tended at certain times in their history to favor Scholastic-style theology and philosophy too much. That hurt their engagement with other intellectual traditions and even with their own times. In fact, Dawson commented in a private letter, "The theological-philosophical monopoly in the universities killed medieval culture and led to the Reformation, and the dictatorship of the theologians at the Sorbonne was equally fatal to French Catholic culture in the 18th century."[231]

---

[230] Leclercq, *The Love of Learning*, 22.

[231] Christopher Dawson to John J. Mulloy, March 15, 1955, University of Notre Dame Archives (Christopher Dawson Papers), folder "Dawson: Christian Culture," Letters of Christopher Dawson on Culture Studies and Catholic Higher Education, 3.

Monastic theology among the Benedictines, by contrast, sought to understand the Bible and the Church Fathers through image, comparisons, and facts; it was more literary and historical, holding to multiple ways of saying the same truth. Monastic theology was less technical and tended to employ common vocabulary. The revelation of God came through history (not through metaphysical reasoning), so monastic theology was inherently oriented toward the study of the past.[232]

This created an opening to historical study among Benedictines by the 1680s, when the French monk Jean Mabillon (1632–1707) entered the scene. Through history "we learn to develop prudence by considering past events," Mabillon wrote; "there we see, as in a mirror, the inconstance of human affairs and the marvelous effects of divine providence in the government of the universe and the church's actions."[233] Mabillon is considered the founder of the sciences of paleography (reading histori-cal handwriting) and diplomatics (critical analysis of historical docu-ments) — two pillars of the science of the past that took shape around 1700. He was a founder of scholarly history, and, like the founders of empirical science at around the same time, he took facts seriously.[234]

Against critics at the time who argued that monks should not con-centrate on study, he set an important precedent for monastic research and engagement with modern thought. In pursuit of historical truth, Mabillon's Congregation of St. Maur (a community of monasteries in France formed after the Council of Trent) began one of the greatest col-laborative research projects of all time. The Congregation of St. Maur widened the scope of the typical vow of stability from a single monastery

---

[232] Leclercq, *The Love of Learning and the Desire for God: A Study of Monastic Culture*, 200-201.

[233] Jean Mabillon, *Treatise on Monastic Studies* (1691; Lanham: University Press of America, 2004), 147.

[234] The Jesuits also contributed to scholarly history at this time. The Bol-landists, named after the Flemish Jesuit Jean Bolland (1596–1665), pro-duced the many-volume *Acta Sanctorum* (*The Lives of the Saints*) based on the most reliable sources of information.

to the whole cluster of monasteries, facilitating the exchange of scholars and students. St. Maur organized intensive academic training for many of its monks, effectively replacing Benedictine manual labor with intellectual work. Spanning over a century, these monks worked in teams preparing critical editions of the Church Fathers and medieval writers, lives of the early martyrs, compilations of monastic history, and secular histories. Ironically, Conflictual Enlighteners hostile to Christianity, such as Edward Gibbon, author of *The Decline and Fall of the Roman Empire*, partly relied on Maurist scholarship for their own work. Even Diderot's *Encyclopédie*—often a bastion for Conflictual Enlighteners—utilized the scholarship of the Maurists.

The Maurists established a one-of-a-kind monastic network of international correspondence to exchange information and manuscripts and researchers even beyond their congregation into Central Europe. This network included an interlibrary loan system allowing monks access to the rarest books on the Continent. Their innovative use of communication networks made them more open to interacting with Protestants and Jansenists.

Empirical study of facts propelled new approaches to Church history and Scripture. Rather than accept facts and traditions from the past at face value, one should approach them with a critical eye, these French Benedictine monks believed. This worked a profound change in the Benedictine mind.

This inner revolution raised awareness of *change* within Catholicism. Change—and thus reform for the better—are possible: a key insight of the Enlightenment spirit. "For the first time in history," wrote historian Ulrich Lehner, "the Church became aware of the fact that beliefs and traditions from the past were not static but developed and grew over time."[235] This shocking reality became a cornerstone of modern Catholicism. One could trace a line from Mabillon to John Henry Newman's

---

[235] Ulrich L. Lehner and Michael Printy, eds., *A Companion to the Catholic Enlightenment in Europe* (Leiden: Brill, 2010), 33–34.

understanding of the development of doctrine to the Second Vatican Council's updating of Church practice and expression. Truth, beauty, and goodness transcend time and place, but their comprehension and expression can change. Pope John XXIII (a historian), who called that council, believed strongly—as did the Maurists before him—that the study of history aided renewal in the Church.

Enlightened Benedictines

Mabillon and his like-minded researcher monks marked one of the key moments in the development of the Catholic intellectual tradition. The strong empirical influence on the Benedictines coming through the new historical-critical methods inspired a wave of scholarship across the Catholic world and prepared the way to receive Enlightenment ideas. For example, excited by the new science of the past, Pope Benedict XIV created institutions in Rome tasked with studying ecclesiastical history, ancient pagan history, liturgy, and medieval and early modern history.

Some of the Benedictines thought of themselves as "enlightened" even at the time, and they were viewed so by other Enlighteners outside the faith, including Protestant scholars in Germany. The *Encyclopédie*, the great Enlightenment project edited by Diderot, praised the Benedictines over the Jesuits as "the most enlightened" among religious orders. (To be fair, though, Jesuits did engage Enlightenment thought too, particularly in France.) For most of the eighteenth century, Enlightenment influence on the Benedictines did not seem to correlate with a decline in religious life, as one might wonder, according to recent scholarship.[236]

---

[236] Edme-François Mallet, "Bénédictins," in *Encyclopédie*, https://artflsrv03. uchicago.edu/philologic4/encyclopedie1117/query?report=concordance& method=proxy&attribution=&objecttype=&q=eclaires&start=0&end= 0&head=Benedictins; Ulrich L. Lehner, *Enlightened Monks: The German Benedictines, 1740–1803* (New York: Oxford University Press, 2011), 27; Derek Beales, *Prosperity and Plunder: European Catholic Monasteries in the*

What did Enlightenment influence on a Benedictine monk look like? Besides historical and biblical scholarship, some pursued interests in electricity, scientific experiments, mechanical engineering, and mathematics. In fact, one of the best-known mathematicians and experts in river hydraulics in Italy, the Benedictine Ramiro Rampinelli, tutored Maria Agnesi in Milan. In England, the Benedictine astronomer Charles Walmesley advised the British government on changing from the Julian to the Gregorian calendar (Protestant countries had dragged their feet in admitting the more accurate "Catholic" calendar inaugurated by Pope Gregory XIII in 1582).

In Spain, the Benedictine Benito Feijoo virtually led the Spanish Enlightenment. He and others sought to advance Spanish culture and intellectual life by writing in a popular vernacular style—forged in salon conversations—rather than in Latin. Feijoo may have been the most-read Spanish author of the century.[237] Inspired by Mabillon's *Treatise on Monastic Studies* to pursue independent intellectual work as a monk, Feijoo popularized scientific and empirical thought. One of his purposes was to debunk pseudoscience, superstition, and improper usage of Aristotle. He appreciated Aristotle's philosophy of nature but refuted the Greek thinker as a model for modern empirical research. Like Lambertini in Italy, Feijoo allied himself with physicians who tried to modernize medicine against the dominant Scholasticism in the universities (in which he himself was educated). He drew support from the writings of Lambertini about the need for rational criteria to evaluate miracles. In addition, one must embrace truth, he believed, no matter if it originated in the mind of a Protestant, a Jew, or a woman. Traditional Catholics scorned Feijoo, but

---

Age of Revolution, 1650–1815 (Cambridge: Cambridge University Press, 2003), 2.

[237] Francisco Sánchez-Blanco, "Benito Jerónimo Feijoo y Montenegro (1676–1764): Benedictine and Skeptic Enlightener," in *Enlightenment and Catholicism in Europe: A Transnational History*, ed. Jeffrey D. Burson and Ulrich L. Lehner (Notre Dame: University of Notre Dame Press, 2014), 321.

he believed a proper skepticism would help rather than hinder religion by making both theology and science humbler. One could modernize Spanish culture by limiting the claims of theology over other disciplines. "Secularizing" the study of nature (i.e., understanding it on its own natural terms) did not diminish faith in the transcendent God.

In Salzburg, Austria, the Benedictines administered the university there as a major site of the Catholic Enlightenment. It was the first European university to teach experimental physics as early as the 1740s. At that time, one of Salzburg's students, the Scottish Benedictine monk Andrew Gordon, created the first electric motor (just *before* Benjamin Franklin!).

In southern Germany and Austria, the Benedictine monasteries commanded considerable wealth in support of vast libraries, scholarly networks, and glorious art and architecture in their churches. They had what it took to engage the Enlightenment in a serious way. Some of them were prince-abbacies in which the abbot governed not only the monastery but also a secular territory, like a feudal lord. These monasteries played important roles in their local communities, providing parishes, education, and employment of all kinds. Some monks even worked for the state as government administrators.

One of these great Benedictine monasteries, Kremsmünster Abbey (founded in the 700s), was known in the eighteenth century for its charity to the poor; its vast, ancient library; its road building; and its remarkable observatory, called the "mathematical tower." Completed around 1758, this eight-story building pioneered high-rise architecture to house an impressive natural-history museum. It was an "encyclopedia in stone"[238] with an implicit hierarchy of the sciences in the ascending order of its seven floors, with geology at the base and astronomy at the top. Paleontology,

---

[238] Aidan Bellenger, "'Superstitious Enemies of the Flesh?' The Variety of Benedictine Responses to the Enlightenment," in *Religious Change in Europe, 1650–1914: Essays for John McManners*, ed. Nigel Aston (Oxford: Clarendon Press, 1997), 151.

mineralogy, physics, zoology, and anthropology occupied intermediate floors. There was a chapel at the top, too, in order to contemplate the meaning of it all. An eighteenth-century Benedictine there used the observatory to make one of the first calculations of the orbit of Uranus. The tower also became famous for its weather station (still operating today!).

German-speaking Benedictines engaged Enlightenment culture through interacting with scholars from different religious traditions, contributing to public discourse, visiting salons, joining academies, giving public lectures, starting journals inspired by Catholic Enlightenment ideals, and even attending popular forms of entertainment outside the monastery (such as theaters). They made initial efforts to utilize the new

The Mathematical Tower of Kremsmünster
Abbey in Austria, completed in 1759.

historical-critical method in biblical studies. They encouraged more frequent Bible reading, rethought papal monarchy in favor of a more collegial ecclesiology, started ecumenical efforts with Protestants, and supported liturgical reform involving simplification of worship and more active lay participation. Some even speculated about vernacular liturgies.

The adaptability of Benedictine monastic culture meant that the Enlightenment shaped even daily life. Take coffee, for example — the drink of the Enlightenment. It brought people together and enlivened their minds. Earlier chapters have shown how this imported drink helped create informal conversations in places from Voltaire's Ferney to Pope Benedict XIV's Caffeaus. There was no structure in the monastery, however, to support such free and open discussions. There were chapter meetings, but these were formal gatherings under the control of superiors, Lehner pointed out. Coffee changed this situation. By 1700, there are records of monks meeting illegally and secretly to share the drink. Superiors saw these informal meetings as subversive and as opportunities for monks to complain or possibly engage in homosexual behavior. Some monasteries, however, managed to cultivate a coffee culture among the monks without subversive implications, Lehner wrote. Therefore, by 1750 or so, most monasteries in Germany allowed coffee. Changing patterns of consumption characteristic of the eighteenth century created challenges to which monasteries had to adapt prudently.[239]

Other aspects of daily life changed, too. At the magnificent Austrian abbey of Melk, monks replaced their traditional rectangular tables for round ones. These new tables better facilitated communication and made monks feel more like ordinary people of the time. Even common understandings of what constituted recreation changed. Some monks felt they no longer enjoyed traditional pastimes. They wanted to play billiards (spreading rapidly at the time) and cards, even for money. Some superiors saw such diversions as a deterioration of religious life, and at least once political authorities intervened to prohibit card playing in

---

[239] Lehner, *Enlightened Monks*, 32–33.

monasteries! By the end of the century, monks argued over hairstyles. Some interpreted the traditional tonsure as representative of Christ's crown of thorns. Enlightened monks pointed out that neither the Bible nor the Rule of Benedict required tonsures; they preferred practicality over tradition in this case. The Enlightenment spirit led many to question old forms of obedience and traditional life. This was dynamite in the very heart of their communal lives, which required careful discernment, as Lehner wrote.[240]

Secularized Monks?

Engaging the Enlightenment changed monastic culture. Through the porous walls of their monasteries, new views and practices sprang up among monks connected to time, space, living and traveling outside the monastery, monastic obedience, and sociability. These developments stretched the very meaning of being a monk and raised troubling questions about Christian identity in the Age of Reason.

For example, the amplification of Benedictine historical scholarship inaugurated by Mabillon and the Maurists affected their way of life. Their enormous research projects demanded more time and more resources than traditional historical annals produced in seventeenth-century monasteries. Research methods resembling those of secular historians encouraged monks to bend the age-old monastic daily schedule. Some saw regular communal prayer times and mealtimes as obstacles to their work. Enlightened monks often requested dispensations and adopted a different rhythm of working and praying than the rest of the monastery, wrote Lehner—one more in tune with the times. One risked losing a sense of religious purpose in one's work.[241]

---

[240] Ulrich L. Lehner, *On the Road to Vatican II: German Catholic Enlightenment and Reform of the Church* (Minneapolis: Fortress Press, 2016), 19.
[241] Lehner, *Enlightened Monks*, 30–31.

More individualistic approaches to time combined with more in-dividualistic approaches to space. This included a new, more modern sense of privacy. Enlightened monks started viewing cells not so much as places apart from others, but as private spheres they could potentially invite guests into for conversation—including even women, in some cases. Women played important roles in salon culture, and some monks adapted to new patterns of interaction between the sexes. In addition, enlightened monks might attempt to deny superiors access to their cells, desks, and correspondence. Once, when an abbot seized the diary of a monk, the religious felt so affronted that he threatened to report the incident to the civil government. The abbot apologized, and the monk requested to be treated simply as a reasonable person, not as a child. On the one hand, such cultural individualism fostered more sincere reflection on the need to discern personal vocation; on the other hand, it could lead monks away from readiness to make personal sacrifices for the sake of their community.[242]

Academic monks sometimes worked and traveled outside the monas-tery as professors in regular contact with the world. They could be found at dinners, theaters, or walking the streets in secular clothes (French jackets, silk scarves, and hats rather than their religious habit). "Secular" is here defined as the world outside the monastery, a world Benedictines viewed with detachment but also with concern. Yet this concern and the willingness to engage created a heightened tension between positive and negative charges, so to speak. Scholarly monks, after the pattern of the Maurists, needed to travel in order to consult resources and scholars at other monasteries. They undertook these journeys not simply for copying documents but also for education and building up the scholarly network. Travel came to be important for broadening the minds of teaching monks while on break from their duties. During the eighteenth century, however, these travels in some cases turned more into vacations and increasingly looked like the Grand Tour around Europe enjoyed by the aristocracy.

[242] Ibid., 55, 102.

One monk from Kremsmünster in Austria, for example, the monastery with the "mathematical tower" described earlier, traveled to Italy on legal business in 1765. He went to Bologna and slipped away from his companions to find the famous Laura Bassi—breaking a monastic rule not to associate with women in private. He wrote: "I was immediately asked to come into a very nice parlour with many mathematical instruments." They chatted in Italian, then in Latin. "I had to work really hard to keep up with her speech [in Latin]," he wrote. She "talked so incomparably beautifully and rapidly, nevertheless sublimely, that I have to confess that I have never heard a man talk like her. This much is certain: she outdid all men I met in Italy in Latin."[243]

All this traveling could lead some monks to lose taste for their monastic life, however. After the 1770s, increasing numbers of monks made unauthorized day trips away from their monasteries to visit family, listen to music, dance, play cards, go hunting, or take walks in the forest.

Like all human beings, monks possessed inalienable rights and duties. The Enlightenment culture of the time, however, changed how they viewed them and the abbot's role. "No longer did monks stay unresponsive when faced with injustice," Lehner wrote; "no longer were they willing to endure inhuman humiliations or remain silent if their rights were violated." At one monastery in southern Germany, for example, a monastic rebellion broke out due to the despotic reign of the abbot, who also pursued love affairs with women. Some monks tried to escape; others petitioned the bishop because they mistrusted the visitation system by other abbots. They believed the other abbots conspired to protect each other from charges of corruption. Eventually the bishop acted, and the guilty abbot was politely forced to resign.[244]

By the later 1700s, worries among monks about abuses of their rights prompted them to publish horror stories about monastery conditions. For example, enlightened Benedictine monks published a journal for their

[243] Ibid., 49.
[244] Ibid., 56.

fellow religious called *Benedictine Museum*. Like a museum, they sought to expose things for public viewing—in this case, what they perceived as abuses of authority and inhuman practices such as communal flagellation. They remained anonymous to protect themselves from their superiors. The first line of the first issue in 1790 appealed to the power of public-ity, much as had Voltaire in the Calas affair. It stated: "Publicity is the most efficient way to further the good of humanity, is the guardian of freedom, and the most just and most secure weapon against despotism." The criticism of an external observer helped superiors see what could be the inhumanity of practices such as self-chastisement.[245]

The editors of *Benedictine Museum* believed that the light of reason needed to expose dark practices going on inside some monasteries—such as in monastic prisons. Prisons were places traditionally used for insane or rebellious monks. But abuses of power led some superiors to store troubling people there and neglect true Benedictine discipline that should appeal to the heart. Housed behind a veil of secrecy, these prisons were places set apart from the reach of civil law. (The Conflictual Enlightener Diderot, friend of Rousseau, was imprisoned in a monastery because his father did not want him to marry a lower-class girl. That left a bad taste in his mouth for all things Catholic. Diderot later wrote a novel to expose corruption in Catholic institutions whose plot included sexual abuse in a convent.) During the eighteenth century, enlightened reformers sought to extend the reach of civil law to all corners of society. Thus, state authorities moved to regulate monastic prison usage and even ban prisons. Some monastic prisons were converted into hospitals. This seemed to one monk "a harbin-ger of Enlightenment in our monastery," he recorded. Jean Mabillon, the Benedictine historian, remarked on how strange it was that monks—who should be models of compassion—had to learn from secular magistrates the humanity they ought to practice toward their brothers.[246]

---

[245] Ibid., 94, 98–99.

[246] Ibid., 109; Terrance G. Kardong, "People Storage: Mabillon's Diatribe against Monastic Prisons," *Cistercian Studies Quarterly* 26, no. 1 (1991): 49.

Enlightenment mentalities also affected the ways monks understood their vow of obedience. "The abbot was still God's vicar for his community," Lehner wrote; "however, obedience to him was increasingly challenged, especially when monks felt betrayed, unjustly treated, or even harassed."[247] More and more monks justified their disobedience by reference to their conscience, increasingly informed by Enlightenment ideals of privacy, freedom, and justice. These ideals led some of them to request more participation in monastic governance and in one case, at least, to draft for their abbot a constitution that included the right of each monk to buy the books he wanted!

One final area of monastic cultural change involved the ideal of enlightened sociability. This was previously a vice for monks, yet at Melk in Austria it became a virtue during the 1780s. Conceiving of their monastery as an open community without boundaries, they abolished holy silence during meals to favor small talk and "community." They made friends with noblemen and intellectuals outside the monastery, founded a Masonic lodge, and freely participated in the entertainment culture outside their community. One monastic critic of developments such as these equated the Enlightenment with atheism. He condemned the new spirit in monks who "anxiously desire to educate themselves according to worldly taste." Instead of rejecting the world, he wrote, they kept a part of it in themselves. He believed that such monks sinned against the Holy Spirit and could never be forgiven. Another critic was concerned that some "enlightened" Catholics had sunk into the deepest ignorance: "after all, they believe that in order to be called erudite one has to deny the Gospel or be ashamed of it."[248] Nevertheless, some monasteries successfully adapted to the new communication patterns of the Enlightenment without losing their religious mission because they possessed strong leadership. At Melk, however, without strong leadership and commitment

[247] Lehner, *Enlightened Monks*, 54, 56.
[248] Ibid., 8, 61; Lehner, *The Catholic Enlightenment*, 140.

to prayer, "the study halls were soon filled with chit-chat instead of serious conversation."[249] Without checks and balances from leaders influenced by *other* ideals, Enlightenment ideals undermined themselves.

The great Benedictine Enlightener Beda Mayr (1742–1794), pioneer of ecumenism, never taught his theology students the new ideas. He believed that the Enlightenment seduced young monks to adopt a libertine lifestyle rather than a monastic one, Lehner wrote. If a monk found Enlightenment ideas on his own, this could be a blessing. Mayr did not encourage this, however, for he knew well the dynamics of living in community. The clash of new and traditional ideas could destroy a monastery. "These German Benedictine reforms anticipated so many later changes in religious life that it is hard not to think of the period covered by Lehner's book as a kind of dress rehearsal for the period after Vatican II," wrote a reviewer of Lehner's book *Enlightened Monks*.[250]

Monastic leaders—and individual monks—had to discern how to engage Enlightenment ideas and practices. This is true today too: how much Internet access and smartphone usage, for example, should be allowed in a monastery? In good Benedictine fashion, this varies according to monastery and is regulated by the principle of moderation: some priest monks and professor monks or sisters are required to utilize digital technology for their work and have different schedules than others. Today, as in the past, one must evaluate how cultural contacts affect a Christian community and its individual members. There must be willingness to conflict, on occasion, with those influences by way of spiritual, intellectual, and practical resistance, as did the Carmelites of Compiègne. The firm resolve of the monks in the eighteenth century was sometimes lacking. The spirit of compromise characteristic of Pope Benedict XIV and other Catholic Enlighteners—so fruitful in many areas—could contribute to a spiritual capitulation.

---

[249] Lehner, *Enlightened Monks*, 102.

[250] Lehner, *On the Road to Vatican II*, 89; Lawrence S. Cunningham, review of *Enlightened Monks*, *Commonweal*, March 9, 2012, 27.

Resistance to this outcome was a matter of the will, but also of the intellect. Perhaps as their monastic ways of life changed, there was a corresponding need among enlightened Benedictines for intellectual integration in such a way as Scholasticism offered. Their non-Scholastic tradition proved quite fruitful, as we have seen, but the challenges of the Enlightenment could easily lead to a breakdown in the relationship between faith and reason, the supernatural and the natural.[251] In the case of Andrew Gordon, for example, the Benedictine inventor of the electric motor, the Jesuits attacked his neglect of Scholasticism they held central to defending the faith. He, in turn, attacked their neglect of experimentation and new ideas for understanding nature. Church authorities who intervened in their bitter dispute did not accept the fears of the Jesuits, but they did instruct Gordon to refrain from teaching metaphysics and theology.

The End of the Catholic Enlightenment

We have seen how Catholic Enlighteners differentiated clearly between spiritual and temporal orders. Muratori, for example, distinguished between rational devotion and superstition, Lambertini between the natural

---

[251] An example of this breakdown of faith and reason among the Benedictines was the highly respected biblical scholar Antoine Augustin Calmet (1672–1757). Voltaire greatly appreciated his biblical commentary and visited him at his monastery. Adopting the Enlightenment ideal of "objectivity," however, Calmet viewed the biblical narratives in a rationalist spirit, "finding in them problems, contradictions, anachronisms, and errors that he tried to harmonize with the findings of historical or scientific research," one theologian wrote. Calmet arrived at orthodox theological conclusions, but his reasoning did not support those conclusions. Thus, his work became a goldmine for anti-Christian writers. In fact, ironically, his commentary "has possibly done more for the rise of disbelief than did all of the eighteenth-century anti-Christian literature." See Marius Reiser, "The History of Catholic Exegesis, 1600–1800," in *The Oxford Handbook of Early Modern Theology, 1600–1800*, ed. Ulrich L. Lehner, Richard A. Muller, and A. G. Roeber (New York: Oxford University Press, 2016), 84.

and the supernatural in miracles and saint making, and Agnesi between the mind and the body — giving equal dignity to women's intelligence. We have seen the fruitfulness of these distinctions in the Museo Profano and the Museo Sacro, for example, that formed the beginnings of the Vatican Museums, in the advancement of anatomy and hospital reform, in the career of Anna Morandi, in Church administration, and in serious engagement with historical and scientific study.

Theoretical *distinction*, however, could lead to practical *separation* — especially in matters of religion and politics. In Germany, some Catholic Enlighteners even adopted a kind of "spiritualist ecclesiology," Lehner called it.[252] Since the core mission of the Church was spiritual, this line of thought held, nothing that happens on the material level can endanger her. Spiritualist ecclesiology played into the efforts of local political rulers to involve the state in marriage law, ecclesiastical property, and the temporal goods of the Church — including monasteries. This had negative and positive effects on the Church, but many Catholic Enlighteners outside the Papal States did not notice the negative ones because they increasingly looked to the state, rather than to Rome, for reform of the Church. This aligned them more and more with national patterns of thinking in their respective locales. By the mid-eighteenth century, even many Benedictines came to support the idea of the state over the church. The Cartesian division of spiritual from temporal, in the political realm, increasingly left the Church in Germany powerless before the whim of the state.

External events weakened the Catholic Enlightenment too. In 1755, one of the deadliest earthquakes in history almost destroyed Lisbon, Portugal. It happened while the faithful attended Mass on the feast of All Saints. Churches caved in, killing and injuring thousands of worshippers. The event seemed inexplicable: Why would God let thousands of Catholics die, even in the very midst of their religious duties?

People across Europe interpreted it differently. Many Christians saw it as an instrument of divine justice. But what was the offense? Voltaire

---

[252] Lehner, *Enlightened Monks*, 162.

asked rhetorically. Did the people of Lisbon sin more than those of Paris? For him, the event challenged the idea that God takes care of the world. Unsurprisingly, for his part, Rousseau interpreted the earthquake in his own way: it proved people should move out of cities and live romantic lives in the country. Catholic Enlighteners tended to interpret it as a tragedy resulting from natural causes. But this offered little comfort. The earthquake was a glaring reminder of the problem of suffering. It seemed to upset the idea of the world as a harmonious rational order championed by Enlighteners of all kinds.

In response, the Portuguese king gave his chief minister, Pombal (1699–1782), almost unlimited power in order to rebuild Lisbon. Pombal, a great enemy of the Jesuits, viewed the order as too rich and too politically involved. He resented one Portuguese Jesuit in particular who claimed that the earthquake represented God's punishment on a sinful political regime. This seemed to attack Pombal's policies, so he pressed Pope Benedict XIV to investigate the Portuguese Jesuits. On his deathbed, and pressured by anti-Jesuit cardinals around him, Benedict authorized the investigation. Unsurprisingly, the resulting report calling for reform was really a condemnation of the order. Pombal confiscated Jesuit property and deported or even executed members of the order. The Portuguese government suppressed the Jesuits in 1759.

Anti-Jesuit feeling spread widely. In 1765, France suppressed the order (remember that Father Adam, an unemployed ex-Jesuit, went to live at Ferney with Voltaire). Spain followed in 1767. Catholic countries pressured the pope to issue a general suppression of the order in 1773. Ironically, Protestant Prussia and Orthodox Russia allowed the Jesuits to survive and carry on their much-respected educational work!

The earthquake and the following Jesuit suppression challenged the idea of the Church as the guardian of rational religion and of her own people. The fall of the Jesuits may have pleased many Catholic Enlighteners and other religious orders that opposed Jesuit missionary methods, theology, and power. But this event signaled a fatal compromise in the Catholic attempt to engage modern culture. Anti-Jesuit Catholics accomplished more destruction of the Church than the Conflictual Enlightenment itself could have dreamed of doing. Catholic fratricide did not bring more enlightenment; it brought less. Reaction set in, polarizing the Catholic world. Church leaders were losing their place at the forefront of the reforming spirit of the age.[253]

The other major external event that indirectly undermined the Catholic Enlightenment was a terrible famine occurring across Southern Europe, especially Italy, from 1763 to 1767. Those suffering in the Kingdom of Naples chewed on bones due to lack of food. Honorable people gave up their honor because of unbearable hunger. These tragic years revealed Italy to herself, one historian wrote. By way of contrast to Enlightenment ideals about public happiness, the famine disclosed the backwardness of Italy's dominant economic mentality, her inefficiency, her poverty, her indifference to the common people, and the incompetence of her administrators. Many had implicitly believed that poverty served a useful function, for peasants would not work unless spurred by necessity. But the famine changed this mentality. In Rome, a vast system of public charity sprang up to help the worst off; but this system distracted from systemic reforms that could have improved the food supply system and the entire papal administration in the long run. People were becoming more aware that perhaps the practice of charity by individuals, local communities, and religious orders was not enough. Public assistance should be organized on additional principles beyond individual and institutional charity. The greatest form of public assistance would be an economic overhaul.

That is exactly what some Italians began to desire. And Portugal seemed to point the way. It was another economically backward country and had expelled its Jesuits due to their economic and political influence. This example led Italians to look more critically at their own governments, often influenced by churchmen. "For the first time, men considered realistically the problem of how to overcome the ancient, age-old rhythms of insufficient harvests, famine, and death," one historian

---

[253] Johns, *The Visual Culture of Catholic Enlightenment*, 318–319.

wrote. Due to this, and to the economic pressure exerted by the famine, Enlighteners in Italy began to desire a new relationship between church and state—one that would result in an independent "political economy" (or "economics" as one might say today).[254]

Political economy originated out of the hope of human betterment in this world through commerce and wealth creation. This ideal—material human betterment on earth—was perhaps the most important contribution of the Enlightenment to Western thought. Self-interested human beings, trading and dealing with each other, would encourage not only a peaceful society but also technological innovation and wider access to material goods by more and more people, proponents held. While some questioned what effects self-interest and wealth might have on a people's virtue, the new political economy held that everyone's lives would nevertheless improve. More individual freedom was needed in economic life to better pursue prosperity, many came to believe. This necessitated reducing state and ecclesiastical involvement in the economy. The weight of these new ideas and new wealth strained and cracked the old social institutions inherited from the Middle Ages. Nevertheless, the new economic freedom had already emerged in practice in Britain—which represented the vanguard of modern economic growth.

One Catholic Enlightener who tried to meet the challenges of economic change was the Catholic priest Antonio Genovesi (1713–1769) of the Kingdom of Naples. He turned from his studies in metaphysics to take up the cause of establishing political economy as a science with its own principles. Genovesi took the first academic chair for political economy ever created—in 1754. He produced truly great and influential work (translated across Europe), such as *Lectures on Commerce* (1765–1767). The famines gave an urgency to his work. They strengthened his case for free trade, spreading new agricultural techniques, and wider land

---

[254] Franco Venturi, "Church and Reform in Enlightenment Italy: The Sixties of the Eighteenth Century," *Journal of Modern History* 48, no. 2 (June 1976): 218, 220.

distribution among small farmers. He looked to Britain as a model of economic development worthy of emulation and warned against Spain[255] as a counterexample of underdevelopment and near-feudal conditions. Political economy should increase commerce for the sake of human happiness. He believed economic thought would be key to spreading Enlightenment culture.

But Genovesi was near the end of his life, and there was no one else to hold together the increasingly divergent Catholic and Conflictual Enlightenments. The 1760s presented many challenges that raised the temperature of debate between the sacral and civic models of culture. "Liberty and competition are the soul of commerce," one Italian political economist wrote in the new Milanese magazine *The Coffeehouse*; "the liberty, that is, that comes from law, and not from license." This recipe would lead to greater wealth and greater social happiness, many believed.[256] There were few Catholic Enlighteners willing to meet the challenges presented by the sciences of society trying to realize the promises of freedom and science for greater economic prosperity.

"Now everyone speaks of Public Economy as if it were Religion," the enlightened Benedictine monk Ferdinando Facchinei lamented in 1764. His criticism of the controversial book *On Crimes and Punishments* (published that year) revealed the new fault line opening over the nature of society. The immensely influential political economist Cesare Beccaria of Milan wrote it. He was influenced not only by Conflictual Enlighteners

---

[255] This was somewhat ironic because Spanish theorists — if not their later practices — first created the modern field of economics during the 1500s. The newly established global trade networks of that century raised profound economic questions, and the theologians of the School of Salamanca established the importance of private property, entrepreneurship, and the free market.

[256] Pietro Verri, "Elements of Commerce," *Coffeehouse* (1764), in Sophus A. Reinert, *The Academy of Fisticuffs: Political Economy and Commercial Society in Enlightenment Italy* (Cambridge, MA: Harvard University Press, 2018), 97.

such as Rousseau and Hume but also by the Catholic Enlighteners Muratori and Genovesi. By arguing against the use of torture and capital punishment, and seeming to separate morality from law, *On Crimes and Punishments* appeared to many an attack on existing structures of society. Voltaire loved it.

Amid the tension between the worldly and the otherworldly, the monk Facchinei condemned the idea that human society could be reformed on its own terms—a fatal assumption of "our very enlightened century," he mocked. He continued: "If our Politics is not a visible part of the true Religion, it will never be a good Politics, but a vague, broken Philosophy." With these words he revealed the essential fault line of the age, between different models of culture. Facchinei believed that one could not consider this earthly world in isolation from the next, as a mere "part" disconnected from the "whole" of eternity, as he put it. Beccaria responded to criticisms such as these in a new preface to a later edition: he did not intend to undermine traditional authority in a radical way, and moral principles, too, not just economic ones, must make for human happiness. The religious, the natural, and the political realms should not contradict one another.[257]

Enlightened Catholics like Feijoo or Muratori might have engaged Beccaria on these points and found a moderate way forward, but they were dead. After them, few Catholic Enlighteners took on the challenges of the rising commercial society of the day, losing significant ground. Indeed, the Roman Inquisition placed Beccaria's work on the Index of Prohibited Books in 1766.

In this context, the Catholic Enlightenment failed because it was not radical enough. Where it *was* radical enough—such as among French priests who joined the enthusiasm of the beginning of the French Revolution in 1789 by casting aside their feudal privileges—it failed because it was not traditional enough.

[257] Ibid., 1, 287.

Unmarked Grave

In the very decade (1760s) when it seemed everyone in Milan and across Europe spoke of getting ahead through "political economy," Maria Agnesi dedicated herself to "voluntary downward mobility," serving the poor.[258] After her father died in 1752, Agnesi quickly moved to renounce her considerable inheritance rights in exchange for an annual salary and the right to live in the family palace. With Maria Agnesi's great text on calculus published in 1749, she considered her mathematical work accomplished. Due also to persistent headaches, she turned away from studies even more. Nevertheless, visitors continued to try to see her. Others sent her questions or essays for comment, but there is no evidence that she ever returned to her studies in a serious way after her father's death. Indeed, one biographer recorded her response to fans who came to see her: "Man always acts to achieve goals; the goal of the Christian is the glory of God. I hope my studies have brought glory to God, as they were useful to others, and derived from obedience, because that was my father's will. Now I have found better ways and means to serve God, and to be useful to others."[259] By recognizing her father's role in her intellectual life, she acknowledged her intimate connections to family and community that—with her cooperation—formed her identity. Later historians portrayed Agnesi with a split identity because they assumed an essential incompatibility between her science and her faith. In reality, however, Agnesi's words revealed the deep continuity of her vocation.[260]

Agnesi increasingly separated herself spiritually and physically from her age in order to devote herself to care for poor and ill women. She refused all invitations to sit for a portrait, so one artist disguised himself and secretly observed her at work in the hospital in order to make a bust. She acknowledged his ingenuity in a card to him. By 1771, she was directing the female section of the Albergo, a charitable institution

---

[258] Findlen, "Calculations of Faith," 282.
[259] Mazzotti, *The World of Maria Gaetana Agnesi*, 145.
[260] Ibid., 293–294.

for urban poor, elderly, and incurables. It was managed by both church and civil authorities—a traditional arrangement of finely balanced institutional powers in Milan. However, from surviving letters, one can see that Agnesi had to struggle with civil authorities over control of the management of the place. She redefined her role to include the power to hire nurses and pay them regularly, as well as discipline unruly patients. She dealt with living conditions and what to do about difficult mental cases. She used her fame to carry out effective fundraising campaigns for the Albergo.

As ideas about church and state changed in German-speaking lands to the north, as discussed earlier, control from Vienna tightened on Milan. Emperor Joseph II, agreeing very much with the "spiritualist ecclesiology" of some German Benedictines, wanted to construct a new church-state relationship. This involved breaking the control of church and civic leaders over local administration, careers, education, and knowledge production in Agnesi's city. It also meant advancing state-controlled "social charity" over the personal-charity model exemplified by Muratori, Agnesi, and many Catholic religious orders, transferring power to state bureaucracy.

Agnesi's struggle with state authorities signaled things to come. Disaster overtook the Catholic world not only due to the French Revolution starting in 1789 but also through the resulting wars. Vienna lost Milan when Napoleon's French army took it in 1796. Agnesi died three years after the invasion. Few took notice. It was not possible to hold large ceremonies, for fear of confrontations with occupying French troops. After a rapid funeral Mass, Agnesi's body was transported by night to a cemetery, where she was buried in an unmarked mass grave like the Carmelites of Compiègne two years earlier. Alongside her lay the bodies of those she had served in the Albergo.

Napoleon's forces pushed on to take Bologna in the Papal States. This was perhaps when Laura Bassi's papers were lost. A student of hers, the devout Catholic anatomist and pioneer of bioelectricity Luigi Galvani (1737–1798), refused to take the oath of allegiance. He believed the French-inspired constitution of the new regime to be atheistic and contrary to his principles. Galvani lost all his jobs in anatomy.

By the late eighteenth century, human dissection less and less expressed the meaning of the whole person in each separate part of the body. *Man a Machine* (1748), by a French Conflictual Enlightener, tried to extend Descartes's mechanistic explanation of the body, redefining humans in purely nonspiritual terms. This eliminated the distinction between soul and body so carefully balanced in the Catholic Enlightenment. In addition, since no soul was found in the body by anatomists, this seemed to give scientific credence to the new materialism (but if the soul is immaterial, how could it be "found"?). So, by the time the French entered Bolgona in 1796, spiritual minds had become material brains. Sadly, the exclusive focus on matter brought back certain anti-woman views. Materialism seemed to prove once again the weakening effects of the female body over her mind, giving scientific weight to traditional misogynism. Dividing bodies into parts without considering their wider meaning induced cultural blindness to relatedness in reality—men to women, morality to technique, individual to community. Those who tried to put these pieces back together again—like Dr. Frankenstein assembling a human being from scattered body parts in Mary Shelley's 1818 novel—often failed to communicate the full dignity of the human person.

Napoleon's troops took Rome in 1798 and demanded that Pope Pius VI renounce his temporal power. He refused and was taken into custody (he would later die a prisoner in southern France). French forces made the pope pay the equivalent of millions of dollars and hand over one hundred of Rome's greatest artworks—including paintings and sculptures from the Capitoline Museum, such as *Capitoline Venus*, donated by Benedict XIV. The French removed altarpieces from churches and invaluable items from the Vatican Archives and from the Museo Profano. They took art from across Italy, then lost or damaged many pieces on transport to France. Their booty was paraded through the streets of Paris. Unsurprisingly, Napoleon's actions—in the name of the "Enlightenment"—meant

that popes for the next 150 years desired to have little to do with enlightened values. Compromise and engagement with the world on its
own terms—high ideals of Pope Benedict XIV—made little sense to
them. The French Revolution, wrote the great nineteenth-century writer
Alexis de Tocqueville, *seemed* to destroy everything because what it did
destroy affected everything else.[261] It felt like the end of an age. Much
of nineteenth-century Catholicism took its inspiration not from the
Catholic Enlightenment but from the awe and mystery of traditions
derived from the Middle Ages.

In Germany, Napoleon forced a surrender resulting in the dissolution
of many of the Benedictine monasteries in 1803. This was a cultural disaster destroying hundreds of thousands of books and scattering unique
collections through auction. Catholic universities and schools closed
across the land. The Catholic intellectual elite disappeared, along with
their research, conversation, networks, and leadership. Only a few monasteries survived. The close of German monasticism "meant the end of a
powerful experiment," Lehner wrote, "namely the engagement of Catholic
thought with Enlightenment ideas and practices."[262] For generations afterward, Catholics did not even acknowledge that such engagement had
ever happened. Dramatic and painful events cast a veil over everything
that had happened before. They forgot the very existence of the Catholic
Enlightenment. Their trauma-induced memory loss fed deep suspicion
of the modern world for the next century and more.

[261] Tocqueville, *The Ancien Régime*, 34.
[262] Lehner, *Enlightened Monks*, 227.

Part 3

Retreat and the Practical Enlightenment

*But our philosopher who knows how to strike a balance between
retreat from and commerce with men, is full of humanity.*

—Dumarsais

*But when you pray, go into your room and shut the door and pray
to your Father who is in secret; and your Father who sees in secret
will reward you. . . . Go therefore and make disciples of all nations.*

—Matthew 6:6; 28:19

*Beware you be not swallowed up in books:
An ounce of love is worth a pound of knowledge.*

—John Wesley

9

Householding

The Third Strategy

Christians interacted with the Enlightenment through both conflict and engagement. Each strategy had strengths and flaws. Through their quiet conflict with the spirit of the age, the Carmelites of Compiègne witnessed to a higher truth. They refused to obey what they judged as unjust. And they would not be pushed around—even in the face of death. However, in other Christians, the conflict strategy could easily become deformed without the counterbalance of the engagement strategy. French Catholic triumphalism and harsh political oppression of their opponents—fruits of a mutant conflictual psychology—contributed to the backlash of the Conflictual Enlightenment and to the very martyrdom of the Carmelites themselves.

In Italy and Germany, the engagement strategy of Maria Agnesi, Pope Benedict XIV, and the Benedictines held out an attractive alternative. Open-mindedness, intellectual achievement, and a spirit of compromise went a long way toward alleviating combative extremes. Religious Enlighteners participated extensively in the Age of Reason. Yet their virtues also contributed to their downfall. They failed to guard the household of faith sufficiently from dangerous influences that existed. This strategy, too, was an incomplete answer to the Enlightenment.

There was yet another possible response to the Enlightenment: ignore it, mind one's own business, and stay home. Turn down Voltaire's dinner invitation to Ferney and walk right on past Pope Benedict XIV's museum of anatomy. Instead, strive to build up Christian culture from within. In other words, *retreat* within one's house to "work from home," so to speak—not a military maneuver backing out of a tough spot, but a spiritual movement inward to nurture the household of faith. From this vantage point, Enlightenment culture and Christian culture ran parallel with each other, not colliding as in conflict or overlapping as in engagement but developing in tandem.

The retreat strategy involved both an inward and an outward movement. Withdrawal from the world sometimes resulted in profound conversions of heart and an outward explosion of evangelical (missionary) energy to "renew the spirit of Christianity among Christians" and beyond. This was how the great evangelist Louis de Montfort (1673–1716) defined the "New Evangelization" of the age.[263] Widespread Catholic missions and Protestant revivals made the 1700s the "Christian century" as much as the century of the Enlightenment.

The third strategy of retreat could overlap with either the first or the second strategy. When it merged with conflict, it produced a Catholic resistance movement in the west of France during the French Revolution. When retreat merged with engagement, it changed political and moral assumptions that supported the American Revolution and Founding and the British abolitionist movement.

The human heart was the personal space where the inward and outward movements of the retreat strategy met. Only a few decades after the English physician William Harvey (1578–1657) famously described the heart as a pump circulating blood around the body, the French nun Margaret Mary Alacoque claimed a profound experience of the Sacred Heart of Jesus through a vision (1673). The heart, as both a secular and a sacred organ, had long served as a metaphor for the inner core of the person and the unity of body and soul. Thus, Catholic devotion to the Sacred Heart of Jesus ran parallel to the spread of Protestant "heart religion" in Pietism and evangelicalism in

---

[263] Louis de Montfort, quoted in *A Course in Montfortian Spirituality* (N.p.: Montfort Missionaries, 2014), 11, http://www.montfort.org.uk/Documents/ Course/A%20Course%20in%20Montfortian%20Spirituality.pdf.

the 1700s to counterbalance the brain as the master anatomical organ in the Age of Reason. Appeal to the heart served as a warning against the dangers implicit in Descartes's "I think, therefore I am," which tended to isolate the mind from the rest of the person. At the same time, Christian heart religion (both Catholic and Protestant) emphasized personal religious experience and the free and individual response to faith. The retreat strategy and its appeal to the heart pled for integration, not distinction, for bringing together, not analyzing apart. It sought to relate faith to all dimensions of life. It could, however, tend toward emotionalism, credulity, and sectarianism if not counterbalanced by either the conflict strategy or the engagement strategy.

Christian Retreat and the English-Speaking World

Our current examination of Christian retreat and religious revival focuses on the English-speaking world for three reasons. First, the British Isles and the American colonies witnessed massive evangelization efforts and were also the prime sites of the Practical Enlightenment. This was the form of the Enlightenment as found among practical people, such as the inventors of steam power (1712) and power looms for weaving cloth (1785). In this sense, the printer and inventor Benjamin Franklin was a classic "Practical Enlightener." He created the lightning rod, bifocals, and the more efficient Franklin stove for heating homes. The Practical Enlightenment lies behind modern economic and industrial development. In a very real sense, it created the modern world.

Evangelists such as John Wesley (1703–1791)—the most effective spokesman and organizer of Methodism—interacted with the Practical Enlightenment. They utilized improved roads and the burgeoning print media culture in evangelization. They also responded to the loneliness and spiritual needs of the marginalized. These were the common people and laborers affected—for good and for ill—by the industry and free-market business practices of the Practical Enlightenment.

The goal: return England to the Christian faith. Wesley strove for this along with his brother Charles (1707–1788) and their friend George

Whitefield (1714–1770). Methodism was not an independent denomination in the eighteenth century but an interdenominational evangelical movement emerging out of the Church of England. It emphasized the possibility of salvation for all people, the experience of the Holy Spirit, and the importance of works of mercy. The three friends were so successful that the Methodist movement spilled over into the Great Awakening (1740s–1750s) in the American colonies and eventually gave birth to the charismatic renewal and Pentecostalism that now affect the lives of five hundred million people globally. The Wesleys and Whitefield changed the shape of the Enlightenment by altering fundamental cultural assumptions about human dignity and political authority.

The friendship (not without tension) between John, Charles, and George was an example of what Joseph Ratzinger called a "creative minority." This is a group of friends "who in their encounters with Christ have discovered the precious pearl that gives value to all life." The convincing model of such creative minorities, Ratzinger continued, attracts and persuades others from many backgrounds. This becomes an opening toward an experience and a knowledge "that cannot emerge amid the dreariness of everyday life." Thus, creative minorities are the first step in influencing the wider culture. They do this both directly and indirectly as they support a Christian civil religion that overcomes the boundaries between denominations and gives voice to the basic religious and moral values that sustain the wider society, Ratzinger wrote.[264]

Wesley himself possessed just such a sociological sense for the importance of little societies of faith in support of wider church structures in which ordinary people could gain participative knowledge of Christian community. Religious societies were highly attractive in an increasingly individualistic, business-minded culture. Understanding how Christians temporarily reversed early eighteenth-century secularization in England, in particular, demonstrates how they adapted to the world's first industrializing, free-market, and consumer society.

---

[264] Ratzinger, "Letter to Marcello Pera," 120, 121.

The second reason to focus on England is the remarkable body of surviving historical sources that document Wesley's work. His journal is one of the great texts of English Christianity. It is to the eighteenth century what the journal of George Fox (Quaker) is to the seventeenth and the *Apologia pro Vita Sua* of John Henry Newman (Catholic) is to the nineteenth. In addition, John's brother Charles Wesley's six thousand hymns changed the course of church singing in the English-speaking world. Christians of all sorts still sing "Hark! The Herald Angels Sing" (1739), "Christ the Lord Is Risen Today" (1739), and "Love Divine, All Loves Excelling" (1747). Finally, hundreds of eighteenth-century evangelical conversion narratives exist that constituted a new literary genre. These allow one to see inside the hearts of ordinary working-class and middle-class people in unique ways.

Third, John Wesley and Protestant Christian culture are of interest because what happened in the English-speaking world exemplifies well both the weaknesses and the strengths of the strategy of Christian retreat. One vulnerability was the "Puritan temptation." This was the desire to "purify" by separating so much from the "world" that one adopted sectarian ways of thinking and a dark view of human nature and the body.

On the positive side, however, the retreat strategy in the English-speaking world centered on households as the engines of Christian culture. This is an important point because social scientists today are beginning to understand more deeply the mutually dependent connection between healthy family life and flourishing religion. Religion is like language: it is learned and practiced in groups. It seems there is something about the way people live in families that makes them more receptive to God. After all, the Christian God entered the world through the "Holy Family."[265] How did this family-faith dynamic work in the age of the Enlightenment? It operated in reverse in the stories of Rousseau and Voltaire: weak households led to loss of faith. How did strong households lead to strong faith? How did people of the time build up Christian culture one domestic

---

[265] Mary Eberstadt, *How the West Really Lost God: A New Theory of Secularization* (West Conshohocken, PA: Templeton, 2013), 5–6, 95, 160–162, 212.

block at a time? How did the retreat strategy — operating through households of faith — affect the eighteenth century as a whole? Answering these questions will require studying both the material and the spiritual foundations of home life. That is where the two cultures — the Practical Enlightenment and Christianity — interacted at the most intimate level.

Householding

Using eighteenth-century court records, advertisements, wills, inventories, and legal records, historian Amanda Vickery showed that the people of northwest Europe in general, and of England in particular, long attributed unique importance to the independent marital home. Marriage meant the construction of distinct households, unlike in southern Europe or China, where married couples were often absorbed within the parental unit, Vickery wrote. Residential autonomy (rented or owned) was central to social respect and personal identity in England.

Enlightenment ideals increasingly influenced households over the course of the century, in terms of personal privacy, rational domesticity, and polite sociability through visiting, drawing-room conversation, and tea drinking. The Practical Enlightenment turned scientific instruments into affordable domestic ornaments and made clock ownership (and pocket watches) common. Time could be controlled as never before. The "enlightened kitchen" emerged as a separate, female domain in which cookware became more versatile and inexpensive.

The household was the "founding social and spiritual unit in society," Vickery commented. "We begin our public affections in our families," the British statesman Edmund Burke wrote in 1790. It was key to politics: taxes, local government, legal administration, and voting rights all depended on householder status. This model of householding was exported to the American colonies.[266]

---

[266] Amanda Vickery, *Behind Closed Doors: At Home in Georgian England* (New Haven: Yale University Press, 2009), 6–8; Edmund Burke, *Reflections*

Thus, when Methodist George Whitefield crossed the Atlantic Ocean to the American colonies and preached his sermon "The Great Duty of Family-Religion" in 1738, colonialists heard and understood him because he spoke their language. Every house is like a little parish, Whitefield said. Every person in the household is under the care of the householder — including apprentices, lodgers, servants, and live-in relatives. Governors of families ought to look upon themselves as obliged to act in three biblical capacities — as a "prophet, to instruct; as a priest, to pray for and with; as a king, to govern, direct, and provide for" the household. To be restored to holiness by the Holy Spirit, he said, heads of families need to pay particular attention to the "spiritual economy at home."[267] The word "economy" often meant in Whitefield's time "householding" or "household management." He was talking about spiritual householding: taking care of the religious needs and practices of a home.

The idea of householding — in a material and spiritual sense — will serve as a metaphor in this chapter for how the retreat strategy worked. Responsibility for provisioning and protection was shared in practice by spouses even if the male householder was the head. He accepted the responsibility of patrolling the boundaries, so to speak. "Shutting in" was a universally recognized nightly ritual of securing weak points such as doors and windows against intruders by internal bolt, padlock, or iron bar. The woman of the house, however, often held the keys, and thus, in practice, it was she who gave admittance — or not — to outside influences. The integrity of the perimeter, Vickery wrote, was central to legal, customary, and spiritual understandings of home.[268]

The house was like the human body in the popular mind: windows were like eyes, doors like mouths, and hearths like breasts. "Apertures

---

on the Revolution in France (1790; Indianapolis: Hackett Publishing, 1987), 173.

[267] George Whitefield, "The Great Duty of Family-Religion" (1738), https://www.milestonedocuments.com/documents/view/george-whitefield-the-great-duty-of-family-religion/text.

[268] Vickery, Behind Closed Doors, 28, 31.

symbolized points of human vulnerability," Vickery wrote. Witches were believed to attack houses through windows, doors, keyholes, chimneys, and hearths, just as demons entered bodies through their orifices. Without openings to the outside world, however, a house was an airless prison. Brick houses built in eighteenth-century London emphasized the importance of their boundaries, guarding them with elevation and iron railings. The Englishman's home was his castle.[269]

In a metaphorical sense, then, householding means *retreating inside to focus on nurturing life*. It means physical and spiritual vigilance about the windows and doors of homes, religious societies, and churches opening to the outside world. More broadly, householding means securing the boundaries of Christian culture — a practice some of the Benedictine Enlighteners from the last chapter should have exercised more vigorously. It was necessary to protect spiritual life in an eighteenth-century world driven by the fragmenting forces of secular interests.

The movement inward was not about fear, but rather prioritization: to focus on the physical and spiritual needs of the human person and to help ordinary church members live out their faith. Householders sought not to conflict or engage but to integrate faith into all aspects of their lives.

Paradoxically, this inward religious movement of retreat contained the seeds of an incredible expansion *outward* through evangelization. This would change not only the Enlightenment, but the whole of modern history. To understand these developments, it is necessary to tell two stories at once about the parallel cultures of the Practical Enlightenment and of Christianity in the eighteenth century.

Parallel Cultures

Benjamin Franklin's autobiography offers a fascinating glimpse of these parallel cultures of Practical Enlightenment and Christianity. Born in 1706, he considered himself an Englishman for most of his life, as did

---

[269] Ibid., 29.

many colonists in North America before the American Revolution. Franklin left Philadelphia to cross the Atlantic Ocean with his friend Ralph in the mid-1720s to continue training as a printer—at "Palmer's, then a famous printing house," he wrote. Ralph—who had many flaws as well as amiable qualities—tried to get work as an actor or a hack writer, meanwhile borrowing money from Franklin. Ralph forgot all about his wife and child back home in the colonies. "I spent with Ralph a good deal of my earnings in going to plays and other places of amusement," Franklin remembered. This reduced them to living "from hand to mouth." Ralph ran off with a fellow lodger, an attractive young milliner (women's hatmaker). That left Franklin with freedom to widen his horizons by making friends with a bookseller, dabbling in "freethought," and conversing with rationalists at coffeehouses. He described himself as under "no religious restraint."[270]

This was London of the early eighteenth century—one of the great cultural centers of the age. The city of around six hundred thousand people attracted young individuals, footloose and fancy free. It was a hub of thought and rapidly expanding communication networks through the printing houses. Franklin was at the heart of it. The Enlightenment culture he found there shaped his whole life.

After Ralph left the picture, Franklin started over with a new job. He moved to Watts's—"a still greater printing house." He worked hard at a press, surrounded by dozens of other workmen, "great guzzlers of beer," he described them. He took only water—to save money and get ahead. He was clever and advanced rapidly.[271]

At the same time, Franklin found a new place to live across from a "Romish chapel" above an Italian warehouse. The law treated Catholics unequally at the time: extra land taxes, no public office allowed, attendance at universities banned. So the few Catholics retreated into their homes. A widow kept the place where Franklin stayed. She had

[270] Franklin, *The Autobiography and Other Writings*, 42, 44.
[271] Ibid., 45.

converted to Catholicism, and they enjoyed conversation together. She told him about another elderly Catholic lady living in the attic who had gone abroad as a young woman to become a nun. But the country did not agree with her, Franklin recalled, so she returned to England and "vowed to lead the life of a nun as near as might be done in those circumstances." She gave away her money, lived simply, and met with a priest every day. The landlady appreciated having her there and let her stay for free.

Franklin visited the lady in the attic. "The room was clean," he wrote, "but had no other furniture than a mattress, a table with a crucifix and book, a stool, which she gave me to sit on, and a picture over the chimney of St. Veronica, displaying her handkerchief, with the miraculous figure of Christ's bleeding face on it, which she explained to me with great seriousness."[272] Little did this elderly lady know that the young American deist Benjamin Franklin would record a glimpse of her retreating lifestyle.

Many years later, on another trip to England and barely surviving shipwreck, Benjamin Franklin wrote to tell his wife how, when he and his companions made it to shore, they heard a bell ringing for church. "We went thither immediately," Franklin wrote, "and with hearts full of gratitude, returned sincere thanks to God for the mercies we had received: were I a Roman Catholic, perhaps I should on this occasion vow to build a chapel to some saint; but as I am not, if I were to vow at all, it should be to build a lighthouse."[273] This was the practical *and* the pious Franklin.

It seems, in fact, that Franklin maintained strong belief in God and the immortality of the soul throughout his later lifetime. He appreciated the importance of religion for social stability and morality, as did most Enlighteners. Despite his Voltairean hostility to clerics and church authority,

---

[272] Ibid., 47.
[273] Benjamin Franklin to Deborah Franklin, July 17, 1757, Founders Online, https://founders.archives.gov/documents/Franklin/01-07-02-0106.

he nevertheless gave money to various churches. He also befriended John Carroll (first Catholic bishop of the United States) and Methodist George Whitefield when the latter came preaching throughout the American colonies—fanning the Great Awakening into flame in 1739. In fact, part of Franklin's fame and fortune came as a result of publishing Whitefield's journal and sermons. Franklin and Whitefield, the printer and the preacher, exemplified the parallel cultures of the Practical Enlightenment and Christianity developing side by side in the eighteenth century.

The Expansion of the Secular

Before the Great Awakening, however, times were tough for religion generally in the English-speaking world. New economic and political forces slowly undermined traditional Anglican culture in England. "It is a melancholy reflection, that our country, which in times of Popery was called the nation of saints, should now have less appearance of religion in it, than any other neighboring state or kingdom," wrote the famous essayist Joseph Addison in 1716.[274] "No religion in England," the French Enlightener Montesquieu wrote in his journal during his visit from 1729 to 1731. "When one man said, in my presence, 'I believe this as an article of faith', everyone began to laugh. There is a committee to review the state of religion; the project is regarded as a joke."[275] The English painter and engraver William Hogarth liked to depict the daily life of common people. His *Sleeping Congregation* (1728) showed a minister's dull sermon putting everyone to sleep.

The established Church of England produced enlightened scholars and enjoyed government support through taxes and appointment of ecclesiastical leaders. It often failed, however, to engage the emotions

---

[274] Joseph Addison, *The Free-Holder*, Friday, April 27, 1716, 176.

[275] Montesquieu, "Notes on England," (1729-1731), https://ouclf.law.ox.ac.uk/montesquieu-in-england-his-notes-on-england-with-commentary-and-translation-commentary/.

*William Hogarth (1697–1764) was a popular English painter,
printmaker, and social critic whose images recorded the lives of ordinary
people. His* Sleeping Congregation *(1728) poked fun at the dull
sermons and sleepy congregations of early eighteenth-century England.
Showing animation or enthusiasm in religion was considered bad taste.
One of the clerics appears distracted by the sleeping woman's bosom.*

and the hearts of the rising proto-industrial populations. The situation
was ripe for the emergence of a populist religious movement, as will be
described in the next chapter.

The increasingly secular cultural situation came about partly due to
hard memories of the religious confusion and extremism of the English
Civil War during the previous century (1642–1651). This conflict pitted

the monarchy (supported by Anglicans and Catholics) against Parliament (supported by Puritans). Parliament won, but their chaotic Commonwealth was only held together by the controlling and even brutal actions of Oliver Cromwell until 1660. Many religious sects formed during this time that claimed direct inspiration from the Holy Spirit. They appealed to religious inspiration to push political agendas. Addison blamed the impiety and decline of religion in his time (1716) on the "extreme of *Cant* and *Hypocrisy*" that took "possession of the people's minds in the times of the great Rebellion [the English Civil War]." Fervent religion led to intolerance and violence, people came to believe. This put Christianity "out of countenance" among fashionable Englishmen.[276] Many responded to the decline of Christianity by absorbing themselves in the increasingly dynamic secular world.

This word "secular" had long referred to members of the clergy living in the world (outside a religious order). During the seventeenth century, however, it came to mean the present and visible world as distinguished from the eternal or spiritual one. "Secular" during the Enlightenment did not yet mean "secular*ism*" (a nineteenth-century ideology at odds with faith). Though the decline of religion in the early 1700s was a setback from the Christian point of view, the expansion of interest in the secular *per se* did not automatically conflict with Christianity. The "Secular Enlightenment," as historian Margaret Jacob called it, did not necessarily imply a wholesale rejection of Christianity. Rather, it created a new "mental space in which to encounter the world on its own terms." Increased attention to the secular world led to an "explosion of innovative thinking about society, government, and the economy," Jacob wrote, which is undoubtedly true.[277] Cultural conditions played a large

---

[276] Addison, *The Free-Holder*, 177. *The Oxford English Dictionary* defines "Cant," according to the usage of the time, as "dark talk" after the manner of thieves, or, "To affect religious or pietistic phraseology."

[277] Margaret C. Jacob, *The Secular Enlightenment* (Princeton: Princeton University Press, 2019), dust jacket, 1.

role in setting the limits of the secular, and those shifted over time. The "Secular Enlightenment" could be in harmony with Joseph Ratzinger's notion of "positive secularity."

The expansion of the secular certainly created both challenges and opportunities for Christian culture. That it *could* conflict with Christianity was obvious, as seen notably in France with the Carmelites. The Conflictual Enlightenment was both real and dangerous, from a Christian point of view. But the expansion of the secular did not *have* to conflict. It might run parallel to Christian culture: sometimes benign, sometimes helpful, and sometimes threatening, but not usually presenting a universal metaphysical clash. I call this secular development the "Practical Enlightenment."

The Practical Enlightenment

The new scientific understanding of nature presented in chapters 6 and 7 was interpreted differently by people within various European cultures. Maria Agnesi in Italy, for example, saw the study of mathematics as an avenue to God. By contrast, the practical people of the English-speaking world tended to see in eighteenth-century science the possibility of material prosperity. They may have also loved God, but they possessed a different ideal of science and its purpose. Whereas Agnesi intentionally wrote her calculus textbook devoid of practical application, English-language textbooks in Newtonian science blended theory and practice due to their strong desire to connect science to technology.

Already by 1680, for example, the Royal Society of London discussed the labor-saving value of machines. The diffusion of Newtonian mechanics through lecture halls, newspapers, and journals led to a mental shift in the public culture of England, historian Margaret Jacob wrote. This happened especially among industrial entrepreneurs and engineers. They began to work together and think mechanically about the productive process. A culture of practical science built a bridge between people with capital and people with mechanical knowledge. This was a

A View of the Iron Bridge (1880) by William Williams. This was the
first iron bridge ever built in the world, over the River Severn in 1779 — a
great engineering achievement of the Practical Enlightenment. Now a World
Heritage Site, it is located near the village of Coalbrookdale. That was where,
in the early eighteenth century, Abraham Darby pioneered the smelting of
iron using coke, a process that was a catalyst for the Industrial Revolution.

monumental change. When traveling in England in 1794, for example,
a French industrial spy wrote to the government in Paris: "I saw with
dismay that a revolution in the mechanical arts ... was developing in a
manner frightening to the whole of Europe, and particularly to France,
which would receive the severest blow from it [due to rising English
dominance]."[278]

This was the Enlightenment of the practical people who especially
thrived among the growing middle class of the English-speaking world.
They believed one could improve human life in little, practical ways by
innovation, experiment, and making "useful knowledge" widely accessible.

[278] Ibid., 4, 6, 165.

Benjamin Franklin was a classic case. His father took him as a boy to watch joiners (carpenters), bricklayers, and other tradesmen at work. As a printer, he cast type, molded lead, made ink, and labored in warehouses in both England and the colonies. He also used every minute of his spare time to read. He worked with his hands *and* his mind—a revolution in the idea of human labor fostered by the Practical Enlightenment. Intellectuals got dirty for the first time in history—with the exception of Benedictine monks, who had beat them to it long before. Nevertheless, this change tended to break down class barriers between different kinds of knowledge and foster the modern culture of innovation.

Besides inventing, Franklin enhanced the Practical Enlightenment by his projects for the public good. He organized street paving in Philadelphia to reduce dust and mud. He formed a library system to promote useful knowledge among the wider population. He created a discussion group "for mutual improvement" among his tradesmen friends. The first members included a clerk, a mathematician, a surveyor, a shoemaker, a mechanic, and a merchant. Their debates about morality, politics, and science were to be "conducted in the sincere spirit of enquiry after truth"—no matter the religious background of members.[279] This was a more democratic form of the salon conversations that represented the shift from a sacral cultural model to a civic cultural model of pluralist participation.

Franklin believed "useful projects" for the public good increased human happiness. Happiness, he wrote, is not produced by great good fortunes that seldom happen. It is created by "little advantages that occur every day." In turn, the desire for happiness in this world increases the drive to work harder. "Early to Bed, and early to rise, makes a Man healthy, wealthy, and wise," he wrote in the essay "The Way to Wealth." Leisure was time for doing something useful. "God gives all Things to Industry."[280]

---

[279] Ibid., 57.
[280] Ibid., 120, 168, 169.

Franklin thus exemplified the "industrious revolution." This is a concept some historians have used to help understand the cultural changes that led to the full-blown Industrial Revolution later in the eighteenth century. As idealized by Franklin, more and more people began to use their time differently than ever before — more "industriously," as one historian put it. They began to give less time to leisure and household production and more to market production — that is, producing things for the market to sell. Instead of working as largely self-sufficient farmers, more and more people strove to make money to buy the consumer goods they needed or wanted to live — the basis of modern life today. Social status shifted away from aristocratic lineage to industrious behavior and patterns of consumption — pursuits open to anyone.[281]

A prominent economic historian summarized the result: "The essence of the Enlightenment's impact on the economy was the drive to expand the accumulation of useful knowledge and direct it toward practical use." This created the world's first consumer society. In fact, the English word "shopping" emerged in the eighteenth century to mean "visiting around to different stores." Retail strategies included advertising, marketing, branding, mail order, dress rental, fashion magazines, fashion dolls, shop design, and window dressing. Widespread paper currency and easy credit facilitated buying and selling.[282]

These cultural changes, along with accessible coal deposits and high labor costs (an incentive to technological innovation), led to the Industrial Revolution in Great Britain after 1750. This was an unprecedented event in human history. Nothing since the discovery of agriculture around

---

[281] Sheilagh Ogilvie, "The European Economy in the Eighteenth Century," in *The Eighteenth Century: Europe 1688–1815*, ed. T. C. W. Blanning (New York: Oxford University Press, 2000), 112, 129.

[282] Joel Mokyr, *The Enlightened Economy: An Economic History of Britain 1700–1850* (New Haven: Yale University Press, 2009), 10; John Styles and Amanda Vickery, introduction to *Gender, Taste, and Material Culture in Britain and North America, 1700–1830*, ed. John Styles and Amanda Vickery (New Haven: Yale University Press, 2006), 2.

10,000 B.C. has more profoundly changed the way humans live out their daily lives, in a material sense. It was the beginning of the modern growth economy that has both raised entire human populations out of poverty and polluted large areas of the globe.

It all started in the eighteenth century with the Practical Enlightenment. Householders had to adapt their family lives and their religious lives to the increasingly mobile and business-oriented environment.

The "Little College" of the Family

One of those who strove for such Christian adaptation was the writer and business entrepreneur Daniel Defoe (ca. 1660–1731). In the very midst of the emergent secular and commercial culture, Defoe represented both the industrious middle class of England and the response of Christian retreat. He is remembered as the author of *Robinson Crusoe* (1719). This popular book was one of the first English novels. It tells of a castaway surviving for years, alone, on an island in the Caribbean Sea through ingenuity and trust in God—the ultimate retreat! This may have reflected Defoe's own sense of isolation and even persecution as a Presbyterian living in Anglican England.

Defoe was the son of a candlemaker. Through his resourcefulness, industry, and winning personality, he became—at one time or another—a merchant, a manufacturer, a journalist, a political agent, an English spy in Scotland, and a business writer. He realized that business could spur scientific innovation and benefit the public, even as he himself experienced both the gains and the losses of the emerging free-market economy. Defoe understood by observation the average man in the different stations of life. He "knew better than most the strain and toil, the skill and resourcefulness and enterprise, on which the continuance of all civilized comforts must depend," one scholar commented.[283] in 1726, Defoe published the first English business manual: *The Complete English*

---

[283] Louis I. Bredvold, *The Literature of the Restoration and the Eighteenth Century, 1660–1798* (New York: Collier Books, 1962), 59.

Tradesman. Necessity is a spur to industry, he wrote, and the need to provide for oneself through business can serve to "humble the minds of those whom nothing else could make to stoop."[284] Benjamin Franklin read the book enthusiastically while in London and later printed and distributed it throughout the American colonies.

Defoe's concerns for both business and religion converged in his household. As he aged, suffering wounds for his faith and his poor financial decisions, he took refuge in his loving family. He was a faithful husband and father. He had married Mary Tuffley, and together they raised seven children. Concerned by what he perceived as the twin dangers of secular culture and "Popery" (Catholicism), in 1727 he wrote *A New Family Instructor*. This work, almost forgotten by scholars ever since, was about passing on Christian faith within a household.

The "Instructor" was the head of the family, "whose Business and Duty is to inform and confirm his Children in right Principles," Defoe wrote. Such formation held great importance for them in an age not only of enlightenment and business, but also of "Modern Heresies"—namely, deism, skepticism, and atheism, he noted. In response to this challenging cultural situation, there was a need to retreat: to foster a Christian way of life within the home.[285]

How? "I have made it my Study for several Years, to find some Family, if it was possible, whose Example might be Historically recommended to the World," Defoe wrote. He found one, but for the sake of decency, he would not name it. He could, however, describe it: they were a middle-class business family living in London, valuing hard work, religion, and education. The father read Scripture to his children daily. He called the whole household together (including servants) for family prayer. After dinner, he

---

[284] Daniel Defoe, "Of the Tradesman Letting His Wife Be Acquainted with His Business," chap. 21 in *The Complete English Tradesman* (1726; Edinburgh: William and Robert Chambers, 1839), http://www.gutenberg.org/files/14444/14444-h/14444-h.htm#CHAPTER_XXI.

[285] Daniel Defoe, *A New Family Instructor* (London: T. Warner, 1727), iv, 5–6.

spent time catechizing the children. Or he talked "familiarly to his Children upon any useful Subject" in an agreeable and pleasant way suitable to their understanding. Thus, his children came to delight in "solid, serious, and profitable Things, as others would do in hearing a pleasant Tune." The Instructor thought of his family as a "little College" where he educated his children "in the Fear and Knowledge of God, in the Love of Religion, and Divine Truth, and in all the best and most improving Parts of Human Knowledge, that he thought suitable to make them wise and religious both together." Thus, "Religion is propagated in Families by the Examples of the Teachers that went before them," he wrote with sociological wisdom.[286]

As a result, they became a happy family. They were "bless'd, and successful too in the World," Defoe wrote. The children showed an "Original Beauty upon their Appearance, a Modesty, Decency, and Sober Behavior, peculiar, as it were, to themselves; which shew'd they had been well Taught." Their formation "is an Ornament, that shines in the Children who are Instructed, and reflects back a Lustre on the Parent Instructing." The rest of the neighborhood loved and esteemed them.[287]

This vision of Defoe might inspire some readers and trouble others. Stable marriages and households really are crucially important to passing on faith and, at the same time, to worldly success and happiness. As the preacher Whitefield said: "Have not people read, that it is God who gives men power to get wealth, and therefore that the best way to prosper in the world, is to secure his favor?" This was not so much the "prosperity theology" of the twentieth century as sound sociological advice and insightful religious marketing.[288]

On the other hand, Puritanical assumptions about disengaging from the world run deep among English speakers. The retreat strategy as illustrated here by Defoe could easily turn in on itself. The internal rhythm of isolated

---

[286] Ibid., 1, 2, 4–5, 10, 11, 12.
[287] Ibid., 2–3, 6.
[288] Eberstadt, *How the West Really Lost God*, 95, 170; Whitefield, "The Great Duty of Family-Religion."

households could get out of balance if detached from the previous strategy discussed, that of engagement. In addition, can one measure success as a parent by the outward behavior of one's children, as Defoe seemed to suggest in these quotations? Can a family be a pure city-on-the-hill example? The pressure of maintaining such an ideal can cause people to judge themselves and others harshly. One can feel permanently dissatisfied with oneself as well as guilty for not constantly living up to certain expectations and standards, as one spiritual writer noted. "That feeling does not originate in God's will but in our damaged psyches," he wrote.[289]

Presenting an idealized image through moralizing can hide interior brokenness—not only from others, but from oneself. Out of pride and "family-olatry," parents can ignore the full humanity of their children and give vent to an indomitable will to control—not only their offspring but even each other. Propping up pious household practices for the sake of "Sober Behavior" might serve to hide emotional neglect and even abuse. Marriage was no shelter from struggle in the eighteenth century, one historian wrote. "The household was the anvil on which the marital dynamic was forged, so sparks flew all about."[290]

Yet Defoe's vision did extend beyond the household. The father's example, in this family case study, "spread itself among other Families; it encourag'd other Masters of Families in the same Street, and in neighbouring Places to do the same; and several of them set about the great and necessary Work of Family Instruction, by his Example." Neighbors would even come and talk with him for advice in better governing their families—which he gave with tenderness, "he being a Man of a large Heart, an extensive Charity, and abounding with a Sweetness of Temper."[291] In the end, Defoe offered a compelling example of Christian retreat in the very midst of the Practical Enlightenment.

[289] Jacques Philippe, *Interior Freedom*, trans. Helena Scott (New York: Scepter, 2002), 38.

[290] Vickery, *Behind Closed Doors*, 193.

[291] Defoe, *A New Family Instructor*, 3, 6, 7.

Thus, spiritual householding not only attempted to pass on faith to the next generation; it aspired to work as a humble leaven among the community. If the family was a bridge between its members and the transcendent, it could also serve as a key sociological structure connecting personal faith to the wider culture. Defoe's example suggests that households could be important avenues through which a religious movement might compete for influence with the expanding secular culture of the day. To test this theory, we must turn to the experience of an eighteenth-century family who left behind enough historical records to enable us to cross its threshold, so to speak, and peer behind its closed doors.

Epworth, England

Let us examine the household of Samuel and Susanna Wesley. Two of their ten surviving children, John and Charles, along with their friend George Whitefield, would change the course of the eighteenth century. Their mission was to return England to the Christian faith. They would "bring Christian fellowship out of the clouds," historian Christopher Dawson wrote, "into immediate relation with the lives of the common people of 18th-century England."[292] As a result, the second half of England's eighteenth century was more religious than the first. It all started in the village of Epworth in rural Lincolnshire, England, the "home of Methodism."

The family lived in the large timber-framed, thatched rectory for the medieval parish church of St. Andrew. Samuel Wesley was the Anglican priest there. He was Oxford educated and committed to his duties. The home was surrounded by three acres of land used for farming and supplemental income.

Unfortunately, some of the locals hated the family, refusing to pay tithe. They burned the family's crops, maimed their livestock, and may

---

[292] Christopher Dawson, *The Dividing of Christendom* (1965; San Francisco: Ignatius Press, 2008).

have even tried to set fire to their house, in an effort to drive them away. They disliked "Royalists" and "academics" like this well-educated man and his wife. They remembered how a local aristocrat, supported by the king, had sixty years earlier drained the surrounding lands for agricultural purposes. This took away their common land, their bird hunting, and many of their local jobs. This lingering resentment in the community made the Wesleys rely even more on their own internal resources.

In 1709, the rectory did burn down, and the family lost everything. They barely managed to rescue five-year-old John from an upstairs window. Resolved to stay at their post, however, they took on a large debt to build a sturdy brick-and-stone house in the style of the Queen Anne era. Quoins emphasized the corners and painted sash windows looked boldly out upon the village. This displayed permanence to the locals. The family would not be leaving. Today, the house is a museum devoted to the Wesley family.

The Rescue of the Young John Wesley from the Burning Parsonage at Epworth, Lincolnshire, *mezzotint by S. W. Reynolds after H. P. Parker.*

Both parents deeply influenced John and Charles, but Susanna is remembered as the "Mother of Methodism" for a reason. Her letters and diary provide fascinating insight into how Christian retreat in the age of the Enlightenment connected personal faith to the wider community by means of the household structure.

Susanna is undoubtedly one of the great Christian women of history. She was the twenty-fifth of twenty-five children. At age thirteen, she left her father's Dissenter church (Daniel Defoe was a member) to join the Church of England. Her father had taught her to think independently and so respected her decision. Susanna had nineteen pregnancies, but due to high infant mortality, only ten children survived. Assisted by servants and wet nurses, she managed the household, gardening, and early education of the children until the boys were sent to school in London around age ten. Amid debt, illness, and helping her children grow up and find spouses, she wrote. Her many letters, her diary, and one publication (against Calvinist predestination) reveal a practical theologian and competent Christian apologist.

Susanna's diary survives in various notebooks and fragments. The mostly undated entries fell between 1709 and 1727, the rectory fire having destroyed earlier documents. It reveals her deep inner life and intellectual interests. She was fascinated, for example, by John Locke's *Essay concerning Human Understanding* (1689). This book held that all knowledge comes through the senses, and it was very influential in the Enlightenment.

She also loved the writings of Blaise Pascal, the great French mathematician and Catholic thinker of the seventeenth century. She had access to a translation of his work. "I have often said that the universal cause of men's misfortunes," she quoted Pascal in her diary, "was their not being able to live quietly in a chamber." Humans have an aversion to home. The human psychology of diversion deflects them from sitting still. They are uncomfortable in the core of who they are as human beings. Without faith, their roving and restless disposition cannot stand the sight of themselves. One of the miracles of Christianity, in reconciling man to

God, Susanna continued jotting down from Pascal, is enabling him to see himself as he is. He can know his deepest vulnerabilities and desires. The Christian faith even "renders solitude and silence more agreeable than all the intercourse and action of mankind," she quoted Pascal. To attain faith, one must regulate passions and banish diversions.[293]

Susanna took up Pascal's challenge. She "professed to renounce the world." From her diary entries, one learns that she set aside regular times during the day for prayer and writing to recollect her spirit—a typical Puritan practice she adhered to as an Anglican. "How inconceivable!" she exclaimed in one entry, simply marked "morning." "How incomprehensibly great is the goodness and patience of the divine Mind toward sinful man!" If one cannot pray, then meditate, she counseled herself. If one cannot meditate, then read to compose the mind. If one cannot read, persevere to retire at the appointed time, accepting no other advantage than "crossing and contradicting your own corrupt and carnal inclinations."[294]

One is sanctified slowly and by imperceptible degrees, she wrote. Good habits "are begot by repeated acts and cannot otherwise be acquired." Good dispositions, she continued, could be induced by the Holy Spirit, but who does not know that good dispositions may be altered or lost by want of care to improve them? Her spirituality blended God's grace and human effort. "'Tis not grace begun, but carried on and improved that will bring us to heaven." One can detect the spirit of the "age of improvement" in these words that would carry over to her sons. She praised God for creating humans as "rational free agents."[295] This was the "rational devotion" also found in the Catholic Enlightenment.

---

[293] Susanna Wesley, "Diary," in *Susanna Wesley: The Complete Writings*, ed. Charles Wallace Jr. (New York: Oxford University Press, 1997), 288. She quoted from Blaise Pascal, *Thoughts on Religion and Other Curious Subjects*, trans. Basil Kennett, 2nd ed. (London: Jacob Tonson, 1727), 191–192. She used the 1704 edition.

[294] Wesley, "Diary," 240, 241, 243.

[295] Ibid., 236, 245.

Susanna's spirituality continually intersected with her sense of vocation. Though eighteenth-century people viewed the husband unambiguously as the head of the family, this did not mean wives counted little. "The married housewife was a pillar of wisdom and worth, with a prominent position" in the hierarchical family, the historian Vickery wrote. In practice, the wife often governed the household in practical matters. Though subject, she was an equal soul in marriage, a bedfellow and domestic ally, together forming the "habit of mutually dependent intimacy," Vickery put it nicely. In a successful marriage, husband and wife usually shared power, and in reality, many men did not want a weak woman anyway. They often desired a "sexy battleaxe" Vickery wrote, commanding and capable, leaving husbands free to pursue their work without distraction.[296]

Samuel may have left Susanna *too* free to manage the household, however. In fact, they once lived apart for a year due to a political disagreement. Susanna refused to say "Amen" to her husband's family prayer for King William III. She believed the king, though a Protestant, was a usurper. So she held loyalty to the line of Stuart kings, though Catholic, deposed in 1688. Samuel said: "You and I must part; for if we have two kings, we have two beds."[297] He moved to London.

Thankfully, King William soon died, and the new monarch was acceptable to both spouses. They lived together again, and John Wesley was born a year later, the fruit of reconciliation. Nevertheless, at least once in her diary, she bemoaned the little help she had from her husband. In all things, however, "when you feel yourself afflicted by pain, sickness, or any other uneasiness, the first thing you do, make an act of submission to the will of God."[298]

Susanna's sense of vocation embraced the entire household. Each child was a talent committed to her for improvement. She advised herself

---

[296] Vickery, *Behind Closed Doors*, 9, 10.
[297] Adam Clarke, *Memoirs of the Wesley Family*, 2nd ed. (New York: Lane & Tippett, 1848), http://media.sabda.org/alkitab-6/wh2-hdm/hdm0386.pdf.
[298] Wesley, "Diary," 236, 239.

in her diary: "Be assured you must give an account at the last great day how you have discharged this trust, and if through your default any soul miscarry, how will you hold up your face in the last judgment?" She once wrote to her husband about how she discharged this trust when he was away for a few months at an annual meeting of the Church of England. "As I am a woman, so I am also mistress of a large family," she wrote. The children and even the servants she viewed as entrusted to her "by the great Lord of all the families both of heaven and earth." She began to think of herself "evangelically," or as an evangelist of the gospel to those around her: "I thought I might ... speak to those with whom I converse with more warmth of affection," she wrote to her husband. "I resolved to begin with my own children."[299]

Therefore, she took "such a proportion of time as I can spare" in the evening to spend with each child separately: "On Monday, I talk with Molly; on Tuesday, with Hetty; Wednesday, with Nancy," and so on, doubling up some of them when necessary. She spoke with John on Thursdays. Since he scarcely survived the 1709 housefire, she recognized something unique in him. "And I do intend to be more particularly careful of the soul of this child [John] ... that I may do my endeavor to instill into his mind the principles of [God's] true religion and virtue," she wrote in her May 17, 1711, diary entry. "Lord, give me grace to do it sincerely and prudently, and bless my attempts with good success." Her prayer would be answered as she supported his future vocation through her own.[300]

In one of the few other dated diary entries, for the evening of May 24, 1711, she wrote of the necessity for some "method in instructing" children. Explain the Ten Commandments, she listed, then principles of revealed religion, and finally discuss the "being and attributes of God."[301]

---

[299] Susanna Wesley to Samuel Wesley, February 6, 1712, in John Wesley, *The Heart of John Wesley's Journal*, ed. Percy L. Parker (Peabody, MA: Hendrickson, 2015), 115–116; Wesley, "Diary," 246.

[300] Susanna Wesley to Samuel Wesley, February 6, 1712, in Wesley, *The Heart of John Wesley's Journal*, 116; Wesley, "Diary," 235.

[301] Wesley, "Diary," 236.

Her care for rigorous method in spiritual householding carried over to the later Methodist movement. In fact, later in life, John asked her to write to him about the rules she observed in educating her family in a Christian way of life. The surviving letter of July 24, 1732, is one of the great documents of Methodism. In it one sees many facets of the household management she practiced.

The many children, Susanna recalled in her letter to John, were taught a "regular method of living," from dressing to undressing to changing their linen, and so forth. From a young age they were taught to fear the rod and "cry softly." Allowed to eat only at mealtimes, they learned to eat and drink what was given them. They were absolutely forbidden to circumvent parents by going secretly to the servants to ask for things.

"In order to form the minds of children," Susanna wrote, "the first thing to be done is to conquer their will and bring them to an obedient temper." She continued: "In the esteem of the world they pass for kind and indulgent, whom I call cruel, parents, who permit their children to get habits which they know must be afterward broken." Conquering the will of children is "the only strong and rational foundation of a religious education," she wrote, significantly. The parent who "studies" to subdue self-will in a child, through both punishment and kind affirmation, "works together with God" in the renewal and salvation of a soul.

The children studied six hours a day at home — and there was "no such thing as loud talking or playing allowed of," Susanna recalled. She taught them their alphabet and how to read. "It is almost incredible what a child may be taught in a quarter of a year by a vigorous application, if it have but a tolerable capacity and good health," she wrote. No girl, she concluded the letter, should be taught to work until she can read well. Putting girls to sewing before they can read perfectly is "the very reason why so few women can read fit to be heard and never to be well understood."[302]

---

[302] Susanna Wesley to John Wesley, July 24, 1732, in Wesley, *The Heart of John Wesley's Journal*, 118-127.

Susanna Wesley possessed amazing powers of organization and resil-ience. However, as in the case of Defoe, certain "occupational hazard signs" pointed to flaws along the road of Christian retreat. One of them was the Puritan temptation to moralistic disengagement from common life, which needs further analysis.

The Puritan Temptation

One of the essential questions of human beings is "How shall we live?" The cultures of the world have long provided traditional insights and customs to help people answer that question. For Christians, the gospel is the supreme law. Yet it does not provide a set pattern because there are multiple ways to live out the gospel. Thus, various collective answers to the question "How shall we live?" create different kinds of Christian cultures.

The historian of ideas Leszek Kolakowski illustrated this in a very helpful manner. "Should we escape from the world as much as possible, avoid contact with its dirty business, and strive after sainthood in isola-tion?" he asked. Should we engage in all sorts of ascetic practices and painful mortifications? Or should we simply avoid major sins and other-wise enjoy earthly life? Should everything in our life, at every moment, be consciously subordinated to the great rule [the gospel], so that when faced with any decision, however trivial and inconsequential, we must ask about its possible relevance to salvation and perform no acts which, no matter how seemingly innocent, do not contribute to this goal?" Or, he asked, has secular life some measure of independence, such that we may do our business without constantly bothering about eternity, if only we do not use it as a pretext for sin?

Answers to such questions depend very much on personal vocation. They are also, however, influenced by different spiritualities and religious cultures. According to a certain "Puritan" type of rigorous spirituality, the answer is clear: whatever human beings do is either for God or against him (and for the devil). Nothing is morally indifferent, Kolakowski summarized. Every thought and act must honor the Creator. People ought to fulfill their earthly duties, of course, but only as a matter of obedience to the commandments, never for enjoyment, for pleasure, for gain, glory, or power, Kolakowski wrote. Our eternal salvation is always at stake. Introspection and ruthless self-examination are constantly required. Rigorist gatekeepers must close the doors of the household of faith (the church) against outside influences, except those strictly necessary. This Puritan temptation took on a "Christian pessimism" about the world.[303]

There is some evidence of this Puritan mentality in the Wesleys. Susanna believed human understanding, will, and affection to be "extremely corrupted and depraved." John once wrote after a tour of the House of Lords: "How was I disappointed! What is a lord but a sinner, born to die!"[304]

In one of the schools John Wesley later managed for preachers' children, he worked out the pedagogical implications of such a rigorous mentality. Strict rules, printed for all to see, controlled their lives. Children rose at 4:00 a.m. for an hour of private devotion. They studied eight hours per day, including five languages, writing, music, and other subjects. "Recreation" involved walking or working in the garden, chopping wood, and so forth. The school did not allow play time. "He that plays when he is a child will play when he is a man," Wesley believed. Play distracted from a serious view of life. More private prayer and a public religious service ended the day. Wesley expelled students who did not keep the rules. Unsurprisingly, however, they were difficult to enforce, and Wesley was never happy with the school as a result. A later critic of the Methodists wrote against their "severe Notions of Christianity" as inconsistent with the "mild and gentle Precepts of the Gospel."[305]

---

[303] Leszek Kolakowski, *God Owes Us Nothing: A Brief Remark on Pascal's Religion and on the Spirit of Jansenism* (Chicago: University of Chicago Press, 1995), 118, 119.

[304] Susanna Wesley to Suky, January 13, 1710, in Susanna Wesley, *The Complete Writings*, 380; Wesley, *The Heart of John Wesley's Journal*, 494.

[305] "Answer to the Foregoing," *Gentleman's Magazine*, May 1739, 257; *The History of Kingswood School*, (London: Charles H. Kelly, 1898), 25–26.

The Puritan temptation—this notion of intensely rigorous spirituality that was down on the world and on the body—applied not only to Protestants. One sees it, too, in the Catholic Pascal (whom Susanna much admired) and the Jansenist movement he supported. Thinking of themselves as traditional Catholics (in France), Jansenists found strong motivations for spiritual withdrawal from the world. They believed, as did Calvin, that human nature is corrupt. It is a rebel that must be violently put in order through moral rigor and discipline. Pedagogical rules based on the depravity of human nature appeared at the seventeenth-century Port-Royal school for girls where Pascal's sister was a nun. Students should think of God only. The less their work pleased them, the more it pleased God. No concessions should be made to the body or worldly life. There is no such thing as innocent diversion, "for to amuse oneself is no less than to abandon God, even for a short time," Kolakowski summarized.[306]

Christian Optimism about the World

Christian pessimism was balanced in the Wesley family, however, by Christian optimism springing from their Anglican background. This emphasized that all human beings are made in the image of God and can choose to cooperate in their salvation. Another source was Enlightenment concern for improvement. And a third source was the works of Catholic spirituality (non-Jansenist) found on the bookshelves at Epworth rectory.

In regard to the last, it seems the saints and spiritual writers of Restoration Catholicism after the Council of Trent packed such punch that they influenced even Protestant England. One could easily obtain Catholic books there. Francis de Sales's *Introduction to the Devout Life* (1609), for example, was almost immediately translated into English. It rapidly gained almost as much attention from Protestants as from Catholics. John Wesley knew it well. Catholic spirituality also influenced him through Brother Lawrence's idea of practicing the presence

---

[306] Kolakowski, *God Owes Us Nothing*, 96, 97.

of God in one's daily life (in *The Practice of the Presence of God*), and through Thomas à Kempis's view of vital religion arising out of the transformation of one's heart as the deepest resource of one's being (in *The Imitation of Christ*).

De Sales believed that the pursuit of holiness did not require withdrawal from the world. Christian retreat might lead one into a monastery, but even there, it oriented one *outward* with a certain optimism—as among the Benedictines studied earlier. Therefore, de Sales is considered a major forerunner of Vatican Council II. Instead of thinking of themselves as abominable and wretched, de Sales wrote, the baptized should deal gently and quietly with themselves when they sin or err. Even a stern rebuke should culminate in loving trust in God. In addition, the pleasure of amusements and diversions is sometimes important for our inner lives. It is a great mistake, he wrote, to be so strict as to eliminate harmless amusements such as games, music, sports, and even dancing. "You will tell me perhaps that you would prefer to be occupied with something more serious and solid," wrote a later spiritual writer, summarizing de Sales. "But God would not prefer it for you," he wrote, directly countering the Puritan temptation. One's pursuit of the devout life, in other words, should not assume that human nature is constantly a rebel in need of violent discipline.[307] Instead, Christian optimism toward the world is rooted in a view of human nature and its desires as broken but good.

As seen in earlier chapters, Rousseau and Voltaire hated the pessimistic view of the human person—and not without good reason. Rousseau grew up in Calvinist Geneva, and Voltaire's brother was a Jansenist. When Voltaire lived in England during the 1720s, just after Franklin was there, he grew excited because it seemed to him that he had found a different view of human nature. Thus, he ended his "Letter Regarding the English

---

[307] Francis de Sales, *Introduction to the Devout Life* (1609; New York: Vintage Books, 2002), 112, 161–162; R. P Quadrupani, *Light and Peace: Instructions for Devout Souls to Dispel Their Doubts and Allay Their Fears*, 10th ed. (1795; Rockford, IL: TAN Books, 1980), 135.

Nation" with a long attack on Pascal (the Jansenist supporter) for showing man in an "odious light," as "all wicked and miserable." English life
demonstrated a different view. Business and prosperity thrived, he saw,
and might even instill a civilizing influence. Natural desires are made by
God and are good. After all, they lead to baby making and commerce,
surely foundations of society. Each creature receives "self-esteem," or
love of self, from nature. Law controls this self-love and religion perfects
it, he wrote. God *could* have made humans who care solely for the good
of others; in that case, a mason would cut stone to please his neighbor.
"But God made things differently. Let us not condemn the instinct that
He gives us, and let us use it as He commands." Thinking about oneself
apart from natural things "means thinking about nothing," Voltaire wrote.
"Whoever wants to destroy the passions [Jansenists, Puritans], rather than
governing them, wants to play the *angel*."[308]

Herein lies one of the spiritual benefits of the Practical Enlightenment for Christians. It provided cultural motivation toward adopting
a more positive view of human nature. It is one thing to *believe* in the
theological goodness of human nature as an abstraction. It is entirely
another matter to *see* the practical fruits of that belief in greater political
freedom, improved roads, and adequate food to eat. "Progress" proved to
the masses of common people for the first time in history the inherent
possibilities of the goodness in human nature. This dealt a deathblow
to the idea of human depravity and limited salvation (predestination),
associated with John Calvin and certain interpretations of Augustine.

If human beings can cooperate in their own religious improvement, as
Catholics and Protestants such as John Wesley believed, then it logically
follows they can cooperate in their own earthy improvement too. Life is
not simply a vale of tears, nor is material poverty a romantic condition.
Christian preachers among the poor more fully realized they needed
to emphasize God's kindness instead of dwelling on his wrath. Among

---

[308] Voltaire, *Philosophical Letters*, 107–108, 116, 120.

Catholics, a more optimistic view of human nature led to a revolution in moral theology away from Jansenist rigorism. The "Enlightenment moral theology" of Alphonsus Liguori (1696–1787), for example, built on the idea of Thomas Aquinas about human beings made in the image of God in possession of liberty.[309] In these ways, certain strands of the Enlightenment reinforced Christian optimism.

The Tree with Many Branches

Cultural values passed not only between Christianity and the Enlightenment but also between different branches of Christianity — as between Catholic spiritual writings and the Wesleys. Joseph Ratzinger wrote how Jesus, in Matthew 13, compared the Kingdom of God to a tree. That tree has many branches in which birds make their nests. "Perhaps the Church has forgotten that the tree of the Kingdom of God reaches beyond the branches of the visible Church," he continued, "but that is precisely why it must be a hospitable place in whose branches many guests find solace." That is a basis for ecumenical orientation.

On that basis, seeing how different kinds of Christian cultures responded to the Enlightenment is deeply informative. As Ratzinger also noted, Protestantism, in particular, possessed a certain "kinship" with the Enlightenment and helped to mold modern culture to a remarkable extent.[310] Indeed, Protestants have inspired certain innovations in Christian culture now appreciated by Catholics: Bible versification (sixteenth century), English-language hymnody (eighteenth century), and homeschooling and healthcare sharing ministries (twentieth century).

Christian retreat must not be inhospitable. It must avoid excessive pessimism about the world. Finding God *within* the heart must not stop

---

[309] Michael Printy, "The Intellectual Origins of Popular Catholicism: Catholic Moral Theology in the Age of Enlightenment," *Catholic Historical Review* 91, no. 3 (July 2005): 456.

[310] Ratzinger, "Letter to Marcello Pera," 117, 119.

there. Love of God must lead to love of neighbor in the tree with many branches.

The Religious Societies

Susanna Wesley's personal prayer life nourished her sense of vocation within her household, but this retreat also connected her inner life to people beyond the domestic threshold. For example, once with her husband away on priestly duties, Susanna led the household in singing psalms and reading aloud sermons in the warm, spacious kitchen. One of the young servants told his parents about the gatherings, and they wanted to come, too. "Then others that heard of it begged leave also: so our company increased to about thirty," she wrote to Samuel. "Last Sunday I believe we had above two hundred. And yet many went away for want of room to stand," she noted. The curate that Samuel had left in charge of the parish was miffed by these meetings. He wrote to Samuel complaining of them, for it was illegal under the Toleration Act of 1689 to gather for religious worship in unlicensed places.[311]

Susanna then wrote to Samuel that she did not care how her actions looked to others. She was endeavoring to draw people to church and to keep holy the Sabbath. "As to its looking particular [unusual], I grant it does. And so does almost anything that is serious, or that may any way advance the glory of God or the salvation of souls." In addition, she wrote to him three weeks later, the meetings "wonderfully conciliated the minds of this people towards us" — once full of resentment — "so that now we live in the greatest amity imaginable." People were returning to church. This was a matter of conscience to Susanna, and she wrote to Samuel she would only cease if he sent her "positive command, in such full and express terms as may absolve me from all guilt and punishment

[311] Susanna Wesley to Samuel Wesley, February 6, 1712, in Wesley, *The Heart of John Wesley's Journal*, 115–117.

for neglecting this opportunity of doing good."[312] Samuel allowed the meetings to continue until his return, and they made an impression on young John that he would not forget.

The sociological importance of such creative minorities as "households of faith" within a larger church structure was not lost on Christians during this time. Catholics had monasteries, religious orders, and numerous confraternities of laypeople such as the ones Maria Agnesi assisted in Milan. These gave them a great advantage during the Catholic Restoration. Without their own version of an order like the Jesuits, Protestants lost considerable ground by 1700.

Samuel Wesley recognized this problem in his published "Letter concerning the Religious Societies." "The Church of Rome owes ... most of the progress she has made of late years, to the several societies [religious orders] she nourishes to her bosom: why may we not learn from enemies?" Indeed, after the destruction of the monasteries in the English Reformation, the English-speaking world had a great need for the "religious societies" starting to spread around the Protestant world. These would promote true piety and Christian charity toward the sick and the poor. They would provide a "bulwark" against the "encroaching world," giving the church strength, beauty, and reputation—like the monasteries of old, he noted. (Samuel may have been impressed by the ruins of a Carthusian monastery just outside Epworth, dissolved under Henry VIII in 1538.) The exemplary piety of the monks and their way of life, he wrote, were "highly instrumental" in first planting and propagating Christianity in Britain. Something like them was needed again.

Samuel proposed an ambitious vision. Religious societies would promote "in a regular manner" the glory of God and the salvation of members and their neighbors. They would be so conducted as to avoid fomenting Christian division and sectarian thinking. He specifically targeted the burgeoning world of "trade and business" as in need of them. People

---

[312] Ibid., 117; Susanna Wesley to Samuel Wesley, February 25, 1712, in Eliza Clarke, *Susanna Wesley* (London: W. H. Allen, 1886), 107–109.

could accomplish so much more when united in groups than singly, he observed. "We see it in trades every day; and why should we not learn from those who are wise in their generation?" Like corporate business ventures, religious societies (as already existed in London) could unleash the energy of spiritual enterprise needed to assist the church in bringing the people of England back to the faith.[313]

Like Catholic third orders for laypeople, Protestant religious societies helped members pursue personal conversion and holiness of life together. They did this through study of Scripture; works of charity for the poor, the ignorant, and the sick; mutual accountability; and even fasting and examinations of conscience. The societies emphasized evangelical zeal and practical Christian living over intellectual acumen. In this way, as one historian wrote, they attempted to "refocus the center of religious sensitivity upon the heart rather than the mind." Thus, they contrasted sharply with the rational spirit of the age.[314]

Samuel started one of these evangelically oriented religious societies in Epworth about the time his son John was born, in 1703. A small group (limited to twelve) would meet to pray, read Scripture, and plan charitable works and the evangelization of neighbors.

Samuel was also involved in the Society for Promoting Christian Knowledge (SPCK), started in 1698 by Anglican clergyman Thomas Bray. Bray believed in the power of the printed word. He wanted to use the rising authority of print media to confront the problems of the day. He and a small group of friends were concerned about widespread ignorance, poverty, and immorality. They met together and decided that the best strategy to confront those problems was to publish and distribute Christian literature. The SPCK raised money to give away millions of Bibles, prayer books, and catechisms. The organization also supported

---

[313] Samuel Wesley, "A Letter concerning the Religious Societies," in Clarke, *Memoirs of the Wesley Family*.

[314] Richard P. Heitzenrater, *Wesley and the People Called Methodists*, 2nd ed. (Nashville: Abingdon, 2013), 20, 22.

charity schools for poor children. Today, the SPCK is the oldest Anglican missionary organization in the world and is still the leading publisher of Christian books in England.

The Road to Aldersgate

Susanna and Samuel's vision of an evangelically oriented Christianity, nurtured in the retreat of home and heart, propelled their two sons John and Charles into their lifelong mission. That mission started during their student days at Oxford as they prepared for ordination. Immersed in the irreligious and deistic environment of the 1720s (when Franklin was in London), they clearly saw the need for little bands of friends to live out the faith in a methodical manner. They met regularly to pray, study, and perform charitable works toward prisoners, the poor, and the elderly. Concerned for proper care of time, John kept a diary as a record and measure of spiritual progress. He purchased religious books from the SPCK to distribute. He also helped organize subsidiary groups that formed spontaneously in connection to his own. A unique blend of faith and life emerged that grew into the Methodist reform movement within the Church of England.

This "Oxford movement" — a hundred years before the later Oxford Movement that produced John Henry Newman — soon propelled John Wesley even to the remote colony of Georgia as a volunteer missionary. In fact, he was part of the wider Protestant missionary movement first emerging in the eighteenth century that would greatly affect modern world history. Christian optimism meant that people could freely choose to accept God's grace or not: thus, there is an evangelical imperative to reach out to others. Accordingly, John Wesley preached in the churches, encouraged religious societies, and published the first English hymn book in the American colonies (1737). Rooted in the psalms, these hymns emphasized God's transcendence and love of human beings. Formed in the bosom of "household" retreat in small groups of people seeking holiness together — both at Epworth and at Oxford — Wesley and his friends committed themselves to building up Christian culture from within.

But his ministry in Georgia did not last long, partly due to missteps on his part. John felt God had humbled him, one historian wrote, to better acknowledge God's direction in his life.[315] John returned to England realizing his own need for deeper conversion. That happened at Aldersgate.

Aldersgate was a ward (precinct) within London. On May 24, 1738, John Wesley walked (unwillingly, he recorded) to a prayer meeting there. As he listened to a commentary on the Letter to the Romans about the change that God works in the heart through faith in Christ, "I felt my heart strangely warmed," Wesley wrote. "I felt I did trust in Christ, Christ alone, for salvation; and an assurance was given me that He had taken away my sins, even mine, and saved me from the law of sin and death." He rejoiced and prayed. Nevertheless, during the following days and weeks, he continued to wrestle with what exactly had happened to him in that Pentecost experience.[316]

Scholars have long debated the meaning of Aldersgate. Wesley himself claimed this was the moment he became a Christian. What he meant, it seems, was that the true core of his person (his heart) was touched by the grace of God more deeply than ever before. His outward Christian actions had been rigidly drilled for decades, all the way back to his youth in the Wesley family household. Now the *source* of those actions, the heart, with its desires and hopes and powers, was changed by the grace of God. Thus, conversion became "not a moment in one's life, but the key to interpreting the meaning of one's life from beginning to end," wrote historian D. Bruce Hindmarsh.[317] It was the heart of the matter.

---

[315] Ibid., 79.

[316] Wesley, *The Heart of John Wesley's Journal*, 66.

[317] William M. Arnett, "What Happened to Wesley at Aldersgate?," *Asbury Seminarian* 18, no. 1 (1964): 11; D. Bruce Hindmarsh, *The Evangelical Conversion Narrative: Spiritual Autobiography in Early Modern England* (New York: Oxford University Press, 2005), 322.

Aldersgate came to represent a different type of conversion than the traditional Anglican conception of gradual spiritual growth throughout life. The evangelical conversion, by contrast, was an inner experience of saving spiritual knowledge said to be gained in no other way. The difference is seen in a letter Susanna wrote to Charles after his experience of evangelical conversion, which happened just days before John's at Aldersgate. "I think you are fallen into an odd way of thinking," she wrote. "I do not judge it necessary for us to know the precise time of our conversion." The Lord works in various ways and by various means in different people. Regeneration begins at Baptism and is not perfected at once. Do not worry overmuch about internal feelings to test the quality of faith, she advised. Rather, faith is known by whether we love God, love neighbor, and obey God's commandments. It is "one thing to have faith," she wrote, "and another thing to be sensible we have it. Faith is the fruit of the Spirit and is the gift of God, but to feel or be inwardly sensible that we have true faith requires a further operation of God's Holy Spirit."[318] Through wise letters such as this, Susanna exerted a subtle influence on the early Methodist movement.

The road to Aldersgate represented a completely different sort of conversion from Rousseau's road to Vincennes. Rousseau's secular conversion led away from God to self in order to find Self. Wesley converted from Self to God. By finding God, he also found self. Rousseau's religious experience, as evidenced by his later work, implied that human beings are basically "good at heart" and do not need Jesus Christ as a personal Redeemer. Redemption comes through emotional pantheism and through state action in the name of the "general will." Wesley's religious experience, on the other hand, began in being "cut to the heart" about personal sin and the need for the mercy of Jesus Christ. Just as in the case of Rousseau, Wesley's conversion experience was a pivotal moment in his life. It is recognized as such within the Methodist community to this day. From 1738 onward, a new power and influence pervaded Wesley's preaching.

---

[318] Susanna Wesley to Charles Wesley, December 6, 1738, in *Susanna Wesley: The Complete Writings*, 176–177.

10

The Heart of the Matter

Nature Abhors a Vacuum

In 2016, British researchers made a fascinating discovery at a private home near Bristol in southwest England. They already knew the oddly shaped structure was an old "fire engine" house, but no one fully understood its significance. The owners of the property let them enter their home to study it. Through historical documents and wood samples from the rafters, the researchers confirmed that the enginehouse (the framework of the home) was built between 1736 and 1738. This makes it one of the oldest surviving structures related to the Industrial Revolution and certainly the oldest surviving and complete enginehouse in the world.[319]

Enginehouses were the supporting structures around the world's first successful steam engines, invented in 1712 by the English ironworker (and Baptist lay preacher) Thomas Newcomen (1664–1729). The mechanical engineer James Watt (1736–1819) later made improvements to this initial engine, making it more efficient. These engines harnessed steam power to pump water out of mine shafts. This invention marked the first utilization of a fuel-based power supply (coal, then oil) that has driven modern societies ever since.

---

[319] David Hardwick, "Investigating the Newcomen Pumping Engine House at Brislington near Bristol," *International Journal for the History of Engineering & Technology* 88, no. 2 (2018): 166–203.

This is how it worked: fire in a boiler heated water to create steam. The steam forced a piston upward in a cylinder, which then operated a beam balance and pump. Next, hot vapor was instantly condensed by letting in cold water, thereby forming a partial vacuum. Since "nature abhors a vacuum" the piston returned to its original position under the force of the atmosphere above it. This was the "power stroke" pumping up water from far below. This up and down movement created a reciprocating mechanical motion of about twelve revolutions per minute. These ingenious machines—like pumpjacks at oil wells today—proliferated across England by the 1730s. This was the Practical Enlightenment in motion, made possible by a scientific culture giving pride of place to mechanics. It profoundly changed the world.

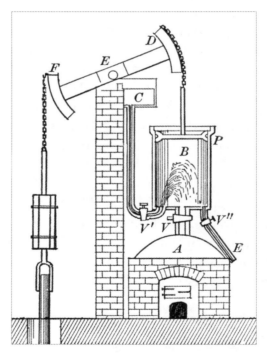

Diagram of a Newcomen Steam Engine
(A = boiler, B = cylinder, E = beam, P = piston).

Down below, in the depths beneath the enginehouses, the colliers—or miners—hewed, hauled, and winched up coal manually. They faced darkness, poisonous air, sudden flooding, roof collapses, and falling accidents. "We have an account from Kingswood [just outside Bristol] that 9 Colliers were kill'd by the Fall of a Mine," stated a 1723 newspaper.[320] Reports usually left out the names of the dead—and any empathy for the emotional trauma of bereft wives and children. "Death makes dreadful havoc in the mines," wrote an unknown poet in a Bristol newspaper:

> Here a rude cottage stands in mould'ring mud
> The bleak wind whistles through its gaping sides
> The children feed upon the floor, naked and starving
> Or with bread and water fed while poor parents,
> lab'ring at the mines
> Are digging night and day to starve along!
>
> Behold! A place dreadful to the traveller benighted!
> In ages past a coalmine four score fathom deep
> What art, what industry, what danger great
> To enter and to empty the bowels of the earth!
>
> How many thousands in the world would not
> For gold descend so low—while Kingswood
> Swarms with those who venture thus for bread?
> And cheerful labour through the darkened day
> Depriv'd of thy blest beams, thou glorious sun![321]

Amid these dreadful conditions, women and children sorted the coal at the surface. Hundreds of packhorses transported it into Bristol to feed

---

[320] *Gloucestershire Journal*, June 10, 1723, Patsy Mac's Genealogy, http://www.genebug.net/glsinquests.htm.

[321] E. W., "Kingswood—A Fragment," *Bristol Journal* (August 10, 1765), in D. P. Lindegaard, *Killed in a Coalpit: Lives of the Kingswood Colliers* (Gloucestershire: South Gloucestershire Mines Research Group, 2016), v.

cooking hearths, soap making, sugar refining, and brass production. There were not enough trees to feed the fires of industry; hence the annual need for more than one hundred thousand tons of coal in the region.

The business writer Daniel Defoe described the Bristol merchants: "As they have a very great Trade abroad, so they have always Buyers at home for their Returns, and such Buyers, that no Cargo is too big for them."[322] A triangular trade route returned large profits: Bristol merchants exported cloth, brandy, and lead to west Africa; transported slaves from there to the New World; then returned to England with rum, sugar, and other raw materials. Banks and insurance companies funded and protected the trading ships, so financial institutions grew. Hundreds of alehouses flourished. All of this brought prosperity and debauchery to Bristol but left the Kingswood colliers in misery.

In 1738, just as construction of the Bristol enginehouse was completed, the Kingswood colliers went on strike. Many of them were squatters and wandering migrants attracted there by industrial employment. They were tough, and they were furious at cuts in wages. The colliers took out their anger by spreading mayhem against the "big city" people in Bristol. They broke into alehouses (drinking and eating without payment), marched through the narrow streets shouting, and smashed coal wagons, spilling their contents about the streets. Soldiers arrived to keep the peace.

"Few persons have lived long in the west of England who have not heard of the colliers of Kingswood," John Wesley wrote in his journal; "a famous people ... for neither fearing God nor regarding man."[323] The Kingswood colliers took pride in the wild independence of their home community just outside the reach of civic jurisdiction. The Bristolians feared the colliers as untamed and ungovernable. But they needed their coal. The growth of industry created jobs but also broke ties of sympathy between classes, fostering restless discontent.

---

[322] Daniel Defoe, *Tour Thro' the Whole Island of Great Britain*, 6th ed. (London: D. Browne, 1761), 2:299.

[323] Wesley, *The Heart of John Wesley's Journal*, 91.

Early in the spring of 1739, as labor unrest continued, the Anglican priest George Whitefield arrived among the unchurched colliers. Having just experienced a profound movement of the Holy Spirit at his ordination, and before he sailed to the American colonies to fan the Great Awakening into flame there, he ministered to the Kingswood mining families. Thousands came to listen. "The Rev. Mr. Whitefield ... has been wonderfully laborious and successful, especially among ... the rude Colliers of Kingswood," the high-circulation *Gentleman's Magazine* reported—"preaching every Day to large Audiences, visiting, and expounding to religious Societies." Whitefield urged his friend John Wesley to come help.

Wesley was shocked at the situation when he arrived in April. "I could scarcely reconcile myself at first to this strange way of preaching in the fields" employed by Whitefield, he wrote in his journal. "I have been all my life (till very lately) so tenacious of every point relating to decency and order that I should have thought the saving of souls almost a sin if it had not been done in a church." Overcoming his reluctance and class prejudices, he "submitted to be more vile," he noted. Wesley began preaching in the open to a people who seemed completely ignorant of the things of God. Therefore, they were "the more ready to cry to God for ... redemption."[324]

Over six thousand people came to hear Wesley in Kingswood on April 8. "Every one that thirsteth, come ye to the waters," he proclaimed—"in the name of the Lord." So many people crowded together indoors a week later to hear him, the floor gave way. One critic wrote to the *Gentleman's Magazine* that if these preachers detained so many of "the Vulgar from their daily Labour, what a Loss, in a little Time, may this bring to the Public!" The "Industry of the inferior People" is the great source of prosperity in any society, he snapped. "For my Part, I shall expect to hear

---

[324] "Bristol," *Gentleman's Magazine*, March 1739, 162; Wesley, *The Heart of John Wesley's Journal*, 70; J. D. Walsh, "Elie Halévy and the Birth of Methodism," *Transactions of the Royal Historical Society* 25 (1975): 15.

of a prodigious Rise in the Price of Coals, about the City of Bristol."[325] But the poor of England had not heard field preachers among them since the days of the medieval Franciscans. Their need was great. The price of coal be damned.

"Nature abhors a vacuum" applies to more than the operation of a steam engine. It reveals the nature of the human heart: "Where there is no vision, the people perish" (Prov. 29:18, KJV). If nothing fills the spiritual vacuum inside human beings, the pistons of the inner engine remain motionless. The twentieth-century psychiatrist Viktor Frankl called this lack of meaning an "existential vacuum."[326] This empty spiritual space can attract anarchic and utopian forces strong enough to reciprocate the pistons of desperate revolt, blind violence, and social revolution.

Alternatively, the vacuum inside can be filled with the hope of Heaven, introducing a new and more peaceful daily life. The Kingswood poet quoted earlier, after giving expression to the terrible sufferings of the miners and their families, then gave voice to the new hope in the hearts of the many miners who embraced the efforts of the preachers who came to them:

> Now when a brother or father falls
> Devotion wafts the parting soul to bliss
> And the black multitude assemble all
> And with united faith
> Unbar the gates of everlasting life
> Courting the entrance of the King of Glory!

This work of evangelization changed the course of the eighteenth century. George Whitefield and John and Charles Wesley, historian Christopher Dawson wrote, "appealed to just those classes which might

---

[325] Wesley, *The Heart of John Wesley's Journal*, 71; "Answer to the Foregoing," *The Gentleman's Magazine*, May 1739, 257.

[326] Viktor E. Frankl, *Man's Search for Meaning: An Introduction to Logotherapy* (1946; New York: Pocket Books, 1963), 170.

otherwise have afforded fruitful soil for the political agitator." The move-ment they founded turned revolutionary forces "into religious channels." A strongly transcendent religious vision left less room in the souls of peo-ple for philosophical and political substitutes of ultimate meaning. "The religious conversion of the individual," Dawson wrote, "took the place of the political revolution of society" in the English-speaking world.[327]

These fascinating insights raise many questions. How did religious revival happen during the age of the Enlightenment? If inner revolution took the place of political revolution, did this mean Whitefield and the Wesleys helped prevent political upheaval in England, as the historian Élie Halévy (1870–1937) thought? If so, then what does one make of the religious revival in relation to the American and French revolutions? Did the religious vision imparted to them mean that the Kingswood col-liers just had to accept injustice because their hope was elsewhere? And what of the fact that early Methodism was itself seen as a revolutionary movement rather than as a conservative force? What exactly was the significance of religious conversion in the eighteenth century? How did religious revival, stemming from Christian retreat, affect the age? How did it interact with the Practical Enlightenment?

These are wide-ranging and important questions. An attempt to answer them requires discussion in three areas: (1) the Christian strategy of retreat that moved from householding to evangelizing a nation did so through five mediums: mobility, field preaching, publishing, music, and institutional thinking; (2) this same strategy interacted with the Enlightenment by utilizing, at times, the strategies of engagement as well as of conflict; and (3) the fruits of a massive "New Evangelization" (in both the Protestant and Catholic worlds) affected the greatest events of the age, including the American and French revolutions and the British abolitionist movement. Starting with a small-scale example will help illuminate these claims.

---

[327] E. W., "Kingswood — A Fragment," in Lindegaard, *Killed in a Coalpit*, 153; Dawson, *The Gods of Revolution*, 136.

How Did Religious Revival Affect the Bristol Area?

John Wesley regularly preached in the Bristol area between 1739 and 1742, and he returned every year for fifty years. Charles Wesley made the city his home. Their preaching (timed to avoid regular church services), along with charitable outreach and the activity of religious societies, attracted not only the Kingswood colliers but also spinners, plasterers, hatters, shoemakers, bakers, servants, shopkeepers, and housewives. The aim was to bring about religious conversion, not start a new church, so the appeal reached across denominational lines to Presbyterians, Quakers, and Anglicans. Anyone could metaphorically walk the "road to Aldersgate."

By the grace of God, "the scene is already changed," John wrote late in 1739. "Kingswood does not now, as a year ago, resound with cursing and blasphemy. It is no more filled with drunkenness and uncleanness and the idle diversions that naturally lead thereto. It is no longer full of wars and fightings, of clamor and bitterness, or wrath and envyings. Peace and love are there."[328]

One important example of change came at the Bristol city prison, Newgate, a place filled with woe. After initial resistance, the Methodists saw chapel attendance and Scripture replace drunkenness and prostitution. The whole place had the "appearance of a quiet, serious family," Wesley wrote.[329] Civil authorities tended to neglect even necessities in prisons during the eighteenth century, but Christians such as John Wesley and others drew attention to much-needed prison reform — giving practical substance to wider Enlightenment humanitarian concern for individuals.

Another example: as hardworking Englishmen, the Kingswood colliers clearly understood their own interests and rights. The colliers knew that political authority should be held accountable, and they utilized supplication, threats, demonstrations of power, and collective violence to do just that. The Wesleys helped to diffuse this potential violence.

[328] Wesley, *The Heart of John Wesley's Journal*, 92.
[329] Ibid., 304.

As Charles Wesley recorded in his journal, riding out of Kingswood one day in 1740, a thousand colliers met him on the road. They were "rising" (marching on Bristol to demonstrate) due to the high corn prices. Charles immediately confronted the colliers, calling on them to desist. The leaders would not listen, however, and violently beat anyone who hesitated to keep going. "I rode up to a ruffian who was striking one of our colliers, and prayed him rather to strike me," Charles wrote. "He would not, he said . . . and was quite overcome." Charles then sought out one of the tallest among the throng to follow him, still trying to deflect the mob energy. "About six more I pressed into Christ's service," Charles wrote. Together they exhorted others to follow them as they marched along singing. They made their way to the Methodist school in Kingswood. "From one till three we spent in prayer that evil might be prevented, and the lion chained," Charles wrote. "Then the news was brought us that the colliers were returned in peace." They had entered Bristol without sticks and went to the mayor with their grievances. Then they returned peacefully. "All who saw were amazed," Charles noted.[330] In his strong stance among them on the road that day, the colliers met a new source of spiritual authority. This was a power that called them to responsibility above the clashing of material interest.

This did not end violence in the area for good, of course. The Kingswood colliers were involved in riots for decades after this incident. However, later accounts from the Bristolian point of view credited the Wesleys for the civilizing effects of their work. The Quaker Sarah Fox praised Wesley in her 1791 diary as "the instrument of civilizing almost from a savage state, the colliers at Kingswood." An official publication noted in 1794 that fifty years earlier, the colliers were barbarous. They were dangerous and spoke in a rude dialect. The efforts of Whitefield and

---

[330] Charles Wesley, *The Journal of Charles Wesley (1707–1788)*, September 22, 1740, Wesley Center Online, http://wesley.nnu.edu/charles-wesley/the-journal-of-charles-wesley-1707-1788/.

the Wesleys, however, had civilized and improved them in "principles, morals and pronunciation."[331]

The coming of a new hope helped the colliers and other marginalized people accept their sufferings and hard conditions. It also led to practical improvements in the world. Far from raising the price of coal, as the earlier critic warned, religious revival had the potential to induce the converted to greater labor. "Gain all you can.... Save all you can.... Give all you can," Wesley preached, distilling his advice for the use of money. Life is not simply a vale of tears. You *can* improve it by using all the gifts God has given you. "It is amazing to observe how few do this," he wrote. A Christian should always try to improve, to do better today than he or she did yesterday. He also cautioned against the dangers of riches, however, and gave away most of his own money.[332]

Religion and Culture

How did religious revival affect people beyond Bristol? The great French historian Élie Halévy argued that the rise of Methodism and the evangelical revival protected England from revolutionary ideology. It secured the social order by encouraging solidarity between the middle and working classes and subsidiarity in the formation of many religious societies and associations. These little groups worked for the reformation of society not so much by revolutionary state action as by voluntary effort and self-government.[333] Personal discipline (virtue) at the local level led to

---

[331] Kenneth Morgan, *John Wesley in Bristol* (Bristol: Historical Association, 1990), 20; Robert W. Malcolmson, *A Set of Ungovernable People: The Kingswood Colliers in the Eighteenth Century* (Kingswood: Kingswood Borough Council, 1986), 6.

[332] John Wesley, "The Use of Money," in *The Sermons of John Wesley: A Collection for the Christian Journey*, ed. Kenneth J. Collins and Jason E. Vickers (Nashville: Abingdon, 2013), 308, 311.

[333] Élie Halévy, *The Birth of Methodism in England* (1906; Chicago: University of Chicago Press, 1971), 51, 74–76; David Hempton, "Wesley in Context,"

public liberty. This interpretation has been debated for decades but it remains influential to this day.

By examining the mediums by which the Wesleys and other evangelists of the day reached masses of common people, one can assess not only Halévy's thesis but also the wider relationship between religion and culture in the eighteenth century.

The First Medium: Mobility

A "medium" is the means by which meaning is communicated. There were limits to how well static church structures and their messages could reach the restless and lonely people of the eighteenth century in England. Broken families and new job opportunities sent many rootless people wandering. In addition, there were not enough church buildings in the places they lived. Someone would have to bring meaning *to* these needy people via the medium of mobility. That someone (among others) was John Wesley.

Loneliness was an impetus for many of the early Methodist conversion stories. The breakdown of households through tragedy and sin created deep wounds in the hearts of many people. In story after story of ordinary people now forgotten to history, children lost their parents, and parents neglected their children. Thomas Taylor and John Mason both were orphaned at age five. Thomas Olivers lost his parents and was shipped off to boarding school, separating him from his brother. One woman wrote that no one formed her early religious sense because her grandmother was dead, her mother was sick, and her father hated being at home. Alexander Mather's father kicked him out of the house. Martha Clagget wrote: "I was almost left to myself, my parents being greatly engaged in worldly affairs." Her husband beat her after she started going to Methodist meetings. Sarah Ryan's father was an alcoholic. He sold

in *The Cambridge Companion to John Wesley*, ed. Randy L. Maddox and Jason E. Vickers (New York: Cambridge University Press, 2010), 73-74.

their family possessions for drink and forced Sarah and her mother into the poor house. Mary Tooth's father died when she was seven, and she also lost five brothers and a sister. Margerit Austin's husband abused her and abandoned her and their two children. Of the surviving conversion letters written in Bristol in the 1740s, only one man and one woman described a positive relationship with a spouse.[334]

Encouraged by the response of the Kingswood colliers, John Wesley took upon himself a single mission: to bring the gospel to people such as these. "I look upon all the world as my parish," he wrote. All his time, all his actions, would serve that purpose. "John Wesley's conversation is good," the man of letters Samuel Johnson wrote, "but he is never at leisure. He is always obliged to go at a certain hour. This is very disagreeable to a man who loves to fold his legs and have out his talk, as I do."[335] Wesley did not have time for that. He was a man of action and spent much of his life on horseback.

Wesley possessed incredible physical stamina and rarely fell ill. His journal recorded many challenges, from roving mobs that might detain him for hours to snowy roads and storms. "The wind rose higher and higher till it was ready to overturn both man and beast," he recorded. Then a violent storm came of rain and hail. It drove through coat and boots and froze his eyebrows. He could scarcely move when he finally reached an inn.[336]

On May 27, 1742, he arrived at Newcastle in northern England. He had scarcely seen such drunkenness, cursing, and swearing—even from the mouths of small children. "Surely this place is ripe for Him who 'came not to call the righteous, but sinners to repentance,'" he wrote.

---

[334] Phyllis Mack, *Heart Religion in the British Enlightenment: Gender and Emotion in Early Methodism* (New York: Cambridge University Press, 2008), 75-76.

[335] Wesley, *The Heart of John Wesley's Journal*, 79; James Boswell, *Life of Johnson* (1791), entry for 1778, https://www.gutenberg.org/files/1564/1564-h/1564-h.htm.

[336] Wesley, *The Heart of John Wesley's Journal*, 175.

John Wesley field preaching in Cornwall,
England. Woodcut, 1888.

Wesley proceeded to the poorest and most contemptible part of town. He began to sing. Soon three or four people looked out to see what the matter was. Then four or five hundred gathered. Then twelve to fifteen hundred. Wesley preached on Isaiah 53:5: "He was wounded for our transgressions, he was bruised for our iniquities" (KJV). "Observing the people, when I had done, to stand gaping and staring upon me, with the most profound astonishment, I told them, 'If you desire to know who I am, my name is John Wesley. At five in the evening, with God's help, I design to preach here again.'"

When the appointed time came: "I never saw so large a number of people together," Wesley wrote. He spoke of the love and healing power of God. "After preaching," he recorded, "the poor people were ready to tread me under foot, out of pure love and kindness. It was some time before I could possibly get out of the press."[337]

Newcastle, which Wesley visited at least fifty times, formed the northern home base of the "Wesley Triangle." This was the geographical framework for his itinerant ministry for fifty years, leading from Bristol to London to Newcastle and back. By the time Wesley died in 1791, he had travelled 250,000 miles by horseback around the English-speaking world and delivered 40,000 sermons. Crowds regularly numbered in the thousands.

This ministry was greatly aided by improvements in infrastructure brought about by "turnpike trusts." The government granted trustees the right to charge tolls on a section of road in order to raise money for improvement. This scheme proliferated and greatly reduced travel times, from around ninety hours between London and Manchester in 1700, for example, to sixty hours in 1760 and to twenty-four hours in 1787. This lowered freight charges, thereby expanding the economy and further increasing mobility. These improvements were part of the transportation revolution of the Practical Enlightenment, and John Wesley took advantage of them.

Wesley often read as he rode along these roads, absorbing and evaluating contemporary thought in the light of Christian faith. "History, poetry, and philosophy I commonly read on horseback, having other employment at other times," he wrote. "How is it that no horse ever stumbles while I am reading?" he wondered in his journal. "No account can possibly be given but this: because then I throw the reins on his neck." In a hundred thousand miles, he remembered only two horses falling while he was reading.[338]

[337] Ibid., 109–110.
[338] Ibid., 386.

He recorded one day reading "with much expectation a celebrated book—Rousseau upon Education. But how I was disappointed!" he continued. "Sure a more consummate coxcomb [a vain and conceited person] never saw the sun! How amazingly full of himself!" Voltaire, too, is a coxcomb, Wesley commented, only he hides it better. Rousseau's book is grounded in neither reason nor experience. The good advice he gives is trite and common, only disguised under new expressions. He thinks he is an oracle, but many of his oracles are palpably false. "Such discoveries I always expect from those who are too wise to believe their Bibles," was Wesley's final judgment.[339]

Wesley's journal is a fascinating record of his movements and observations about the ordinary people of the eighteenth century. He wrote affectionately of the "earnest, loving, simple people" who crowded around him. He also noted elegant congregations, but he expected little good to be done among them. "For we begin at the wrong end: religion must not go from the greatest to the least, or the power would appear to be of men," he noted. "I was a little out of my element among lords and ladies," he wrote on another occasion. "I love plain music and plain company best."[340]

So Wesley prioritized the marginalized: the wild colliers, the blasphemous soldiers, and the stupid and violent people who threw potatoes or drove their oxen through his audience, trying to disrupt the preaching. Once he walked straight into the midst of an angry mob in London and proclaimed the name of the Lord. Wesley told them they could not escape the face of God and that they should all join in prayer for his mercy. "To this they readily agreed," he summarized. He often marveled in his journal how the power of God either "tamed the wild beasts" of the people (their passions) or "chained them up." As he began preaching, the silence "spread farther and farther till I had a quiet, attentive congregation," he wrote on one occasion. Wesley's shocking message that holiness and salvation are open to *everyone* affirmed the dignity of

[339] Ibid., 384–385.
[340] Ibid., 279, 339, 467.

Gin Lane (1751), by William Hogarth, depicts a scene of urban desolation
in London. These were the marginalized Wesley tried to reach.

those on the margins of society. While there were few African slaves in
England, this truth reached even African American slaves on the other
side of the Atlantic Ocean, among whom Methodism spread widely later
in the century. Wesley felt great compassion for such as these — all the
more, because others seemed to despair of them.[341]

[341] Ibid., 95, 335.

The Second Medium: Field Preaching

In the Christian tradition, strong evangelical preaching is the fruit of faithful intimacy with Christ. Like the Apostle Peter's preaching in Acts 2:37, it clearly delineates sin and cuts "to the heart," convicting sinners and moving them toward conversion. It is also bold in its proclamation of the Risen Christ as divine and thus worthy of giving him one's whole heart and life.[342]

Field preaching seems to have arisen among the earliest Methodists in Wales, then spread to Whitefield and Wesley. It became the characteristic apostolate of the movement. "In the name of God," Wesley wrote, "let us, if possible, secure the present generation from drawing back to perdition! Let all the preachers that are still alive to God join together as one man, fast and pray, lift up their voice as a trumpet ... and exhort them instantly to repent."[343]

This spiritual mission was accomplished with the help of practical methods. John Wesley's *Directions concerning Pronunciation and Gesture* for lay preachers was printed in Bristol in 1749. The "medium I recommend," he wrote about use of one's voice, "ought not to drop, but to flow along ... like a gliding stream, not as a rapid torrent." The body should communicate the message of the words in "a natural and graceful manner, as various circumstances may require."[344] For his part, George Whitefield made regular use of his training in theater during his preaching.

Preachers often looked for places of optimal acoustics. They spoke under trees or alongside church walls to project their voices better. One of the best places Wesley frequented was at the village of Gwennap in the copper-mining district of southwest England. Nearby was a pit caused by the collapse of a mine shaft underground. Wesley described it as a

---

[342] Robert Barron, "Called out of Corruption and into Christ," YouTube video, 18:28, posted May 3, 2020. https://www.youtube.com/watch?v=AtOv-YdXR0M.

[343] Wesley, *The Heart of John Wesley's Journal*, 487.

[344] John Wesley, *Directions concerning Pronunciation and Gesture* (1749; Bristol: William Pine, 1770), 6, 10.

"round, green hollow, gently shelving down," about fifty feet deep and two or three hundred feet wide. This formed a natural amphitheater. He stood at one side with people both below him in the pit and spreading away above the pit sometimes to a considerable distance. Wesley preached there eighteen times during the decades of his ministry. In the right weather conditions (calm and clear), he reported an audience of up to twenty or thirty thousand people who, upon later inquiry, could all hear "even to the skirts of the congregation! Perhaps the first time that a man of seventy had been heard by thirty thousand persons at once!" he wrote in 1773.[345]

This question of numbers and hearing in an age before microphones is an interesting one. The Gwennap pit is still used for religious purposes, and two thousand people can sit inside it comfortably. But thirty thousand, as claimed by Wesley and by newspapers? The skeptical Benjamin Franklin himself wondered about reports of thousands listening to George Whitefield in the American colonies. "He had a loud and clear voice," Franklin wrote, describing Whitefield, "and articulated his words and sentences so perfectly that he might be heard and understood at a great distance." Franklin wondered just how far that distance was:

> Being among the hindmost in Market Street [among the audience in Philadelphia], I had the curiosity to learn how far he could be heard by retiring backwards down the street towards the [Delaware] river, and I found his voice distinct till I came near Front Street, when some noise in that street, obscured it. Imagining then a semicircle, of which my distance should be the radius, and that it were filled with auditors, to each of whom I allowed two square feet, I computed that he might well be heard by more than Thirty Thousand. This reconciled me to the newspaper accounts of his [Whitefield] having preached to 25,000 people in the fields.[346]

[345] Wesley, *The Heart of John Wesley's Journal*, 359, 427.
[346] Franklin, *The Autobiography and Other Writings*, 101–102.

Once again, the parallel Enlightenment and Christian cultures met in the ever-practical Franklin. It seems possible, then, that hundreds of thousands of people did indeed hear the messages transmitted to them through mass revivals and missions in the eighteenth century.

How Did Listeners Respond?

Some ignored the field preachers or walked away from them, shaking their heads. For others, the message initiated a chain reaction of religious experience that led to conversion. There is a remarkable (and rare) account of how this worked in the memoir of a certain Nathan Cole. He was a Connecticut carpenter and farmer. The news spread that George Whitefield was preaching at Philadelphia "like one of the Old apostles" and that great crowds were converted to Christ. "I felt the Spirit of God drawing me by conviction; I longed to see and hear him, and wished he would come this way [Connecticut]."

On October 23, 1740, Cole was out in the fields working. Suddenly, a messenger arrived saying that Whitefield was going to preach that very morning in a town nearby. Cole dropped his tools and ran home to alert his wife and fetch his horse. The couple rode horseback as fast as they could, "all the while fearing we should be too late to hear the Sermon, for we had twelve miles to ride double in little more than an hour" he wrote. As they approached, they heard a low, rumbling thunder. A cloud was rising. It was the sound and dust of thousands of horses' feet as a multitude converged into the main roads. Every horse, covered with foam and sweat, "seemed to go with all his might to carry his rider to hear news from heaven for the saving of Souls," Cole wrote; "it made me tremble to see the Sight, how the world was in a Struggle." The land and the banks of the river swarmed black with people and horses for miles. The fields were all deserted. Then, seeing Whitefield afar off set him into a "trembling fear.... And my hearing him preach, gave me a heart wound." Cole went home pondering deeply. Not long after this, he took up the Bible on a sleepless night and read John, chapter 15, about Christ the true vine and the Father the gardener. "My heart and Soul were filled as full as they Could hold with Joy and sorrow;... now every thing praised God; the trees, the stone, the walls of the house and every thing I could set my eyes on, they all praised God."[347] This was the power of the Great Awakening across the colonies. The simple prose and emotional detail of this memoir make it one of the most remarkable texts of eighteenth-century America.

Others, too, wrote about how the spoken word of the field preachers convicted their hearts. One who heard John Wesley in Bristol around 1742, Elizabeth Halfpenny (nothing is known about her), initially thought he was a Catholic, probably because of his apostolic view of the church (guided by bishops) and his emphasis on good works. She recorded hearing him preach on the death of Lazarus, "when I found Such work in my heart as I never felt before," she wrote. Halfpenny "Saw the Necessity of a Thorough Change of Life, a Blessing so great that I knew not how to Praise God for." She recorded experiencing forgiveness for her sins, the word of God sinking into her heart, and the wish that "I may have no head knowledge, or wisdom of my own, but that Wisdom which flows from God."

Wesley's words pierced the heart. A certain John Nelson remembered the first time he heard Wesley preach: "As soon as he got upon the stand, he stroked back his hair, and turned his face toward where I stood and I thought fixed his eyes upon me.... It made my heart beat like the pendulum of a clock; and, when he did speak, I thought his whole discourse was aimed at me. When he had done, I said, 'This man can tell the secretes of my heart.'"[348]

---

[347] Nathan Cole, "Memoir," in *The Great Awakening: A Brief History with Documents*, ed. Thomas S. Kidd (1771; Boston: Bedford/St. Martin's Press, 2008), 60–64.

[348] Kenneth Morgan, "Methodist Testimonials Collected by Charles Wesley in 1742," in *Reformation and Revival in Eighteenth-Century Bristol*, ed. Jonathan Barry and Kenneth Morgan (Bristol: Bristol Record Society, 1994), 93, 94; Mack, *Heart Religion in the British Enlightenment*, 77.

A certain Elizabeth Downs of Bristol graphically recorded in rough prose what happened to her while listening to John Wesley preach. She was a "Constant hearer of the word and as duly Communicated" but had not yet "Experienced any thing of the work of God in my Soul." John Wesley's preaching and prayers, however, cut her to the heart in conviction of sin and induced religious experiences remarkably like Catholic mystics in other parts of the world: "I felt myself so drawn to Christ. I thought I was thrusting my head into the wounds in his side.... I felt my heart Clipt as though an hand Graspt itt. The Greater he was in power the stronger I felt my pain. Att last itt Extorted strong Groans from me. I was not able to sitt but Laid my self on the floor. The Excessive pain and workings of my heart made me think itt was Death pangs." Her conversion, however, was not instantaneous. She recorded twists and turns in her emotional and spiritual life afterward. At one point, "the Devil came upon me Like a roaring Lyon," she wrote, "telling me twas all Delusion what I had received and I had deceived my soul." Then in an interesting application of rationality: "I began to reason with him [the devil] how can this be [delusion]. Nature Could not work this in me. I surely have had a foretaste of heaven and that[,] thou [the devil] could not Give me."[349]

Unusual phenomena regularly accompanied Wesley's evangelization ministry, such as murmurs, groans, outcries, trembling, convulsions, and falling down (called being "slain in the spirit" today). "While I was speaking," he recorded matter-of-factly, "several dropped down as dead, and among the rest such a cry was heard of sinners groaning for the righteousness of faith as almost drowned my voice." He considered these manifestations often to be simply the natural human responses to the supernatural power of the Holy Spirit convicting people internally of sin and the need for conversion.[350]

---

[349] Morgan, "Methodist Testimonials," 85, 86, 87, 89.
[350] Wesley, *The Heart of John Wesley's Journal*, 111, 295.

Rethinking the Enlightenment

Enthusiasm and Enlightenment

All this greatly shocked polite society. Considering themselves rational, orderly, and contained, many wondered how a movement like this could happen in an enlightened age. Field preachers who went "trolling about the kingdom," mocked one critic, tended to "unsettle and pervert weak Minds." They "daily misled" and "greatly injured" many thousands of innocent persons. The "spirit of delusion" they raised would lead many to think everyone's word is a separate revelation. This "is a Procedure destructive of all Order and Religion, and dangerous to the Peace and Safety of the State," the critic wrote. What was really disturbing, he continued, was that these men—Whitefield and the Wesleys—were liberally educated at Oxford. They should know better![351]

The central charge against them was fomenting fanaticism or "enthusiasm." This was understood to be false belief in the inspiration of the Holy Spirit, irrational attribution of everyday occurrences to divine intervention, and uncritical acceptance of "religious experiences." Writers, artists, and Anglican bishops linked what they saw as the internal threat of Methodism with the most detested external threat (Catholicism) and mocked both groups for their dangerous appeals to emotion.

Wesley took this in stride. Remarkably, he *was* well educated, and yet he accepted the label "enthusiast" by using it to designate a vigorous and earnest faith. He tried to bridge the divide between brain and heart, between "intellectual religion" of the educated classes and "popular religion" of the lower classes. This was the secret of his success.

Wesley acknowledged that it could indeed be dangerous to regard "extraordinary circumstances" too much. But it was also dangerous to regard them too little, "to condemn them altogether; to imagine they had nothing of God in them, and were a hindrance to his work." Human psychology is more multidimensional than some of the rationalists and

---

[351] "Observations on the Conduct of the Rev. Mr. Whitefield," *Gentleman's Magazine*, May 1739, 239–241.

deists of the age imagined. On either side of conscious human reason resides two other domains of human psychology that Wesley often met in his ministry. There is the subrational lower region of unconscious instinct and mob psychology. And there is the superrational level of spiritual experience — "which is the sphere not only of religion but of the highest creative forces of cultural achievement — the intuitions of the artist, the poet and the philosopher," the historian Christopher Dawson wrote. The Age of Reason tended to forget about these two levels. Not Wesley. He had seen how God's power could use personal experience to convince people of sin "suddenly and strongly" and to encourage those who already believed. "God begins His work at the heart; then 'the inspiration of the highest giveth understanding,'" he wrote. In some cases, it was true, "nature mixed with grace" (i.e., human psychology and imaginings also shaped religious experience). And in others, Satan mimicked the work of God in order to discredit the whole work. One had to apply discerning reason to each case.[352]

The "Wesley quadrilateral" provided the standards of evaluating what was happening: Scripture, tradition, and reason (the cornerstones of traditional Anglican faith) should temper personal religious experience, he believed. The latter had to be judged in terms of the other three. Thus, crucially, experience did not reveal new truths, but it could confirm Scripture and add to the discernment of truth in one's life. Without the other three, too much focus on religious experience could lead to emotionalism, morbid introspection, and anti-intellectualism. Extrabiblical revelation, millenarian predictions, or fanciful revelations of special authority Wesley judged as false religious experience because they violated the quadrilateral. For example, one man "who had received a sense of the love of God" a few days before went riding through his town, driving the people before him. He shouted that God told him he was to be king and that he would

---

[352] Wesley, *The Heart of John Wesley's Journal*, 198, 295; Christopher Dawson, *The Historic Reality of Christian Culture: A Way to the Renewal of Human Life* (London: Routledge & Kegan Paul, 1960), 92.

tread all enemies underfoot. "I sent him home immediately to his work," Wesley wrote, "and advised him to cry day and night to God that he might be lowly in heart, lest Satan should again get an advantage over him."

John Wesley brought religious enthusiasm and the Enlightenment into conversation in the English-speaking world. Wesley believed that faith is knowable through the senses—much like Catholics who touch relics, view Christian archaeological artifacts in museums, or recognize healing miracles. But in Wesley's case, the "facts" and the "senses" detecting them were largely *internal religious experience* and *internal senses* of the "heart"—conceived as the seat not merely of affectivity but also of self-knowledge. In this way, Wesley owed something to John Locke's *Essay concerning Human Understanding*, which held that all knowledge comes by way of the senses. Locke's book was tremendously influential during the Enlightenment. Wesley applied Locke's secular account of knowledge to religion and evangelization as he tried to make faith relevant to his generation: faith is knowable through the internal senses of the human heart.

"Is it now in your power to see, or hear, or taste, or feel God?" he asked in his *Earnest Appeal to Men of Reason and Religion*. "Is it in your power to burst the veil that is on your heart, and let in the light of eternity? You know it is not. You not only do not, but cannot (by your own strength) thus believe. The more you labour so to do, the more you will be convinced, *it* [faith] *is the gift of God*." The experience of this gift from God, however, *does* pierce that veil and *does* bridge that gulf between human beings and the supernatural world, making faith perceptible internally.[353]

The Third Medium: Publishing

Printing began well before the Enlightenment, around 1450, with Johannes Gutenberg. However, just as infrastructure improvements supported

---

[353] Wesley, *The Heart of John Wesley's Journal*, 128; John Wesley, *An Earnest Appeal to Men of Reason and Religion*, 8th ed. (1743; London: G. Whitfield, 1796), 6.

Wesley's horseback preaching ministry, so too did crucial changes to the English-speaking press in the eighteenth century. In 1695, the Licensing of the Press Act (1662) lapsed. This ended censorship and restrictions on the number of printers. A printing monopoly was replaced by a competitive commercial model. Dozens of printing houses had started operating by the time young Benjamin Franklin worked in London during the 1720s. The first true daily newspaper, the *Daily Courant*, started in 1702.

Besides this emerging literary marketplace, rising literacy, cheap paper, and regular mail routes also contributed to an explosion of cheap mass printing. Everything from news to practical science, folk medicine, and pornography circulated widely among the people. Unbound tracts and pamphlets dealing with the events of the moment flew off the presses. Authors would often respond to each other in this "paper public sphere," debating issues within a community that sometimes spilled over into the broader population—as in digital media today.[354]

Christians immediately moved in to take advantage of the new print culture. The Society for the Promotion of Christian Knowledge, mentioned in chapter 9, generated hundreds of thousands of religious publications. As soon as Whitefield arrived in the American colonies in 1739, he burst into the news and dominated the newspapers all during the 1740s. In 1740 alone, he inspired one-third of all printed works published in the colonies. Franklin capitalized on this in his printing business, for the Great Awakening was also great business.

Wesley was well educated and expressed himself in clear, forceful writing. He wrote, edited, or abridged some four hundred works—and not just on religious topics. He produced a compendium of folk medicine and—drawing from the work of Benjamin Franklin—a commentary

[354] Paula McDowell, "Media and Mediation in the Eighteenth Century," Oxford Handbooks Online, March 2017, 7–8, https://www.oxfordhandbooks.com/view/10.1093/oxfordhb/9780199935338.001.0001/oxfordhb -9780199935338-e-46.

on electricity. By means of both, he sought to offer healing remedies to common folk.

As a young man, Wesley had resolved to serve God through writing and editing so as to be read by common people. "We see (and who does not) the numberless follies and miseries of our fellow creatures," he wrote. "We see on every side, either men of no religion at all, or men of lifeless, formal religion. We are grieved at the sight," he continued. He proposed a religion worthy of the God who gave it, the religion of the love of God and of all mankind. "This love we believe to be the medicine of life, the never-failing remedy, for all the evils of a disordered world, for all the miseries and vices of men." Toward this end, he published. In *The Imitation of Christ*, by Thomas à Kempis, which he edited for devotional use, he even tried to influence *how* people read religious books. One should do it leisurely, seriously, and with great attention. Allow time for the "enlightenings of divine grace." Remember what is read, and reflect on how to put it into practice, he advised. Wesley understood the power of the printed word to change lives and ultimately change the wider society.[355]

The historian Christopher Dawson remarked on the significance of Christian participation in the English literary marketplace.[356] It must be emphasized that Christians successfully checked the influence of the deists toward dechristianization. The defenders of orthodoxy, Dawson

---

[355] Wesley, *An Earnest Appeal*, 3; Isabel Rivers, "John Wesley as Editor and Publisher," in *The Cambridge Companion to John Wesley*, ed. Randy L. Maddox and Jason E. Vickers (Cambridge: Cambridge University Press, 2009), 147, 149.

[356] Great English Christian writers of the age included Bishop William Warburton; essayist Jonathan Swift, who is regarded as the foremost prose satirist in the English language; William Law, whose *Serious Call to a Devout and Holy Life* (1729) was in many ways the seed of the Methodist movement; Bishop Joseph Butler, who influenced moral and economic thinking and Enlighteners such as David Hume and Adam Smith; Samuel Johnson, perhaps the greatest man of letters in English history; and the poet and hymnodist William Cowper.

wrote, "proved to be better writers and abler controversialists than their critics." The English rationalists had no Voltaire, as did the French, so the tables were turned. Eighteenth-century English Christians of all shades of religious opinion—like G. K. Chesterton, C. S. Lewis, and Ronald Knox in the twentieth century—stepped up to nurture the faith within Christian culture. Importantly, they also engaged the wider spirit of the age. These two strategies of retreat and engagement together meant the English Enlightenment "did not lead to the defeat of Christianity," Dawson wrote.[357] This was a remarkable achievement.

The Fourth Medium: Hymns

Music is one of the most primal and fundamental aspects of human culture, deeply shaping consciousness. "Singing a hymn, again and again," one music historian wrote, "means that the text becomes lodged in the memory, captured, experienced and re-experienced, sometimes with a new awareness or a deeper sensibility."[358] To "learn by heart" is to give something a deep personal indwelling. Hymns connect the intellect (words) to the physical (body) and to the soul. They are the only poetry most people know. If the medium of the *hymn* spreads among thousands and thousands of people, one can say truly that sound shapes society.

Charles Wesley's more than six thousand hymns and John's editing and compilation of dozens of hymnals not only represent one of their greatest legacies to English-speaking Christianity but also demonstrate a central thrust of their retreat strategy. From a poetic ability cultivated in

---

[357] Dawson, *The Dividing of Christendom*, 240, 241. Alexis de Tocqueville seemed to agree with this assessment. Christian writers took advantage of the free-market publishing world in England, turning to print to debate those theories hostile to the church, which were "rejected by the efforts of society itself without any interference from government." See Tocqueville, *The Ancien Régime*, 155.

[358] J. R. Watson, *The English Hymn: A Critical and Historical Study* (New York: Oxford University Press, 1997), 20.

internal retreat, an outward movement or religious influence exploded across the wider culture.

John Wesley first encountered the power of hymn singing aboard ship during a storm while crossing the Atlantic Ocean (1735). He was heading to the colony of Georgia as a missionary. As the sea broke over the ship, split the mainsail in two, and poured in between the decks, Wesley found himself greatly shaken. Screams arose from the English on board, but the German Moravians calmly kept on singing psalms. They were a Protestant group who integrated personal piety, missionary outreach, and music into their daily lives. "Were you not afraid?" Wesley asked one of them afterward. "I thank God, no," he replied.[359] Wesley was moved. He started studying German so he could talk with them, join their singing, and translate their songs.

While Catholic Masses of the time often incorporated chants or trained choirs, Protestants started incorporating into their liturgies beautiful and simple hymns involving the whole congregation (not professionally trained). That was the key, and the Wesleys knew it. Catholics followed, realizing that hymns provide an excellent opportunity for catechesis. Though Charles Wesley did not create the genre of the English hymn, he developed the form "in a more complex, elegant and elaborate way than any who had come before him and, arguably, set the standard for those who were to follow," wrote one scholar.[360]

As an Anglican, Charles created a liturgical hymnody for the church year. This included Advent ("Come, Thou Long Expected Jesus," 1744), Christmas ("Hark, the Herald Angels Sing," 1739), Easter ("Christ the Lord Is Risen Today," 1739), Ascension ("Hail the Day That Sees Him Rise," 1739), and an entire hymnal for Pentecost (1746).

---

[359] Wesley, *The Heart of John Wesley's Journal*, 29.

[360] Andrew Pratt, "The Influence of Charles Wesley on Contemporary Hymnody," in *Charles Wesley: Life, Literature and Legacy*, ed. Kenneth G.C. Newport and Ted A. Campbell (Peterborough, UK: Epworth, 2007), 395.

In his "Directions for Singing," John advised: "Above all sing spiritually. Have an eye to God in every word you sing. Aim at pleasing him more than yourself, or any other creature." One should see that one's heart is not "carried away with the sound," he directed, "but offered to God continually."[361]

Charles wrote only the poetry of the hymns, not the tunes. For those, the Wesleys turned to the German chorale, classical and folk melodies, and psalm melodies. The aim was to express clearly the words so they could be understood. The hymns integrated theology with personal experience—a new departure for the English hymn. The Wesley brothers resolved to achieve this connection while maintaining literary integrity. As John wrote in the preface to his *Collection of Hymns*: "In these hymns there is no doggerel; no botches; nothing put in to patch up the rhyme; no feeble expletives. Here is nothing turgid or bombast, on the one hand, or low and creeping, on the other. . . . Here are, allow me to say, both the purity, the strength, and the elegance of the English language; and, at the same time, the utmost simplicity and plainness, suited to every capacity." Charles insisted on genuine poetic quality to raise the masses up to its level, rather than writing down to their lowest level, one scholar noted. By joining the spirit of poetry to the spirit of piety, the hymns, John believed, would quicken devotion, confirm faith, and kindle and increase love of God and man. In addition, their clear message offered "strong cautions" against prevalent errors of the day, he wrote, subtly guarding the family of faith.[362]

One can see some of these qualities in Charles Wesley's very first hymn. He wrote it immediately after a profound personal experience of

[361] John Wesley, "Directions for Singing," no. 7 in *The United Methodist Hymnal* (Nashville: United Methodist Publishing House, 1989), vii.

[362] John Wesley, *A Collection of Hymns, for the Use of the People Called Methodists* (London: John Mason, 1779), 4–5; Richard D. Dinwiddie, "Two Brothers . . . Who Changed the Course of Church Singing," *Christianity Today*, September 21, 1984, 33.

Pentecost on May 21, 1738, three days before John's Aldersgate experience. During a time of prayer with others, Charles reported in his journal, the Spirit of God came and "chased away the darkness of my unbelief."[363] He began to write a hymn in order to express the beauty and truth of his experience. "Oh how shall I the goodness tell,/ Father, which Thou to me hast show'd?" he wrote. His burgeoning sense of mission appeared: "Shall I, the hallowed cross to shun/ Refuse His righteousness t'impart/ By hiding it within my heart?" He warmed to his theme: "Outcasts of men, to you I call,/ Harlots, and publicans, and thieves!/ He spreads His arms t'embrace you all." Here, one historian commented, he fused his verses with widespread social concerns of the day for rising prostitution and thievery as well as unjust taxes.[364]

This musical mission to sinners welled up like a wave across the English-speaking world. The subtle power of song drew people out of the loneliness of the age. One convert, Thomas Olivers, remembered the following experience:

> When the public preaching was over on a Sunday evening, and I, along with the multitude, was shut out from the society, I used to go into the field at the back of the preaching-house, and listen while they sang the praises of God. I would then weep bitterly at the thought, that God's people were there, praising His name together, while I, a poor and wretched fugitive, was not permitted to be among them.

On another occasion, hymn singing saved a woman's life. She was so overcome with affliction that she went out one night to drown herself in the London water-supply canal. John recorded in his journal how, as she went by a Methodist chapel, "she heard some people singing. She stopped and went in; she listened awhile, and God spoke to her heart."

---

[363] Wesley, *Journal*, May 21, 1738.
[364] Watson, *The English Hymn*, 221, 222, 227.

Wesley commented: "She had no more desire to put an end to her life, but to die to sin and live to God."[365]

The Fifth Medium: Institutional Thinking

One could preach, write, and sing to thousands, but if no structures were in place to support them afterward, all could be lost. This is what happened in Wales, Wesley noted. Without religious societies, discipline, order, and enough connections between people, "the consequence is that nine in ten of the once-awakened are now faster asleep than ever."[366] The work of social organization had to follow on revival.

Thus, much of John Wesley's attention went to building up religious societies. Whereas the likes of Rousseau believed that institutions chain up the free expression of individual authenticity, Wesley held institutions to be central to the social nature of human beings. He grasped the importance of *institutional thinking*, attentive to common ends and rule following. Following rules created the basis for predictability in conduct. Predictability, one political scientist wrote, enhances trust and participatory knowledge. The resulting chain of relationships "amounts to a civilized way for people to live together."[367]

The religious societies nurtured the life of faith through mutual accountability, confession, and Christian fellowship. They were voluntary associations of farmers, shopkeepers, soldiers, clergymen, and eccentrics. Members were united by a common faith and religious experience as well as a strict system of inspection and discipline through which Wesley exercised highly centralized control.

In this, Wesley was an organizational genius. His movement was an "amazing achievement," Christopher Dawson wrote, which could

---

[365] Mack, *Heart Religion in the British Enlightenment*, 76; *The Heart of John Wesley's Journal*, 180.

[366] Wesley, *The Heart of John Wesley's Journal*, 331.

[367] Rousseau, *Emile*, 43; Hugh Heclo, *On Thinking Institutionally* (Boulder: Paradigm, 2008), 188.

be compared only to the most centralized religious orders such as the Jesuits. ("Ay, he is a Jesuit; that's plain," someone in an Irish audience once said after hearing Wesley preach. "To which," Wesley recorded, "a popish priest who happened to be near replied aloud, 'No, he is not; I would to God he was.'")[368]

---

[368] Dawson, *The Dividing of Christendom*, 223; Wesley, *The Heart of John Wesley's Journal*, 188.

11

Revolutions of the Soul

Edmund Burke's Prophecies

If religious revival pervaded the Age of the Enlightenment in the English-speaking world, what effects did it have on the wider culture? Did religious revival help prevent revolution in England? If so, what about America and France, where revolutions broke out in 1775 and 1789?

To answer these questions, let us begin with Edmund Burke (1729-1797). He was an Anglo-Irish statesman and political thinker. Born in Ireland to a Catholic mother and a Protestant father, Burke served as a member of Parliament in London from 1766 to 1794. In his writings and in his speeches, he engaged Enlightenment themes, such as the nature of human society and religious toleration. Burke empathized strongly with American grievances against British taxation in the years leading up to the American Revolution. In fact, he gave a famous speech in Parliament in 1775 called "Conciliation with the Colonies." He understood that the Americans simply wanted to defend their traditional "rights of Englishmen."

Despite his empathy for the Americans, Burke later opposed the French. He published the influential (and prophetic) book *Reflections on the Revolution in France* in 1790, one year into the French Revolution. To the surprise of everyone, he virulently attacked events in France and the French quest for liberty as completely misguided. Why did he support the Americans but not the French?

Burke perceived significant differences between the American and French revolutions. The French "have found their punishment in their success," Burke wrote: "laws overturned; tribunals subverted; industry without vigor; commerce expiring; the revenue unpaid, yet the people impoverished; a church pillaged, and a state not relieved; civil and military anarchy made the constitution of the kingdom; everything human and divine sacrificed to the idol of public credit, and national bankruptcy the consequence." As one historian wrote, if Burke had written this in 1793 during the Reign of Terror, there would have been nothing extraordinary about it. But to have seen the true nature of the French Revolution in 1790 was extraordinary.[369] How did he do it?

The first answer is Rousseau. Burke knew the French writer through books and indirectly through mutual acquaintances. Rousseau was a writer of "great force," Burke admitted, and it was to him that the revolutionary leaders looked for a new religion and a new morality to displace Christianity. This was the emotional pantheism emerging from Rousseau's religious experience covered in chapter 2. "Him they study; him they meditate; him they turn over in all the time they can spare from the laborious mischief of the day or the debauches of the night. Rousseau is their canon of holy writ," Burke wrote.

Burke characterized this new religion as the "philosophy of vanity." In this he echoed Wesley's critique of Rousseau. Vanity was the motivating principle of Rousseau's heart, based on the evidence of his words and his actions, Burke judged. The sentimental virtue of his best-selling novel and his self-publicized neglect of his own children inculcated selfishness. Rousseau's example undermined the actual virtues needed to sustain households, and thus society. It is domestic trust and familial fidelity that "form the discipline of social life," Burke wrote insightfully. Thus, the French revolutionary leaders were cunning. They saw in Rousseau's attack on the family an avenue for breaking down the "train of our natural feelings" in

---

[369] Burke, *Reflections on the Revolution in France*, 34; Niall Ferguson, *Civilization: The West and the Rest* (New York: Penguin, 2011), 151.

human society. This shattering would open the possibility of an attempted "regeneration of the moral constitution of man." The French Revolution sought nothing less than to remake human nature in the line of Rousseau.[370]

Burke divined in Rousseau's *Social Contract* (1762) other dangerous ideas. The so-called "General Will" of the people disallowed partial associations (subsidiary groups, such as religious societies and political parties). It worked against traditional Christianity, which separated spiritual and temporal power. All power should unite in the General Will itself to create the true reign of virtue, Rousseau believed—as did Robespierre, who led the Reign of Terror. The General Will should dominate even fundamental rights to property and religion—a view incarnated in the Declaration of the Rights of Man and Citizen already at the outset of the French Revolution in 1789.[371]

The second answer to why Burke defended the Americans but attacked the French was the divorce between head and heart he discerned across the English Channel. Still impassioned by Descartes, French elites operated under the assumption that all problems, even political ones, could be solved by the spirit of mathematical clarity and simplicity. But their hot heads made for cold hearts. The "nakedness and solitude of metaphysical abstraction" separated universal principles (such as "liberty," "equality," and "fraternity") from wisdom and real life, Burke charged. This led to a "savage atrocity of mind." Rousseau's powerful rhetorical expression of universal benevolence for all mankind, for example, was matched by a heart "incapable of harboring one spark of common parental affection." In other words: "Benevolence to the whole species, and want of feeling for every individual with whom the professors come in contact, form the character of the new philosophy," Burke wrote.[372]

---

[370] Edmund Burke, "A Letter to a Member of the National Assembly," in *The Best of Burke: Selected Writings and Speeches of Edmund Burke*, ed. Peter J. Stanlis (1791; Washington, D.C.: Regnery, 1963), 615-622.

[371] Ferguson, *Civilization: The West and the Rest*, 151-152.

[372] Burke, *Reflections on the Revolution*, 7, 134; Burke, "A Letter to a Member of the National Assembly," in *The Best of Burke*, 617.

Burke then issued a string of astonishingly accurate predictions:

1. The mindset in France would lead to laws "supported only by their own terrors." Then: "In the groves of *their* academy, at the end of every vista, you see nothing but the gallows." (Burke's only failure here was to forecast the gallows rather than the guillotine as the Revolution's choice mode of execution.)

2. The domination of the Catholic Church was "preparatory to the utter abolition, under any of its forms, of the Christian religion."

3. Burke prophesied that the experiment across the Channel would not last long. The regime would devolve into oligarchy and then "military democracy—a species of political monster which has always ended by devouring those who have produced it."

4. Then military insurrection would threaten the very nation itself.

5. The whole situation would end up in military dictatorship.[373]

Burke published those words in November 1790, and his predictions soon came to pass:

1. The guillotine was first used in April 1792. The Reign of Terror ensued from 1793 to 1794, during which the Carmelite nuns of Compiègne perished.

2. With the downfall of the Church came the anti-Christian Cult of Reason enforced during 1793 and 1794. This was the first political religion of the modern age, complete with its own rites, temples, and martyrs.

3. The Committee of Public Salvation—an oligarchy—formed in 1793.

4. In February of 1793, military conscription sparked military insurrection in the Vendée region of western France, threatening the very nation through civil war.

---

[373] Burke, *Reflections on the Revolution*, 68, 109, 130, 173, 186, 193.

5. After more governmental turmoil, France resolved itself into
    military dictatorship under Napoleon in 1799.

Burke's political prophecies came true, just like the religious prophecy
that motivated Mother Teresa of St. Augustine and her Carmelites to
remain obedient unto death.

Religious Revival in France

Was there religious revival in France, as there was in the English-speaking
world? If so, what role did it play in the French Revolution? A revival
did emerge in the west of France, at least, especially in the region called
the Vendée. There, the Catholic revivalist Louis de Montfort and the
missionary order he founded in 1705 (the Company of Mary) renewed
popular religion much as the Methodists did in England. One of his
central motivations was his belief that personal union with Jesus Christ
can best be achieved through devotion to his mother, the Virgin Mary.
The manuscript for his famous *True Devotion to Mary* was hidden at a
farm during the French Revolution and was rediscovered and published
only in 1843. Montfort also spread devotion to the Sacred Heart of Jesus.
In one of his hymns, he wrote, "O Sacred Heart, set us ablaze," and in
another, "We offer you our hearts / Take them and sacrifice them / At
the foot of your altar."[374] The devotions and the brotherhoods Montfort
established survived him, and the veneration of his legacy spread widely.
In particular, the Company of Mary gave 430 parish missions throughout
western France from 1718 to 1781. Notably, these were the parishes that
rose in rebellion in 1793 against the French Revolution.

The religious issue was central in this rebellion, which "sprang directly
from the faith and emotion of the soul of the people," Dawson wrote.

---

[374] Quoted in H. M. Guindon, "Sacred Heart," in *Jesus Living in Mary: Handbook of the Spirituality of St. Louis de Montfort* (Litchfield, CT: Montfort
Publications, 1994), EWTN, https://www.ewtn.com/catholicism/library/
sacred-heart-12788.

Sacred Heart Patch from the French Catholic and Royal Army, 1793–1794. The French regime viewed possession of these hearts as a sign of betrayal and rebellion. In fact, discovery of hearts among the possessions of the Carmelites of Compiègne served as incriminating evidence against them.

"Nothing could have been more democratic than this war against the Revolution." When the church bells rang, the farmers and laborers of western France took up their rosaries, their Sacred Heart emblems, and their guns or pitchforks to march on the enemy. When the battle was over, they returned to the fields.[375]

The Catholic rebels were eventually crushed, and their heroic efforts left an ambiguous legacy. On the one hand, they witnessed to the real divide separating Christian culture from Enlightenment culture. They believed clear boundaries demarcated the household of faith that needed defending, to the death if necessary. Since their time, anyone who has ever struggled against other political religions of the modern world has inherited the mantle of their honor.

On the other hand, more than one hundred thousand people died. Both sides were locked in a fight to the death over fundamental values. This testified to the total breakdown in the search for common ground. Why, in the Catholic countries of Europe, Joseph Ratzinger wrote, "is there such a sharp opposition between Catholics and secularists?" Unlike in the English-speaking world, why did a "civil religion" fail to develop, with common values transcending any one denomination?[376]

The answers to these questions are complex. Though England had already passed through a political revolution in 1688, rejecting absolute

---

[375] Dawson, *The Gods of Revolution*, 80.
[376] Ratzinger, "Letter to Marcello Pera," 109, 113, 116.

monarchy, the situation was very different in France during most of the 1700s. As shown in earlier chapters, the French absolute monarchy undermined local governance and patriotism. Alliance with the Catholic Church made the Church partly into a political institution, and an accomplice in persecution. This situation created a lot of resentment. The greater social and political freedom of the English-speaking world allowed a chaotic cacophony of voices to blow off steam, so to speak. France, by contrast, was a pressure cooker. French deist, Protestant, and Catholic leaders attempted to come together around common civil-religious values during the 1780s—as in the Edict of Versailles (1787), for example. This edict granted non-Catholics in France the ability to practice their religion openly as well as civil status, which included the right to contract marriage without having to convert to Catholicism. But this was too little, too late.

The Conflictual Enlightenment had gained a penetrating power in France during the century. Excluded from real political experience and influence by an absolute monarchy, Conflictual Enlighteners created a literary form of politics in their heads. They lacked down-to-earth, commonsense experience that could have modified their imagined society in which everything appeared simple, just, and reasonable, political thinker Alexis de Tocqueville wrote. In addition, Conflictual Enlighteners tended to view reason as the antithesis of religion. "Reason is to the philosopher what grace is to the Christian," the great French *Encyclopédie* declared. "Grace determines the action of the Christian; reason determines that of the philosopher." Finally, Conflictual Enlighteners tended to look down on common people as lazy and irrational—though, as readers saw at Ferney, Voltaire was an exception in his concern for those around him. Nonetheless, Conflictual Enlighteners generally lacked shared values with much of the rest of the country.[377]

---

[377] Tocqueville, *The Ancien Régime*, 142, 143; César Chesneau du Marsais, "Philosopher" *The Encyclopedia of Diderot & d'Alembert Collaborative Translation Project*, trans. Dena Goodman (Ann Arbor, MI: University of Michigan Library, 2002), http://hdl.handle.net/2027/spo.did2222.0000.001.

Rethinking the Enlightenment

Some French Catholics tried to find common ground with the Revolution. Adrien Lamourette (1742–1794), for example, was a Catholic priest who supported religious tolerance. He played a public role in the Revolution through salons and clubs and political alliances. He believed one could support the Revolution *and* Christianity. He became more and more radical, however, coming to see the Revolution as the fulfillment of the gospel and calling for the elimination of all Church property. This put him out of touch with most other French Catholics, and in order to avert the growing polarization by 1791, Lamourette appealed to "enlightened Christians" to back his middle-ground approach.[378]

But by then, there was no middle ground. There was no pro-revolution, pro-Christian party identifying with the Enlightenment as an audience for Lamourette's appeal. The Catholic Enlightenment in France had failed to link social classes together. In fact, it had driven them apart by its attack on the Jesuits. Some ordinary Catholics in France attempted to engage revolutionary values by reinterpreting them according to their traditional religious assumptions. For example, one historian wrote, when town officers at Saint-Bris, southeast of Paris, tried to enforce a departmental decree closing the church, Catholic villagers gathered before the doors. They demanded the right to assemble peaceably and worship the "supreme being." Due to their persistence, the major eventually gave up and recommended that they be allowed to worship freely.

But such efforts did not bridge the cultural chasm. The French Revolution had appropriated the *sacred* for the state, forcing Christianity into a defensive mode.[379] Thus, the retreat and evangelization movements of missionaries such as Montfort overlapped with a conflictual strategy rather than the engagement strategy as predominant in the English-speaking world. Religious revival in western France armed the people against political tyranny, as they saw it. Without realistic possibility for

---

[378] Sorkin, *The Religious Enlightenment*, 294.

[379] Suzanne Desan, *Reclaiming the Sacred: Lay Religion and Popular Politics in Revolutionary France* (Ithaca: Cornell University Press, 1990), 1–2.

engagement, the overlap of retreat and conflict strategies eventually led to the noble but tragic outcome of Catholic rebellion and mass death in the Vendée in 1793. The cultural divide apparent in these events in France between Catholicism and secular culture, lamented by Ratzinger, persisted for generations.

The American Situation

In contrast to France, the retreat strategy of Christians in the more socially mobile English-speaking world overlapped with engagement. They fostered a public sphere in which Christianity had an important place. John Adams told the officers of the militia of Massachusetts in 1798, "Our Constitution was made only for a moral and religious People. It is wholly inadequate to the government of any other." "I stop the first American I meet, either in his own country or elsewhere," Alexis de Tocqueville wrote decades later, "and I ask him whether he thinks religion useful to the stability of laws and good order in society. He answers without hesitation that a civilized society, especially a free one, cannot last without religion."[380]

The Practical Enlightenment dominating the English-speaking world was easier to get along with than the Conflictual Enlightenment in France. Practical Enlighteners in America looked more to the commonsense realism of the Scottish Enlightenment for inspiration than the speculations of Rousseau or Descartes. The Scottish Enlightenment was marked by Christian fidelity, serious intellectual sophistication, and concern for practical improvements to individuals and society. It greatly influenced America by Americans who studied in Scotland and by Scottish immigrants.

The Scottish Presbyterian minister John Witherspoon (1723–1794), for example, crossed the Atlantic to become the president

---

[380] John Adams, To the Massachusetts Militia, October 11, 1798, Founders Online, https://founders.archives.gov/documents/Adams/99-02-02-3102; Tocqueville, *The Ancien Régime and the Revolution*, 154.

of the College of New Jersey (Princeton). There he educated James Madison (1751–1836), an American Founding Father who played an important role in drafting and promoting the Constitution of the United States of America (1787) and the Bill of Rights (1789). Madison absorbed "commonsense" philosophical realism from his Scottish-Enlightenment education under Witherspoon as well as a notion of fallen human nature.

The Scottish Christian philosopher Thomas Reid (1710–1796) defined common sense as follows: "If there are certain principles, as I think there are, which the constitution of our nature leads us to believe, and which we are under a necessity to take for granted in the common concerns of life, with out being able to give a reason for them; these are what we call the principles of common sense; and what is manifestly contrary to them, is what we call absurd." Principles *taken for granted* among ordinary people — such as the principle of noncontradiction, "self-evident" truths in the Declaration of Independence (1776), unalienable rights endowed by a Creator — these first principles employed by the American Founders implied *limits* to reason. Common sense was the starting point of reason, not the creation of it. In this spirit, the diverse group of American Founders were "practical Enlighteners" who founded the United States as a practical project of check-and-balance rather than as a land of ideological purity. In fact, Madison attacked those "theoretic politicians" who tried to do just that.[381]

If the nature of the Practical Enlightenment in America helps explain the differences between the American and French revolutions, so, too, does understanding the character of the religious revival in America called the Great Awakening (1740s–1750s). This was the first common

---

[381] Thomas Reid, *An Inquiry into the Human Mind: On the Principles of Common Sense*, 4th ed. (1764; London: T. Cadell, 1785), 52; James Madison, "The Federalist Papers: No. 10" (1787), Lillian Goldman Law Library Avalon Project, https://avalon.law.yale.edu/18th_century/fed10.asp. Reid's motto, "common sense," also gave the title to the most popular pamphlet calling for independence, by Thomas Paine (1776).

experience shared by Americans. As embodied in the friendship of Franklin and Whitefield, it encouraged alliances between different groups and engagement with the Practical Enlightenment in the decades before the Revolution. The Great Awakening was of such significance that the historian Thomas Kidd called George Whitefield "America's spiritual Founding Father."[382] As John Adams wrote in 1818: "The [American] Revolution was effected before the War commenced. The Revolution was in the Minds and Hearts of the People. A Change in their Religious Sentiments of their Duties and Obligations."[383]

The Great Awakening encouraged the formation of nonstate churches. In doing so, it changed political culture in the colonies in two ways. First, Americans began to conceive of the chain of political authority as extending not from God directly to the ruler to govern the people and the church, as European absolute monarchists claimed. Rather, in practice, if not always in theory, Americans saw the source of political authority leading from God through the "Laws of Nature" to the collective people. The people then consent (tacitly or expressly) to entrust political authority to the state. This arrangement allows them to hold the state accountable *and themselves accountable.*[384]

By encouraging the formation of nonstate churches, the Great Awakening encouraged both deists and evangelicals to cooperate toward jurisdictional separation of church and state in the United States. This

---

[382] Thomas S. Kidd, *George Whitefield: America's Spiritual Founding Father* (New Haven: Yale University Press, 2014). Whitefield was the most famous man in the American colonies and—along with John Wesley—in Britain too (other than the monarch). In addition, Whitefield was the key figure in the first generation of American evangelicalism (3).

[383] John Adams to Hezekiah Niles, February 13, 1818, Founders Online, https://founders.archives.gov/documents/Adams/99-02-02-6854.

[384] The Catholic thinker Orestes Brownson argued that this view of the origin of political authority as sketched here is the correct one. See his *The American Republic: Its Constitution, Tendencies and Destiny* (1865; Wilmington, DE: ISI Books, 2003), 87.

looked new at the time, but in reality, it represented a recovery of a deep tradition of Christian thought back to the early Church. "There are two … by which this world is governed, the sacred authority of priests and the royal power," Pope Gelasius I wrote in 494. Gelasius's language of "the two" was a Christian revolution against the sacral political model of the ancient world that joined religion and politics. "The very distinction between religious observance and government was a Christian innovation," one political scientist wrote. He termed this the "Christian apostasy" from the long-accepted religion-joined-to-politics paradigm of the ancient world. It was *modern* thinkers such as Thomas Hobbes (1588–1679) and Rousseau who tried to *undo* this Christian separation of church and state. They wanted to create an all-powerful leviathan, fusing them together. Insofar as the U.S. Constitution and the American Founders sought to preserve a sphere not subject to the state and over which God is sovereign, the Americans stood in the tradition of Pope Gelasius rather than the modern tradition.[385] Ironically, Protestants helped recover this very Catholic tradition.

The American Revolution was not an overthrow of existing society and an attempt to regenerate human nature, as in France. Therefore, a thriving, if imperfect, civil religion took shape. While it broke down over the question of slavery by the time of the Civil War (1861–1865), it was nevertheless composed of certain shared moral and religious assumptions such as the importance of religious freedom. Despite deep-seated antipathy toward them, Catholics eventually managed to gain a seat at the table too. Catholics had created the first law guaranteeing the "free exercise" of religion in America as a practical device to attract settlers to Maryland in their Toleration Act (1649). Thanks to the alliance between the Protestant Great Awakening and the Practical Enlightenment, this principle of religious freedom spread widely.

---

[385] Paul R. DeHart, "The First Amendment Didn't Separate Church and State—Christianity Did," *Public Discourse* (April 25, 2018): 6, 7, 8, https://www.thepublicdiscourse.com/2018/04/21381/.

John Carroll (1735–1815), America's first Catholic bishop, found the new arrangement quite satisfactory. He wrote a letter to an English friend and fellow priest in 1779. Most of the American states had adopted a system of toleration, he wrote, by which Catholics could even hold civil and military posts. "I am heartily glad to see the same policy beginning to be adopted in England and Ireland [the Papists Act of 1778]; and I cannot help thinking that you are indebted to America for this piece of service. I hope it will soon be extended as far with you as with us."[386] Carroll understood that few Catholics outside the United States strongly supported religious freedom. But the positive experience of religious freedom by Carroll and by Catholics in America after him slowly changed their values. Arguments based on revelation and reason in favor of religious freedom slowly coalesced from the Enlightenment onward into firm and widespread Catholic commitment to religious freedom. Thus, the American Catholic bishops eventually made a unique contribution to the Second Vatican Council on the topic of religious freedom. The legacies of retreat and conflict in France contrasted very much with the legacies of retreat and engagement in America.

What about England?

How did religious revival affect England beyond the Bristol area? Did revival prevent revolution, as historian Halévy surmised? Did the conversion of the individual take the place of the political revolution of society, as Dawson wrote?

As the French Revolution raged during the early 1790s, thousands of working-class demonstrators in industrial England took to the streets to show their support for the "rights of man" that they thought the Revolution represented. Radical propaganda spread through lecturers, songs, the press, and political clubs in Yorkshire. This was a region where steam

[386] John Carroll to Charles Plowden, February 28, 1779 in Peter Guilday, *The Life and Times of John Carroll* (Westminster: Newman, 1954), 110.

engines drained mines and life was hard, just as in the Bristol region. Violence and demands for political reform broke out.

Interestingly, at the same time, Methodism also spread rapidly in Yorkshire. From 1792 to 1796, one of the most dramatic outbursts of mass revival in the history of Methodism happened in that part of England. "The Lord saw that, in Yorkshire, we were in too great a union with the world," one writer of the time put it.[387] Thus, rival hopes clashed: revolutionaries focused on this world, revivalists on the next. The latter won. No revolution happened. Methodism replaced French-inspired radicalism, as Halévy claimed.

While many factors led to the de-escalation of tensions in Yorkshire, not just the rise of Methodism, the Marxist historian E. P. Thompson interpreted events there differently than Halévy. Thompson blamed Methodism for the part it played in undermining the revolutionary spirit in Yorkshire and beyond. He was the son and grandson of Methodist missionaries and was sent as a boy to the Kingswood boarding school started nearly two centuries earlier by Wesley. Reacting against what Thompson perceived as a restrictive religious worldview, he became a Communist. Christian belief in Heaven is the last hope of the defeated and the despairing, he wrote. It merely eases the pain of the poor in a heartless world and prevents their real liberation.[388]

It is true that one could interpret the actions of John Wesley in this way. More than anyone else, he mingled with the masses of working-class people and *could* have encouraged them to revolt against injustice. But he did not do so. He preached the Kingdom of God not of this world. In fact, he ejected from the religious societies people who did not obey civil laws. He opposed, for example, numerous English commoners who expressed sympathy for the Americans as the revolution there got started. "England

---

[387] John Baxter, "The Great Yorkshire Revival 1792-6: A Study of Mass Revival among the Methodists," in *A Sociological Yearbook of Religion in Britain*, ed. M. Hill (London: SCM, 1974), 63.

[388] E. P. Thompson, *The Making of the English Working Class* (New York: Pantheon Books, 1963), 369, 370, 381–382.

is in a flame!" he wrote in November 1775, "a flame of malice and rage against the King, and almost all that are in authority under him. I labor to put out this flame."[389] Wesley was no revolutionary, as Halévy praised and Thompson denounced. Did Wesley's work, then, simply perpetuate social injustice in England? Or did it keep the peace and help people accept the new economic conditions?

In 1782, Wesley visited four new factories for spinning and weaving cloth set up in his hometown of Epworth. The Industrial Revolution was picking up steam. Many young women and youngsters worked there. Their whole conversation was "profane and loose," Wesley found. Some of the workers ended up at a prayer meeting, however, and they were "cut to the heart." They did not rest until they had gained their companions. The whole scene was changed in three of the factories, Wesley wrote. God put a new song in their mouths. They turned from blasphemy to praise, from cursing to gratitude, better able to cope with the circumstances of their work.[390]

Traditional religion could indeed thrive in the new industrial environment. When Wesley died in 1791, there were seventy thousand committed Methodists, though the movement clearly influenced far more beyond that. By contrast, there were twelve hundred revolutionary Jacobins in France in 1790. In other words, more people were attracted by the religious revival in England than by Jacobin clubs across the English Channel. The Methodist movement, one historian wrote, was "unquestionably effecting a great moral revolution in England."[391]

Changing the World

Aiming at Heaven did not require discounting earth. In Christianity, Christopher Dawson pointed out, the tendency to world-renouncing

---

[389] Wesley, *The Heart of John Wesley's Journal*, 438.
[390] Ibid., 473–474.
[391] William E. H. Lecky, *A History of England in the Eighteenth Century* (New York: D. Appleton, 1878), 2:652.

asceticism coexists with a tendency toward social activity. It is the tension between these two poles that gives dynamism to Christian culture.

In this spirit, Edmund Burke wrote in his *Reflections on the Revolution in France*, true lawgivers ought to have a "heart full of sensibility." They ought to be ready to feel compassion for suffering. However, they must not hate vice so much that they come to love people too little. "A disposition to preserve [society] and an ability to improve, taken together, would be my standard of a statesman," he wrote.[392]

Such a statesman was found in the English abolitionist leader and astute politician William Wilberforce (1759–1833). "Religion ... is seated in the heart, where its authority is recognized as supreme" he wrote after his evangelical conversion. "Christianity calls her professors to a state of diligent watchfulness and active services."[393] Wilberforce's 1797 book *A Practical View of Christianity* was the *Mere Christianity* of the day. Like C. S. Lewis's 1952 work of apologetics, Wilberforce's book made a deep impression in his time. As a member of Parliament and friend of Prime Minister William Pitt the Younger, Wilberforce also led the British abolitionist movement that succeeded in ending the slave trade in 1807 and slavery in the British empire in 1833.

Britain not only dominated the international slave trade; she harbored slaves within her shores, as hundreds of newspaper ads for missing slaves testified during the 1700s. The story of the British abolitionist movement extends far beyond the confines of this book. But key events of the formative period, from 1785 to 1792, are a fitting place to show how the Christian strategy of retreat interacted with *both* conflict and engagement in England.

The African writer, former slave, and Methodist convert Olaudah Equiano (c. 1745-1797) published his autobiography[394] in England in 1789, depicting the horrors of slavery. The multiple editions of this widely

---

[392] Dawson, *The Historic Reality of Christian Culture*, 77; Burke, *Reflections on the Revolution*, 138, 148, 150.

[393] William Wilberforce, *A Practical View of Christianity* (Dublin: Robert Dapper, 1797), 117–118, 124.

[394] *The Interesting Narrative of the Life of Olaudah Equiano* (1789).

read book (it was one of the last books Wesley read before he died) helped to galvanize the abolitionist movement, made up of thousands of other (white) evangelical Christians.

The road to Aldersgate, in other words, led to a religious movement that changed culture. In effect, thousands of converted hearts and minds shifted certain implicit assumptions of the later eighteenth century about slavery and the human person. These changes then led to new kinds of social action, affecting the hearts and minds of the next generation. In this cultural dynamic of spiritual influence and modified behavior, one can see not only that reason purifies religion but that religion purifies reason. The misuse of reason in the Practical Enlightenment had justified slavery in the first place. Enlightened and upstanding citizens of Bristol all participated in the trade as a major source of wealth. The progress of civilization and of the Practical Enlightenment itself seemed to depend on slavery. But over time, religion (among other factors) prodded reason to take fuller account of the dignity of the human person, or progress is not progress.

Two consequential events in this story were the evangelical conversions of Wilberforce and of the high-society literary figure Hannah More (1745–1833) in the late 1780s. She was a poet and playwright who became a popular writer against slavery. After their conversions, she and Wilberforce both retreated into their homes away from the world for some time to reflect and nurture their newfound spiritual growth. They were also concerned about their public reputations. What would English polite society think? Elites of the day pressured one to keep faith private. Each wrestled with what to do. They could either turn away from the world of politics and literature to pursue their lives of newfound faith more directly, or they could keep their positions in society. "Can a serious Christian act in the world without compromising faith?" one historian summarized their problem. That question haunted Wilberforce during the winter of 1785 to 1786.[395]

---

[395] Christopher L. Brown, *Moral Capital: Foundations of British Abolitionism* (Chapel Hill: University of North Carolina Press, 2006), 383.

Both Wilberforce and More consulted the ex-slaver John Newton (1725–1807), now an evangelical Anglican priest. He had written the hymn "Amazing Grace" in 1772. Newton convinced them to stay in public life. To More, in her country retreat away from London, he wrote that one finds peace in faith when one finds a principle of action. "So far as our hearts are right," he told her, "all places and circumstances which his wise and good providence allots us are nearly equal." She realized that religion does not require one to retreat in such a way as to hide from the world. "The mischief arises not from our living in the world," she wrote in 1788, "but from the world living in us; occupying our hearts, and monopolizing our affections. Action is the life of virtue, and the world is the theatre of action." The real problem for someone in her position was how to create a space for godliness in public life. That could create conflict with some people around her. "The Christian life is a warfare," Newton wrote to More. "Much within us and much without us must be resisted." It was about this time that Wilberforce, too, found a new clarity. He wrote in his journal on October 28, 1787: "God Almighty has set before me two great objects, the suppression of the slave trade and the reformation of manners" (i.e., morality).[396] How could he reach the upper echelons of society as Wesley had reached the lower?

Retreat to Clapham

Wilberforce chose to continue an active political life in London. However, he needed a place of regular retreat to be with family and friends. In 1792, he moved to Clapham, a village just outside the city. Here the "Clapham Group" formed around the household of Henry Thornton, a devout economist and banker. The haphazard and inclusive Clapham Group eventually included two dozen leaders from the highest levels of

---

[396] Ibid., 384; Robert Isaac Wilberforce and Samuel Wilberforce, *The Life of William Wilberforce* (London: John Murray, 1839), 1:149.

business, clergy, politics, and literary culture (including Hannah More). Some lived elsewhere and regularly visited, while others purchased houses near each other around the village common. The Christ-centered community frequented Holy Trinity Anglican church. Clapham functioned something like a lay monastery, one scholar wrote: "retreating from the world in suburban seclusion with like-minded believers in order to better infiltrate and impact society for Christ."[397] They took delight in each other's families and marriages. They wandered freely in and out of each other's homes and gardens, discussing how to end slavery and other social problems. They operated under the assumption that cultural change had to precede and accompany long-lasting political change. They were motivated by the desire for religious action in the public sphere, and they had the money, the talent, and the connections to make it happen.

Engage the Times

The public lives of the Clapham Group were grounded in their households. This was undoubtedly a source of vitality. They loved to entertain and socialize, however, balancing retreat with engagement. The fact that they seemed to know everyone was very important to their eventual success. Through their networks, they created numerous voluntary associations, formed strategic alliances with those who shared Enlightenment values of benevolence and personal freedom, gathered evidence about the conditions of slaves and the slave trade, and made maximum use of the public media of the day. This resembled the public outcry Voltaire mobilized in the Calas affair. Thousands of evangelicals (especially

[397] Rhys Bezzant, "'The Better Hour Is Near': Wilberforce and Transformative Religion" (conference paper, September 2013) 10, ResearchGate, https://www.researchgate.net/publication/258632052_'The_Better_Hour_is_Near'_William_Wilberforce_and_Transformative_Religion.

Methodists) supported what became one of the first grassroots human rights campaign in the English-speaking world.

The Clapham Group engaged the Practical Enlightenment through friendship with the unitarian Josiah Wedgwood (1730–1795). He was famous for industrializing the manufacture of pottery. He pioneered methods of marketing and meeting the increasing consumer demands of English society for tableware and other goods driving the Industrial Revolution. He made a popular anti-slavery image in 1787 that brought public attention to abolitionism. A kneeling slave appealing to Heaven for help appeared with the motto, "Am I Not a Man and a Brother?" Over the years, this image appeared on artifacts made in ceramic, metal, glass, and fabric such as snuffbox lids, shoe buckles, hair pins, pendants, and bracelets. (This suggested an important tactic used by social pressure groups ever since to communicate their messages by material things such as T-shirts.)

First produced in 1787 by Josiah Wedgwood,
this antislavery medallion became a popular
icon for the British abolitionist movement.

Most Enlighteners disliked slavery but remained passive or even condoned it in the face of powerful vested interests — such as the rising sugar industry. In other words, the abolitionist movement did not result inevitably from Enlightenment ideas. Motivated by Christian faith, the Clapham group and their allies took advantage of a sense of imperial crisis after the American Revolution to lead a mass movement that would push moral opinion into moral action.

Conflict with Principalities and Powers

The Practical Enlightenment sometimes contributed to the exploitation of people — such as miners near Bristol and the slaves who were traded from that city as property. Thus, at times, the Practical Enlightenment conflicted with Christianity. This provoked war, spiritual and otherwise.

In 1788, for example, the aging John Wesley gave an abolitionist sermon in Bristol. Entrenched interests hated the abolitionist movement, and it was by no means safe to challenge their power. The text of the sermon is lost, but it was likely based on Wesley's pamphlet *Thoughts on Slavery* (1774). This was widely read and made Wesley one of the first prominent figures of the English-speaking world to stand against slavery. The pamphlet appealed both to reason and to the rhetoric of the heart in a way that set the pattern for later abolitionist writing. "Are you *a man?*" he addressed the slave trader directly. "Then you should have an *human* heart. But have you indeed? What is your heart made of?" he asked. "When you squeezed the agonizing creatures down in the ship, or when you threw their poor mangled remains into the sea, had you no relenting?" Here Wesley may have referred to the widely known *Zong* massacre of 1781. The crew on a British slave ship, the *Zong*, threw 130 living slaves overboard due to a water shortage. They later made an insurance claim based on their lost property. "Do you feel no relenting *now?*" Wesley continued in his pamphlet. As in the evangelical conversion experience, he appealed to a personal emotional response. "If you do not, you must go on.... Then will the Great GOD deal with *You*, as you have dealt with *them*, and require all their blood at your hands."[398]

If this was how he gave his sermon in Bristol in 1788, then one can understand why a great disturbance broke out during it. Wesley recorded: "About the middle of the discourse, while there was on every side attention still as night, a vehement noise arose, none could tell why, and shot like lightning through the whole congregation." There was a panic and benches ended up smashed to pieces. Wesley blamed "some preternatural influence. Satan fought, lest his kingdom should be delivered up."[399] Supporters of the slave trade may have had something to do with the disturbance too.

Three years later, in 1791, and only one week before his death, John Wesley wrote his last letter. It was to William Wilberforce, who in 1789 had given his first major speech in the House of Commons on the abolition of the slave trade. In that speech, Wilberforce described in detail the appalling conditions in which slaves traveled from Africa across the Atlantic Ocean. Some argued, he said, the slave trade was necessary for the development of the West Indies. "I could not believe that the same Being who forbids rapine and bloodshed, had made rapine and bloodshed necessary to the well-being of any part of his universe," he said. The truth was clear when viewing the evidence in light of the laws of God: the slave trade should be abolished. Wilberforce's opponents included the powerful West India lobby group. This linked merchants, planters, shipbuilders, and financiers, to members of Parliament representing slave ports, such as Bristol. The West India lobby group held considerable power and managed to delay the vote on Wilberforce's proposal. This derailed antislavery momentum and prevented legislation for decades, during which Wilberforce and his allies never quit fighting. It was during

---

[398] Brycchan Carey, "John Wesley's *Thoughts upon Slavery* and the Languge of the Heart," *Bulletin of the John Rylands University Library of Manchester* 85, nos. 2–3 (2003): 283.
[399] Ibid., 277.

this time of defeat and discouragement in 1791 that Wesley wrote the following to Wilberforce:

February 24, 1791

Dear Sir:

Unless the divine power has raised you up to be as Athanasius against the world, I see not how you can go through your glorious enterprise in opposing that execrable villainy which is the scandal of religion, of England, and of human nature [slavery]. Unless God has raised you up for this very thing, you will be worn out by the opposition of men and devils. But if God be fore you, who can be against you? Are all of them together stronger than God? O be not weary of well doing! Go on, in the name of God and in the power of his might, till even American slavery (the vilest that ever saw the sun) shall vanish away before it.

… That he who has guided you from youth up may continue to strengthen you in this and all things, is the prayer of, dear sir,

Your affectionate servant,

John Wesley[400]

---

[400] John Wesley to William Wilberforce, February 24, 1791, Asbury Theological Seminary, https://place.asburyseminary.edu/cgi/viewcontent.cgi?referer=&httpsredir=1&article=1009&context=engaginggovernmentpapers; William Wilberforce, "Abolition Speech," in *The Parliamentary History of England, from the Earliest Period to the Year 1803* (London: T.C. Hansard, 1816), 48–49.

Conclusion

A Strategic Vision of Enlightenment and Christian Cultures

....

Why Does the Enlightenment Matter?

As a powerful and diverse cultural movement, the Enlightenment did not simply oppose reason to faith. Anti-Christian rationalism fueling the French Revolution was not the whole story. Even at the dinner party in Voltaire's Ferney château, religion occupied a seat at the table.

Since the Enlightenment was a cultural movement and not just a set of ideas labeled "anti-Christian," a wide population—not simply elite thinkers—participated in it. There was the Practical Enlightenment of tradesmen and engineers that changed the material face of the modern world. It inculcated not only mechanical thinking but also realism, common sense, and practical mindedness about human affairs—especially in the English-speaking world. At the Constitutional Convention of 1787, for example, Benjamin Franklin urged delegates to drop their animosities. "Can a perfect production be expected?" he asked. "Thus I consent," he said, "to this Constitution because I expect no better.... The opinions I have had of its errors, I sacrifice to the public good."[401] This was the Practical Enlightenment striving to bring diverse people together in common and useful projects from improving roads to founding a country.

---

[401] Benjamin Franklin, "Constitutional Convention Speech," in *Colonies to Nation, 1763–1789: A Documentary History of the American Revolution*, ed. Jack P. Greene (1787; New York: W. W. Norton, 1975), 546.

Rethinking the Enlightenment

The Enlightenment also fostered a culture of conversation. It created new spaces for networking with people and ideas—such as coffeehouses, where the stimulant caffeine replaced the depressant alcohol. A certain code of politeness tried to elevate human interactions. For example, in his daily paper the *Spectator*, the Enlightener Joseph Addison endeavored to "enliven Morality with Wit, and to temper Wit with Morality." He proposed to utilize innocent and "improving Entertainment" to impart "sound and wholesome Sentiments" that would enrich readers' conversation. This could lift people up from the prevailing vice and folly of the age.[402] In this way, the Enlightenment worked against the kinds of boorish disrespect and ideological divisiveness sometimes characteristic of the public sphere.

The Three Strategies

The Enlightenment is a fascinating example of the relationship between religion and culture. As common ways of life, Christian culture and Enlightenment culture both conflicted and overlapped with each other—or diverged altogether. Christians interacted with the Enlightenment through conflict, engagement, and retreat. Each of these strategies possessed different emphases, strengths, and weaknesses.

Strategy 1: Conflict

The Carmelites of Compiègne modeled a sophisticated and inspiring type of conflict with the Enlightenment. They trusted in the Holy Spirit, combatted the spirit of the age, and triumphed over the temptation to compromise. They refuted error by their witness, thereby preserving their identities until the end.

We have seen other examples of conflicts. The French priest and apologist Nicholas Bergier combated the ideas of Rousseau. French peasants

---

[402] Addison, *Spectator*, March 12, 1711.

of the Vendée fought the French Revolution. Politicians such as Edmund Burke and William Wilberforce took the battle into enemy lines when they defended religion and human dignity in the British Parliament.

Christian conflict during the Enlightenment displayed not only heroism and doctrinal clarity, however. In a negative sense, it also revealed tendencies toward closed-mindedness, viewing opponents as enemies, and politicizing disagreements. A conflictual mentality even affected relations among Christians. For example, as we have seen, Catholics in France persecuted Protestants, then fellow Catholics (Jansenists), then other fellow Catholics (Jesuits), and then Enlighteners (who became increasingly angry and "conflictual"). The discordant attitudes exported beyond French borders contributed to the polarization of the whole of Catholic Europe and its empires. The Conflictual Enlightenment formed — and in some places triumphed — partly in response to these weaknesses and internal divisions within Christian culture.

The tensions of conflict produced a crisis of faith. They also unexpectedly enriched faith. The messy, uncomfortable duels between faith and reason stirred up the dust of combat in the public arenas of the time. This yielded greater practical appreciation for religious freedom and toleration. Humanitarian modifications were made to criminal law. "It is necessary for the very life of religion, viewed in its larger operations and its history, that the warfare should be incessantly carried on," John Henry Newman wrote a century later. Paradoxically, conflict of forces, of faith and reason, and of willful intellects and wild passions, could purify each other in that "awful, never-dying duel," he continued. That is why the world of secular rationality and the world of religious belief "need one another and should not be afraid to enter into a profound and ongoing dialogue, for the good of our civilization," Pope Benedict XVI said.[403]

---

[403] John Henry Newman, *Apologia pro Vita Sua* (1864; London: J. M. Dent & Sons, 1949), 226; Benedict XVI, Address in Westminster Hall.

Strategy 2: Engagement

Maria Agnesi, Pope Benedict XIV, and numerous Benedictine monks engaged the Enlightenment on its own terms. They demonstrated faith both *during* the Age of Reason and *faith in the Age of Reason* itself, in many of its methods and goals. They were open to the true, the good, and the beautiful wherever it could be found. Catholic Enlighteners took up the challenges of rationalism and empiricism to make important distinctions between the natural and the supernatural, thus defending the proper autonomy of different kinds of knowledge.

Catholic Enlighteners were convinced that Christian faith is born from a Great Fact: Jesus Christ in history. They held that faith in him and in human nature is renewed again and again by analysis of "little facts" — archaeological remains from the early Church, perhaps, or the anatomy of the human body. As a result, the Vatican Museums emerged in Rome and the Academy of Sciences in Bologna. The engagement of mathematics, history, and medicine overlapped with Enlightenment reason and kept faith relevant to the new generation.

Ludovico Muratori showed how "rational devotion" could purify Christian faith and practice. Rational devotion oriented piety rightly toward God and neighbor and away from superstition. Enlightenment spirituality emphasized the importance of the brain for holiness.

The Catholic Enlightenment prioritized open-mindedness and the spirit of compromise. Even Benedictine monasteries did not isolate themselves from the world. Their doors remained open to the Divine Logos coming from the outside. Pope Benedict XIV conducted important Church administration from his coffeehouse, engaging others and resolving problems with compromise and humor.

A key challenge emerged, however, in engaging the Enlightenment. This was tension between fame and modesty, reason and tradition, and love of earthly life and the desire of Heaven. Maria Agnesi and Laura Bassi successfully balanced these tensions. Others stumbled, however, such as certain monks as they overindulged in the Enlightenment spirit. That spirit could at times infiltrate hearts and monasteries in a way that lessened or even destroyed Christian identity. In this way, there was a failure to nurture and guard the thresholds and windows of Christian culture.

Strategy 3: Retreat

Thus, the need for spiritual retreat became apparent. Christians needed not only to conflict and engage with their times but also to nurture and guard Christian culture from within—to withdraw from the world into households, religious societies, and churches. This sheltering strategy tried to integrate faith into all dimensions of life. "Householding" pled for synthesis, rather than analysis. It sought to unify instead of to distinguish.

Daniel Defoe wrote about retreat, and Susanna and Samuel Wesley lived it. Two of their sons, John and Charles, emerged from the sanctuary of their family household to build up Christian culture in the English-speaking world in an impressive way. They employed mobility, preaching, publishing, hymns, and institutional thinking. This "New Evangelization" of the Enlightenment era utilized achievements of the Practical Enlightenment. It merged with the engagement strategy in the English-speaking world to work a moral revolution. This changed basic assumptions about political authority and human dignity. Christians allied to win the American Revolution, to found a regime that clearly distinguished between church and state, and to end slavery in the British Empire. In France, by contrast, Christian retreat and the legacy of evangelization by Louis de Montfort allied nobly with the conflict strategy. Christian forces in the west of the country coalesced around the Sacred Heart of Jesus as a symbol of resistance to totalitarian claims of the Conflictual Enlightenment.

Notably, religious revival benefited not only religion but also the Enlightenment. Revival confronted the Age of Reason with the importance of the human heart. It preserved awareness of those levels of human psychology both below and above rational consciousness. By alliance with the engagement strategy, religious revival fostered a broad civil religion of common values. It helped preserve public freedom by prompting believers to restrain and govern themselves through the practice of virtue. "Of all the dispositions and habits which lead to political prosperity, religion and morality are indispensable supports," George Washington said. "And let us with caution indulge the supposition that morality can be maintained without religion."[404] In addition, religious revival provided a check on the pretensions of the all-encompassing state, making possible reasonable politics rather than mythological politics filled with utopian dreams.

The retreat strategy contained weaknesses, however. Emphasizing the heart over the brain fostered intense emotionalism and introspection. Where intellectual engagement was lacking, this left a weak basis for sustaining long-term faith. Integrating life based solely on faith risked overstepping the proper autonomy of the secular order and of different fields of knowledge. This could create confusion and feed superstition. That was why many Catholic Enlighteners and Anglican bishops in England, for example, viewed popular missions with suspicion. They simply fed fanaticism. Pope Benedict XIV, however, thought the public benefit of popular missions outweighed the dangers of misplaced enthusiasm. John Wesley agreed.

Intellectual engagement with the Enlightenment was necessary to balance the other weaknesses in the retreat strategy too. Fear of human nature for the sake of "holiness" led to joyless rigidity and a Christian pessimism that scandalized Voltaire and others who saw the goodness of natural human desires. Without engagement, the Puritan temptation could lead to "pseudo-retreat" from the world based on moral self-righteousness. "These are narrow minds," Diderot wrote in the *Encyclopédie*, "deformed souls, who are indifferent to the fate of the human race and who are so enclosed in their little group that they see nothing beyond its special interest."[405]

---

[404] George Washington, Farewell Address (1796), Our Documents, https://www.ourdocuments.gov/doc.php?flash=false&doc=15&page=transcript.

[405] Denis Diderot, "Encyclopédie," in *The Portable Enlightenment Reader*, ed. Isaac Kramnick (1755; New York: Penguin Books), 19.

Redeeming the Time

There is a need for all three strategies. There was in the eighteenth century, and there is today. Conflict without engagement is senseless. Engagement without conflict is weak. Either strategy without retreat lacks wisdom. Retreat without conflict or engagement is stultifying.

Each of the strategies represents a different intention. They all seek to live out the relationship between religion and culture and between personal faith and public life. But the emphasis differs with each one. Since every person cannot pursue every strategy constantly with equal effectiveness, there is need to discern which is necessary at the time. The vocation and talents of individual people or of whole cultures indicate which strategies make the most sense for them. The porous boundaries between strategies mean that it is possible to migrate from one to the other, depending on the season. Carefully integrating even two of the strategies could make for a more effective and psychologically sound relationship between religion and culture. When different parts of the Kingdom of God pursue *all* of them, however, a tough, intellectually sophisticated, and evangelically oriented Christianity can emerge—as it did in the Age of the Enlightenment.

Works Cited

Adams, Geoffrey. *The Huguenots and French Opinion, 1685–1787: The Enlightenment Debate on Toleration*. Waterloo: Wilfrid Laurier University Press, 1991.

Adams, John. To the Massachusetts Militia. October 11, 1798. Founders Online. https://founders.archives.gov/documents/Adams/99-02 -02-3102.

Addison, Joseph. *Spectator*, March 12, 1711. https://www.gutenberg.org/files/12030/12030-h/SV1/Spectator1.html#section10.

———. *The Free-Holder*, April 27, 1716.

"Answer to the Foregoing." *Gentleman's Magazine*, May 1739, 253–257.

Arnett, William M. "What Happened to Wesley at Aldersgate?" *Asbury Seminarian* 18, no. 1 (1964): 6–17.

Baillie, Marianne. *First Impressions on a Tour upon the Continent in the Summer of 1818, through parts of France, Italy, Switzerland, the Borders of Germany, and a part of French Flanders*. London: John Murray, 1819.

Barron, Robert. "Called out of Corruption and into Christ." YouTube video, 18:28. Posted May 3, 2020. https://www.youtube.com/watch?v =At0v-YdXR0M.

Baxter, John. "The Great Yorkshire Revival 1792–6: A Study of Mass Revival among the Methodists." In *A Sociological Yearbook of Religion in Britain*, edited by M. Hill, 46–76. London: SCM, 1974.

Bayle, Pierre. *A Philosophical Commentary on These Words of the Gospel, Luke 14.23, 'Compel Them to Come In, That My House May Be Full.'* 1686; Indianapolis: Liberty Fund, 2005.

Beales, Derek. *Prosperity and Plunder: European Catholic Monasteries in the Age of Revolution, 1650–1815.* Cambridge: Cambridge University Press, 2003.

Beccaria, Cesare. *On Crimes and Punishments, and Other Writings.* 1764; Toronto: University of Toronto Press, 2008.

Becker, Carl L. *The Heavenly City of the Eighteenth-Century Philosophers.* New Haven: Yale University Press, 1932.

Bellenger, Aidan. "'Superstitious Enemies of the Flesh?' The Variety of Benedictine Responses to the Enlightenment." In *Religious Change in Europe, 1650–1914: Essays for John McManners,* edited by Nigel Aston, 149–160. Oxford: Clarendon Press, 1997.

Benedict XIV, Pope. *Heroic Virtue: A Portion of the Treatise of Benedict XIV on the Beatification and Canonization of the Servants of God.* 3 vols. 1734–1738; London: Thomas Richardson and Son, 1851–1852.

Benedict XVI, Pope. Address in Westminster Hall. September 17, 2010.

———. Papal Homily at the End of the Year for Priests. June 11, 2010.

Bezzant, Rhys. "'The Better Hour Is Near': Wilberforce and Transformative Religion." September 2013. https://www.researchgate.net/publication/258632052_'The_Better_Hour_is_Near'_William_Wilberforce_and_Transformative_Religion.

Bien, David D. *The Calas Affair: Persecution, Toleration, and Heresy in Eighteenth-Century Toulouse.* Princeton: Princeton University Press, 1960.

Blum, Carol. *Rousseau and the Republic of Virtue: The Language of Politics in the French Revolution.* Ithaca: Cornell University Press, 1986.

Böckmann, Aquinata. "Openness to the World and Separation from the World according to the *Rule* of Benedict." *American Benedictine Review* 37, no. 3 (1986): 304–322.

Bonet-Maury, Gaston "The Edict of Tolerance of Louis XVI (1787) and Its American Promoters." *American Journal of Theology* 3 no. 3 (July 1899): 554–565.

Boswell, James. *Life of Johnson.* 1791. https://www.gutenberg.org/files/1564/1564-h/1564-h.htm.

Braudel, Fernand. *The Structures of Everyday Life: The Limits of the Possible. Civilization and Capitalism, 15th–18th Century.* Vol. 1. New York: Harper & Row, 1981.

Bredvold, Louis I. *The Literature of the Restoration and the Eighteenth Century, 1660–1798.* New York: Collier Books, 1962.

"Bristol." *Gentleman's Magazine,* March 1739, 162.

Brown, Christopher L. *Moral Capital: Foundations of British Abolitionism.* Chapel Hill: University of North Carolina Press, 2006.

Brownson, Orestes. *The American Republic: Its Constitution, Tendencies and Destiny.* 1865; Wilmington, DE: ISI Books, 2003.

Burke, Edmund. "A Letter to a Member of the National Assembly." In *The Best of Burke: Selected Writings and Speeches of Edmund Burke,* edited by Peter J. Stanlis, 609–622. 1791; Washington, DC: Regnery, 1963.

———. *Reflections on the Revolution in France.* 1790; Indianapolis: Hackett Publishing, 1987.

Bush, William. *To Quell the Terror.* Washington, DC: Institute of Carmelite Studies, 1999.

Carey, Brycchan. "John Wesley's *Thoughts upon Slavery* and the Languge of the Heart." *Bulletin of the John Rylands University Library of Manchester* 85, nos. 2–3 (2003): 269–284.

Cavazza, Marta. "Between Modesty and Spectacle: Women and Science in Eighteenth-Century Italy." In *Italy's Eighteenth Century: Gender and Culture in the Age of the Grand Tour,* edited by Paula Findlen, Wendy Wassyng Roworth, and Catherine M. Sama, 275–302. Stanford: Stanford University Press, 2009.

———. "Laura Bassi and Giuseppe Veratti: An Electric Couple during the Enlightenment." *Contributions to Science* 5, no. 1 (2009): 115–124.

Chadwick, Owen. *The Popes and European Revolution*. New York: Oxford University Press, 1981.

Clarke, Adam. *Memoirs of the Wesley Family*. 2nd ed. New York: Lane & Tippett, 1848. http://media.sabda.org/alkitab-6/wh2-hdm/hdm0386.pdf.

Clarke, Eliza. *Susanna Wesley*. London: W. H. Allen, 1886.

Clendening, Logan, ed. *Source Book of Medical History*. New York: Dover, 1942.

Cole, Nathan. "Memoir." In *The Great Awakening: A Brief History with Documents*, edited by Thomas S. Kidd, 60–64. 1771; Boston: Bedford/St. Martin's Press, 2008.

Collins, Jeffrey. "Pedagogy in Plaster: Ercole Lelli and Benedict XIV's *Gipsoteca* at Bologna's Instituto delle Scienze e delle Arti." In *Benedict XIV and the Enlightenment: Art, Science, and Spirituality*, edited by Rebecca Messbarer, Christopher M. S. Johns, and Philip Gavitt, 391–418. Toronto: University of Toronto Press, 2016.

Condorcet. *Outlines of an Historical View of the Progress of the Human Mind*. 1795; Philadelphia: Lang and Ustick, 1796.

Copleston, Frederick. *A History of Philosophy*. Vol. 4 of *Descartes to Leibniz*. Garden City, NY: Image Books, 1960.

A Course in Montfortian Spirituality. Montfort Missionaries, 2014. http://www.montfort.org.uk/Documents/Course/A%20Course%20in%20Montfortian%20Spirituality.pdf.

Cranston, Maurice. *Jean-Jacques: The Early Life and World of Jean-Jacques Rousseau, 1712–1754*. New York: W. W. Norton, 1982.

Cunningham, Andrew. *The Anatomist Anatomis'd: An Experimental Discipline in Enlightenment Europe*. Farnham, Surrey, UK: Ashgate, 2010.

Cunningham, Lawrence S. Review of *Enlightened Monks*. *Commonweal*, March 9, 2012.

Cupillari, Antonella. *A Biography of Maria Gaetana Agnesi, an Eighteenth-Century Woman Mathematician, With Translations of Some of Her Work from Italian into English*. Lewiston, NY: Edwin Mellen, 2007.

d'Holbach, Baron. *Good Sense without God: Or Freethoughts Opposed to Supernatural Ideas.* 1772; London: W. Steward, ca. 1900. https://www.gutenberg.org/files/7319/7319-h/7319-h.htm.

Daniel-Rops, H. *The Church in the Seventeenth Century.* London: J. M. Dent & Sons, 1963.

Darnton, Robert. *The Great Cat Massacre, and Other Episodes in French Cultural History.* New York: Vintage Books, 1984.

Davidson, Ian. *Voltaire: A Life.* New York: Pegasus Books, 2010.

Dawson, Christopher. *The Dividing of Christendom.* 1965; San Francisco: Ignatius Press, 2008.

———. *The Gods of Revolution.* 1972; Washington, DC: Catholic University of America Press, 2015.

———. *The Historic Reality of Christian Culture: A Way to the Renewal of Human Life.* London: Routledge & Kegan Paul, 1960.

———. *Progress and Religion: An Historical Enquiry.* 1929; Washington, DC: Catholic University of America Press, 2001.

de Sales, Francis. *Introduction to the Devout Life.* 1609; New York: Vintage Books, 2002.

"Declaration on Religious Freedom." In *The Teachings of the Second Vatican Council,* 366–383. Westminster, MD: Newman Press, 1966.

Defoe, Daniel. "Of the Tradesman Letting His Wife Be Acquainted with His Business." Chap. 21 in *The Complete English Tradesman.* 1726; Edinburgh: William and Robert Chambers, 1839. http://www.gutenberg.org/files/14444/14444-h/14444-h.htm#CHAPTER_XXI.

———. *A New Family Instructor.* London: T. Warner, 1727.

———. *Tour Thro' the Whole Island of Great Britain.* 6th ed. London: D. Browne, 1761.

DeHart, Paul R. "The First Amendment Didn't Separate Church and State—Christianity Did." *Public Discourse* (April 25, 2018): 1–9. https://www.thepublicdiscourse.com/2018/04/21381/.

———. "Madisonian Thomism." *Public Discourse* (January 23, 2017). https://www.thepublicdiscourse.com/2017/01/18427/.

Desan, Suzanne. *Reclaiming the Sacred: Lay Religion and Popular Politics in Revolutionary France*. Ithaca: Cornell University Press, 1990.

Descartes, René. *Discourse on Method, and Related Writings*. Translated by Desmond M. Clarke. 1637; New York: Penguin Books, 1999.

Diderot, Denis. *Encyclopédie*. In *The Portable Enlightenment Reader*, edited by Isaac Kramnick, 17–21. 1755; New York: Penguin Books.

Dinwiddie, Richard D. "Two Brothers ... Who Changed the Course of Church Singing." *Christianity Today*, September 21, 1984, 30–34.

Donato, Maria Pia. "The Mechanical Medicine of a Pious Man of Science: G. M. Lancisi's *De subitaneis mortibus* (1707)." In *Conflicting Duties: Science, Medicine and Religion in Rome, 1550–1750*, edited by Maria Pia Donato and Jill Kraye, 319–352. London: Warburg Institute, 2009.

Duffin, Jacalyn. *Medical Miracles: Doctors, Saints, and Healing in the Modern World*. New York: Oxford University Press, 2009.

Du Marsais, César Chesneau. "Philosopher." *The Encyclopedia of Diderot & d'Alembert Collaborative Translation Project*. Translated by Dena Goodman. Ann Arbor: Michigan Publishing, University of Michigan Library, 2002. http://hdl.handle.net/2027/spo.did2222.0000.001.

Eberstadt, Mary. *How the West Really Lost God: A New Theory of Secularization*. West Conshohocken, PA: Templeton, 2013.

Erdozain, Dominic. *The Soul of Doubt: The Religious Roots of Unbelief from Luther to Marx*. New York: Oxford University Press, 2016.

Ferguson, Niall. *Civilization: The West and the Rest*. New York: Penguin, 2011.

Feser, Edward. *Aristotle's Revenge: The Metaphysical Foundations of Physical and Biological Science*. Neunkirchen-Seelscheid, Germany: Editiones Scholasticae, 2019.

Findlen, Paula. "Calculations of Faith: Mathematics, Philosophy, and Sanctity in 18th-Century Italy." *Historia Mathematica* 38, no. 1 (2011): 248–291.

———. "Science as a Career in Enlightenment Italy: The Strategies of Laura Bassi." *Isis* 84, no. 3 (1993): 441–469.

———. "The Scientist and the Saint: Laura Bassi's Enlightened Catholicism." In *Women, Enlightenment and Catholicism: A Transnational*

Biographical History, edited by Ulrich L. Lehner, 114–131. New York: Routledge, 2018.

Finocchiaro, Maurice A. *Retrying Galileo, 1633–1992*. Berkeley: University of California Press, 2005.

Fontaine, James. *Memoirs of a Huguenot Family*. New York: George P. Putnam, 1853.

François, Bernard, Esther M. Sternberg, and Elizabeth Fee. "The Lourdes Medical Cures Revisited." *Journal of the History of Medicine and Allies Sciences* 69, no. 1 (2012): 135–162.

Frankl, Viktor E. *Man's Search for Meaning: An Introduction to Logotherapy*. 1946; New York: Pocket Books, 1963.

Franklin, Benjamin. *The Autobiography and Other Writings*. 1791; New York: Signet Classics, 2001.

———. "Constitutional Convention Speech." In *Colonies to Nation, 1763–1789: A Documentary History of the American Revolution*, edited by Jack P. Greene, 545–547. 1787; New York: W. W. Norton, 1975.

Galilei, Galileo. "Letter to Castelli." In *The Essential Galileo*, edited by Maurice A. Finocchiaro, 103–109. 1613; Indianapolis: Hackett Publishing, 2008.

———. "Letter to the Grand Duchess Christina." In *The Essential Galileo*, edited by Maurice A. Finocchiaro, 109–145. 1615; Indianapolis: Hackett Publishing, 2008.

Gay, Peter. *The Enlightenment: The Rise of Modern Paganism*. New York: Vintage Books, 1966.

Gregory, Brad S. *The Unintended Reformation: How a Religious Revolution Secularized Society*. Cambridge, MA: Belknap/Harvard University Press, 2012.

Guido, Joseph J. "A Clergy Sex Abuse Survivor's Story and Its Lessons for Restoring Faith." *America*, August 31, 2018. https://www.americamagazine.org/faith/2018/08/31/clergy-sex-abuse-survivors-story-and-its-lessons-restoring-faith.

Guilday, Peter. *The Life and Times of John Carroll*. Westminster, MD: Newman Press, 1954.

Guindon, H. M. "Sacred Heart." In *Jesus Living in Mary: Handbook of the Spirituality of St. Louis de Montfort*. Litchfield, CT: Montfort Publications, 1994. EWTN. https://www.ewtn.com/catholicism/library/sacred-heart-12788.

Halévy, Élie. *The Birth of Methodism in England*. 1906; Chicago: University of Chicago Press, 1971.

Hanrahan, James. "Creating the 'Cri Public': Voltaire and Public Opinion in the Early 1760s." In *Voltaire and the 1760s: Essays for John Renwick*, edited by Nicholas Cronk, 145–158. Oxford: Voltaire Foundation, 2008.

Hardwick, David. "Investigating the Newcomen Pumping Engine House at Brislington near Bristol." *International Journal for the History of Engineering & Technology* 88, no. 2 (2018): 166–203.

Harth, Erica. "Cartesian Women." *Yale French Studies* 80 (1991): 146–164.

Haynes, Renée. *Philosopher King: The Humanist Pope Benedict XIV*. London: Weidenfeld and Nicolson, 1970.

Heclo, Hugh. *On Thinking Institutionally*. Boulder: Paradigm, 2008.

Heilbron, John L. "Benedict XIV and the Natural Sciences." In *Benedict XIV and the Enlightenment: Art, Science, and Spirituality*, edited by Rebecca Messbarger, Christopher M. S. Johns, and Philip Gavitt, 177–205. Toronto: University of Toronto Press, 2016.

Heitzenrater, Richard P. *Wesley and the People Called Methodists*. 2nd ed. Nashville: Abingdon, 2013.

Hempton, David. "Wesley in Context." In *The Cambridge Companion to John Wesley*, edited by Randy L. Maddox and Jason E. Vickers, 60–76. New York: Cambridge University Press, 2010.

Hindmarsh, D. Bruce. *The Evangelical Conversion Narrative: Spiritual Autobiography in Early Modern England*. New York: Oxford University Press, 2005.

The History of Kingswood School. London: Charles H. Kelly, 1898.

Jacob, Margaret C. *The Secular Enlightenment*. Princeton: Princeton University Press, 2019.

John Paul II, Pope. *Fides et Ratio: On the Relationship between Faith and Reason*. Boston: Pauline Books & Media, 1998.

————. "Lessons of the Galileo Case." *Origins* 22, no. 22 (November 12, 1992): 370–374.

Johns, Christopher M. S. *The Visual Culture of Catholic Enlightenment.* University Park, PA: Pennsylvania State University Press, 2015.

Johnson, Claudia Durst, and Vernon Johnson. *The Social Impact of the Novel: A Reference Guide.* Westport, CT: Greenwood, 2002.

Kant, Immanuel. "What Is Enlightenment?" In *The Portable Enlightenment Reader,* edited by Isaac Kramnick, 1–7. 1784; New York: Penguin Books, 1995.

Kaplan, Benjamin J. *Divided by Faith: Religious Conflict and the Practice of Toleration in Early Modern Europe.* Cambridge, MA: Harvard University Press, 2007.

Kardong, Terrance G. "People Storage: Mabillon's Diatribe against Monastic Prisons." *Cistercian Studies Quarterly* 26, no. 1 (1991): 40–57.

Kidd, Thomas S. *George Whitefield: America's Spiritual Founding Father.* New Haven: Yale University Press, 2014.

Knott, Sarah, and Barbara Taylor, eds. *Women, Gender and Enlightenment.* New York: Palgrave Macmillan, 2005.

Kolakowski, Leszek. *God Owes Us Nothing: A Brief Remark on Pascal's Religion and on the Spirit of Jansenism.* Chicago: University of Chicago Press, 1995.

Kramnick, Isaac, ed. *The Portable Enlightenment Reader.* New York: Penguin Books, 1995.

Lecky, William E. H. *A History of England in the Eighteenth Century.* New York: D. Appleton, 1878.

Leclercq, Jean. *The Love of Learning and the Desire for God: A Study of Monastic Culture.* New York: Fordham University Press, 1982.

Lehner, Ulrich L. *The Catholic Enlightenment: The Forgotten History of a Global Movement.* New York: Oxford University Press, 2016.

————. *Enlightened Monks: The German Benedictines, 1740–1803.* New York: Oxford University Press, 2011.

————. *On the Road to Vatican II: German Catholic Enlightenment and Reform of the Church.* Minneapolis: Fortress Press, 2016.

Lehner, Ulrich L., ed. *Women, Enlightenment and Catholicism: A Transnational Biographical History*. New York: Routledge, 2018.

Lehner, Ulrich L., and Michael Printy, eds. *A Companion to the Catholic Enlightenment in Europe*. Leiden: Brill, 2010.

Lev, Elizabeth. *How Catholic Art Saved the Faith: The Triumph of Beauty and Truth in Counter-Reformation Art*. Manchester: Sophia Institute Press, 2018.

Lewis, C. S. *Surprised by Joy: The Shape of My Early Life*. London: Collins/Fontana Books, 1955.

Lindegaard, D. P. *Killed in a Coalpit: Lives of the Kingswood Colliers*. Gloucestershire: South Gloucestershire Mines Research Group, 2016.

Logan, Gabriella Berti. "The Desire to Contribute: An Eighteenth-Century Italian Woman of Science." *American Historical Review* 99, no. 3 (June 1994): 785–812.

Mabillon, Jean. *Treatise on Monastic Studies*. 1691; Lanham: University Press of America, 2004.

Mack, Phyllis. *Heart Religion in the British Enlightenment: Gender and Emotion in Early Methodism*. New York: Cambridge University Press, 2008.

Madison, James. "The Federalist Papers: No. 10." (1787). Lillian Goldman Law Library Avalon Project. https://avalon.law.yale.edu/18th_century/fed10.asp.

Malcolmson, Robert W. *A Set of Ungovernable People: The Kingswood Colliers in the Eighteenth Century*. Kingswood: Kingswood Borough Council, 1986.

Mallet, Edme-François. "Bénédictins." In *Encyclopédie*. https://artflsrv03.uchicago.edu/philologic4/encyclopedie1117/query?report=concordance&method=proxy&attribution=&objecttype=&q=eclaires&start=0&end=0&head=Benedictins.

Maritain, Jacques. *Three Reformers: Luther, Descartes, Rousseau*. London: Sheed & Ward, 1928.

Mazzotti, Massimo. "Maria Gaetana Agnesi (1718–1799): Science and Mysticism." In *Enlightenment and Catholicism in Europe: A Transnational*

History, edited by Jeffrey D. Burson and Ulrich L. Lehner, 289–306. Notre Dame: University of Notre Dame Press, 2014.

———. "Maria Gaetana Agnesi: Mathematics and the Making of the Catholic Enlightenment." *Isis* 92, no. 4 (December 2001): 657–683.

———. *The World of Maria Gaetana Agnesi, Mathematician of God*. Baltimore: Johns Hopkins University Press, 2007.

McDowell, Paula. "Media and Mediation in the Eighteenth Century." Oxford Handbooks Online. March 2017. https://www.oxfordhandbooks.com/view/10.1093/oxfordhb/9780199935338.001.0001/oxfordhb-9780199935338-e-46.

McNeil, Gordon H. "The Cult of Rousseau and the French Revolution." *Journal of the History of Ideas* 6, no. 2 (April 1945): 197–212.

Messbarger, Rebecca. "Faith, Science and the Modern Body: Anna Morandi's Studies of Human Anatomy in Wax." In *Women, Enlightenment and Catholicism: A Transnational Biographical History*, edited by Ulrich L. Lehner, 98–113. New York: Routledge, 2018.

———. "The Art and Science of Human Anatomy in Benedict's Vision of the Enlightenment Church." In *Benedict XIV and the Enlightenment: Art, Science, and Spirituality*, edited by Rebecca Messbarger, Christopher M. S. Johns, and Philip Gavitt, 93–119. Toronto: University of Toronto Press, 2016.

———. *The Lady Anatomist: The Life and Work of Anna Morandi Manzolini*. Chicago: University of Chicago Press, 2010.

Messbarger, Rebecca, and Paula Findlen, eds. *The Contest for Knowledge: Debates over Women's Learning in Eighteenth-Century Italy*. Chicago: University of Chicago Press, 2005.

Messbarger, Rebecca, Christopher M. S. Johns, and Philip Gavitt, eds. *Benedict XIV and the Enlightenment: Art, Science, and Spirituality*. Toronto: University of Toronto Press, 2016.

Mokyr, Joel. *The Enlightened Economy: An Economic History of Britain 1700–1850*. New Haven: Yale University Press, 2009.

Montesquieu. "Notes on England." (1729–1731). Oxford University Comparative Law Forum. https://ouclf.law.ox.ac.uk/

montesquieu-in-england-his-notes-on-england-with-commentary-and-translation-commentary/.

————. *The Spirit of the Laws*. Chicago: Encyclopedia Britannica, 1952.

Moore, John. *A View of Society and Manners in France, Switzerland, and Germany*. 2nd ed. Vol. 1. London: W. Strahan, 1779.

Morgan, Kenneth. *John Wesley in Bristol*. Bristol: The Historical Association, 1990.

————. "Methodist Testimonials Collected by Charles Wesley in 1742." In *Reformation and Revival in Eighteenth-Century Bristol*, edited by Jonathan Barry and Kenneth Morgan, 77–104. Bristol: Bristol Record Society, 1994.

Muratori, Lodovico Antonio. *The Science of Rational Devotion*. Translated by Alexander Kenny. 1747; Dublin: James Byrn, 1789.

Neill, Thomas P. *Makers of the Modern Mind*. Milwaukee: Bruce, 1949.

Newman, John Henry. *Apologia pro Vita Sua*. 1864; London: J. M. Dent & Sons, 1949.

————. *An Essay on the Development of Christian Doctrine*. London: Longmans, Green, 1906.

Northcote, James Spencer. *The Roman Catacombs: A History of the Christian City beneath Pagan Rome*. 1877; Manchester: Sophia Institute Press, 2017.

O'Brien, Louis. *Innocent XI and the Revocation of the Edict of Nantes*. Ph.D. diss., University of California, Berkeley, 1930.

O'Connor, Siobhan M. "Confessions of a Catholic Whistleblower." *First Things* (November 22, 2018). https://www.firstthings.com/web-exclusives/2018/11/confessions-of-a-catholic-whistleblower.

"Observations on the Conduct of the Rev. Mr. Whitefield." *Gentleman's Magazine*, May 1739, 239–242.

Ogilvie, Sheilagh. "The European Economy in the Eighteenth Century." In *The Eighteenth Century: Europe 1688–1815*, edited by T. C. W. Blanning, 91–130. New York: Oxford University Press, 2000.

Orieux, Jean. *Voltaire*. Translated by Barbara Bray and Helen R. Lane. New York: Doubleday, 1979.

Paine, Thomas. *The Age of Reason*. 1794; London: Freethought, 1880.

Palmer, R. R. *Catholics and Unbelievers in Eighteenth Century France*. 2nd ed. New York: Cooper Square, 1939.

The Parliamentary History of England, from the Earliest Period to the Year 1803. London: T. C. Hansard, 1816.

Pascal, Blaise. *Thoughts on Religion and Other Curious Subjects*. Translated by Basil Kennett. 2nd ed. London: Jacob Tonson, 1727.

Pearson, Roger. *Voltaire Almighty: A Life in Pursuit of Freedom*. New York: Bloomsbury, 2005.

Philippe, Jacques. *Interior Freedom*. Translated by Helena Scott. New York: Scepter Press, 2002.

Pilling, Terry. "Ethereal Delights." *Engineering Quarterly* (Spring 2019): 6–8.

Pink, Thomas. "Conscience and Coercion: Vaticans II's Teaching on Religious Freedom Changed Policy, Not Doctrine." *First Things* (August 2012). https://www.firstthings.com/article/2012/08/conscience-and-coercion.

Pomata, Gianna. "The Devil's Advocate among the Physicians: What Prospero Lambertini Learned from Medical Sources." In *Benedict XIV and the Enlightenment: Art, Science, and Spirituality*, edited by Rebecca Messbarger, Christopher M. S. Johns, and Philip Gavitt, 120–150. Toronto: University of Toronto Press, 2016.

Pratt, Andrew. "The Influence of Charles Wesley on Contemporary Hymnody." In *Charles Wesley: Life, Literature and Legacy*, edited by Kenneth G. C. Newport and Ted A. Campbell, 395–413. Peterborough, UK: Epworth, 2007.

Printy, Michael. "The Intellectual Origins of Popular Catholicism: Catholic Moral Theology in the Age of Enlightenment." *Catholic Historical Review* 91, no. 3 (July 2005): 438–461.

Quadrupani, R. P. *Light and Peace: Instructions for Devout Souls to Dispel Their Doubts and Allay Their Fears*. 10th ed. 1795; Rockford, IL: TAN Books, 1980.

Ramelow, Anselm. "Not a Miracle: Our Knowledge of God's Signs and Wonders." *Nova et Vetera* 14, no. 2 (2016): 659–673.

Ratzinger, Joseph Cardinal. *Christianity and the Crisis of Cultures*. Translated by Brian McNeil. San Francisco: Ignatius Press, 2006.

———. *Church, Ecumenism, and Politics: New Endeavors in Ecclesiology*. Translated by Michael J. Miller et al. San Francisco: Ignatius Press, 2008.

———. "Letter to Marcello Pera." In *Without Roots: The West, Relativism, Christianity, Islam*, 107–135. New York: Basic Books, 2006.

Reid, Thomas. *An Inquiry into the Human Mind: On the Principles of Common Sense*. 4th ed. 1764; London: T. Cadell, 1785.

Reinert, Sophus A: *The Academy of Fisticuffs: Political Economy and Commercial Society in Enlightenment Italy*. Cambridge, MA: Harvard University Press, 2018.

Reiser, Marius. "The History of Catholic Exegesis, 1600–1800." In *The Oxford Handbook of Early Modern Theology, 1600–1800*, edited by Ulrich L. Lehner, Richard A. Muller, and A. G. Roeber, 75–88. New York: Oxford University Press, 2016.

Rivers, Isabel. "John Wesley as Editor and Publisher." In *The Cambridge Companion to John Wesley*, edited by Randy L. Maddox and Jason E. Vickers, 144–159. Cambridge: Cambridge University Press, 2009.

Roero, Clara Silvia. "M. G. Agnesi, R. Rampinelli and the Riccati Family: A Cultural Fellowship Formed for an Important Scientific Purpose, the *Instituzioni analitiche*." *Historia Mathematica* 42 (2015): 296–314.

Rousseau, Jean-Jacques. *The Confessions*. 1782; New York: Modern Library, n.d.

———. *The Confessions of J. J. Rousseau: With the Reveries of the Solitary Walker*. Vol. 2, London: J. Bew, 1783.

———. *The Confessions, and Correspondence, Including the Letters to Malesherbes*. Translated by Christopher Kelly. *The Collected Writings of Rousseau*. Edited by Roger D. Masters Christopher Kelly, and Peter G. Stillman. Vol. 5. Hanover: Dartmouth College, 1995.

———. *Emile, or On Education*. Translated by Allan Bloom. 1762; New York: Basic Books, 1979.

————. "On the Social Contract." In *The Basic Political Writings*, edited by Donald A. Cress. Indianapolis: 1762; Hackett, 2011.

————. *The Social Contract and Discourse on Inequality*. Edited by Lester G. Crocker. New York: Pocket Books, 1967.

Rule and Constitutions of the Discalced Nuns of the Order of Our Blessed Lady of Mount Carmel. Dublin: Cahill, 1928.

Ruprecht, Louis A. *Winckelmann and the Vatican's First Profane Museum*. New York: Palgrave Macmillan, 2011.

Russell, Bertrand. *Autobiography*. New York: Routledge, 2009.

Saint-Simon, Duc de. *The Age of Magnificence: The Memoirs of the Duc de Saint-Simon*. 1788; New York: Capricorn Books, 1964.

Sánchez-Blanco, Francisco. "Benito Jerónimo Feijoo y Montenegro (1676–1764): Benedictine and Skeptic Enlightener." In *Enlightenment and Catholicism in Europe: A Transnational History*, edited by Jeffrey D. Burson and Ulrich L. Lehner, 309–325. Notre Dame: University of Notre Dame Press, 2014.

Scotti, Dom Paschal. *Galileo Revisited*. San Francisco: Ignatius Press, 2017.

Shea, Diane. "Effects of Sexual Abuse by Catholic Priests on Adults Victimized as Children." *Sexual Addiction & Compulsivity* 15 (2008): 250–268.

Sorkin, David. *The Religious Enlightenment: Protestants, Jews, and Catholics from London to Vienna*. Princeton: Princeton University Press, 2008.

Stuart, Joseph T. "*Dignitatis Humanae* and the New Evangelization." *Newman Rambler* 10, no. 1 (Fall 2013): 6–14.

Styles, John, and Amanda Vickery. Introduction to *Gender, Taste, and Material Culture in Britain and North America, 1700–1830*, edited by John Styles and Amanda Vickery, 1–34. New Haven: Yale University Press, 2006.

Talmon, J. L. *The Origins of Totalitarian Democracy*. New York: Frederick A. Praeger, 1965.

Taylor, Charles. *A Catholic Modernity?* Dayton: University of Dayton, 1996. http://ecommons.udayton.edu/uscc_marianist_award/10/.

Thompson, E. P. *The Making of the English Working Class*. New York: Pantheon Books, 1963.

Tocqueville, Alexis de. *The Ancien Régime and the Revolution*. 1856; New York: Penguin Books, 2008.

The United Methodist Hymnal. Nashville: United Methodist Publishing House, 1989.

Venturi, Franco. "Church and Reform in Enlightenment Italy: The Sixties of the Eighteenth Century." *Journal of Modern History* 48, no. 2 (June 1976): 215–232.

Vickery, Amanda. *Behind Closed Doors: At Home in Georgian England*. New Haven: Yale University Press, 2009.

Vidal, Fernando. "Miracles, Science, and Testimony in Post-Tridentine Saint-Making." *Science in Context* 20, no. 3 (2007): 481–508.

Voltaire. *Age of Louis XIV. The Works of Voltaire*. Vol. 12. 1751; New York: St. Hubert Guild, 1901.

———. "Alzire." Translated by William F. Flemming. In *The Works of Voltaire*, vol. 9, 4–62. New York: E. R. Dumont, 1901.

———. *God & Human Beings*. Translated by Michael Shreve. 1769; Amherst: Prometheus Books, 2010.

———. "Philosophical Dictionary." In *The Portable Voltaire*, edited by Benn Ray Redman, 53–228. 1764; New York: Penguin Books, 1977.

———. *Philosophical Letters*. 1733; Indianapolis: Hackett, 2007.

Wagniére, Jean Louise. *Historical Memoirs of the Author of the Henriade*. Dublin: R. Moncrieffe, 1777.

Walsh, J. D. "Elie Halévy and the Birth of Methodism." *Transactions of the Royal Historical Society* 25 (1975): 1–20.

Washington, George. Farewell Address. 1796. Our Documents, https://www.ourdocuments.gov/doc.php?flash=false&doc=15&page=transcript.

Watson, J. R. *The English Hymn: A Critical and Historical Study*. New York: Oxford University Press, 1997.

Wecter, Dixon. "The Soul of James Boswell." *Virginia Quarterly Review* 12. no. 2. (Spring 1936). https://www.vqronline.org/essay/soul-james-boswell.

Wesley, Charles. *The Journal of Charles Wesley (1707–1788)*. Wesley Center Online. http://wesley.nnu.edu/charles-wesley/the-journal-of-charles-wesley-1707-1788/.

Wesley, John. *A Collection of Hymns, for the Use of the People Called Methodists*. London: John Mason, 1779.

——. *Directions concerning Pronunciation and Gesture*. 1749; Bristol: William Pine, 1770.

——. *An Earnest Appeal to Men of Reason and Religion*. 8th ed. 1743; London: G. Whitfield, 1796.

——. *The Heart of John Wesley's Journal*. Edited by Percy L. Parker. Peabody, MA: Hendrickson, 2015.

——. "The Use of Money." In *The Sermons of John Wesley: A Collection for the Christian Journey*, edited by Kenneth J. Collins and Jason E. Vickers, 302–311. Nashville: Abingdon, 2013.

Wesley, Susanna. *The Complete Writings*. Edited by Charles Wallace Jr. New York: Oxford University Press, 1997. See esp. "Diary," 197–301.

——White, Andrew Dickson. *A History of the Warfare of Science with Theology in Christendom*. Vol. 2. 1896; New York: D. Appleton, 1910.

Whitefield, George. "The Great Duty of Family-Religion." 1738. https://www.milestonedocuments.com/documents/view/george-whitefield-the-great-duty-of-family-religion/text.

Wilberforce, Robert Isaac, and Samuel Wilberforce. *The Life of William Wilberforce*. London: John Murray, 1839.

Wilberforce, William. *A Practical View of Christianity*. Dublin: Robert Dapper, 1797.

Wilde, Norman. "On the Conversion of Rousseau." *International Journal of Ethics* 26, no. 1 (October 1915): 54–71.

Wilken, Robert Louis. *The Christian Roots of Religious Liberty*. Milwaukee: Marquette University Press, 2014.

——. *Liberty in the Things of God: The Christian Origins of Religious Freedom*. New Haven: Yale University Press, 2019.

Wilson, Christie Sample. *Beyond Belief: Surviving the Revocation of the Edict of Nantes in France*. Bethlehem, PA: Lehigh University Press, 2011.

Ziegler, Gilette. *At the Court of Versailles: Eyewitness Reports from the Reign of Louis XIV*. New York: E. P. Dutton, 1966.

Image Credits

19. *Carmelites of Compiègne*, first half of the 19th century, private collection: Heritage Image Partnership Ltd / Alamy Stock Photo (2AG7W19).

37. *Tomb of Jean-Jacques Rousseau* (1778), by Jean Michel Moreau the Younger: The Art Institute of Chicago, public domain.

50. *Voltaire Welcoming His Guests*, by Jean Huber: Wikimedia Commons, public domain.

65. *Voltaire Playing Chess*, by Jean Huber (Wikimedia Commons, public domain)

93. Cartoon of a French dragon intimidating a Huguenot, by Godefroy Engelmann, after a design of 1686: Wikimedia Commons, public domain.

123. *Kneeling Carmelite Nun*, attributed to Jean-Baptiste de Champaigne, 17th century, Bequest of Professor Alfred Moir, public domain, https://collections.artsmia.org/art/33429/.

138. Salon gathering, by Fray Pedro Subercaseaux Errázuriz: Wikimedia Commons, public domain.

139. Maria Gaetana Agnesi, Italian mathematician: Wikimedia Commons, public domain.

181. Pope Benedict XIV (1741), by Pierre Subleyras: Wikimedia Commons, public domain.

201. *St. Camillo de Lellis Saves the Patients at the Ospedale S. Spirito in Rome during the Tiber River Flood in 1598*, by Pierre Subleyras: photo by Danilo Boccetti and Francesca Leonetti for Himetop—The History of Medicine Topographical Database (himetop.net).

204. Capitoline Venus: © José Luiz Bernardes Ribeiro, CC BY-SA 4.0, https://commons.wikimedia.org/w/index.php?curid=53996071.

213. *Self-Portrait*, by Anna Morandi (wax, 1770s): CC BY-SA 3.0, https://commons.wikimedia.org/w/index.php?curid=30705872.

228. The Mathematical Tower of Kremsmünster Abbey in Austria: H. Raab (User:Vesta)—own work, CC BY-SA 3.0, https://commons.wikimedia.org/w/index.php?curid=8040688.

260. *The Sleeping Congregation*, by William Hogarth: Minneapolis Institute of Art, Wikimedia Commons, public domain.

263. *A View of the Iron Bridge* (1880) by William Williams: Wikimedia Commons, public domain.

271. *The Rescue of the Young John Wesley from the Burning Parsonage at Epworth, Lincolnshire*, mezzotint by S. W. Reynolds after H. P. Parker: Wellcome Collection; attribution 4.0 International (CC BY 4.0).

290. Diagram of a Newcomen Steam Engine: Wikimedia Commons, public domain.

301. John Wesley field preaching in Cornwall, England, woodcut, 1888: Photo 12/Alamy Stock Photo (HTMJ6X).

304. *Gin Lane* (1751), by William Hogarth: Wikimedia Commons, public domain.

326. Sacred Heart Patch from the French Catholic and Royal Army, 1793–1794: Wikimedia Commons, public domain.

340. Josiah Wedgwood, antislavery medallion: Wikimedia Commons, public domain.

Index

About the Author

Joseph T. Stuart, Ph.D., is Associate Professor of History and Fellow of Catholic Studies at the University of Mary in Bismarck, North Dakota. His research and publications concern the life and work of cultural historian Christopher Dawson, the cultural history of the Great War, and the Enlightenment of the eighteenth century. He views the Enlightenment as an epic moment in the prolonged dialogue between faith and reason in the history of Christianity. He believes culture is the driving force of history, and that cult — in the sense of worship — is the wellspring of culture. Dr. Stuart sees the vocation of the historian as enriching the world of the present through knowledge and preservation of the past. An award-winning teacher and pedagogical innovator, Dr. Stuart has practiced land surveying in two states, farmed onions in Texas, lived in Canada and Scotland, and co-produced an original play, *North Dakota Voices of the Great War*, in 2018 to mark the one hundredth anniversary of the armistice ending World War I. Most importantly, Dr. Stuart is married to Barbara, and together they are blessed with three wonderful children. They live in Bismarck, North Dakota, where they square-foot garden, acquire at least a book per day for their family library, and marvel at the community and family with which God has blessed them.

Sophia Institute

Sophia Institute is a nonprofit institution that seeks to nurture the spiritual, moral, and cultural life of souls and to spread the Gospel of Christ in conformity with the authentic teachings of the Roman Catholic Church.

Sophia Institute Press fulfills this mission by offering translations, reprints, and new publications that afford readers a rich source of the enduring wisdom of mankind.

Sophia Institute also operates the popular online resource CatholicExchange.com. *Catholic Exchange* provides world news from a Catholic perspective as well as daily devotionals and articles that will help readers to grow in holiness and live a life consistent with the teachings of the Church.

In 2013, Sophia Institute launched Sophia Institute for Teachers to renew and rebuild Catholic culture through service to Catholic education. With the goal of nurturing the spiritual, moral, and cultural life of souls, and an abiding respect for the role and work of teachers, we strive to provide materials and programs that are at once enlightening to the mind and ennobling to the heart; faithful and complete, as well as useful and practical.

Sophia Institute gratefully recognizes the Solidarity Association for preserving and encouraging the growth of our apostolate over the course of many years. Without their generous and timely support, this book would not be in your hands.

www.SophiaInstitute.com
www.CatholicExchange.com
www.SophiaInstituteforTeachers.org

Sophia Institute Press® is a registered trademark of Sophia Institute.
Sophia Institute is a tax-exempt institution as defined by the
Internal Revenue Code, Section 501(c)(3). Tax ID 22-2548708.